SHAKA ZU

The late E. A. Ritter was born in Dundee, Natal, where his father was a magistrate. He grew up with the Zulus, playing among them as a child and making numerous friends. In fact Zulu was the first language he spoke, and, like his father, he gained over the years the respect and confidence of these people. Through his personal association with such royal Zulus as Njengabantu, he learned the true story of their great leader Shaka, which had been passed on from generation to generation by word of mouth. Long urged by both Zulus and Europeans to write this great story, he drew upon his own unique knowledge to do so.

E. A. Ritter

SHAKA ZULU

PENGUIN BOOKS

PENGUIN BOOKS

Published by the Penguin Group
Penguin Books Ltd, 27 Wrights Lane, London w8 5tz, England
Viking Penguin, a division of Penguin Books USA Inc.
375 Hudson Street, New York, New York 10014, USA
Penguin Books Australia Ltd, Ringwood, Victoria, Australia
Penguin Books Canada Ltd, 2801 John Street, Markham, Ontario, Canada l3r 1b4
Penguin Books (NZ) Ltd, 182–190 Wairau Road, Auckland 10, New Zealand

Penguin Books Ltd, Registered Offices: Harmondsworth, Middlesex, England

First published by Longman 1955
Published in Penguin Books 1978
7 9 10 8

Copyright © E. A. Ritter, 1955
All rights reserved

Printed in England by Clays Ltd, St Ives plc
Set in Linotype Juliana

Except in the United States of America,
this book is sold subject to the condition
that it shall not, by way of trade or otherwise,
be lent, re-sold, hired out, or otherwise circulated
without the publisher's prior consent in any form of
binding or cover other than that in which it is
published and without a similar condition
including this condition being imposed
on the subsequent purchaser

CONTENTS

5

Contents

INTRODUCTION

THIS book attempts to portray Shaka, the founder of the Zulu nation, as the Zulus saw him, particularly at the turn of the last century. By writing a biography rather than a general history it has been possible to incorporate the established traditions of the Zulus which the older generations described in the vivid and dramatic style peculiar to their nation. To find a suitable English idiom for the reproduction of that style would have required literary genius, to which the author does not pretend. But he has done his best to echo it.

Almost every evening Zulu fathers spoke to their children of the traditions of the Zulu nation, which they in their turn had learned from their fathers. In much the same way must the Old Testament stories have been passed on orally for generation after generation until at last, perhaps not until as late as 800 B.C., they were written down. The earliest chronicles of all peoples were presumably oral: they were none the less chronicles for that, and the author has not hesitated to refer, occasionally, to the Zulu oral tradition as a chronicle, and to the elders who spoke it as chroniclers.

In order that the reader may understand how the author came to have access to a tradition which would normally have been heard only by Zulu children, it will be necessary – the necessity is one he welcomes – to say something of his father, Captain C. L. A. Ritter.

In 1876 President Burgers of the Transvaal Republic tried to quell the Ba-Pedi chief Sekukuni and failed. He then called for volunteers who would be required to equip and supply themselves with everything needful for a campaign, and in return for a year's service they were each promised a farm. The response came exclusively from foreigners living in the Transvaal and a mounted force of some 200 men came into being under the command of von Schlikmann, a former Prussian officer. This heterogeneous body called itself the 'Filibusters'. Captain C. L. A. Ritter, the author's father, joined them.

Captain Ritter was born in 1833; he had been a lieutenant in the Hanoverian army, had joined the British army in the reconstituted King's German Legion, and fought in the Crimea. In 1857 he came to South Africa as a captain in the British Army. With other legionaries he was stationed on the turbulent Kaffrarian frontier of the Cape Colony in the combined rôles of settler and border guard. After joining the Filibusters he soon became one of the principal officers.

The Transvaal Republic was meanwhile heading for bankruptcy and on 12 April 1877 it was annexed to the British crown by Sir Theophilus Shepstone.

The Filibusters had given a good account of themselves but were unable to dislodge Chief Sekukuni from his rocky stronghold. A strong British military expedition failed likewise. It was after this that Sir Theophilus Shepstone and Sir Garnet Wolseley commissioned Captain Ritter to raise a regiment of Swazi warriors. This he did. The Swazis were closely related to the Zulus and armed like them with stabbing spear and shield. Sekukuni's stronghold was then besieged by British troops together with Captain Ritter's regiment, Ritter being the only European among them. In the subsequent storming of the stronghold one side was allocated to the Swazis and they were the first to breach the defences. Captain Ritter told the author that the resulting butchery was revolting, for the blood-maddened Swazis could not be stopped and spared neither man, woman nor child. Sekukuni managed to get away through one of the subterranean caves which honeycombed the whole stronghold, but was soon afterwards captured alive in another cave.

Captain Ritter was thereafter appointed 'Native Commissioner' over the whole area and after the first Boer War and the resuscitation of the Transvaal Republic, he was transferred to Natal as a Magistrate. He there had, as his head native court orderly, one

Njengabantu Ema-Bomvini, then about seventy years of age; his father, Mahola, was one of Shaka's fellow-soldiers in Dingiswayo's *Izi-cwe* regiment. Mahola had handed down to his son a wealth of detail about Shaka.

The author was born in 1890 and his first language was Zulu, learned from his nurses. He was a frequent if not daily listener to Njengabantu's recitals of Shaka's deeds. He would sit in Njengabantu's hut evening after evening, surrounded by the latter's children, taking in every word with the same rapt attention as the other listeners. Thus was laid the foundation of his being able to see Shaka as the Zulus saw him. By frequent repetition of the same episodes these became as firmly impressed on the author's young mind as Biblical history is on that of the ordinary Christian child. Perhaps rather more so on account of the dramatic events and telling. This created an undying interest in all things Zulu, and a thirst for accumulating all the knowledge possible about them. Fortunately his father was much interested in all the battles of natives against natives, and gathered a rich store of material when the events were relatively fresh.

The author had other direct sources: his maternal grandfather, the Rev. C. W. Posselt, founder of many mission outposts, came to South Africa in 1842 and provided much useful information which was then readily available. For example, from the Ngwane chief, Zikali, son of the redoubtable Matiwane, who accompanied his father in all the dreadful tribal migrations described in one chapter of this book. The Rev. C. W. Posselt opened his first Natal mission station in Zikali's territory, and thus saw much of him and his son and successor Ncwadi. Captain Ritter was the first magistrate appointed to administer this tribe at Upper Tugela.

The most valuable source of direct information the author had was, however, Chief Sigananda Cube, who was born about 1810 and died shortly after the Zulu rebellion in 1906, in which he had taken part as a leader. As a boy Sigananda had often served Shaka as an *u-dibi* (mat-carrier and general body-servant) and could therefore give a first-hand account of Shaka's appearance and general manner as well as confirming the accounts of Njengabantu, who was well known to him. Sigananda is accepted by Pika Zulu, Shaka's grand-nephew and custodian of the Zulu Royal Family's unwritten history, as the leading exponent of that history at the time of his death. When the author forgot his Zulu manners and became too importunate in his questioning, the old man would exclaim, with the dignity of a judge, '*Tula mfana! lalela nxa ku kuluma abadala.*' That is, 'Silence, boy! Listen when your elders speak.' But he did grumblingly concede that, for a European boy, the author's manners were tolerable.

When a part of the Zulus rebelled in 1906 the author fought against them as a trumpeter in the mounted Natal Carbineers. This enabled him to witness their bravery in battle, and although their regimental training had been suppressed for a generation it was amazing to see how well they kept their traditional battle formations and faced a hail of bullets with nothing but assegais and shields. From a fifty-foot-high precipice flanking the Mangeni Valley the author had a grandstand view of the epic encounter between Captain Lonsdale's Natal Native Contingent, armed with shield and spear, and similarly armed Zulus. The Zulus were a remnant broken by several encounters with Colonial troops lower down, yet in ones and twos they attacked the advancing line of Lonsdale's force, and several times scattered their attackers until, one by one, collapsing from their wounds, they would lie, an elbow on the ground and their head supported on their hand, proudly awaiting the traditional *coup de grâce* and disembowelling.

Having passed the official interpreter's examination in Zulu, he joined the Native Affairs Department of Southern Rhodesia at the age of seventeen. At twenty-one, having passed the Cape of Good Hope University examination in Civil Service Law (Lower) and that for proficiency in the Sindebele (Matabele) language, he became Registrar of Natives and J. P. of Bulawayo, then the premier town of Southern Rhodesia. (For origin of its name see text.) In 1913 he resigned and went exploring, following many of the trails of the great conquerors who, through Shaka, drove outwards from Zululand and fanned out over southern Africa up to the equator. Great was his joy to find, here and there, a few aged ring-headed *indunas* (headmen) who still spoke the Zulu tongue and were the ruling aristocrats in a sea of alien tribes conquered by their fathers.

So much for the author's oral sources: as to his literary sources the reader is referred to the bibliography at the end of the book.

Spelling and Pronunciation

For the sake of non-South African, English and American readers, the spelling of Zulu names has been slightly modified in some cases. For example, the battle of Gqokli is unpronounceable by those who have not mastered Zulu orthography and has been rendered Qokli, which still enables purists to pronounce the q click, although not as richly as with the g included. Also names like Nkandhla and Mdhlaka have been modified by dropping the h, a modern university usage which makes the author shudder. Long words have been broken up with hyphens to facilitate pronunciation. The new usage of spelling the prefix of a name with a small letter followed by a capital looks so monstrous to non-Zulu eyes that it has been eschewed. But the author frequently separates the prefix from the word, in, e.g. *u-dibi*, simply to make pronunciation easier. The u prefix has been dropped altogether where the word is preceded by the English definite article *the*, as otherwise the author would be committing bilingual tautology ! Readers wishing to pronounce Zulu words are reminded that all vowel sounds are long ... a=a in *far*; e=a in *made*; i=ee in *feet*; o=o in *note*; u=oo in *moon*.

In the original text of his work every reference to literary sources was given by numerals in the text related to an elaborate bibliography. The author's literary adviser and publishers persuaded him to drop this in respect to the appearance of the pages and to content himself with a simpler bibliography at the end of the work. He agreed reluctantly, for he is deeply conscious of his debt to numerous writers, historians and scholars. An appendix has also been included dealing with anthropological, medical and other matters of interest concerning Zulu social life.

The original text has been modified in another respect. To certain passages the author's literary adviser objected that they were too imaginative-seeming for biography, and that it was extremely important to avoid any question of a fictitious element in a work of serious purpose. To this the author replied by an explanation: as has been explained his first sources were oral, and when Zulus give an account of an historical event their method is not dry reportage, it is more akin to drama, and the feelings and words of all protagonists are recounted as in epic poetry. It was the author's wish to tell his story as nearly as possible as it was told to him rather than to extract from his material an elegant narrative. He had his Zulu readers much in mind. But it was rightly pointed out to him that he must also consider his English and American readers. A compromise was reached. It is hoped not an unhappy one. But if at any point the non-South African reader be tempted to exclaim 'How could he know that?' (for example, when he gives an account of Ntombazi's feelings upon being shut up with a hungry hyaena), the answer is that the Zulu chroniclers knew – as the poets who wrote the sagas *knew*.

The Author's Thanks to Helpers

The author finds it very difficult to express his thanks adequately to his many helpers; nor is it easy to know in what order to name them. He will therefore do so in chronological order, disregarding the degree of magnitude of help received. It was Mr H. S. Coaker, 'uncrowned King' of Ladybrand, who, having heard the author narrate some events of Shaka's life, insisted that he write this book, and assisted him materially in doing so. The book would, however, have been stillborn but for the help of Major J. E. M. Cuthbertson, O.B.E. (South African readers will know him affectionately as 'Uncle John'). His assistance has been invaluable: he was not only principal editorial representative of the *Star* and *Argus* newspapers in Pretoria for a generation, but a power in the land as a close friend of the late Field-Marshal J.

C. Smuts and General J. B. M. Hertzog and other Cabinet Ministers, as well as several Governors-General and Overseas Ministers-Plenipotentiary. It was Major Cuthbertson's hope that the book he helped to bring into being would do something to improve race-relations by giving the Whites a better insight into the sterling qualities of the Zulus and the Nguni race as a whole. Mrs Cuthbertson ('Auntie Gladys' to South African readers), of whom the Zulus say, when she is absent, *Li-guqubele!* the heavens are overcast!, was also of immeasurable help with constructive advice and comment.

Through Major Cuthbertson the author secured a valuable ally in Mr J. S. M. Simpson, editor of the *Natal Daily News*, who brought his penetrating mind and long experience to bear on many problems which would have confounded the author.

The author is greatly indebted to Mr William Campbell, J.P. of Durban. His name is a household word in South Africa and far from unknown overseas. Among his many appointments and distinctions which it is unnecessary to mention, one must be recalled: Mr Campbell is Hereditary Tribal Councillor of the Ama-Qadi tribe, his Zulu name being Ntaba-Kayi-Konjwa, The-Mountain-which-is-not-pointed-at (out of respect).

The author was extremely grateful for access to the incomparable collection of Africana belonging to Miss Killie Campbell. It includes a copy of every book and paper published on South Africa; unpublished documents, MSS. and letters, numerous albums of photographs, and the paintings of native life which she has commissioned artists to make before civilization sweeps these things away. With her usual enthusiastic generosity Miss Campbell put her treasures completely at the author's disposal.

The author wishes to acknowledge that much of his desire to place the Zulus and their kings in their true historical light was due to the late Mr F. W. T. Posselt, formerly native Commissioner and Magistrate in Southern Rhodesia.

Thanks are also due to Colonel Noel Poulton, O.B.E., V.D., E.D., to Mr John L. Gallagher and to Mr Lynn Acutt. For the peace in which to work a great deal is owing to Mr and Mrs John Pearce of Umhlanga Rocks, and for the maps to Mr Clifford V.

Weirich. And it is true to say that this book would never have emerged from the muddle of illegible scrawl into which the author had got it had it not been for the patient help over a very long period of time by the most loyal of unofficial secretaries, Mrs F. E. Wood and her sister Miss Madeline Pearce.

E.A.R.

CHAPTER 1

Zululand and the Zulus in the late Eighteenth Century

BEFORE proceeding with the mighty drama of Shaka's life it is necessary to give the background of the Zulus and Zululand in the days of his father, Senzangakona. When the time came for the passing of that chieftain in 1816 it marked the end and the beginning of two distinct periods in East Nguni* political history.

The transition would be painful. The primordial system of numberless clans and independent chieftains would, amidst much wailing and bloodshed, be demolished, and upon and out of its ruins would be built up a nation ruled by a despot. Yet, despite these drastic political changes, the social habits of the people would mostly continue undisturbed.

Geographically, Zululand rises steeply from the Indian Ocean in a series of terraces, first of coastal bush-covered plains, then of swelling park-lands, then of broken hill country girdled with many dense forests and, finally, of high and open prairies, all intersected by river torrents in bushy valleys. In Shaka's time a land free everywhere to all, to roam and hunt and cultivate at pleasure; with neither roads nor bridges, nor towns, nor any mode of artificial conveyance or inter-communication, but dotting the

---

*The term is generic and covers all the tribes speaking Zulu or its derivative languages in a similar manner that 'Teutonic' covers the Vikings, Norsemen, Danes, Norwegians, Swedes, Dutch, English and Germans, as distinct from the Slavonic, Celtic or Latin Europeans. The Zulus and the neighbouring clans were the purest Nguni, as the Scandinavians are the purest Teutonic 'race' today. The language differences in the various Nguni nations and clans were, however, very slight and certainly fewer than the different county dialects in England today, whilst many of the clans spoke in the identical tongue.

landscape on every hillside were human habitations, each consisting of a circle of beehive huts enclosed within a fence, and themselves surrounding a central cattle-fold – each such circle the homestead of a single polygamous paterfamilias, each hut the one-roomed residence of one wife and her children.

The single homestead, popularly called kraal, was the basic unit of the old Zulu State, a microcosm of the whole clan system. For the Zulu clan was but the multiplication of minor families thrown off from a common ancestral source, still represented in the person of the reigning chieftain – each cast-off kraal thus becoming in itself an independent, yet still subject, unit and, by exogamous marriage, a potential future sub-clan. For within each kraal were many huts, each with its separate family of mother and children, or marriageable, or married, sons, the nucleus of further homes and each holding its allotted rank within the family circle, all being ruled by a common head, at once father and kinglet, who governed all alike with unrestricted power of life or death, a benevolent despotism of protection, discipline and care. The father jealously retained his supreme control but it was the prerogative of elder sons always to be consulted by him in matters of general home management.

In passing now from the kraal to the clan we shall find that the structure and governance of the latter ran on the same lines as the former, save that here the separate huts, senior and junior, have become separate kraals, of major or minor status; and the common kraal-head, the common clan-head or chieftain, the clan, indeed, being nothing more than a magnified kraal or family.

A number of kraals, in any one clan, situated in a single, easily demarcated neighbourhood (as along a particular river valley) was, for the convenience of better government, grouped together as a ward and placed under the supervision of a local headman, *umnumzana*, who functioned at once as a petty magistrate and a Member of Parliament possessing authority to adjust all minor disputes and acting as the voice and ears of his people in the lower rank (or House of Commons) in the Parliament of the clan. A number of such headmen and their wards were again grouped together, forming what might be called counties, over each of which presided a still higher official or district headman, *induna*, who in turn acted as county judge for the trial of major cases or appeals from the lower courts, and posed as senior representative of his people in the national Parliament (or House of Lords). Above all these local and county courts was the Supreme Court of the chieftain and his chosen Ministers, who constituted at once the Cabinet of the Government, the King-in-Council, and the highest seat of justice in any case brought before them on appeal by any commoner of the land. Each, in this triple series of officers and court, was provided with a junior official, equivalent to our policeman, for the summoning or arrest of offenders, and in cases of contempt the higher court had always a body of warriors at their disposal. Trials were held as necessity arose.

Once in every year, about our Christmas time, the Royal Assembly or National Parliament, *umkosi*, was held at the Great Place, or Capital, of the clan, at which the King proclaimed new laws and made pronouncements from the throne. The entire male population of the land was required to attend this annual Panathenaea – young men, in full-dress regimentals, as ornaments and onlookers; headmen, to receive their orders, to state local grievances, to solicit favours, to seek or offer advice and to discuss administrative matters in general with the chief.

When Shaka came to the throne, the year after Waterloo, there were in what we now call Zululand (including the Vryheid district) more than fifty independent clans, some with several subordinate sub-clans, all speaking the same language and observing the same customs, each clan descended from a progenitor, and all together from a single still more ancient ancestor.

The Zulu daily life of a hundred or a thousand years ago was very much what it is today. In the Zulu social system every kraal is self-contained and self-supporting, and by a tradition that bears the force of law, the work of the home is clearly, though far from equally, divided between its male and female inmates. It is the peculiar province of the males to provide and maintain the fabric of the kraal: of the females to provide the family and support it, in other words, to find the food. The men work as the

artisans and herdsmen; the women as the housekeepers and culti-
vators. Was agriculture an invention of the female sex? Certainly
much evidence may be found among primitive peoples that it was.
To the Zulu man it falls to build the hut and keep it in repair;
to erect and renew the various fences of the cattle-fold and kraal;
to hew down the bush and cut the long grass from such spots as
the females are to cultivate; to milk the cows and generally tend
all stock. In these duties it is important to note that all take part,
from the kraal-head, even the chief himself, down to the smallest
boy. All who have passed the age of infancy, that is, who are already beyond their sixth year, be they male or female, must work,
or be ready to do so when called upon, the males under the direction of the father (or guardian), the females, of the mother.

Besides the aforesaid duties pertaining to the general mainten-
ance of the home, every man has every day some small private
task of his own, wherewith, in a leisurely way, to while away his
time – a skin-covering to patch or make, a new stick to pare or
polish, a hatchet or assegai to whet, his hair or head-ring to have
dressed, a snuff-box or body ornament to manufacture, a wooden
post to seek and fell in the forest, a medicinal herb for himself or
family to search for on the veld, a visit, friendly or on business, to
pay some neighbouring kraal. Then, again, many of the elder men
are constantly engaged with special offices, professions or trades –
of doctoring, divining, metal-working, wood-carving, basket-
making, stock-castrating, skin-dressing, head-ring-making, shield-
manufacturing, or travelling as messengers of the headmen. And
when no more urgent business presents itself, an occasional hunt,
a visit to a wedding-dance or beer-drink, a courting expedition in
search of an exogenous girl to woo or to a sweetheart already won,
add spice and variety to daily life.

The boys, up to the age of about sixteen, go out with the cattle
after sunrise, returning with them, first, towards midday, for
milking, and finally in the evening about sundown, thus spending
the whole of their days in the exhilarating sunshine and free life of
the open veld. In winter, often very cold weather, the younger
boys are permitted to remain in the home, but the elder have to
stick manfully to their tasks – a fine, healthy life that can hardly

result otherwise than in weeding out the weak and producing a vigorous and robust type of manhood.

To the wives and their daughters falls the duty of keeping house and cultivating the fields. Immediately after break of day – in summer as early as four o'clock in the morning – they cheerfully shoulder their hoes and wend their way to plant or weed in their gardens. As each wife is allotted her own separate hut, and often her own separate milch-cow, so also does she receive her own separate garden-plots to be attended by herself and her daughters and to furnish foodstuffs for the family. Throughout the early morning while their mothers and elder sisters are in the fields, the smaller girls, tasks appointed, are busily engaged minding and feeding the babies, sweeping out the huts and surrounding yard, fetching water in gourds from the neighbouring spring or stream, while one of the elder daughters crushes the boiled maize or prepares other food for the approaching meal. Two good meals a day – in times of dearth only one – are the normal Zulu dietary, the first at about eleven o'clock in the forenoon, when the cows come back from the veld and the workers come home from the fields, the last in the evening before sleeping.

The hut to which each family returns to rest or sleep is a dome-like structure of compactly arched wattles covered externally by a thick layer of thatch, and resting upon a floor, twelve feet or more in diameter of hard, dry and smoothly polished earth, with an oval, slightly sunken, fireplace in the middle. For the meal each takes his or her appropriate place according to sex and seniority, males on the right of the hearth, as one enters the hut, with the elders nearest the semi-circular doorway, females and children on the left. From a rack each withdraws a rolled sitting-mat of rushes and squats thereon with legs adjusted in regulated fashion according to sex; for it would be ill-mannered to sit upon the ground within a hut. Before each group, male and female, a daughter of the house places a common bowl of food – boiled maize-grains, toasted maize cobs, sour clotted milk, boiled sweet potatoes, a mash of pumpkins, fermented sorghum porridge, or some other of their forty-odd varied dishes – with a requisite number of clean wooden spoons standing round it on the ground, the ladles resting on its rim. Hurried and greedy eating is severely checked in children. Before the meal all hands are washed in a special earthen basin, and after it mouth and teeth are rinsed with water.

The rougher home-jobs having been performed before the meal, the younger men may now anoint their bodies, already washed at the river, with a pomade of fragrant herbs, don their gala dress of beads and feathers and be off to flirt with the girls. The females, during the hours of midday heat, employ themselves with light household duties or private pastimes, such as mat-making or bead-work; then, later on, they again shoulder their hoes, or betake themselves to the bush for firewood.

A Zulu home in olden times was to many so-called civilized homes a model of discipline and manners. Amidst the crudest of surroundings, the highest of social virtues flourished, the children thus receiving salutary and effective lessons by precept and example.

The dominant rule was that of complete submission to parental authority; and that authority was drastically enforced. Unquestioning, unanswering obedience to the supreme power was demanded without distinction of all alike – of mothers, of sons (some of them already middle-aged men with families of their own), of every child. Every failure to obey was immediately followed by a penalty inflicted without mercy; while persistent insubordination might lead to the disgrace of expulsion, and open revolt might even terminate in death. And what each inmate of the kraal saw practised by the father, he in turn practised in his own regard, demanding of all his juniors the same measure of obedience as was demanded of him by those above. Alongside, or out of, this practice of complete submission was gradually evolved something more than mere respect, almost a holy awe – *Ukwe-Saba*, or fear, as the Zulus call it, for those above one. And this again was mutual and universal, the little boys revering the big boys; the bigger boys the men; and all, their parents.

The child mind having been thus once reduced to this happy state of perfect docility, it was now capable of being moulded in a hundred other fashions. By precept and by example the child was led, or forced, into innumerable ways of proper behaviour – how it should be sympathetic and generous towards its companions, treating the little ones with consideration, and unselfishly sharing every good thing with all; how it should accustom itself to its share in the tasks of daily life, by herding the calves, by minding the babies, by fetching firewood and water; how it should take a pride in personal appearance, in cleanliness and neatness; how boys should associate with the males of the kraal and grow manly, and the girls with their mothers and grow womanly. There were rules of etiquette governing almost every phase of Zulu daily life – how to deport oneself before elders; how to behave at meals; how to respect the places and property of others. In such ways as this were habits of order and orderliness, of civility and cleanliness, of unselfishness and self-respect, of industry and sexual propriety constantly encouraged and gradually acquired in this admirable and efficient school of precept and practice.

Zulu mothers were hard-working folk, who had little time for playing with their children. From the age of four, and earlier, boys and girls, but especially the latter, were largely left to their own devices and thrown upon their own resources. Within the limits of the kraal and immediate surroundings, the little ones might roam and mind themselves. The bigger boys, of course, went out with the stock, and spent the day hunting on the hills and partly feeding themselves on roots and berries. Yet all the while they must remain alert, on sentinel duty, guarding and guiding the herds of cattle or goats – a century ago ferocious beasts of prey were common – each bearing an increased weight of responsibility according to his age. Thus upon the gentler habits of respectfulness, obedience, generosity and decency were superimposed the manlier virtues of love of freedom, of sense of duty and responsibility, of trust and trustworthiness, of self-reliance, self-control, and self-defence.

Meanwhile, too, the thorough study of nature was quietly proceeding, and a large amount of nature knowledge being gradually accumulated. The small girls, by minding the babies, were learning human anatomy, and the care of children; and domestic art and science, equal to their needs, alongside their mothers in the home and on the field. Out on the veld the boys were busy studying the nature of plant and tree, the habits of insects, the peculiarities of rocks, and could soon interpret the meaning of the winds and clouds and mists; and could give the names of the grasses and the medicinal uses of many trees and herbs; could describe the qualities of the different kinds of wood, the shapes of the different types of leaf, and explain the bodily structure of insect, bird and beast within their little world. Thus, through the ages this admirable system of forming character and imparting knowledge continued, until at length was evolved a Zulu race noble of heart, dignified of bearing, with refined manner, and learned in natural science – qualities, alas ! rapidly corrupted or destroyed by the advance of European civilization.

Two or three years after having reached the period of sexual maturity, *uku-tomba* – which occurs with the Zulus anywhere between the age of fourteen and a half and nineteen years – the boy moved up another rung on the scholastic ladder – he passed, as it were, from the preparatory school to the college. With other lads of like age, he would go up to *kleza* (i.e. drink milk squirted direct from the udder into his mouth) at one or other of the numerous military kraals, there to tend no longer his father's but the king's herds. This was an established institution in every boy's upbringing, needed, it was said, to ensure his growing well, in which no doubt the copious supply of milk at this particular period of life materially aided.

During the two or three years of his stay in the military kraal, milk-drinking and cattle-herding, he had been confined entirely to male society, that of the young soldiers of the clan. Now at length he was to graduate. So soon as there seemed to the king a sufficiency of unenlisted youths in the military kraals, a brand-new guild or regiment, *i-buto*, was created for their enrolment, with a brand-new barrack-kraal for their reception and a brand-new uniform (generally some novel head or body decoration of fur or tails or feathers) for their distinction.

Life and manners in a Zulu military kraal were much as they

are, and ever have been, in other barracks. The spirit of joviality, comradeship and *esprit de corps*, ever strong in the African nature, was here at its best. While ease and freedom were enjoyed, stern discipline continuously reigned; but it was a wholly moral force, the young men being thrown entirely on their honour, without standing regulations and without supervision; and they seldom dishonoured that trust. They were there for the sole purpose of fulfilling the king's behests. They acted as the State army, the State police, the State labour gang. They fought the clan's battles, made raids when the State funds were low – the State funds, of course, being the king's cattle; they slew convicted, and even suspected, malefactors and confiscated their property in the king's name; they built and repaired the king's kraals, cultivated his fields and manufactured his war shields; for all of which they received no rations, no wages, not one word of thanks. It was their duty to the State as men, and they did it without question or complaint. Save for a few Royal oxen slaughtered perhaps once a week, no State provision was made for the body's needs. The 500 to 2000 warriors crowded within a single barrack-kraal must provide for themselves how, when and where they could, finding a meagre sustenance by the mutual sharing of occasional 'parcels' of grain from home or by drawing on the extraordinary hospitality – one of the most admirable traits in the Zulu character – of neighbouring families.

In such ways as this was each and every individual of the Nguni clan, boys and girls, maids and men alike, taught obedience, first to father, then to king; to be docile, disciplined, self-sacrificing even to the supreme test of offering one's life on the field of battle.

The art of war, prior to the wonderful efficiency later attained by the martial genius of Shaka, had remained throughout unaltered in its most unsophisticated form. For, on rare occasions, misunderstandings did arise between clan and clan, and peaceful efforts providing no remedy, recourse must be had to arms. A day having been mutually arranged beforehand, each clan turned out *en masse* to enjoy the excitement. A score or two of warrior youths – for single clans were mostly small be-

fore the union – bearing assegais and shields, marched proudly
and gleefully forth, with as many women and girls to stand behind and cheer. Each party, drawn up at a distance from the
other, would send forth its chosen braves to single combat in the
arena. Such a champion falling wounded would become the prize
of the victors and be taken home by them to be ransomed, perhaps before sundown, with a head of cattle, like a mere captured
woman. Or, again, each party might stand there before the other
in battle array and provoke their rivals to action by pungent
abuse, shouting at them not the Philistinian challenge, 'We
defy the armies of Israel this day', but the ruder jibe, *Ya-ntsiniza
ya-ti sina* (The dog merely shows its gums and snarls – afraid to
bite) or *Ya'ntsini za'nja, nje-ya nje-ya nje-ya* (It is but a dog bar-
ing its teeth, like that one over there, yes! over there). Then the
javelins would fly, each warrior returning the darts of his rival,
until at length the defeated took to their heels and fled, whereupon a rush would follow for male and female prisoners and
enemy cattle, the former to be subsequently ransomed, the latter
to be permanently retained.

CHAPTER 2

Shaka: birth and exile

SHAKA was an unwanted child, his birth the consequence of a lack of self-control on the part of his parents while they were taking advantage of the Nguni institution called *uku-hlobonga*. There were various traditional ways in which advantage could be taken of this institution but in all of them the same purpose was served – the release of sexual tension among young, unmarried people, without conception resulting. The diary of Henry Francis Fynn (see Bibliography) contains a full description of the several practices under this heading.* No conception resulted unless the partners lost their heads. If, for that reason, deflowering of the girl and pregnancy followed, a fine of three cows was payable by the man to the girl's father (but in Shaka's reign the penalty was death for both partners). However, such disasters were rare, while the technique allowed a complete and synchronized orgasm to both partners. If it failed to do so, the man was held to blame.

It was this 'customary' intercourse which was allowed in 'the fun of the roads' (*ama hlay endlela*), which was also known as *ake nishaye inyoka enhleleni*, which literally translated means, 'Do strike a snake in the road', in which form it was put as a request.

In the 'wiping of the axe' ceremony by a warrior who had slain an adversary *uku-hlobonga* only was permitted. Under no

---

*The technique of this customary form of sexual intercourse confined it to a phallic contact beginning at the clitoris, proceeding through the labia majora and minora to the fourchette. The ejaculation occurred on the perineum, the girl keeping her thighs closely locked throughout.

circumstances was it allowed between members of the same clan. This was in conformity with the exogamous rule of marriage.

Shaka's father, Senzangakona, a young Chieftain of the Zulu clan, is said by the Zulu tradition to have come upon his mother, Nandi, while she was bathing in a woodland pool and, fired by her beauty, to have boldly asked for the privilege of *ama hlay endlela*. To this, after some banter and mutual teasing, she consented, both parties lost their heads and broke the rules governing casual intercourse, with the result that three months later Nandi realized that she was pregnant.

As soon as Nandi's pregnancy was discovered, a messenger was rushed off bearing a formal indictment against the young Zulu chief. But Mudli, Ndaba's grandson and chief elder of the clan, indignantly denied the charge. 'Impossible,' said he, 'go back home and inform them the girl is but harbouring *I-Shaka*.'* But in due course Nandi became a mother. 'There now !' they sent word to the Zulu people over the hills; 'there is your beetle' (*I-Shaka*). 'Come and fetch it for it is yours.'

And reluctantly they came, and deposited Nandi, unwedded, in the hut of Senzangakona; and the child was named U-SHAKA – the year 1787.

The unhappy Nandi was now not only illicitly a mother but, what was worse, within the forbidden degrees of kindred – her mother being Mfunda, daughter of Kondlo, the Qwabe chief, with whose clan intermarriage with the Zulus was taboo. But Senzangakona, being a chief, 'could do no wrong', and without the wedding-feast – there being no ceremonial celebration of the coming of a bride already with child – Nandi, doubly dishonoured, was quietly installed as the chief's third wife.

Love for Nandi had been but a transient fancy. She soon found herself unwelcome and neglected. Happily Mkabi, 'great wife' at the Esi-Klebeni kraal, to whom, as *Um-Lobokazi* (young wife), Nandi had been entrusted, was closely related to Nandi's

---

* An intestinal beetle held both then and now to be a common cause of the suppression of the menses.

mother. So she took her under her own particular care and displayed towards her an especial sympathy.

Nevertheless the relationship between husband and wife was never happy for long. There was a reconciliation, resulting in the birth of Shaka's sister Nomcoba, followed by another estrangement. Shaka's first six years were overshadowed by the unhappiness of a mother he adored. At the age of six he went out to care for his father's sheep, with the other herd-boys; in a moment of negligence he allowed a dog to kill a sheep, his father was angry, his mother defended him, and they were dismissed from Senzangakona's kraal.

Shaka now became a herd-boy at his mother's I-Nguga kraal in E-Langeni-land, twenty miles away from his father's kraal. He was immediately subjected to much bullying by the elder boys, and what hurt him more deeply still was that his dear mother felt herself to be disgraced through the dismissal by her husband, and tongues were not wanting to rub this in. Thus, his years of childhood in E-Langeni-land were not happy.

Zulu children dearly like to lick the porridge spoon – with them an oar-shaped piece of wood for stirring. The bullies of the family would find great fun in thrusting this stirrer into the fire and then, when almost burning, ordering Shaka to lick off the porridge, saying: 'Come, eat this, that we may see whether thou be indeed a chief'; or, when he would return from herding the cattle for his midday meal, they would force him to hold out both his little hands, extended side by side like a saucer, into which they would pour boiling collops and compel him to eat, threatening him with punishment if he allowed the food to drop. If he did let it drop they tried to force him to eat it like a dog or starve, and because his fierce, proud nature rejected this indignity in spite of every punishment, it goaded the bullies to additional vindictiveness. And when on the veld each moulded for himself a little herd of clay cattle, and led forth their respective bulls to fight, each boy pushing his puppet by the hand, they would grow jealous of his skill.* Later, they would complain of him to their parents.

* Bryant, *Olden Times in Zululand and Natal.*

Modern psychology has enabled us to understand the importance in after life, of a child's unhappiness. Perhaps we may trace Shaka's subsequent lust for power to the fact that his little crinkled ears and the marked stumpiness of his genital organ were ever the source of persistent ridicule among Shaka's companions, and their taunts in this regard so rankled that he grew up harbouring a deadly hatred against all and everything E-Langeni.

One day in particular, when he was about eleven years old, two older herd-boys flung the deadly insult at him: '*Ake ni-bone umtondo wake; ufana nom sundu nje*' (Look at his penis; it is just like a little earth worm !').

With a yell of rage Shaka flung himself at the two much bigger boys, and so fierce was his attack that, although they were armed with similar sticks to his own, he beat them savagely and nearly killed them before the other herd-boys could pull him away.

Nevertheless he began to brood deeply over this deficiency which, as all herd-boys paraded in the nude up to the age of puberty, was so painfully apparent. Nothing could be more humiliating to a Zulu than this. It led to a feeling of hopeless inferiority, and deep, resentful brooding, from which may well have derived that need to dominate first his family, then his tribe, at last a vast empire. He became anti-social to a marked degree, which made him very unpopular with everyone, and already his fierce, unconquerable nature led him into one rebellious act after another, and he found an outlet for his seething mind by trying to excel in every field of rivalry, to counteract the scathing ridicule he seemed to see in the eyes of everyone.

'Never mind, my *Um-Lilwane* (Little Fire), you have got the *isibindi* (liver, meaning courage) of a lion and one day you will be the greatest chief in the land,' Nandi would tell him. 'I can see it in your eyes. When you are angry they shine like the sun, and yet no eyes can be more tender when you speak comforting words to me in my misery.' So the Zulu chroniclers give her words.

When Mkabi, the 'Great Wife' of Senzangakona, who had befriended Nandi, came on a visit with her sister-in-law Mkabayi, and Langazana, the fourth wife of Senzangakona, both like-

wise cheered him up, and quoted instances in which retarded
development had been fully made up at the time of puberty.
To his dying day Shaka never forgot these consolers, and when
he came into power he placed them in the very highest positions in the land – veritable reigning queens of his military
kraals, and maintained them there to the end.

It was during a visit of his relatives that Shaka greatly distinguished himself whilst out herding cattle. He attacked and
killed a black mamba which had bitten and killed the prize bull
of the cattle he was herding, a feat requiring great courage, and
skill; he was then thirteen. He was summoned before the E-Langeni Chief Mbengi who, before the assembled people, said to him,
'Boy! Today you have done a brave man's deed.' And he gave
Shaka a goat. The boy shared it that night with his family and
the other herd-boys; his pride was great but his hatred of the
E-Langeni remained unchanged.

At the age of fifteen it became apparent that Shaka was
attaining puberty,* and that he would soon have to go to Senzangakona's Royal kraal to go through the ceremony prescribed
for all boys at that age, and to be presented by his father with
his first *umutsha* (front apron), for up to the age of puberty all
Zulu boys remained naked. Shaka was overjoyed to perceive that
he was now developing on perfectly normal lines.

On experiencing his first nocturnal emission the boy would
steal out of his hut before dawn and secretly let all the cattle out
of the kraal and drive them out of sight. Such was his way of
publicly announcing the event.

After sunrise he would be joined by the other herd-boys.

* Some two years before puberty a Zulu boy had to undergo a
small operation. It was invented by Zulu boys themselves to replace
the older, but now obsolete, ordeal of circumcision. The boy would
engage one of his comrades to cut his penial fraenum – the ligament
attached to the prepuce. It was preferably done with the sharp peel
obtained from the 'imfe' sugar cane. Its effect was to prevent an
unseemly protrusion of the glans, and by loosening the prepuce, to
facilitate the wearing of the prepuce-cover after puberty.

Meanwhile at home his sisters and neighbouring girls collected a number of switches. Milking-time at midday came and passed; but no cows came home. Then the girls, armed with their switches, were mustered and despatched to bring both cows and nude truant back. A brisk battle, in which sticks and switches were liberally used all round, naturally ensued out on the veld between the rival sexes; but soon the bigger girls rounded up boys and cows and drove them all scampering back home.

In the kraal the boy was given various medicines by his father and finally water which had been heated with a red-hot axe. The nude boy was then given his *umutsha*, or loins girdle. Thereafter older boys and girls subjected him to a rough ragging similar to the initiation rites practised by some schools. Innumerable ceremonies followed, including a period of isolation, washing and finally feasting.

During these puberty rites and afterwards, the boy acquired much detailed knowledge of female physiology.

Girls were kept secluded on the occasion of their first menstruation and sometimes for months afterwards.* Thereafter a feast would be arranged and the girl's favourite youth, known as the 'Greeter of the Little Bird caged-in-her-trap', would invite her to come out to the feast.

The Zulus did not practise any of the barbarous initiation methods, such as clitoridectomy, which were used by some Central African tribes.

In due course Shaka went to Senzangakona's kraal and went through the ceremonial rites of puberty. But when his Royal father presented him with his *umutsha* he rejected it with disdain, and otherwise succeeded in getting himself so generally disliked that his early return to his mother became imperative.

Shaka had a very definite reason for deciding to continue living unclothed. He wished it to be known that he was now physically adequate. In particular he wanted all his associates of the E-Langeni tribe to see and know this, and especially his former

* Girls used a sanitary towel known as *um-tabane* and married women a vaginal tampon called *isi-vato*. They were made from soft, absorbent and aromatic herbs.

tormentors, who would now, if anything, be envious of him. Public outcry, however, presently compelled him to dress at least like a Zulu gentleman, to adopt the *um-ncedo*, that is foreskin cover, an ingenious rounded little contrivance about one inch in diameter, resembling in shape a miniature basin, made of palm leaves and very light. A Zulu considers himself fully dressed if he appears garbed in one of these, and Shaka did not mind this concession to public opinion, because it could not disguise the fact that he was now 'normal'.

He still harboured one other great grievance against the world, namely the way his mother had been treated, especially by Senzangakona, and those of the E-Langeni tribe who referred to his illegitimate birth. A flaming determination spurred him on to exalt his mother and all those who had befriended her, and on the other hand to revenge himself on all those who had slighted Nandi and ridiculed him. Behind these resolutions was the driving force of an iron will, backed up by an exceptional physique. This, then, was the character of the boy at the age of fifteen and a half years.

The other herd-boys disliked him intensely, especially the elder ones who were one or two years older than he, because he surpassed them all in their sports and undertakings, and with easy arrogance usurped the leadership in everything. The younger boys partly adored him as a hero, and partly hated him for his unrelenting disciplinary code, and his tireless energy – which he expected everyone to emulate.

About the year 1802 a famine afflicted E-Langeni-land, and Nandi now found herself unable to provide food for her children. It was the calamitous famine of *Madlatule* (Let one eat what he can and say nought), when people lived on *ama-hlukwe* (fruit of the arum lily), on *uboqo* roots (*Ipomoea ovata*) and other wild plants. Nandi, with her children, set out for Mpapala, at the sources of the Amatikulu river, where, among the Ama-Mbedweni folk (sub-clan of Qwabes), there dwelt a man, Gendeyana, to whom she had already borne a son, named Ngwadi. She was affectionately received, and there for a while they all remained.

In this strange kraal, Shaka, now over fifteen, held no rightful place, and both his father's and his mother's people were pressing for his return. So on his mother's advice he went, it is said, to Macingwane, of the Cunu clan, his father's dreaded neighbour. Senzangakona is supposed – the report is doubtful – to have sent presents to the Cunu chieftain 'to induce him to betray his trust and destroy his guest. This the chief nobly refused to do, informing Shaka that he could no longer afford him protection.'*

Nandi now sent the boy to her father's sister, in Mtetwa-land, near the coast. Neither Shaka nor his mother was a person of any consequence at this period; indeed, as destitute vagrants, they were everywhere despised. But the headman, under King Jobe, in charge of the district in which they settled was Ngomane, son of Mqombolo, of the Dletsheni clan, and with him they soon became acquainted. He treated Nandi and her son with a kindness which Shaka never forgot, and there in a real 'surrounded by home' sympathy Shaka at last had come to rest.

This was about the year 1803 and Shaka about sixteen years of age. 'Six years of happy youth were passed in the sunshine and tranquillity of that kindly Mtetwa home.'†

Shaka now became one of the herd-boys in headman Ngomane's ward. Owing to his unusual size, intelligence and drive he was classed as a senior, and he now donned the *umutsha*, and the *ibetshu* (an apron of soft skin and similar size) to cover his buttocks. He also acquired several light hunting assegais and a small shield made of black cow-hide, about eighteen inches long and twelve inches wide.

He spent much time practising the throwing of these spears until he could make sure of piercing a tuft of grass fifty yards away in two throws out of every three. He had, of course, had years of practice in the herd-boys' favourite game of *uku gwaza insema* (to transfix or spear the *insema*, a tough round tuber about the size of a small football). This game consists of rolling the *insema* down a steep declivity past a line of boys armed with sharpened sticks which they throw like spears at the fast-rolling and bounding *insema*. Once they become proficient in this they can spear running rabbits and small buck in the same way.

* Bryant, *op. cit.*   † Bryant, *op. cit.*

Shaka soon assumed the absolute leadership of his gang of herd-boys and delighted in encouraging good marksmanship in the *insema* games, and stick fights, which resembled the English single stick bouts except that the Zulu boy was armed with two sticks, and used the one in his left hand principally to parry blows. There were stringent rules governing these bouts; for instance, the adversaries must not hit each other on the knuckles, or lose their temper, nor were any thrusts allowed.

Shaka loved nothing more than a mass-fight with rival groups of herd-boys, and so well drilled and disciplined was his own group that he had soon beaten all the other groups and formed alliances with which he controlled them all. Restless and super-active as he always was, there were periods when he would sit apart from the other boys morosely brooding, and, perhaps, dreaming dreams of conquest and empire.

It must be remembered that these boys were living in an age when every kind of African wild beast still roamed the land. Leopards frequently made raids on the small stock. The boys, with the dogs, would then sometimes hold them at bay in a cave or thicket, or up a tree, and the younger boys would be sent out post-haste to mobilize the adult males, who would arrive with spears and more dogs and not infrequently the leopard would be killed after a savage fight, with much mauling of the dogs and some of the men.

When Shaka was nineteen, on one such occasion a leopard had been treed. He did not wait for the men to be summoned, but with two throwing-spears and a heavy club he approached to within fifteen yards of the snarling beast glaring down at the dogs. His first spear pierced the ribs of the beast but a little too far back to hit the heart. The leopard came down, and with characteristic charging grunts came straight for him, with the pack of yelping dogs at its heels. Nothing but death will turn a charging leopard, but Shaka coolly changed his remaining spear to his left hand, and grasped his great club in his right. In an instant the leopard had run with its chest into the unwavering spear pointed at it, and simultaneously Shaka brought the club crashing down on its skull, killing it instantly.

When the men arrived they were loud in their praises of the brave deed, and decided that Shaka himself should take the skin to the headman, Ngomane, for transfer to the king – all leopard skins being the perquisite of Royalty.

Ngomane, who had taken a great liking to the strapping boy and his intelligent, forceful personality, presented him, as a special favour, with a cow, the first which Shaka had ever owned. Proudly he drove it home where his foster-father, Mbiya, with whom he was staying, gave him a warm welcome. Shaka venerated him profoundly, and presently it will be seen how much Shaka's dreams were coloured by this foster-parent. From Mbiya he received the only fatherly love he had ever known.

At twenty-one Shaka stood some 6 ft 3 in., with a robust and magnificently proportioned body which seemed to be all muscle, sinew and bone. His appearance was commanding and dignified, and the fire and intelligence of his eyes showed that here was a Zulu chief indeed.

Although now a young man of great energy and action he spent much of his time alone, dreaming and brooding. His poverty was intolerable to his proud spirit, and his burning thoughts of revenge against all his former tormentors obsessed him. With this obsession went his overwhelming desire to reward all those who had been kind to Nandi and himself.

CHAPTER 3

The young soldier – Pampata – The assegai

THE Chief of the Mtetwa tribe, with whom Shaka dwelt, had been Jobe. His sons had conspired against him, one had been put to death and the other, Godongwana, had fled. He changed his name to Dingiswayo (The Wanderer). When Jobe died, Dingiswayo returned and became chief in 1809. He revived the *Izi-cwe* (Bushmen) regiment by calling-up Shaka's age-group, including Shaka. Thus Shaka became a soldier.

His regiment had its own kraal, *Ema-Ngweni*, and their captain was Buza. Shaka was issued with an oval shield 5 ft. 9 in. by 3 ft. and three throwing assegais. He wore the uniform – white ox-tails at ankles and wrists, a kilt of fur strips, a skin cap with black widow-bird plumes, and ox-hide, *izi-xatuba*, sandals.* No rations were issued, the soldiers depending on foraging and on 'food parcels' from home, which, in Shaka's case, were brought to him by his sister Nomcoba and her friend Pampata who had been very kind to him and his family ever since they arrived, when, at eleven years of age, she brought them their first meal in Mbiya's kraal. She was Shaka's greatest admirer and supporter from the first moment of their meeting, and she prophesied his greatness.

Since Dingiswayo played Philip to Shaka's Alexander it is necessary to say something of this remarkable man. In exile among the Hlubis, people of Lala and Swazi stock, he distinguished himself by bravery and initiative, and became a headman under King Bungane. A white man arrived at Bungane's kraal, riding a horse and armed with a gun, neither of which had ever been seen before.† Dingiswayo volunteered to guide him to the coast, but

* See Appendix.

† Probably Dr Cowan, sent on an exploring mission by Lord

35

on their way King Kondlo of the Qwabes had the white man killed. Dingiswayo possessed himself of horse and gun – he had already possessed himself of much knowledge by talking with his charge – and thus equipped returned to his tribe and assumed the chieftainship.

Dingiswayo was a remarkable man, capable, observant, thoughtful, imaginative and ambitious. His early trials and travels had given him a valuable and appropriate education. 'They had brought him into contact with other peoples and other ideas, and had led him to observe and to ponder upon many evils in the surrounding social and political system.'* His mind and his view of life were broad and his bearing towards other people tempered with exceptional altruism and benevolence. His projects and ambitions, once he found himself in power, were not confined, as they otherwise would have been, within the narrow limits of the small Mtetwa patch over which he reigned. They were wide, and concerned with the welfare of those in need outside.

He had no doubt talked of politics with Dr Cowan and thus greatly broadened his mind. Once in power he opened trade with Delagoa Bay, founded several industries and reorganized the army into disciplined regiments which were soon as superior to the armies of his adversaries as the Roman legions to the Celtic hordes. By this means Dingiswayo had soon either conquered or persuaded all the surrounding tribes into a commonwealth under the *Pax Mtetwa*. His overlordship was light and tactful, his administration enlightened, and his preference always for diplomacy rather than force; he ultimately united, in a single political system, all the Zulu-speaking clans south and west of the Black Umfolozi river.

In the Izi-cwe regiment which took part in Dingiswayo's conquests Shaka soon distinguished himself. Abandoning traditional fighting methods, Shaka used a throwing-spear as a stabbing weapon, closing with the enemy instead of standing off from him.

Caledon, Governor of the Cape, 1806. Robert Moffat reports him as passing through Bechuanaland in 1807.

* Bryant, *op. cit.*

Finding that his sandals hampered him, he discarded them, which gave him superior speed. Parrying his opponent's thrown assegai with his shield, he would charge forward, hook the enemy's shield aside with his own, and stab him to death with the dreadful war-cry of '*Ngadla!*' 'I have eaten!' On one such occasion he would have been surrounded and cut off by the enemy, but was rescued by two comrades imitating his new method – Nqoboka and Mgobozi-ovela-entabeni: he did not forget them.

Shaka's commander, Buza, and in fact the whole regiment, did not fail to note the prowess of the young warrior; he was allowed to lead the *giya* or victory dance. Shaka was pleased with his progress, but pondered deeply over the fact that he constantly broke the light throwing assegais with his mighty stabs into the opposing warriors' bodies. But the custom of hurling an assegai, mostly without any effect, at a distant foe, was to him as though merely throwing one's weapon away. According to the chronicle, it was then that he conceived the idea of a single, massive-bladed assegai with a stout, short handle. This would mean fighting at close quarters, with deadly physical and psychological effect.

Having killed in battle, it was Shaka's duty to *sula izembe*, to 'wipe the axe', that is, to have intercourse with a woman. Until he had done so he was unclean, could not enter the social life of the tribe, could drink no milk, and must observe other taboos; thus, a woman, if unmarried, accosted by any warrior for this ceremony, was morally bound to agree with it. It was the soldier's duty to take the first suitable woman who came his way, but according to the Zulu chroniclers Shaka so contrived matters that the first girl he 'saw' was Pampata and that she, in her turn, had managed to put herself in his way. Her presence in his vicinity when he was known to be seeking to 'wipe the axe' was certainly no accident. She had, from the first, a very high opinion of Shaka's future, as of his person. For his part, Shaka not only found her beautiful; he found, what counted with him above beauty, that she was an able and intelligent woman, that she had, in his own words, 'a mind shrewder than that of a ring-headed councillor'. Moreover, he was grateful to the girl for the charity with which she had treated himself, his mother and sister, when they were starving vagabonds.

In short, the issue of this contrived meeting, planned by Pampata, could be in no doubt. The pair are said to have made love lying upon Shaka's great shield of ox-hide. And afterwards the girl prophesied that her lover would rule all the world they knew.

Like other great conquerors, Shaka began his career by reforming not only tactics, but weapons. His own prowess as an infighter had shown him what was needed, but, as we have seen, he had found the throwing spear dangerously fragile when used as a striking or thrusting weapon. He was determined to get his stabbing blade, which, however, had to conform with the very definite specifications formulated in his mind. He had tried out various types of heavy hunting spears but always there was something lacking, even if he shortened the handle or had a new one made for the blade. At last he decided to have his own assegai specially made, and whilst he was about it, to start from the very beginning, namely with the smelting of the crude iron-ore. Only the very best smelter and spear-smith would be employed to ensure that his exacting requirements would be met.

The Mbonambi clan, south-eastern neighbours of the Mtetwas, were the most renowned blacksmiths and one of their best craftsmen was Ngonyama (Lion), and to him Shaka went with his problem. Ngonyama was both smelter and blacksmith and like all his brotherhood he had his kraal in a wild and lonely part of the countryside. All the people shunned the locality in which such a smelter lived and particularly if he was a smith as well. There was a very good reason for this, as it was an open secret that these craftsmen used human fat when they forged their best blades, and whenever a man (or child) mysteriously disappeared, the smiths were believed responsible. Shaka on the other hand preferred to beard Ngonyama in his own den, in spite of his particularly sinister reputation which was supposed to account for the excellence of the spears in which he specialized. Armed with three types of the heaviest spears he could procure, and his war-shield, Shaka set off for the 'Lion's' kraal, which was situated in a clearing surrounded by a gloomy forest. Without any hesitation he boldly approached and entered through the open gateway, giving a dignified greeting to all the astonished inmates he passed, as he proceeded to the 'great hut' at the upper end. In the open court-yard in front of this hut he beheld the squatting figure of a man of consequence – he wore the head-ring of a benedict – whom he at once recognized as the kraal-head.

With upraised hand Shaka politely saluted him with the customary words 'Sakubona baba' ('We saw you, my father') – and standing to attention silently, calmly looked direct into the eyes of the kraal-head, who was indeed Ngonyama.

'*Sakubona*' came the dignified response after the usual slight pause. After an interval of silence, which is never embarrassing as it is the hallmark of good manners, the kraal-head inquired after the well-being of his visitor, who replied courteously, and then in his turn put the same question, which was answered likewise.

With these formalities over Shaka squatted at a respectful distance (about four yards) from Ngonyama, who, after a meas-ured pause, inquired whether he had travelled far, thus giving Shaka an opportunity of introducing himself. A conversation on topical subjects now followed, but not a word was said of the thoughts uppermost in both their minds – the reason for this un-usual visit. Although Shaka did not wear a single scrap of leopard skin to indicate that he was of Royal blood, Ngonyama intuitively knew that he was speaking to no ordinary man. He sensed a great potential chief, and in those days it was always wise to be at least friendly, but non-committal, to avoid the disastrous mistake of backing the wrong or losing party. Shaka might be anything from a bold man seeking refuge where no one would search for him, to a chief in disguise.

Shaka now told him exactly what he wanted, and why, and his fervour soon infected the old 'Lion', who agreed that none of the existing blades would quite answer Shaka's purpose. He proposed to reshape a heavy *isi-papa* or buffalo spear, but Shaka would not hear of it, and demanded freshly smelted or virgin iron which should be transformed into the tempered blade he wanted, 'with all the magic at your disposal incorporated with it,' he added significantly.

Although Shaka had introduced himself with perfect honesty as an ordinary warrior of Dingiswayo's army, and a member of the then quite insignificant Zulu clan, the blacksmith was so impressed by his visitor's personality that he instinctively felt he was dealing with Royalty – and no ordinary Royalty at that.

'What you want, Zulu, you shall have,' responded the 'Lion' at last. 'But it will take time, for we might as well start at the very beginning. A new furnace shall be equipped with new bellows to ensure that the iron is of the best. The blade will be tempered with the strongest fats, and in your hands it will ever be victorious. It will cost me a lot, but for you I will do it for the price of one heifer, and that you may send to me when you are satisfied with my work, and in your own good time.'

Shaka was delighted, for his one worry had all along been the question of price, as he only possessed the cow he had received from Ngomane for killing the leopard unaided, and the progeny of that cow. Outwardly he did not show his delight, or the gratitude he felt towards the old 'Lion' for virtually giving him credit for an unspecified time. He clinched the bargain gravely and then added meaningly, 'Maybe that one heifer you will receive from me will fill your kraal.'

The 'Lion' understood, and replied: 'I am but sending my corn ahead' – a Zulu saying which signifies forethought, as that of a person travelling who sends food ahead.

Ngonyama's first act was to provide the new bellows according to immemorial practice. He selected the five best goat rams from his numerous flock, and these were taken to the place where he had his smelting furnace and smithy in a gloomy defile next to a running brook within the forest. Here with the help of many assistants all five animals were simultaneously skinned alive. Only the skin on the head and below the knees was left on. Then the goats were released and allowed to run about within an enclosure. None of the spectators was in the least perturbed at their suffering, but watched them all with intense interest. As one by one they died their skins were put aside, as being of no use for the bellows, which could only be made from the skin of the last surviving goat, whose tenacity of life proved its superior vitality. And so this harrowing scene proceeded until the last goat died and its skin was duly selected; its flesh was reserved for the smith and his furnace attendants, and certain medicines for initiating the new furnace. The other four goats provided the inmates of Ngonyama's kraal with a welcome supply of meat, and their skins went to the smith's skilled helpers, although that of the fourth goat to die could be used as a reserve bellows, and, when goats were scarce, probably all their skins could be used for this purpose.

In order to impress Shaka with the pains he was taking Ngonyama had invited him to be present at the skinning, after first fortifying him with special medicines. As the making and drying out of the new furnace and the preparation of the skins for bellows would take some time, Shaka returned to his military kraal at Ema-Ngweni, and a day was fixed when he should pay his return visit to view the actual smelting of the iron-ore, and all further stages up to the finished blade. This request to witness everything was only granted as a special favour.

In due course Shaka returned to Ngonyama's kraal on the third day after the new moon, having obtained special extended leave from Buza, the commander of his regiment.

Shaka beheld the new furnace with great interest. It is, by ancient lore, supposed to represent a female, which remains unfruitful until it is fertilized by the male. A furnace charged with iron-ore and charcoal, even if fired, will produce nothing, the smelters argue. But applying the fertilizing agent in the form of air supplied by the bellows, and the furnace in due course produces pig-iron. To conform with this idea the aperture at the base of the clay furnace for the ingress of the air from the bellows, and the egress of the pig-iron, is made in the form of the human pudendum distended as at child-birth. Into this is inserted the clay nozzle of the bellows. It is given a phallic shape. The back of the nozzle is connected with the bellows by means of long horns, which enable the operator to put a reasonable distance between himself and the heat radiating from the furnace. The furnace is made of special clay and is cylindrical in shape, with an outside diameter of about two feet, and about three feet high, the upper twelve inches tapering inwards. When once charged with crumbly iron-ore and charcoal mixed, it is kept going continuously by refills from the top. The ore generally used is laterite (*umgubane*), which is widely distributed in South Africa. It is a ferruginous, crumbly, honey-combed rock, which is readily broken into any desired size.

Whether a limestone flux was added cannot be ascertained, but Ngonyama, with many incantations, kept on sprinkling a whitish, gritty powder into the open top of the furnace. Possibly, this may have been ground oyster and mussel shells from the near-by sea-shore. It was maintained, at all events, that this 'medicine' was very powerful, and made all the difference between a good or bad result.

Shaka remained during the two days required by Ngonyama's assistants to smelt and beat out a clean bar of iron – using granite blocks as hammers, and a granite anvil. Then he watched the master-smith continue the work of beating out the bar into a blade using iron hammers. When the work approached comple-tion, there came a pause, and the expectant, nervous air of the smiths warned Shaka of some impending and important event. He retired a little from the forge and put himself on guard. There was a silence broken only by the friendly chatter of the brook. Ngonyama squatted, idle but tense, by the forge.

And Shaka understood that he awaited The Nameless One.

The coming of this purveyor of power was announced by a low and mournful two-note howl which caused Ngonyama to start and his people to tremble. The signal was repeated and drew near. The two forge assistants hurriedly covered their heads with a goatskin each, an example which was immediately followed by the two at the furnace. The former were visible by the light which came from the glow of the forge, which they did not cease to supply with air from the bellows, near where they now sat with bowed and covered heads. There was a rustling in the near-by undergrowth followed by a horrible noise of crunching and rend-ing as of some great carnivore devouring bones and flesh, and an evil stench floated towards the trembling, waiting group. Again there was silence, which tortured all the cowering assistants and was not without effect even on Ngonyama the Lion and Shaka. Then came blood-freezing, cackling laughter, a demented demon enjoying the sight of the tortures of Hell. The assistants moaned; Ngonyama shuddered; Shaka perspired. The cackling stopped as abruptly as it had started. At last, a voice:

'I smell a hidden person. Who is the stranger in your midst, and what does he here?'

The chroniclers say that, thus challenged, Shaka boldly answered The Nameless One; that the sorcerer was amused and pleased by the young soldier's courage, and prophesied a magnificent future for him, and willingly helped him. The Nameless One would have appeared to Shaka as a shrewd, powerful, middle-aged man with a fur cape of pelts about his shoulders. Around his middle and hanging half way down his thighs, he wore strips of fur. Altogether, except for the tails hiding his face, there was nothing unusual in his dress; had there been, it would have betrayed his macabre profession. In his right hand he carried a heavy spear, and in his left a strong polished club and a goatskin bag. He belonged to the dreaded fraternity of *inswelaboyas*, which literally means 'Those who lack hair'. They were secret murderers and general purveyors of human fats, and other parts, which provided the 'strong medicines'. Their agents were supposed to be monstrous hyaenas on which they rode about at night, in the peculiar manner of having one leg thrown over the back of these fabulous animals, whilst with the other leg they walked or ran on the ground.* The friction caused on the inner side of the suspended leg was reputed to rub off all the hair in that area. Zulus are only sparsely covered with hair except on their heads, but should a man have been so unfortunate as not to have had any hair on the inside of his legs he was immediately suspected of being an *inswelaboya*, generally with fatal results to himself unless he chose to live as an outlaw in some remote forest and, in all probability, to become a practising *inswelaboya*. Many blacksmiths were undoubtedly *inswelaboyas* themselves, but as long as they could maintain the benefit of some doubt, they clung to it.

*Cf. the Wendigo legends of N. America.

43

In due course Ngonyama made some selected purchases, the price and its place of delivery being arranged for in cryptic terms, which were only understood by the seller and the buyer. Shaka was greatly impressed by all he saw and heard. As yet he was too unsophisticated, and had not yet learned how much chicanery and deception were used by the occult professions throughout the country.

It is said that when the *inswelaboya* rose to leave, he turned towards Shaka, scrutinized him deliberately and long, and failing to make any visible impression on him said, 'You are a man. Already I see a chief of chiefs. Ngonyama here will make you the weapon which will blaze your trail. See that he deviates not from what you have in mind. Farewell!' And he was gone – so suddenly and silently that he appeared to have been swallowed by the darkness. There came a patter as of padded feet, which receded with great speed, and within a short time the howl of a questing hyaena was heard from far away.

The work of forging the blade continued. Again and again Shaka voiced his dissatisfaction, and with the exacting demands of genius insisted on every little detail of his conception being carried out. The night was far spent before he was satisfied with the shape, weight and balance of the blade, and there now only remained to be done the final refining and tempering, and of course the most important detail of all, the addition of the 'strongest medicine'.

A deep hush preceded this ceremony, for it was regarded as a consecration which would fortify the blade and endow it with magic powers similar to those of King Arthur's sword 'Excalibur'.

Ngonyama, having produced 'IT', that is, the reputed human heart, liver and fats, began an incantation which he kept up whilst the rough blade was heated at the forge just below red heat. Thereupon 'IT' was placed on the granite anvil and the blade was brushed over the various human remains. The sizzling of the fleshy parts, and especially of the fat, was regarded as an acknowledgement by the spirits of the blade and those of its intended owner; for did it not resemble the hissing of the ancestral spirits when they took corporate form in the shape of nonvenomous snakes? Shaka accepted this simple logic when Ngonyama explained it to him, for were these not the beliefs he had imbibed with his mother's milk, as all his ancestors had before him? It would be heresy to think otherwise. As the blade cooled the sizzling stopped, and Ngonyama announced that the spirits were satisfied. So was Shaka; but long afterwards, this, and numerous similar happenings, made him think, until he became first an agnostic and then a heretic, who openly flouted most of the superstitious beliefs of his countrymen.

With the magic rites completed, Ngonyama once more became a practical and ardent blacksmith, and again the forest resounded to his hammer blows as he put all his craftsmanship into finishing and refining the blade. It was now about cock-crow, but Ngonyama did not cease his toil until the light of dawn. Then he began polishing the blade whilst an assistant climbed into a high tree growing well above the defile, from which vantage point he would be able to see the sun's first rays and announce the fact to his master. 'It (the sun) is approaching,' was his first deeply intoned and far-carrying shout. 'It is on the verge of appearing,' was his second message. 'It stabs,' came the final and joyful announcement.

Thus was born the blade which was the model of others which were destined to sweep irresistibly over half a continent. As Shaka held it in his hand and gazed at it with admiration his eyes shone, but not yet had he finished with his tests. He tried it for its 'ring' and vibration, and its resiliency, and as it had not yet been sharpened he gave a part of its forward edge a good rub on a hard sandstone provided for that purpose. It took a lot of rubbing before it became sharp, razor sharp, as Shaka demonstrated by shaving a few of the sparse hairs which grew on his arm. Then at last he was satisfied and expressed his gratitude to the smith.

There followed the hafting of the blade by a visiting expert. For this purpose a hardwood, either *Brachylaena discolor*, *Grewia occidentalis* or *Halleria lucida*, was used. It was Shaka who, by trial, fixed the length of the shaft. The hafter then drilled a long hole in the wood with a red-hot piercing tool (*isipiselo*), which was filled with the juice of a bulbous root (*Scilla rigidifolia*). The slightly heated, pointed shank of the blade was then thrust in and, when cool, was glued into place by the *scilla* juice. The haft was then bound with tough bark and finally the skin of the tail of a freshly slaughtered ox was drawn over the binding, where it dried and shrank, making a perfect hand-grip and fastening blade to haft very firmly.

Every type of Zulu assegai has a specific name. As yet Shaka did not name his blade. That was only to come after he had first killed in battle with it. He then called it 'Ixwa'. No one knows what the name means, but it may have an onomatopoeic origin to illustrate the sucking sound it made when it was withdrawn after a deep body thrust. This sound was due to the slight fluting of the blade, which made it cling to the flesh it had pierced. 'Ixwa', pronounced with the Zulu 'X' click, which is analogous to the sound made by a driver urging on his horse, does suggest such a withdrawal sound.

CHAPTER 4

The new weapon – New tactics – Promotion

VERY soon the Izi-cwe regiment was doctored again for war. The biggest black bull available was driven into the cattle-kraal of the military barracks, and for an hour chased round and round. Then the regiment hurled itself on the animal with bare hands. Some of them were hurt, but the rest of them got a grip on the bull, wherever they could, and threw it to the ground. Then using the horns as levers they twisted its neck till the spinal cord was broken. The witch-doctors then got busy and cut off the parts required for the medicine – a mixture of herbs and stewed bull's meat made into a soup. The rest of the bull was roasted.

The warriors then filed past the witch-doctors, who gave each one some of the decoction to drink, while some of it was sprinkled over the person with an ox-tail. Now the warriors each had to go to a deeply dug pit and vomit, and thereafter repair to the cattle-kraal. Here bits of the roasted bull were thrown into the air, and each warrior had to catch a piece and eat it. After each one had partaken of this meat, whatever remained of the bull was completely incinerated, and the ashes buried.

In the following campaign Dingiswayo took personal command of the Ize-cwe regiment, brigaded with the Yengondluvu regiment. The year was 1810 and Shaka twenty-three years old. When the army marched its destination was only known to senior officers. Its first halt, after reaching the Umhlatuzi river, was present-day Melmoth. Zulu armies were fed by a supply of cattle 'on the hoof' and some grain.

Much interest was displayed by Shaka's comrades in the fact that he wore no sandals, and in the single massive stabbing-assegai which he carried instead of the usual three throwing spears.

Nqoboka, Shaka's friend, foresaw that, bare-footed, Shaka would outrun his detachment and might be cut off among the enemy. Shaka maintained that all the army should go bare-foot and be armed as he was. Such an army would conquer all the tribes of Zululand. And he would prove it.

'Dadewetu! (by our sister!),' he swore, 'this day will I prove my words or feed the vultures!'

Then Nqoboka and Mgobozi-ovela-entabeni swore to discard their sandals and follow Shaka should he need them.

As darkness gathered the brigade moved forward again, but at a slower tempo. Long before dawn the objective was reached – the kraal of Pungashe, chief of the Butelezi tribe. At the first streak of dawn the three regiments closed in, but found their quarry flown. Soon, however, Dingiswayo's scouts reported that the Butelezis were massing some five miles away, and with all speed the army advanced in this direction. Presently they came upon the Butelezis, who were only some 600 strong, but in a commanding position, in a narrow valley of a tributary of the White Umfolozi. Their cattle were behind them, and behind these were the women and children.

Dingiswayo ordered Buza, with the Izi-cwe regiment, to march up to within 100 yards of the Butelezis, and then despatched a herald to summon them to surrender, in view of the overwhelming force confronting them. He promised them an amnesty if they would acknowledge his overlordship.

He was met with jibes and insults, and then the most renowned Butelezi warrior stepped forward some twenty yards, and shouted 'Go dog, to your toothless master and tell him to send someone who can fight with me, and not a yapping cur like you.'

Instantly young Shaka bounded forward, and faced him at a distance of fifty yards. In stentorian tones he then called out: 'You dried-out old cow's bladder full of wind, I will make you eat your words, and my assegai too. Now fight.' Then with mighty strides Shaka advanced on him. This was something entirely new to the Butelezi warrior, and in fact to all the spectators on both sides. A single combat, or a general fight, was hitherto always conducted with the opponents some forty-five or fifty yards apart, each side hurling their spears at each other, and returning those which had been thrown, until one or the other side had had enough and fled; if they were then pursued, and dropped their remaining spear or spears, it was a token of surrender, and the captive's life would be spared.

With Shaka striding up to him, the Butelezi warrior was nonplussed and somewhat flurried. At thirty-five yards' distance, he hurled his first spear, which glanced harmlessly off Shaka's shield. Shaka now broke into a swift charge, with his shield held at a slant to enable him to see what was coming. At fifteen yards he caught the second spear on his shield, and two seconds later he closed with his man. In an instant he had hooked the left side of his shield round the left edge of his opponent's shield, and with a mighty wrench to the left deprived the warrior of any opening for the light spear in his right hand, thus at the same time exposing his opponent's left armpit; into this, with a mighty swinging stroke from the right, Shaka struck his broad-bladed spear with such force that its point not only went through heart and lung, but actually came out under the right armpit. As the Butelezi fell over dead in the direction of the thrust, Shaka used the weight of his falling body to disengage his spear, as he roared, 'Ngadla !'

The two opposing forces were spellbound. Greater still was their astonishment when they now perceived Shaka, singlehanded, advance across the remaining twenty yards which separated him from the Butelezis.

It was then that Nqoboka and Mgobozi threw away their sandals, and with the utmost speed proceeded to 'cover the back' of their comrade. This was the signal for the whole of Shaka's guild, or company of fifty, to follow suit, immediately to be followed by the whole Izi-cwe regiment.

Within a short time the bewildered Butelezis broke before the surge of the Izi-cwe regiment, and fled for protection amongst their cattle drawn up behind them, and only the timely arrival of Dingiswayo and his indunas stopped the carnage which would otherwise have resulted, especially with Shaka in the van.

Chief Pungashe submitted with his whole tribe, and agreed to accept the suzerainty of Dingiswayo and to pay a moderate fine in cattle.

In the short encounter some fifty Butelezis were slain, including Bakuza, son of Senzangakona and his tenth wife, Sondaba, and therefore Shaka's half-brother. Dingiswayo's losses were about twenty, for the Butelezis were no mean fighters.

After some twenty head of cattle had been killed for the victors and the vanquished, Dingiswayo told Buza, the commander of the Izi-cwe regiment, to present Shaka to him. He had already had a very favourable report on his first battle, and was greatly impressed by what he had seen that day.

At his first glance into the sharp and intelligent eyes of the huge young warrior, he instantly recognized a leader. After putting a number of questions to him, he was agreeably surprised at the prompt and clever replies. He then questioned Shaka on the matter of fighting without sandals, and with a single stabbing assegai, and conceded that Shaka was right as far as war only was concerned, but for the time being he was content to fight in a less sanguinary way, and to achieve his aims by persuasion with the minimum employment of force. However, after conferring with Buza and Ngomane, he there and then promoted Shaka to Captain of 'one hundred', or the equivalent of a leader of two 'guilds', and also presented him with ten head of cattle.

Dingiswayo ordered the Izi-cwe regiment to parade before him in the front line, with the other two regiments in the rear. He then addressed the Izi-cwe regiment and thanked it for the day's work: he called for Shaka, Nqoboka and Mgobozi to stand forward. He first thanked Shaka and made known his promotion and present, and the whole regiment acclaimed this recognition of their favourite, for not only as a fighter, but also a dancer, songster and punster he was held in high esteem. He confirmed the praise names *Nodumehlezi*, and *Sigidi*. Then it was the turn of Nqoboka and Mgobozi. They too were thanked for their prowess, and then given a present of three head of cattle each; and the regiment as a whole were given the present of a hundred head of cattle.

Senzangakona, the Zulu chief and Shaka's father, on hearing the calamitous news that his favourite son Bakuza had been killed, and the Butelezis defeated, lost no time in making his submission to Dingiswayo. Hitherto the Butelezis had with almost monotonous regularity defeated Senzangakona, and he therefore logically argued that it was no use fighting the conquerors of the Butelezi.

Dingiswayo now wheeled northwards, and took the Dlamini clan by surprise. In the resulting scrimmage their chief, Nyanya, son of Sogidi, was killed and the whole tribe submitted to Dingiswayo. This action took place on the Macanca flats behind the Esi-Hlalo Mountain. Shaka and his 'one hundred' did practically all the fighting, and completely outshone the rest of the regiment. Led by Shaka, with his terrifying war-cry *Si-gi-di!*, they were irresistible.

The neighbours of the Dlaminis, namely the Mbateni, under Chief Kali, son of Shandu, were then subdued.

Next Dingiswayo marched on the capital of Donda Wesi-Ziba, chief of the Kumalo clan. He surrendered straight away.

The Eba-Tenjini, Ema-Ngadini, and E-Langeni had previously been mopped up before Shaka went on active service.

Satisfied with its work inland the Mtetwa expedition turned towards home. Shaka was now the star brave of the whole Mtetwa army, and he and his lieutenants Nqoboka and Mgobozi formed the most formidable trio of warriors they had ever known.

Of Shaka's personal prowess at this time the Zulu tradition has many stories, the most famous of which is that of the Mad Giant. This ferocious solitary had built himself a kraal on a hill in the ward of Shaka's friend Ngomane. He was of gigantic stature. Raiding the surrounding herds for meat, he terrorized the district. Expeditions were sent against him, but he showed his contempt for them by waiting before his kraal smoking hemp in his *gudu* and then charging out to kill and maim with his colossal axe. Regarded as a supernatural, the bravest feared him. But Shaka met and killed him in single-combat, a match of wit and strength which was to become the substance of a Zulu epic. Shaka sent the giant's ten head of cattle to Ngomane, while Mgobozi took charge of his weapons.

The chroniclers have also much to say of Pampata at this time. They say that, while Shaka was away campaigning, she daily visited Nandi and Nomcoba. Shaka's mat in his own hut at Mbiya's kraal was kept standing against the wall at the back. This must be done for every warrior on active service, for if the mat falls, he falls. Pampata very naïvely, and without any precedent to guide her, had made doubly sure by skewering the mat to the wall. Every day she swept the hut and made a little fire in it. To ensure Shaka's safe return she also spent nearly all her scanty stock of beads to purchase charms and medicines from the witch-doctors. Pampata was leaving nothing to chance. Nandi and Nomcoba, who were just as anxious, were deeply touched by Pampata's solicitous care for Shaka's welfare, but one day Nandi had perforce to remonstrate with her in a kind and motherly way.

'Child, you cannot dispose of any more beads for medicines and charms. Why, you will soon be quite naked.'

'Then I will wear my string girdle in place of the beads,' Pampata answered.

The return of the army was heralded by the praises of Nodumehlezi, which swept through the country like wildfire.

At first Pampata was puzzled as to why Shaka should have been outshone by this new warrior. With Nomcoba she hurried with a parcel of food to Ema-Ngweni, the Izi-cwe regiment's military kraal. The regiment was just returning and they learnt with dismay that Shaka had left them some way back to go by a short-cut and fight the Mad Giant. Pampata was bitterly disappointed and sorely troubled for his safety, nor did it dispel her gloom when she heard that Nodumehlezi was one and the same person as Shaka. His promotion and the present of cattle he had received left her without solace in the numbing fear which clutched her heart at the thought of Shaka's perilous venture.

They left the food at Ema-Ngweni and hurried back home. Pampata argued that Shaka, or, dread thought, his party without him, would first report to Ngomane, who lived close to their own kraal.

Reaching Nandi, she implored her help to raise more funds

immediately for more protective medicines. Although Nandi too felt very anxious, she put on a bold front and said, 'Nay, fear not, my child, our *Um-Lilwane* knows well how to take care of himself, for though he is surpassing brave, he is never rash.'

They all repaired to Mbiya's hut and made report. He was delighted to hear that Nodumehlezi was one and the same person as Shaka, whom he regarded with the utmost affection, but he too looked grave when he heard of Shaka's venture. It being now noon, and the cattle back from the early grazing, he forthwith gave orders for the killing of an ox, as a propitiatory offering to the spirits, and sent for a renowned *isanusi* (witch-doctor) living close by. That worthy was not long in coming, having 'smelt' much meat and beer. On the way to Mbiya's he questioned the messenger and soon knew why he was being summoned with such precipitate haste. When he was asked by Mbiya to 'throw the bones' and to divine the trouble, it was easy for him, especially as his running comments, clothed in innuendo, must, after each sentence, be acknowledged by all around him with the exclamation '*Siya vuma*' ('We admit it'). As he gets nearer the mark the exclamations get louder, exactly like the parlour game in which an object is hidden whilst someone steps outside, who, when he returns, is guided to find it by someone playing louder music as he gets 'warm', or closer to the hidden object, and fainter when he moves away.

It was Pampata with whom, when he returned, Shaka 'wiped the axe', and it was she who dressed the wound he had received from the Giant.* It is said that Shaka now told the girl that she, after his mother, was dearest to his heart and that once again she prophesied greatness, saying that he would soon be a commander and then *induna*, supreme commander under the King; and also that he would succeed to Senzangakona as chief of the Zulus.

Shaka was now summoned by Ngomane to appear before Dingiswayo with Nqoboka and Mgobozi – the latter carrying the late

* Crushed herbs developing moulds were used as dressing and a remarkably high proportion of cures of even serious wounds was obtained.

Giant's accoutrements. The ten head of cattle had long since been delivered to the king by Ngomane. At the Royal kraal Shaka found Dingiswayo seated in a chair, carved out of a solid block of wood, in front of his 'great' hut. He was surrounded by his *indunas* and a detachment of warriors. Shaka approached, saluted and sat down. 'Welcome! Nodumehlezi,' said Dingiswayo. 'I have heard reports of your great deed, but would now hear everything from your own mouth.'

'Baba Nkosi!' (My Father, Chief!) 'as commanded by you I took a *viyo* (platoon) of warriors with me, including Nqoboka and Mgobozi. We proceeded to the Mad Giant's abode and spent the greater part of the day in learning his habits. Near sunset we approached and I killed him. These are his accoutrements. We also took ten head of cattle from him, with such and such markings. These cattle were delivered to Ngomane, who transferred them to the Royal herd. The Giant's kraal was destroyed by fire.'

'Is that all you have to report of so great a deed?' exclaimed Dingiswayo.

'Oh Chief, what more is there to say? I am but a warrior who makes his report.'

'Nodumehlezi, you are as modest as you are great! I now call on Nqoboka and Mgobozi to give us an account.'

Nqoboka now gave a graphic description of the fight to a spellbound audience. He went through all the actions in perfect imitation of the actual happening with a mounting hyperbole. Then Mgobozi gave his version, and not to be outdone, he so added to the horrible appearance and shouts of the Giant, that all the people present were staring with open mouths.

Dingiswayo presented all the accoutrements to Shaka as well as all the cattle he had taken, together with another fifteen – all cows. Thus with the ten cattle he had received for the Butelezi battle and his original cow and progeny, Shaka now was the owner of close on forty head, and quite an *umnumzana* (master, or important person).

Dingiswayo then invited him to partake of meat and beer, and to stay the night, as there were some things he wished to discuss with him.

As usual Shaka was very moderate with the beer, nor did he over-eat. For many hours that afternoon and evening he was closeted with Dingiswayo in the latter's council hut.

First of all Dingiswayo touched on the subject of the succession to the Zulu chieftainship, especially now that Senzanga-kona's favourite son and nominee, Bakuza, was no more. He revealed to Shaka there and then that he would press with all his weight for the early nomination of Shaka as chief designate. He would try diplomatic means if possible, but failing that would apply forceful persuasion. Shaka could look upon himself as the next chief of the Zulus.

He also told him that during or before the next campaign he intended to promote him to be regimental commander, as Buza now wished to marry, and therefore to be released from active soldiering. This would also insure that Shaka did not expose his person nearly as much in hand-to-hand fighting, as he was too good a man to lose, for without question he was marked out for generalship.

Shaka was elated at Dingiswayo's words and expressed his gratitude.

Dingiswayo then spent a considerable time in explaining his policies, and Shaka listened with the utmost concentration. He expressed no views of his own unless he was asked.

The Zulus say that in the course of this conversation, Dingiswayo told Shaka of a great White civilization which had established its advance posts many moons' journey to the south, and an allied civilization which had an outpost at Delagoa Bay. That beyond the seas the White men were far more numerous than all the Ngunis combined, and that their armies there were uncountable, and armed with death-dealing staffs which vomited thunder, smoke and death, and still bigger ones like logs (cannon) which were the most fearsome of all. He stressed the importance of keeping on friendly terms with the Whites, as quite apart from their death-dealing instruments, they had powerful medicines to heal, though, strange to say, none for witchcraft.

Above all they had an orderly system of government, in which all lesser chiefs acknowledge one supreme chief as head over all, which did away with petty fighting and ensured peace for the whole land. Their system of justice ensured a fair trial for every man, chief and commoner alike, and the death sentence was only inflicted for treason, murder and the most serious crimes. They had, however, abrogated the death sentence for witchcraft, which they said they no longer believed in, an absurdity he could not grasp. They had, too, discontinued the death sentence for theft, which at one time was even inflicted on mere boys who had prank-ishly stolen but a fowl, or its equivalent in value. But instead of the good Nguni practice of a good switching for such boyish mischief, they had the horrible punishment of incarceration in stone houses, where, deprived of all freedom and sunshine, they had to linger on a poor diet for many moons or even years. This was execrable.*

When the audience was concluded, Shaka saluted and retired to a hut which had previously been assigned to him and his com-rades. This audience took place at Dingiswayo's O-Yengweni kraal, situated on a ridge between Tzangonyana and Dondota – between the En-Tseleni and Umfolozi rivers.

Next morning Shaka and his companions started on the return journey, proudly driving the twenty-five head of cattle before them. Mbiya, Nandi, Nomcoba and Pampata were all delighted at this latest and richest home-coming. Shaka immediately made arrangements for an ox to be slaughtered as an offering to the ancestral spirits, and it greatly pleased his mother and himself to be in a position at last of giving a real party. He then arranged with Nandi to barter an ox for all the beads and bangles they could get for it. Out of these, ample presents were earmarked for Pampata, not only to recoup her for her sacrifices, but also to give her a fine additional trousseau.

Shaka and his warrior comrades Nqoboka and Mgobozi then returned to Ema-Ngweni, the military kraal. Here the daily army routine was resumed and Shaka, with his 'one hundred' com-mand, became an assiduous disciplinarian, teaching them new

* The authority for this conversation is Zulu oral tradition. General Zulu opinion of nineteenth-century European civilization seems here to have been given form as the sayings of a folk-hero.

evolutions in rapid massing and deployment; he split them into three groups – a central, compact, large group with two smaller ones on each flank, deployed into encircling horns. Here was the beginnng of the famous central 'head' and 'chest' formation with the outflung 'horns', which became the characteristic Zulu battle array.

The regiment now participated in several peaceful expeditions as a show of force to some of the conquered tribes, to 'warm up' the loyalty of those chiefs who were inclined to become forgetful and lukewarm.

On the return of one of these, Dingiswayo addressed the regiment and informed the men that their old commander, Buza, now wished to retire and settle down to married life. This news was heard with general regret, but when Dingiswayo went on to say that their future commander would be one of them – a warrior mighty in battle, dance and song – all eyes began to turn to Shaka, and when Dingiswayo revealed that it was he indeed, there was enthusiastic acclamation by all, for he was not only the hero of the whole regiment but the most popular warrior of all. Nqoboka took over Shaka's 'one hundred' but Mgobozi wished to remain a private warrior.

CHAPTER 5

*Campaign against Zwide – Unprecedented generosity
– Dingiswayo pardons Zwide against Shaka's
advice – Shaka's refusal to consider marriage*

ZWIDE, chief or king, of the very powerful Ndwandwe tribe
had his domain north and east of the Black Umfolozi river. He
was very ambitious and had lately become somewhat rebellious.
He had begun to copy Dingiswayo's methods of raising an army
by a *levée en masse*, and, having himself subdued some smaller
neighbouring tribes, he had considerably augmented his fighting
strength by forcing them into vassalage.

Zwide had been previously subdued and captured by Dingiswayo, and as usual, magnanimously released. Hereafter Zwide
thought he would try his martial strength on a very small antag-
onist, Zwangendaba, a puny sub-chief of the Ema-Ncwangeni
tribe which lived eastwards of the Ndwandwes towards the
Indian Ocean. The result was so disgraceful that Zwide himself
was captured by the enemy. Zwangendaba magnanimously released him and had him escorted home accompanied by a present
of cattle.

Zwide, defeated and humiliated, determined on revenge. 'One
of his "half-mothers", Nowawa, animated by a nobler sentiment,
endeavoured to dissuade him from so ungrateful and risky a
resolve. Her pleadings were in vain. Not to be outdone, she decided on measures more impressive than words. So when the
army was marshalled in the cattle fold preparatory to departure,
she wildly rushed into the enclosure – a place strictly taboo to
the female – and standing there in the midst of the encircling
warriors, deliberately disrobed before them and exposed her
naked body. Such a heinously wicked act, thought Zwide, could
not but be of evil omen – in which opinion the frightened army
agreed; and all accordingly stayed at home.'

Zwide then made up his mind to regain his reputation in another direction. He knew that Dingiswayo's force was patrolling the upper districts. He sent to their commander for help in punishing, as an incorrigible law-breaker, Mlota, chief of the Ema-Ntshalini, living near the Ntabankulu. Help was granted and with his army thus reinforced, Zwide attacked the Ema-Ntshalini, killed Mlota, and achieved a victory. Mlota's skull was added to the collection at the back of his mother Ntombazi's hut, where all such trophies were religiously preserved, conferring on the owner a kind of occult prestige.

Since this event Zwide had become so arrogant that Dingiswayo decided to teach him a lesson. He therefore mobilized his three regiments, each 600 strong, doctored them for war, and marched northwards over the Umfolozi river towards Nongoma, where Zwide's capital lay. Shaka marched in the van with his newly disciplined Izi-cwe regiment. On the first day they bivouacked on the banks of the Umfolozi, and Shaka first of all attended to the wants of all his warriors, by seeing that they each received an adequate ration of meat.* In those days each warrior in addition to his arms and shield, carried a sleeping mat and his own supplies of meal or grain.

Shaka now joined the other two regimental commanders and the headmen who were in attendance on Dingiswayo, and the heads of the contingents supplied by allied tribes. Presently the campaign was discussed and Shaka remained silent whilst his seniors gave their opinions. In fact he said nothing until he was invited by Dingiswayo to speak.

Shaka then said that in the next battle the army should be

---

* Cooking fires were kindled with the *pehla* (boring) stick, which consisted of a hard stick some 2 ft. long which was inserted into a small hole cut into a soft piece of wood about 4 in. × 2 in. × 1½ in. The soft wood was held on the ground by the feet of the operator. The stick was now rapidly twirled between the hands, causing such friction that presently it made the soft wood glow and the dried moss placed around and in the hole would be blown upon until it ignited. Two men generally manipulated the twirling of the stick in order to ensure constant friction.

drawn up with a central head and chest, with half a regiment on each side thrown out as enveloping horns to ensure the complete annihilation of the enemy force. Only thus would they gain the complete submission of the remnants of the tribe, and do away with the periodical reconquests necessitated by the present easy-going methods which had proved to be so futile and inconclusive. Moreover, in future campaigns the broad-bladed, stout stabbing assegai should replace the light throwing spears, and sandals should be discarded to increase the mobility of the warriors.

Dingiswayo conceded the advantages in an *impi ebomvu* (red war, or war to a finish), but emphasized again that he did not wish to destroy, but merely to teach a lesson, whereupon Shaka sharply rejoined, 'Which will never be learned'.

The rest of the council voted solidly against Shaka, as they saw no good in these innovations. The elderly commander or colonel of the 'Old Guard' or Yengondlovu regiment attacked the idea of going without sandals, and discarding their throwing spears for a clumsy stabbing assegai; it would be the ruination of the army, and as for the idea of having encircling horns, he dismissed it by saying such a thing had never been heard of before. Shaka fiercely defended his ideas, even against Dingiswayo, for it was a feature at these *i-bandla*, or councils of war, that everyone was entitled freely to voice his opinions, even against the chief or king. Shaka always knew when to beat a retreat, and when he realized that on the one side he was up against the stone wall of ultra-conservatism, and on the other against Dingiswayo's humanitarian – and to him misplaced – idea, he ceased to waste his arguments.

After another night march they reached the upper waters of the Um-Mona river, a left tributary of the Black Umfolozi river. Early in the morning the scouts and spies came in to report that Zwide's army was massing a few miles ahead near one of his principal kraals. They also reported the approach of three other considerable contingents which were all converging on Zwide's capital. Shaka was in almost complete charge of the intelligence department, which, at his request, Dingiswayo had entrusted to him. He had already sent out a screen of scouts, and beyond them trusty spies chosen from tribes other than Dingiswayo's Mtetwas. Shaka now urged immediate action, and to strike before Zwide's mobilization was complete. This advice was unanimously accepted by Dingiswayo and the war council.

Shaka's request to lead the vanguard with his young Izi-cwe regiment as they were the fleetest, and because he was in charge of the intelligence, was also granted. On coming up with the enemy the elderly Yengondlovu were to form the centre, with the tribal contingents behind them in support. The I-Nyakeni were to hold the right of the line and the Izi-cwe the left. This had been Shaka's idea and, without the war council knowing it, was in fact the head, chest and horns formation in disguise. After Dingiswayo had adjured the dynamic Shaka on no account to take Zwide's life and to kill as little as possible, the army started to advance rapidly.

When they saw Zwide's army it was about two miles ahead in a strong position on a steep hillside or ridge near Nongoma. When about a mile away from Zwide's army they saw on their left, and slightly to the rear, also about one mile away, Zwide's western contingent approaching, about 500 strong. These were mostly his Ntshalini and Nxumalo allies.

Shaka immediately sought Dingiswayo at the head of the Yengondlovu regiment and asked for permission to intercept them, in order that when Zwide saw them being attacked he might be tempted to leave his strong position to come to their aid. That would bring on a battle of movement which Dingiswayo's better-disciplined army would be able to exploit to the utmost. Dingiswayo instantly gave his permission and slowed down his advance.

The Izi-cwe regiment now advanced rapidly, making for a point mid-way between the approaching contingent and Zwide's right flank. The enemy contingent in its turn now broke into a fast run to try to cross the interception point before Shaka reached it, and cut them off from Zwide's protecting army. In the latter a great commotion was now apparent, and presently their right flank and centre broke and came tearing down the hill to succour their allies, and, as they thought, to catch the Izi-cwe regiment in a pincers movement. Their timing, however, was bad, and Shaka had crossed the intersection point by the time they had covered only half the distance to it. Then he wheeled to the left and struck the head of the contingent and crumpled up their streamlined formation, which now began to run in the opposite direction. Nevertheless there was some fighting, and although of a running nature, it slowed down, the Izi-cwe regiment and soon the leading warriors of Zwide's main army were only 400 yards behind Shaka's rear. In the meantime Dingiswayo had not been idle, and had brought up at the double the rest of his army, towards the interception point and a little nearer to Zwide's original position.

Shaka barely had time to complete the rout of the Ntshalini and Nxumalo contingent, and to 'about-face', before Zwide's leading Ndwandwes were upon him. When the pressure became too great he retired slowly, but almost at once this pressure on him was relaxed, as Dingiswayo with his whole army pounced on the left flank of the advancing Ndwandwes. Now Shaka in his turn pressed forward and threw an enveloping left arm around the Ndwandwes' right flank, which had really become their rear as they had to turn to meet Dingiswayo. The battle became an utter rout for the entrapped Ndwandwes, especially the forward ones. By the time Zwide's tardy left wing arrived on Dingiswayo's right the action was practically over and the Ndwandwe left wing was in its turn broken up. The whole battle was a series of brilliant tactical moves which had succeeded in breaking up the enemy in detail. Perhaps 'strategical' would be the more correct description, as, with short-range weapons, a turning movement of a mile, or even less, can be classified as such.

One of Shaka's maxims was: 'Follow a defeated enemy ruthlessly and put the fear of Shaka into him.' With tireless energy the Izi-cwe followed up the remnants. Shaka was especially eager to catch the other two contingents he had knowledge of, but these, hearing from fugitives of the shocking defeat of the main body, were moving away and homewards as fast as they could travel.

On returning to headquarters Shaka learnt that Zwide had been captured and safely handed over to Dingiswayo; Shaka believed that it would have been better had Zwide been killed, and had intended to kill him if he got the chance; events were to prove him wise.

Zwide's casualties were some 500 killed and an equal number wounded out of a total force of about 2500 engaged. Though high for the form of warfare then waged – a form which was rising in intensity – it was still low in comparison with the warfare which would develop later on. For one thing the wounded were not killed, and many prisoners were taken – a warrior dropping his shield and remaining spears being deemed to have surrendered.

Dingiswayo's total casualties were surprisingly low, less than a third of Zwide's.

Comrades of the wounded men on both sides stayed with them to see what could be done for them. Not then had the Zulu Spartan and logical method been adopted of putting out of his misery a hopelessly wounded friend, at the latter's implied or spoken consent. Nor were the enemy wounded killed as they were later on. Shaka saw to it that all the wounded in his regiment received every possible care, although he saw no sense or logic in prolonging the agonies of those with mortal hurts.

The *inyangas* or healing doctors were summoned, who prepared herbal decoctions mixed with the contents taken from the small intestines of the numerous oxen which had been killed for food, and as a sacrifice to the spirits. After boiling the whole and adding some gall, each wounded warrior had to take three sips. They then had to point a stick at the enemy, after spitting on it, and call out *Yize* ('Come on'). This had to be repeated three times. Thereafter they were given an emetic. The wounds were then dressed with the crushed leaves of *u-joye* (*Datura stramonium*), a powerful poultice with high medicinal values, and the quality of developing moulds. These practical and psychological methods generally resulted in astonishingly rapid cures.

When Dingiswayo and his *i-bandla*, or war-council, met that evening full and unanimous recognition was accorded to Shaka for his personal share in the great victory, as well as the outstanding merits displayed by his Izi-cwe regiment.

The elderly commander of the Yengondlovu gave unstinted praise to the Izi-cwe, for their very effective 'close in' fighting, and their new 'left hook' method of forcing their opponents' shields to one side, so causing them to expose their sides for a fatal thrust. Of Shaka he said, *Nodumehlezi* was *Sigidi* (One Thousand) indeed, inasmuch as he was worth 1000 men, and that he was the *Nkalakata* (anything huge and outsize) whose plumed head was visible above all others wherever the fighting was thickset. Finally he declared that Shaka was not only the greatest warrior the army and country had ever seen, but he also had *ikanda*, i.e. a head, and young as he was everyone in future would do well to listen to him, and that he, for his part, 'would eat all his words' which he had uttered about Shaka at an earlier meeting.

Dingiswayo underlined and emphasized everything the old commander had said, and as a mark of his esteem promised Shaka a very generous allocation of the cattle about to be collected from Zwide. Shaka thanked him, and the whole assembly joined in the thanks. It is a universal Nguni custom for all those present to thank the donor for a gift to one of them, as if each and all of them were the one and only recipient of the gift.

Shaka once more thanked his sovereign, but pointed out that it would be better for his own personal reward to be decreased, with a corresponding increase for his individual warriors who had all fought well that day, for it was better to please many than one person only. This liberality* struck his audience dumb, and again they looked on him with wonderment. Such altruism on the part of a commander in favour of his private soldiers simply was not known, and it made history not only at this meeting, but in the unfolding future. Nevertheless after the first murmurs of incredulous astonishment, Shaka was loudly acclaimed. Dingiswayo alone was not astonished, but smiled his understanding and approval.

He then asked Shaka what he should do with Zwide and the

* See Fynn, in Bird's *Annals of Natal.*

Ndwandwe tribe. Shaka's fierce reply was immediate: He bade his King kill Zwide and Ntombazi, and all Zwide's male heirs. Zwide was treacherous and would never forgive his defeat and mortification. If Dingiswayo did not kill him, then one day Zwide would kill Dingiswayo whose skull would join the evil-smelling collection in Ntombazi's hut. As for her, she was *umtagati*, a witch and should be impaled on a pole of her own kraal and then roasted with faggots of grass.

For the rest, burn the Ndwandwes' kraals, collect their women, children and cattle and settle them in Mtetwa-land. Their men will soon follow them and the whole community be incorporated in Dingiswayo's people.

Shaka said: 'Strike an enemy once and for all. Let him cease to exist as a tribe or he will live to fly at your throat again.' If, he said, there must be war, let it be *impi ebomvu* – total war. But treat generously those who submit without war.*

Shaka received much support from the other councillors, especially the regimental commanders, but others awaited their cue from Dingiswayo, who once more conceded many points to Shaka, especially his reference to the 'protecting shadow'. However, his policy remained one of conciliation and he still hoped to attain his ends with the minimum of bloodshed, misery and destruction. He proposed to fine Zwide 2000 oxen and a small number of cows. This, with the heavy losses of men and prestige in the battle, he felt, would be a salutary lesson to him, and would also have a far-reaching effect on all the neighbouring tribes. Ultimately Dingiswayo's counsels prevailed. Had he been outvoted he would probably have closed the meeting, sent most of the opposition on some errand or duty, and then called another meeting which would contain a predominant number of his sup-

---

* That Shaka lived up to this when he came into power is shown by the fact that all those tribes who submitted to his hegemony were left in undisturbed possession, but naturally had to furnish their quota of warriors. To mention but a few: Chief Zihlandlo and his E-Mbo tribe. Chief Jobe of the Sitole clan. The Qungebini, the Ntombelas, the Langeni, the Sokulus, the Mtetwa tribe and all their tributaries, the Dubes, Celes, Ema-Ndlazini and many more.

porters, who would enable him to get a clear majority. The absent or out-voted counsellors, would, in their turn, be expected to pay a solatium or fine to their chief and king.

The army was now quartered in Ndwandwe-land until the fine was paid, and for some time afterwards helped the Ndwandwes to drink their beer and eat their corn and cattle. Dingiswayo encouraged merry-making with the idea of promoting friendships.

In due course the occupation ended and the army returned home. The chroniclers have much to say of his meeting with Pampata but more to the point, they recall at this stage a remarkable conversation with his mother, Nandi. It was not his practice to confide even in her, but upon his return from the campaign against Zwide, the young General took his mother aside and, it is said, spoke as follows:

'*Mame!* (mother) soon I will be able to sleep more restfully like other men, for the time is now approaching when you will be a great *inkosikazi* (chieftainess), aye, perhaps the greatest in the land. For that has always been my aim from the day when Senzangakona drove us into the wilderness. You shall be the head of your own great kraal, and a power in the land. Whom you frown upon will be as good as dead, and those who live under your shadow will wax beyond all others. Whom you forgive will be forgiven. Take of all my cattle as you please, for they are yours as much as they are mine. Stint not yourself and your friends, and mark well, that your true friends are all those who were kind to you in your distress and poverty, and not those who now merely come to eat your meat. Take special care of Pampata, for though I shall never marry, she will be, after you, always nearest to my heart.'

Nandi was shocked, as she had fondly imagined she would be a grandmother some day, and although Pampata was a commoner, there was no reason why she should not be affiliated to the *I-Kohlo* 'Left House', or even the *Indlun-Kulu* 'Great House'. Shaka tried to explain his deeply rooted aversion to heirs, who on reaching manhood were always a potential danger to the ruling chief.

Nandi's gathering distress and tears moved him strangely, and presently his own eyes were wet. '*Mame!* it is a great grief to me that for the first time in my life I have caused you tears; I, the very person who was pledged to see you shed no more. Let an ox be killed to wipe away your tears, and strengthen your stomach with good cheer, so that your heart may once again feel sweet. Take many oxen more to those who barter them for beads, then bedecked in finery beyond all women's dreams, your teeth will shine again in happy smiles and bring comfort to my aching heart. Then, perchance, as time goes on, and my unfolding plans take shape, you will agree with me, or, who knows, perhaps *I* will agree with *you*?'

Nandi was now completely mollified and the party broke up for home. The sight of another score of Shaka's oxen and a few cows being driven ahead of them added to her rising feeling of security. Four times that number of oxen had been given to the regiment by Shaka alone out of his 'prize money', in addition to Dingiswayo's own gift of 300 head.

Many people may find it hard to believe that so ruthless a conqueror as Shaka later became could be moved by his mother's tears, but we have the testimony of Henry Francis Fynn, who knew him intimately at the zenith of his power.*

The truth is that Shaka was a most unusual product of his race. He was highly emotional and sentimental behind a façade of iron self-discipline. The fact that he was the finest composer of songs, the leading dancer and the wittiest punster suggests the artist, who would naturally have a highly strung nature, and be more sensitive than the common run of the Nguni race.

* See Bird's *Annals of Natal*, i, 67.

CHAPTER 6

Senzangakona reconciled – The Zulu chieftain
– Rewards and punishments

ABOUT this time Mbiya, Shaka's foster-father, became seriously ill. Shaka visited him every evening, a distance of ten miles there and back, in spite of a strenuous day with the warriors whom he led in every exercise. Shaka summoned the best doctors to retard Mbiya's decline, and promised them large rewards if they should succeed, and he frequently sacrificed an ox to Mbiya's ancestors; only a council meeting called by Dingiswayo, at his O-Yengweni kraal would keep Shaka from Mbiya's side.

It was now about the year 1814, and Shaka approximately twenty-seven years old, when Dingiswayo sent his headman Ngomane to Shaka's father Senzangakona, chief of the Zulu clan, bearing this message : 'The "Great One" directs us to inform you that Shaka, your son, is with him and he requests an explanation thereof.' Sensangakona understood the hint and immediately hurried to Dingiswayo's kraal with an appropriate escort, and some of his wives.

He was given a great welcome, and in the usual Nguni way entertained with lavish hospitality, and the customary ceremonial was held to celebrate his first appearance at court. While the principal dance, known as the *inkondlo*, of Dingiswayo was going forward, the irrepressible Shaka – still quite unrecognized by his father – danced with such surpassing art and verve as to attract the admiration of the whole assembly. 'Hau !' said Senzangakona, 'Who is that fine, tall young man of light-brown skin, dancing so exquisitely?' To which Dingiswayo replied, 'That is Nodumehlezi, of Nome, of Jobe.'

Whether or not his suspicions had already been aroused, Senzangakona ventured to inquire,

'And where, then, is Shaka?'

68

'Oh Chief,' said Dingiswayo, 'he is afraid to appear !'

After the dance, it being a hot day, Dingiswayo prompted Senzangakona to refresh himself by a bathe in the near-by river. Shortly afterwards he suggested the same thing to Shaka and some young men who were with him. After they had removed their scanty coverings Shaka saw his father enjoying a bathe near by, and startled his young companions with the cry 'There is the chief.' Thereupon they all picked up their trappings and fled, except Shaka, who, when asked his name, boldly responded 'I am Shaka.' Senzangokano then discovered that the young man and famous warrior he had admired so much was his own son.

'So pleased did Senzangakona show himself at the fine appearance and excellent reputation of his new-found son, that it became apparent to all that the latter was bound to become the favourite. This was precisely what Dingiswayo was aiming at; for how better could he reinforce his political structure than by securing on the several tribal thrones his own selected partisans?'*

Dingiswayo, however, wished to make assurance doubly sure, by magic. He had a good stock of charms for every emergency and he now took Shaka into his confidence. All sorts of charms were thereupon sprinkled on the path Senzangakona would tread, on his mat, and most of them over Shaka himself to fortify his own person. The combined effect should give Shaka complete ascendancy over Senzangakona; and it did, for when it was hinted to Senzangakona that he was bewitched, his resistance was lowered and the psychological stimulant it gave to Shaka strengthened his own overpowering personality.

Amongst the Royal Ngunis the rule of primogeniture was not regarded and the favourite son of the chief or king was usually appointed as successor. Nevertheless Shaka now had four weighty claims, viz.: (1) He was the eldest surviving son in the Indlun-Kulu (Great House); (2) His prowess as a warrior and capacity to rule were unquestionable; (3) His father favoured him; (4) And, most potent factor of all, Dingiswayo wished him to succeed.

Shaka was now promoted to Commander-in-Chief of all

Bryant, op. cit.

Dingiswayo's armed forces, and a member of the Inner Council. As such, he insisted on visiting each military kraal in rotation to tighten up the discipline and extend the drill with rapid forced route marches. In fact he constituted himself an Inspector-General of the Forces.

One of his first duties as Commander-in-Chief was a very pleasant one, viz.: to install his old comrade-in-arms, Nqoboka, as chief of the Sokulu clan. Nqoboka had been ousted by his brother Nondlovu many years previously, and had then taken refuge with the Mtetwas. Nondlovu now disobeyed a summons to appear at Dingiswayo's court and it was decided to remove him and replace him with Nqoboka, who was accordingly given an adequate force to carry out this decree: Shaka installed the new Chief after a short, decisive battle in which Nondlovu was killed. In those days a kraal was not totally 'eaten up' as it was in the ruthless days to come. Nqoboka gave a feast to Shaka and his force before they departed, and they remained the closest lifelong friends.

Towards the end of 1815 Senzangakona's health rapidly declined, and early in 1816 he died. Weak and wasted, he had in the end given way to the incessant importuning of his eighth wife, Bibi, to appoint her son Sigujana as his successor.

When a Nguni chief dies it is always given out that he is 'indisposed', to enable his successor to grasp firmly the chieftaincy and if necessary to 'remove' any opposition there may be. The dead body is wrapped in a black bull's hide, and kept in the chief's hut, where it is constantly guarded in front of a fire which is not allowed to go out. To counteract the dreadful stench the watchers plug their nostrils with the stink plant, *umsuzwane* (*Lippia asperifolia*).

Although kindly and civil in the business of their daily lives, the Ngunis concealed in their social system many remnants of their primordial barbarism. When Senzangakona died, a cruel and ancient rite was celebrated – his private body servants were caught, ceremoniously killed, and their bodies placed in the grave in order that their spirits might keep the chief company. The work was done by men of strong criminal repute, *abatakati abakulu* (great sorcerers), who were not subsequently killed, but were banished into the wilderness, for ever thereafter beyond the pale of society.

In due course the day for the burial arrived and a nine-foot-deep grave was dug. From the floor of the grave a lateral excavation was now made extending three feet sideways, and about four feet high, running the whole length of the grave. The site of the grave was in the Mpembeni Valley known as *Makosini* (The Place of the Chiefs) where Senzangakona's seven ancestors lay buried.

Now they waited for nightfall and the rising moon. The two body servants of Senzangakona sat bound in the hut facing the corpse of their master. Hlati, their slayer, entered and gave each a long draught of the strongest beer, an inadequate anaesthetic. It was the killer's business to break up and kill the victims without breaking the skin.

Presently a party of men shorn of all ornaments entered the hut, carrying a roughly made bier on which the King's body was placed. As they left the hut Hlati entered with his assistants. The hour of doom had struck for the servants. They were led after the funeral cortège with hands bound behind their backs. Near the procession's tail walked Sigujana, the new chief, followed by the doomed men. They arrived at the grave and the body was deposited beside it. Next it was lowered on the bier with ropes. The body, which immediately after death had been tied in a sitting posture, was deposited in this position in the niche or cave dug into the side of the grave, with the feet parallel to its length. The back of the corpse leant up against the upper end of the grave within the overhang. The dead chief's accoutrements were placed beside him and at his feet. In front of him cooking pots and beer were placed.

The whole burial party stood in motionless silence. Sigujana, the new chief, stepped forward, and motioned to Hlati to begin. The bier was now placed on its side, and held in this position by its original bearers. The first victim was seized and held face downwards, with his knees across the edge of the bier. A terrific leverage was placed on the leg, for it must be broken at the knee.

The performance was repeated with the two elbows, which were also broken in the direction opposite to the natural flexing. The victim was left moaning on the ground with a stifling hand over his mouth.

The whole dreadful performance was then repeated with the second victim, and when he too was left moaning on the ground, the slayers turned again to the first victim.

He was made to sit up. A rawhide thong was wound round his neck with some six feet on either side left unwound. These loose ends were now pulled tight by Hlati's helpers, and when the victim was nearly strangled, a slayer took a heavy stick and struck the tautly drawn thong, which broke the spinal cord. The process was repeated on the other victim; then both were bound into a sitting position and lowered into the grave. Here they were deposited at the feet of the dead chief, sitting, and facing him. The grave was then filled up, and a cairn of stones built over it, and the whole covered with thorn bushes. A platoon of warriors guarded the grave from a little distance, and day and night this watch was kept for many moons, until the *ukubuyisa* (bringing back the spirit) ceremony had been performed.

When Shaka and Dingiswayo heard that Sigujana had appropriated the chieftaincy by prevailing upon the dying Senzangakona to nominate him, the former was furious, and the latter much annoyed, as he had not been advised or consulted. Shaka now called his younger half-brother, dearer to him than all, Ngwadi, son of Nandi by her second marriage to Gendeyana. It was arranged that he should see Sigujana and tell him to get out of the way betimes. Sigujana was obdurate, and one day when they were both bathing, an altercation arose and ended in a fight to the death in which Sigujana perished. Others assert that Shaka instructed Ngwadi to ingratiate himself with Sigujana, and then to assassinate him with hirelings. Shaka, though revengeful, had his own code. Ngwadi was a plain, honest, but doughty warrior as witnessed by his death, when he, though surrounded, slew eight warriors before he was killed. Finally, Dingiswayo would not have countenanced it, and why should that noblest of all Ngunis have stooped to a treachery when he had the means at his disposal to chase away, capture or kill this petty chief in fair fight?

Dingiswayo now summoned Shaka and told him to take over the chieftaincy of the Zulu clan. He put at his disposal the 2nd Izi-cwe regiment (subsequently known as 'Ngomane's Own'), which had recently been formed under Shaka's energetic recruiting policy for the expansion of Dingiswayo's armed forces. He also provided him with an imposing staff, headed by Ngomane and Dingiswayo's own nephew, Siwangu of Mbikwane. At the head of this triumphal and irresistible force Shaka entered his father's Esi-Klebeni kraal – the home of his childhood days.

With his immense size – perfectly proportioned – and in his full gala dress, his regal, dignified bearing, the easy grace of all his movements, his piercing eyes set in a strong, stern face, and the general look of authority, made plain to all that here was a warrior-king indeed.

A murmur of admiration arose from the whole assemblage as they viewed him in his gala uniform, which in itself was imposing and set him off to the greatest advantage. 'Round his bare head he wore a circlet of stuffed otter skin, bearing within its circumference bunches of gorgeous red loury plumes, and erect in front, a high glossy blue feather, two feet in length, of the blue crane. Hanging over his shoulders and chest was a fringe three inches long of manufactured "tails" of spotted genet and blue-grey monkey fur. Depending from the hips almost to the knees, and completely encircling the body, was a kilt of numberless similar "tails" of the same furs. Above each elbow were bound four dressed ox-tails concealing the arms beneath a glossy white fringe a foot in length. Similar white ox-tails, fastened beneath the knees, covered the lower leg to the ankles. Carrying in his left hand an oval ceremonial ox-hide shield, four feet long and snow white in colour tempered by a single black spot and in his right a polished assegai.'*

Ngomane now advanced to address the headmen of the Zulu clan, who, each with their following, had been assembled for the occasion.

*Fynn, op. cit.

'Children of Zulu! Today I present to you Shaka, son of Senzangakona, son of Jama, descended from Zulu, as your lawful chief. So says the "Great One" (Dingiswayo) whose mouth I am. Is there anyone here who can contest the righteousness of this decision? If so, let him stand forth and speak now, or hereafter be silent.'

There was a hushed silence but in the background someone scowled and made as if to speak, and then with one look at Shaka, kept a frozen silence. It was Dingane – Shaka's half-brother by Senzangakona's sixth wife Mpikase – who was then a youth of some nineteen years, and had just returned from a visit to Qwabeland, with hopes of acquiring the chieftaincy himself.

'No one speaks,' said Ngomane, 'then salute your chief.'

'Ba-ye-te! Nkosi.' The Royal salute was shouted. The Izi-cwe regiment gave one thunderous stamp with the right foot to show their approval, but could not join in the salute as they were Dingiswayo's men.

Shaka now ordered many oxen to be killed for a big and generous feast. His own cattle had been brought up by his half-brother Ngwadi and a party of men who had also escorted Nandi, Nomcoba and Pampata, who had all been breathless witnesses of the day's great event. They were now the guests of Mkabi and Langazana, the first and fourth wives of the late Senzangakona, and well-proven old friends.

Before the eating had started, Shaka summoned an *i-bandla* or State council, to which he gave peremptory orders to be carried out immediately. Such hustling was unknown to the Zulus – a quick and active doer being phenomenal among them.

Finding that he had no army, Shaka at once called up the whole manhood of the Zulus capable of bearing arms. Breaking up traditional guilds, he brigaded all men between thirty and forty into the *Ama-Wombe* regiment. These men being head-ringed and married, he allowed them to retain their social status, housing them in a new kraal on the Nolele stream, which was called *Belebele*. The Belebele was placed in charge of Mkabayi, Shaka's maiden aunt, a woman of formidable character.

The age-group twenty-five to thirty men, head-ringed but not yet married, lost their status and head-rings and became 'youths' again (*izinsizwa*). They were brigaded as the *Jubingqwanga*, together with such of the 1790–95 age-group as were not yet head-ringed and whose regiment was called U-Dlambedlu. The whole became known as the Izim-Pohlo, the Bachelors' Brigade, and their kraal was commanded by Mkabi and Langazana, Senzangakona's widowed queens.

But the first regiment which was completely Shaka's own creation was the U-Fasimba, consisting of all the idle twenty-year-old youths. On them he could impose his mark. With them he built his new kraal, of which they became the garrison. And henceforth they were known as Shaka's Own.

The place Shaka selected for his new capital was an agreeable spot on the right bank of the Mhodi stream, a tributary of the Umkumbane, and with a heart still brooding over the bitter wrongs suffered in childhood, he named the new kraal Kwa Bulawayo* (at Place of the Killing) in ominous remembrance of those tearful times. This first Bulawayo was a small affair compared to the second Bulawayo which he built in later years in the Umhlatuzi Valley, seventeen miles from Eshowe, and which consisted of 1400 huts. The first Bulawayo had at most 100 huts but was designed to accommodate more in the near future, and ultimately may have consisted of twice the original number of huts.

Within one month of taking over the chieftaincy, Shaka had established himself at his new Bulawayo kraal. He was now firmly in the saddle. His warriors were being licked into shape with the utmost rigour, and Dingiswayo's 2nd Izi-cwe regiment was still standing by to make sure that there would be no interference from neighbouring tribes. Ngonyama the Lion and other renowned Mbonambi blacksmiths were imported to make the new

---

* Mzilikazi, one of Shaka's generals and founder of the Matabele nation, later named his own 'Great Place' Kwa Bulawayo, which is still the name of the capital city of the Matabeleland Province in Southern Rhodesia, but without the prefix. 'Kwa', namely Bulawayo. 'Kwa' means 'At.'

broad-bladed stabbing assegais as fast as they could turn them out – principally by converting two light throwing spears into one massive *ixwa*. The hocus-pocus and secrecy were cut out and the blacksmith's trade turned into an open and flourishing industry under the supreme direction of Ngonyama, who throve exceedingly as an armourer.

The day had now come to deal out retribution to all those of the tribe who had wronged Nandi and Shaka in bygone days, and those who had opposed him in obtaining the chieftaincy.

At the head of the kraal there stood a shady tree, and here Shaka placed his judgement seat, which consisted of a large bundle or roll of mats. On either side of him, on the ground, squatted his councillors or headmen. Next to them on either side stood the specially selected slayers armed with unusually heavy clubs, known as *izin-tsulungu*. Drawn up behind Shaka and the councillors in crescent formation stood a carefully selected half company of the Fasimba regiment – the Royal Guards in embryo.

First to be brought up for trial was Mudli, Shaka's paternal uncle, the same Mudli, who, when Nandi was found to be pregnant, had sent back the infamous message that 'She is but harbouring an I-Shaka (an intestinal beetle)'.

The Zulus say that on Shaka's left front was Nandi, seated on a big mat. Then Mudli was led forward by two guards. He was a tall, stately, dignified but somewhat corpulent man of sixty years or so. At fifteen feet he and his escort halted, and in perfect unison all three lifted their right hand and gave the Royal salute 'Ba-ye-te! Nkosi' (Hail, Oh Chief!) and then squatted on their haunches.

In a soft, gentle voice Shaka said: 'Sakubona (Greetings), Mudli. I have long hungered to hear a little more wisdom from your mouth concerning those obnoxious insects – those I-Shaka. Now what was the message you sent to my mother's E-Langeni people?'

'I remember not, Oh Chief,' replied Mudli.

'Then as elder of the tribe and bestower of names will you please explain to me why I was called "Shaka"?'

There was no response. Shaka turned to his mother and said: '*Mame* ! (mother) you see how his silence convicts him?'

Then Shaka turned to Mudli again and asked in the same gentle tones, 'Tell me, my uncle, why were you always so consistently unkind to my mother? Why did you always slight her? Tell her, for you see her, and she would like to know.'

Again there was no response.

'Now tell me,' went on Shaka, 'why did you, after my reconciliation with my father, try to influence him against me wherever you could? Why did you support Sigujana, and even after his death fail to extend a welcome to me?' Mudli still preserved a dignified silence.

Then Shaka's voice dropped almost to a whisper as he said, 'A little heated iron or some other methods which we know of may make you speak.'

'I have nothing to say, Oh Chief,' replied Mudli at last.

'Do you hear, Mother, he has nothing to say; now speak.'

'He treated me grievously whenever he could,' answered Nandi.

'That, Mother, is enough,' said Shaka. Then rising to his full stature, Shaka, contorted with rage, roared at Mudli, 'You are condemned to death, and your going shall not be easy. Furthermore, know, all people, whosoever is not kindly to Nandi here, my mother, is already as good as dead and they shall die the "hard way".* On the other hand all those whom Nandi, the *Ndlovukazi* (The Female Elephant – a courtesy title conferred on Queens in a Nguni State), smiles upon, shall grow fat in my shadow. You slayers there, hold Mudli while we consider these other cases.' Shaka sat down and called for the next case, amidst a deadly

---

*From time immemorial the Nguni races have killed those found guilty of witchcraft in the following manner. The victim is held down, and four sharpened sticks, each twelve inches long, are driven up his rectum, and hammered out of sight. The unfortunate person is then left on the veld to die a slow and agonising death.

Others than sorcerers, condemned to this form of death, were usually rendered unconscious first by having their heads twisted, which in itself in most cases resulted in a speedy death.

silence. The shocked spectators now knew what manner of chief they had. Mudli's rank and relationship had not saved him.

One by one a dozen people who had slighted Nandi or opposed his chieftaincy, or both, were brought before Shaka. Each one was peremptorily questioned for a few minutes, and sentenced to death by clubbing. In the case of one who had opposed Shaka, Nandi intervened, and pointed out that he had been kind to her. Shaka retracted the death sentence and gave him an ox. When the cases were finished, Shaka turned on the condemned men and asked them if they had anything to say. He told them to note well that he was not touching their families or cattle.

'This I have to say, son of my brother,' replied Mudli in measured tones, 'I fear not death, for often I have faced it on the field of battle. Nor do I fear pain, but for Royal blood to die a felon's death, that brings shame not only on the one who dies, but on all those of the same blood.'

'Well spoken, Mudli,' returned Shaka, 'I would never have you killed like a sorcerer. I said that your going would not be easy. But a warrior's death you shall have.'

'Ba-ye-te ! Nkosi !' responded Mudli with a sincere ring of thanks in his voice. And tradition says that he was taking a last pinch of snuff when the Headman approached him, not with a club, but with a spear.

'It is a warrior's death for you as the Ndlovunkulu (Great Elephant) has decreed. But hurry not, Baba (My Father), for the last pinch of snuff is sweet, and maybe you have a message for those you will see no more.'

'I thank you, Headman; and this is the message I would like you to convey to my sons, and all my kin.' He paused, as he took another pinch of snuff, with the same deliberation he would have employed at an ordinary council-meeting. 'Tell them, and hearken too all ye young warriors, that the Zulus now have a chief of chiefs – aye, greater even than Zulu (Heaven) himself, from whose loins we all sprang, and whose name we now all bear. Tell them I was blind not to have seen this long ago, and that I deserve my fate for getting in the path of the Great Elephant, who is now stamping me flat, but has spared my kraal. Tell them I die gladly now, for our Great Elephant will stamp out our lifelong enemies, the Butelezis, who have so often inflicted grievous humiliations on us, and he will eat up all the surrounding tribes, and make the Zulus great. Finally, tell them that it is my wish, and my command, that they fight for the new chief till they die. So speaks Mudli, son of Nkwelo, of Ndaba, who is now going to eat earth. Now, Headman, do your work.'

There was a pregnant silence. They all liked the old man and greatly respected him, but they knew, too, that he had committed the mistake of mistakes in Nguni usage, by backing the wrong bull, and his life was therefore forfeit.

The headman approached with a spear in his hand. Mudli looked straight ahead and past him. In one quick flash the spear was raised and plunged under the left nipple diagonally and horizontally through the chest.

Slayers and warriors gazed in silence, which was presently broken by the platoon commander, 'Hau! Indoda' ('A Man indeed').

CHAPTER 7

*Making of an army – Retribution – The E-Langeni
punished and annexed*

SHAKA now lived at his Bulawayo kraal. At the top end of
the kraal he had fenced off some twenty huts, which were his
own private preserve and the beginning of the *Um-Dlunkulu*,
or seraglio, for his women, or 'sisters', as he called them. For the
time being he lived there alone with his mother, sister, Pampata
and attendants. Most of the other eighty huts were taken up
by the young Fasimba regiment who were to develop into the
famous Royal Guards, Shaka's Own.

Shaka was tireless in getting his little army into shape. Nearly
every day he visited one of his two other military kraals and woe
betide the defaulters. His kingdom was so small – a paltry ten
miles by ten – that from his central position he could reach any
of its confines within an hour.

To understand the task which presently lay ahead of Shaka
with his 'army' or rabble of 500 men, which he had inherited,
the following comparison may assist in forming a picture. In
1879 – sixty-three years later – to conquer Zululand it required
a British Army of 20,000 Imperial foot soldiers and cavalry armed
with breech-loading rifles, cannon and rocket batteries, in addition to Colonial mounted troops and thousands of Natal Native
levies, many of them armed with rifles. It further needed more
than 1000 ox-drawn wagons capable of carrying three tons each
to provide the commissariat. Nor did the British Army have to
look for the Zulus, for without exception it was the latter who
attacked, and yet the campaign lasted for a full six months due
to the initial grave disasters of the British.

It was the nation and military machine which Shaka had
created which resisted the British.

Nevertheless Shaka had to fight the same war-like forebears

before he could forge the different tribes into a homogeneous Zulu nation and in the beginning he had only those 500 untrained men armed with light throwing spears to help him to accomplish his task. His tiny kingdom was surrounded on all sides by infinitely stronger tribes and confederations, who, through the wars of Dingiswayo, had acquired a progressively mounting military efficiency and ferocity. Now, whereas the British Army had to conquer only the area at present known as Zululand – some 10,000 square miles – Shaka brought under his direct rule an area more than ten times as great, whilst his 'Shadow' hovered over territory twelve times greater still, or 120 times as large as present-day Zululand, of which Shaka's original inheritance only formed one per cent, i.e. about 100 square miles.

Shaka's particular genius lay in his meticulous personal attention to detail, and sheer hard work. If at all possible he always insisted on inspecting everything himself. In every one of his critical battles he insisted on personally reconnoitring the ground and the disposition of the enemy forces. He invariably checked all reports by producing collateral evidence. He was a firm believer in the maxim: 'It is the master's eye which makes the cow grow fat.'

Two months after his accession Shaka called all his 'regiments' together for general manoeuvres. The combined forces totalled only about 500 men. He told them of the virtues of the one short, heavy stabbing assegai in place of the light throwing one, and arranged to demonstrate this.

The Fasimba, and the next youngest, the U-Dlambedlu, now had the new weapon, known as the *ixwa*, issued to them. The smiths had not yet forged enough for the whole army but were kept busy converting the throwing assegais. The youngsters of the Fasimba, as Shaka had calculated, took up the new weapon with enthusiasm, soon to be followed by an older group, until it had penetrated to the oldest and most conservative regiments.

Next Shaka ordered all his regiments to discard their sandals. There was consternation, especially among the older groups, but he pointed to his own unshod feet, and in a contest demonstrated his own superior speed and that of some other unshod warriors over all those who wore sandals.

A month later Shaka noticed that there was still a lot of ill-will and murmuring against the abolishing of the sandals. He instructed the Fasimba regiment to collect many basketsful of *nkunzanas*, the three-pronged 'devil thorns' which always have one prong pointing upwards, and are sometimes encountered in considerable numbers in certain localities which are avoided by all those travelling barefoot. Their spikes average three-sixteenths of an inch.

When enough of these 'devil thorns' had been collected, Shaka ordered them to be strewn over the Bulawayo parade ground. All the regiments were then ordered to parade a little aside of the ground covered with the thorns. Shaka then addressed them: 'My children, it has come to my ears that some of you have dainty feet and this has sorely grieved my heart. In my fatherly kindness I have decided to help you to harden your feet so that you will never have occasion again to complain about them. The parade ground has therefore been strewn with *nkunzanas* which you will proceed to stamp out of sight with your bare feet. Now, my children, it is my will that you should do this with gusto, to prove how gladly you obey my commands. Those who hesitate, or who stamp gingerly, will be disobedient to my commands, and disobedience merits death. My slayers are at hand. Now go to it with a will.'

The regiments gritted their teeth and, chanting their war song and led by Shaka himself, spread over the parade ground. Shaka's feet, however, from long exposure were hard, horny and impervious. Now he turned and faced them, and as he led in the stamping, his eagle eye at once picked out those who were hesitant. These he approached with his slayers, and bidding them stand forward, had them clubbed to death. And so he went, searching up and down the lines, but after half a dozen examples had been made, all the warriors stamped with a frenzy in which they vied to outdo each other.

When Shaka was satisfied that the thorns had been stamped

out of sight he dismissed the parade with the words, 'I thank you, my children, for your zeal in carrying out my will, which you will soon learn is the only law in your lives and in the land I rule. Now take these oxen and eat heartily, and let there be generous measures of beer, which you will find awaiting you. For you have done your duty and deserve reward.'

According to the Zulu chronicler, during the drinking and talking among the men which followed, the Fasimba taunted the older regiments, there were mutual insults, and fighting broke out in which the Fasimba – urged on, some say, by Mgobozi! – gave a very good account of themselves. After Shaka, warned by Pampata, had appeared and stopped the fighting, it is said that Mgobozi told his chieftain : 'Baba, before another moon is past you will have an army of men. The Fasimba will stamp out a burning kraal for you. The older men feel sore where the *nkun-zanas* pricked them, but that is nothing. They feel still more sore where my boys jabbed them. That, too, is nothing, and will pass in a few days. The greatest of their hurts, however, is in their hearts, and they will never get over that until, in a real battle against outside enemies, they can get their honour back by excelling the Fasimba. Today's fight was the finest thing that could happen, and when the "Great One" ordered all the strong beer and meat, and threw us as close together as a man and his wife, I had a little dream that my Father had it in his heart, that a little rivalry would not come amiss for the better training of the older men. They will now drill with their whole hearts in their work.'

Shaka now listened to much sage advice, and at last he was prompted to offer Mgobozi the post of Commander-in-Chief under himself. To this offer Mgobozi replied: 'Nay, my Father, that would be a mistake, for when I am in a battle I see only my own assegai and the man before me, and I forget all else. A small command at most I could manage in battle. To drill your army in peace, and to advise you in council, that I could do, but when it comes to fighting, then just let me be your leading warrior who starts the killing.'

Shaka respected Mgobozi's views on any matter connected

with warfare, and rarely checked his garrulousness. But his principal, unofficial adviser in civil affairs was unquestionably Pampata. She supplied him, during frequent nocturnal visits, with all the current rumours, trends of opinion, criticism or approval of his policy, all that was passing in the mind of his people. Her intuitions were remarkable and always a source of pleased surprise to Shaka. She read his thoughts and always anticipated his wishes. She was now twenty-four years old, and he five years older.

Pampata apparently early resigned herself to the fact that she would never be his wife but determined to be his first and principal woman and a power behind the throne. She became necessary to him because she knew how to make herself so, and if she were absent it was not so much her body that he missed, as her mind, her shrewd conversation, and her ability to foretell events by reading Shaka's mind. And because of her close alliance with his mother Nandi, the most powerful influence in his life, Pampata could exercise restraint over him.

Shaka, having effected all his reforms in his own tribe, proposed to extend his reformative and retributive activities. He had dealt with individuals; now he would deal with clans, beginning with the E-Langeni, of which his own mother was a daughter, in which he and she had spent those first hideous years of exile and sorrow, and where they had been so cruelly treated. His army was now a war machine indeed. He marshalled it and made a night march of twenty-five miles over the Mtonjaneni Heights to E-Langeniland. Before dawn he had silently surrounded the Esiweni kraal, the capital of Makedama, the E-Langeni chief. As soon as it became light the chief was summoned to surrender, and he did so without any waste of time.

Shaka ordered all the inhabitants to be brought before him, and singled out all those who, so many years before, had inflicted untold misery on his mother and himself. Some other kraals which harboured his youthful tormentors had also been surrounded by detachments of the army, and their inhabitants were also brought up for scrutiny and judgement.

All those with whom Shaka had old scores to settle were now brought before him and the rest were liberated, but ordered to attend the trial and its sequel as spectators. Some three dozen of those selected were paraded before their accuser and judge.

Gently Shaka reminded them of their boyhood days, and recalled incident after incident in a way which was truly astonishing. One by one he tried them, and some he told to stand over to the left, occasionally one was ordered to the right. Each one was asked if he could remember one single act of kindness he had shown towards Shaka, his mother or his sister. One of them claimed to have fetched for Nandi a specially good *imbogoto* (water-worn, round grinding-stone) from a distant place, and Shaka told him to stand apart. One other averred that he had saved from death by fire a little pet goat-kid belonging to Nomcoba. This man too Shaka told to stand apart. No other claims were made. The men on trial were all three to eight years older than Shaka, who was then twenty-nine.

Shaka now began his indictment against the accused. From the gentle way he started none of them guessed what was coming. Beginning with the man who had given his mother a grinding-stone he remarked that this had been a voluntary act of kindness, a faint echo of which lingered in his memory, now that he had been reminded. He therefore told the man that inasmuch as he had done this for Nandi, his mother, he had done it for Shaka too, and that his bullying of the latter would be wiped from his memory. He was therefore free to go, and would receive an ox as a present; before he left, however, he bade him tarry in order to see how much he owed to that one *imbogoto*.

Turning to the second suppliant, Shaka said to him sternly, 'You did but a herd-boy's duty in saving the kid from the fire. Wherefore you have no claim. Join those others on the right.'

The whole group on the right were now led before Shaka, who addressed them as follows: 'Little did you reckon many years ago that the young herd-boy whom you bullied and sneered at, and often whipped quite needlessly, would one day have you in his power as I have you now. It is true you were not as mercilessly cruel as those on the left, nor did any of you, to my knowledge, insult my mother. The time has come, however, for you to pay your debt and that you shall do by "eating earth" (to be dead) before this sun has set. In my mercy I have decreed that you shall die quickly by the club. Before you leave this earth, however, I want you to watch the going of these others on my left, and then you will die praising me for the kindness I have shown to you.'

Whilst this was being done Shaka called for two bowls of water, and then deliberately disrobed in front of all the gathering. The bound men on the left were ordered to approach and squat on their haunches. Shaka then arose and towered over them.

'You will all die,' he roared. Then after a dreadful pause he resumed in deep, even tones, 'Before I tell you the manner of your going there are some things I have to say to you. You are such a filthy collection of *utuvi* (excrement) that the very sight of you contaminates me, and I must wash before I proceed.' Very deliberately he now poured water over his head, and rinsed his whole body carefully, until the first bowl was empty. Then he reminded them of how they had sneered at his bodily inadequacy and bade them note that they had lied.

'This is the death I have in mind for you. The slayers will sharpen the projecting upright poles in this cattle-kraal – one for each of you. They will then lead you there, and four of them will pick you up singly and impale you on each of the sharpened poles. There you will stay till you die, and your bodies, or what will be left of them by the birds, will stay there as a testimony to all, what punishment awaits those who slander me and my mother.' As the anguished victims were led away Shaka taunted them with 'Hlalani gahle' ('Sit you well!' not the customary 'Salanigahle!' i.e. 'Stay you well'). Then he ordered the second bowl of water, and again washed his whole body to 'cleanse it from the last defiling look, of those he had sent to their doom.

Shaka did not come to gloat upon the indescribable agony of his victims. In fact it was a remarkable trait that he always, if possible, tried to avoid witnessing executions, except those comparatively humane head-twistings, which were sometimes carried out in his presence, when he issued a summary death sentence.

After a time Shaka sent orders to the slayers to end the death agonies of the victims by placing bundles of grass under them and firing them. As the flames licked about them, those who were still conscious shrieked out in their death agonies, which were now short-lived.

Thereupon each of the twelve condemned to death by clubbing walked to his end with a loud exclamation of 'Baba Nkosi' (Father Chief), and was dispatched with one crushing blow to his skull.

Makedama, the chief of the E-Langeni, was a docile man and he, with his whole tribe, submitted meekly to Shaka's demands; these were a close alliance, indistinguishable from incorporation with the Zulu clan. Dingiswayo, who was kept advised by Shaka, closed at least one eye to this arrangement, as it lay within his policy to form the Zulu, and neighbouring clans, into a strong bastion between the powerful Ngcobos, Cunus and Qwabes on one side and the Ndwandwes and Ngwanes on the other.

Many fantastic tales, utterly without foundation, have been woven around Shaka's act of retribution against the E-Langeni. Dr A. T. Bryant, that incomparable authority, and all reliable writers agree that Shaka impaled and burnt a selected number of his former tormentors but nothing more. After all, the E-Langeni were his mother's people, and he was therefore half an E-Langeni himself, and far from being vindictive against the tribe as a whole he actually and naturally accorded the tribe special privileges, the more so as its chief, Makedama, was his pliant tool. Through the E-Langeni, who were about equal to the Zulus in numbers, Shaka immediately doubled the forces at his disposal. Shaka was never a fool, whatever else he may have been, and for popular-fiction writers to assert that he marched the whole E-Langeni tribe – man, woman and child – over a precipice to their destruction – a tribe, be it noted, who as a whole acclaimed him as their hero – is not only nonsense, but cheap sensationalism. Because of this and other utterly unfounded stories, fed to

a gullible public, has grown the untold number of fantastic legends which claimed almost every precipice and waterfall in Zululand and the Natal coast as a place of execution used by Shaka for individuals. regiments, and even tribes.

CHAPTER 8

The second conquest – The harem established

ON returning to Bulawayo from the E-Langeni expedition, Shaka continued to concentrate on the building up of his armed forces. He received considerable reinforcements from the Qungebeni and E-Langeni clans, who were sent by their chiefs in complete bodies of the same age-groups, later becoming attached to Shaka's regiments as separate wings or companies, according to their ages. He had formed friendly alliances with the neighbouring Sibiya and Gazini clans, whose chiefs encouraged their young men to volunteer their services; and with the Qungebeni on his northern frontier, subsequently incorporated with the Zulus.

Soldiers of fortune from many parts of the country were attracted by the fame of *Nodumehlezi*. These included Mdlaka, son of Ncidi of the Gazini clan, who in a few years rose to be Shaka's generalissimo, and Nzobo, son of Sobadli of the Ntombela clan, who also became a leading general. Dingiswayo also allowed a number of his men to transfer to Shaka's service. The new levies were rigorously drilled and (as soon as these became available) were armed with the broad-bladed stabbing assegai. They too had to discard their sandals, and were given one month in which to harden their feet.

Shaka now turned his eye to his western boundary, where Chief Pungashe had referred to him jeeringly as 'Dingiswayo's poor-man'. That settled it! He would teach him! This was the man who had so frequently captured his father, and heaped insults and indignities on him and the whole Zulu clan. Moreover, here was an opportunity of testing his new fighting methods. He sent an ambassador to Pungashe, demanding an apology. Pungashe told him to return to Shaka and tell him, 'Barking pups are silenced with a switch!' War was accordingly declared in the easy-going, good old-fashioned way. The opposing forces faced each other at the appointed place in the battle array. Many Butelezi women were standing some distance behind their men, 'to enjoy the fun', and also carried much beer to celebrate the coming victory.

Shaka commanded his troops in person. The Fasimba, now numbering over 300, were in the front centre, with the Belebele immediately behind them. Thus these two bodies formed the 'head and chest'. On either side of the Fasimba were drawn up half the Izim-Pohlo or 'Bachelors' Brigade'. Just before the action started they were rapidly extended to form the enveloping 'horns'. Shaka's total force numbered about 750 men.

Pungashe's Butelezis, about 600 strong, were drawn up in four or five lines, with a total frontage of about 200 yards. Pungashe himself sat at a safe distance on a knoll far behind his force. Before Shaka appeared this used to be the practice of all chiefs – to keep out of danger.

Shaka, through his spies, knew almost to a man the strength of the Butelezis. The numerical superiority of his own he tried to hide as much as possible by keeping his men more densely formed, with instructions to hold their shields at the 'carry' by their sides.

He now roared out the order to extend to the proper fighting formation. When this had been done he shouted the second order, 'Show shields!' (i.e. to hold them broadside on). The psychological effect of this was to give the impression that his force had been suddenly more than doubled, as if by magic.

The two forces were about 100 yards apart. Shaka ordered the 'horns' to deploy, and for some moments the Butelezis gazed in astonishment. Then the whole centre advanced with a measured stride. Mgobozi was in the van of the Fasimba. Shaka stood behind them but immediately in front of the Belebele, and, more than half a head taller than the rest, he had a clear view of the whole field.

When they had advanced to within sixty yards of the Butelezis, the Zulus gave their terrible war-cry '*Si-gī-di!*' and charged right on to the bewildered Butelezis, who were barely able to discharge a desultory shower of ineffective throwing spears before the

Fasimba were amongst them with their deadly stabbing blades. In a very short time the first line of the Butelezis melted away amidst a chorus of 'Nga-dlas!' from the exultant Zulus. Mgobozi was in the thick of it, and with his 'left hook' with the shield, time and again he would expose the left nipple of his opponent and drive his blade in just below it, as he yelled to his men 'Stab, lads, stab!' Soon the Butelezis were a flying mob of panic-stricken fugitives. But flight availed them nothing, for the speedy, bare-footed killers kept up with them, and in fact ran circles around their clumsily shod opponents.

The two converging 'horns' were closing in on them too, and within these 'horns' were the now terrified women spectators. It was useless for a Butelezi warrior to throw down his spears and expect the age-old custom of making him a prisoner to be observed. Armed or disarmed, he was instantly slain. Drunk with battle-lust and the sight of blood, the Zulus came up to the surrounded women, among whom some Butelezi warriors had rushed for cover. A frenzied butchery of the screaming women now began, and within a short space of time the last one had shrieked out her life.

Every wounded enemy warrior was now finished off. Then his abdomen was opened 'to enable his spirit to escape'. Pungashe and half his personal attendants alone escaped by running down a wooded watercourse leading to the White Umfolozi river. The other half of his attendants acted as decoy, and drew their pursuers away until they were overtaken and slaughtered to a man.

The Zulu forces were now sent out in every direction to round up the Butelezi women, children and cattle; to kill off all the old and useless of both sexes, and to burn every hut.

The Zulu dead and wounded were astonishingly few. Friends attended the latter, and those who were beyond help were, before sundown, dispatched with a single stab through their hearts. Consent to this new Spartan method was tacitly implied, or taken for granted in those beyond speech.

Surveying the day's results, Shaka had no further doubts: a new order of warfare had been inaugurated in Nguni-land. The chief had certainly escaped, but he had been compelled to abandon his tribe and was now a fugitive abroad. As it later turned out, he sought refuge with Zwide, the chief of the powerful Ndwandwe tribe. When Pungashe complained to Zwide that he had been driven from hearth and home, and his tribe had been destroyed by the Zulu chief, Zwide sneeringly inquired, 'What is the size of this chief who can drive away another chief as great as you?' 'A mere boy,' replied Pungashe, 'but his fighting is as irresistible as fire; the like of which I have never seen before; and, moreover, led in person by himself.' Zwide was astonished, and not a little perturbed. He is reported to have had Pungashe assassinated later on, but this cannot be confirmed. At any rate Pungashe disappeared from the stage.

All the neighbouring tribes now looked with respect and awe on Shaka. He incorporated the whole Butelezi tribe in the Zulu, E-Langeni and Qungebeni clans. The vacant lands of the Butelezis he peopled with families from his own and allied tribes. The captured cattle, however, went to Dingiswayo, under whose paramountcy Shaka was supposedly acting; but to his protégé he allowed a goodly portion.

The unmarried Butelezi women became Shaka's 'crown property' – about 100 – aged from eighteen to twenty years. He divided them into three groups of approximately even numbers, and apportioned one group each to the military kraals of the Belebele and the Esi-Klebeni, the former under his maiden aunt Mkabayi, and the latter under the late Senzangakona's first wife Mkabi, and fourth wife Langazana. The third group he placed under Nandi to form the nucleus of the Um-Dlunkulu (Those of the Great House), the name he gave to each one of his seraglios at each of his military kraals. These maidens of the seraglio he called his 'sisters', and under no circumstances did he allow them to be referred to as his wives. At Bulawayo, Nandi was responsible for their good conduct, and one of her duties consisted in a careful pudendal inspection of each girl at the time of her 'moon', to make sure she was not pregnant, and that any signs of tampering with the hymen corresponded with Shaka's own recollection of each individual case. Even when, at the zenith of his power, his 'sisters' reached the prodigious number of 1200 in his various seraglios (Fynn says 5000), it is perfectly astounding how he knew the history of each.

In order to grasp this it is necessary to illustrate the average Zulu's powers of memory when applied to cattle. The Royal herdsmen of the Zulu kings had as many as 5000* head of cattle in one herd. They did not count them for the simple reason that they could not. Yet if one were missing they knew at once, for among the fifty herdsmen or so that were in charge one would at once miss from his particular bunch of approximately 100 head a familiar face or body. To him each cow and calf were as individualistic as 100 women and children are to the headman of a large kraal. The present-day Basuto herdsman in charge of 1000 merino sheep is even more remarkable. Although the sheep look as alike as peas to the European, the herdsman, without counting, will notify the loss of one single sheep and describe its characteristics!

Shaka liked to have his herds of cattle assembled in uniform colours or markings. Thus there would be pure white herds, or pure black and pure red. Thereafter there would be uniform mixed colours. This to a European would make it far more difficult to distinguish one from the other, but to the Zulu it made no difference at all. The Zulu nomenclature for various coloured cattle runs to over 300 – an incredible number when we compare it with the scanty dozen or so names we have for the different colours of cattle and horses combined. As the Zulu did not read, all his waking thoughts were concentrated on the surrounding objects that interested him most, which, starting from his childhood days, first included plant, bird, animal and insect life, and then later cattle, women and war.

In this way he built up for himself without a single borrowing, as recorded in Dr A. T. Bryant's monumental dictionary, a vocabulary of some 19,000 words – truly a stupendous feat for an unwritten language and falling short by but 1000 words of the vocabulary used by Shakespeare. These 19,000 words were of a necessity used by the Zulus in their daily talk, for, being unwritten, they could not otherwise have been preserved. Again, it is strange, but true, that it was the womenfolk of the nation who

*Fynn counted 5654 in one average herd.

were the most erudite exponents of the language, as, in addition to the ordinary vocabulary, they had to master all the additional words dictated by the *hlonipa** custom.

Finally the Zulu language has eight different classes of nouns governing the inflections of each verb and adjective. In one of the most complicated but exact grammars in the world, although unwritten until the European came, every Zulu then, as now, spoke with perfect grammatical exactitude, and ungrammatical speaking is utterly unknown to the Zulu.

A little prior to the battle against the Butelezis, Nqoboka, Shaka's old comrade-in-arms, and now chief of the Sokulus, seventy miles away at the coast, had sent Shaka two of the best damsels of his tribe. After the battle the chiefs of the neighbouring Qungebenis, Ntombelas, Gazini, E-Langeni and Sibiyas each sent two or more of their prettiest girls to grace Shaka's seraglio. These, numbering about a dozen, were also quartered at Bulawayo.

To give tone to his Court Shaka had brought to Bulawayo his half-sister Nomzintlanga, the daughter of Mkabi, and the Nkosazana, or Princess Royal, of the Zulus. Shaka had a special regard for her because, with her mother, she had been kind to him in his childhood days and subsequently he put her in charge of one of his numerous military kraals.

Shaka had from now onwards many affairs of State to attend to. Through conquest and friendly alliances he had half a dozen tributary clans. In point of numbers and territory the Zulu sphere of influence had quadrupled within the space of a year, and Shaka lost no time in consolidating his position. The army too had grown to a strength of 2000 and the Fasimba regiment was 800 strong. In spite of his rigorous discipline his forces were daily augmented by a steady stream of soldiers of fortune, freebooters and men who had to flee from their clans for one cause or another.

The secret of his popularity was his great liberality to his soldiers at the expense of his tributary chiefs and the personal attention he gave to the needs of his warriors. Lastly, like his

*See Appendix.

contemporary, Napoleon, who told his soldiers that they each carried a Field-Marshal's baton in their knapsacks, Shaka let his warriors know that there was no limit to their promotion, irrespective of their clan or social status, provided only that they had proved their merit. Thus he made Mdlaka of the Gazini clan commander of the Fasimba, and Nzobo of the Ntombelas commander of the Izim-Pohlo.

Shortly after the Butelezi battle Shaka had summoned Mgobozi to his council hut for a special talk. They discussed the battle and its significance for Shaka's new fighting methods. Mgobozi approved of this introduction of 'total war', but not of the slaughter of the women. He is said to have pointed out to his chief that this was a wanton waste, and that he could have done with some of the women himself, 'When you, Great Elephant, permit me to marry'.

Permission to marry was granted, and the Army was delighted to hear of Mgobozi's reward. Within a short time he had put on the head-ring, selected a kraal-site within two miles of Bulawayo, and asked for audience of the 'Great Elephant'.

The 'August One' was having his customary bath in public at the head of the Bulawayo kraal. There were many people seeking audience and Mgobozi, having saluted with 'Bayete !', joined the crowd. 'Several page-boys brought water in gourds which they held vertically above their heads, and then handed them to Shaka with both arms extended. First he rinsed his body with water, and then another page-boy approached with a large black wooden dish.'* From this Shaka took a paste of fat and ground millet corn, and 'soaped' the whole body with it. A bowl of water was now held before him and he washed the paste away. All this time he was carrying on a running conversation with those around him. As soon as the water had dried on him a page-boy presented a basket of cosmetics. 'From this His Majesty took a lump of red ochre paste with which he smeared his whole skin, and then rubbed it in until it had almost disappeared. A final application of native butter made the body resplendent with a beautiful ruddy, silky gloss, as became a king.'*

* Fynn, *op. cit.*

Shaka now proceeded to his dressing-room – likewise *al fresco*, in the cool shadow of a tree. There in the shade he comfortably donned his kilt of furry tails, with armlets, leglets and tippet of silky white cow-tails; then, seated in his chair of state – consisting of a huge roll of *induli* matting – had his head and body bedecked with red loury plumes, and fancy coloured beadwork. Beside him throughout the ceremony stood a page-boy bearing the royal umbrella – a large white ox-hide shield – to ward off any intruding sun-rays.

Although it is customary for Zulus of every rank to wash in public, at any convenient stream, it was an innovation of Shaka's to raise this act into a public ceremony which took place at his court every day at about 10 a.m., when the crowds around him – of both sexes – were at their greatest.

Shaka now motioned Mgobozi to approach. 'By my sister! Mgobozi, you have lost no time in putting on your head-ring, and well it becomes you as my "inner councillor". Have you selected the site for your kraal?'

'Yebo Baba.'

'Where is it?'

'On the hillside facing the river down there.'

'Good; then let us proceed to erect it. Let the whole Fasimba turn out, and before nightfall your kraal should be up. How many huts do you propose to erect?'

'Nay, my Father, that is for you to say. I have but put in a few sticks as markers – nothing but a rough indication for a hut or two.'

Arrived at the site Shaka beheld an innumerable array of 'markers'. First a large outer circle, with a smaller inner one (for the cattle-kraal), and in the space between, some twenty smaller circles had been marked to denote the places for the huts.

Even Shaka was astonished. 'Mgobozi! are these the "one or two huts" you so casually mentioned, or do my eyes deceive me and I see the plan for a fair-sized military kraal?'

'Nay, Great Elephant, 'tis but planning for future expansion as you daily drum into me, and, as my Father knows, I am but his obedient dog.'

'Mgobozi, if I let you pour any more cream on my tongue my Bulawayo kraal will rank second to yours. But know, all you people, and the regiments here assembled, that Mgobozi may have his plans carried out, for on many a day he protected my back in the thick of battle, and but for him I should not be here. Now set to, all of you, and get the kraal finished by tomorrow. Call in the women all round to assist.'

Shaka then turned to Mgobozi : 'We now come to the question of women. How many shall they be?'

'My Father, I have spoken to one or two, and they looked not unkindly at me, but their fathers have hearts of stone, which nothing would melt but a look from you, or the necessary number of cattle from me.'

'When you say one or two, Mgobozi, that means twenty in plain language, as I have learnt to my cost !'

And twenty, according to the tradition, was the number of Mgobozi's brides, for it was Shaka's policy to demonstrate that a man who served him well, although not of the Zulu people and, as in the case of his famous drill-instructor, a member of a tribe so primitive that they had not the use of metals, could rise to great wealth and position. It was Shaka who paid the *lobola* (dowries) for Mgobozi's wives, although he need not have done so. For, autocrat though he was, even at that time of his reign, he could not then, or at any time, run counter to the custom of the land. True, he could have a man rich in cattle and maidens 'smelt out' and executed as a sorcerer (*umtagati*) or on some other pretext, and confiscate all his property, but that was within the bounds of immemorial custom.

CHAPTER 9

Mgobozi married – Death of Mbiya

ALTHOUGH Mgobozi emerges from the Zulu spoken chronicle as the great fighter, and the hammer of Shaka, he also stands in this unwritten epic for comedy: and the matter of his wedding to twenty brides has become the subject of a hundred high-spirited anecdotes. It is said that he had made the most reckless promises of seniority to all the maidens he approached. In every Zulu kraal the precedence of the wives is strictly regulated by the position of the huts, which are arranged in three sections or 'houses'. The 'Great House' ranks first. Thereafter come the 'Left House' and then the 'Right House'. Then again there may be any number of affiliated huts to any of these 'Houses', and the precedence of the occupants is determined by the position the huts occupy. Therefore no amount of attention to the occupant of hut number two can take away the fact that in precedence she ranks after the occupant of hut number one – although it would be a great compensation to be shown more attention.

Mgobozi is said to have told all twenty of his betrothed that wherever her hut was placed in his kraal, there he would be found and to have become involved in a series of ludicrous situations in consequence. As Shaka said,

'Mgobozi, you are in the cooking-pot, with twenty pairs of hands to hold down the lid !'*

At the wedding, Shaka acted as proxy father and the whole Fasimba regiment was present, not regimentally, but as individual guests.

Nandi and her household had collected the appropriate women-folk to help in the coming entertainment of the bridal parties.

* A multiple wedding was entirely contrary to Zulu practice: here, as in other matters, Shaka departed from tradition and rules.

These, as was customary, all had a bathe in one or other of the streams or rivers they had to cross on their way. Several parties actually performed their ablutions within distant view in the Umkumbane river. They were mostly girls of the same age-group as the bride. A number of older men accompanied them and also washed, slightly apart from them. The Zulus say they like a person to *nuka 'manzi* ('to smell of water'), and Shaka himself was the greatest exponent of this idea. In their natural state they were one of the cleanest races, free from all vermin and body odours.

After washing, the girls anointed themselves with *amaka* prepared from fragrant *impepo* leaves crushed and pounded with fat and said to possess aphrodisiac powers.

Shortly after sunset the bridal parties arrived, each bride carefully hidden in the midst of her age-group girl companions. The bride now began to sing the *ihubu* of her sib (i.e. song of family circle in its widest sense), in a low, impressive chant, with rhythmical movements of the body, and after a while the rest of her party of girls joined in. The sib song is an invocation to the ancestral spirits.

'The bride never goes empty-handed to her home. In addition to the various cooking and other utensils, mats, and hoe, she is accompanied by one or more *ukwendisa* cattle, according to the wealth of her father, and these are virtually a gift to the bridegroom's kraal; but most important of all, are the presents consisting of beads, mats, baskets, etc., which the bride gives to all the important members of the bridegroom's kraal.'*

Shaka acted as proxy father, and Nandi and some other matrons as 'mothers' of Mgobozi, whilst the Fasimba took the place of Mgobozi's 'brothers', and the daughters of the matrons acted as his 'sisters'. The gateway to the kraal was barred with a log until each bridal party had thrown a piece of meat over it as an entrance fee. Having done this, Mgobozi's proxy father gave each bridal party a present of the *isiwukula* goat to be slaughtered for their breakfast next morning.

Mgobozi's 'father', 'mothers', 'brothers' and 'sisters' on one

* Dr E. J. Krige, *The Social System of the Zulus.*

side, now vied with the bridal parties on the other side, in continuous exchange of presents to engender a spirit of friendliness all around. As the moon was nearly at the full there was sufficient light for all practical purposes.

Each bride was then escorted to her hut* where she would remain in seclusion with a little girl from her own kraal as sole companion till dawn, consuming such refreshments as she had brought along with her.

The bridal parties, without the brides, now assembled on the right side of the kraal, and those representing the groom on the left side. Both parties then returned to the entrance of the kraal, where, facing each other, they began to *Qubushela*. This custom is remarkable for its insulting references by one party to the other. 'Things that could not possibly be said at ordinary times are now shouted out and not resented.'† The bridegroom's honour is attacked, to be answered by jeers questioning the bride's chastity.

Twenty pairs of groups now created a deafening din by drumming, clapping the hands and singing, with the women on both sides yelling at the top of their voices. Refreshments of beer and grilled meat were brought at intervals and the pandemonium continued till dawn.

During all this time Mgobozi sat secluded in one of the huts annexed to the 'Great' hut, for as bridegroom he could not participate in the festivities until the next day.

Shaka left early and deputed his duties as 'father' to Mdlaka, the new commander of the Fasimba.

At dawn the bridal parties each collected their bride, who, surrounded by her age-mates, proceeded into the surrounding country, where each selected a place and killed and ate the presentation goat, given to them on the previous evening. Beer was sent to them from Mgobozi's kraal. Thereafter each party repaired to the river to wash and put on their finery.

With the morning well advanced, the bridegroom parties like-

* The term 'hut' is flexible and may include one or more additional huts as annexes to 'The hut'.
† Dr E. J. Krige, *op. cit.*

wise dressed up, arrived to invite the bridal groups to come back
to the kraal to begin the proper wedding dances. Each bride now
wore around her arms and legs white cow-tails which distinguished her from her following, who still hid her from the
view of all outsiders. 'The most noticeable distinguishing mark
of the bride is her veil, made of twisted fig leaves which hang
down from her head in strings, and cover her face as far as the
mouth. On her head she wears black finch plumes. In her hand
she carries a toy assegai which she will point upwards at her
husband-to-be during the dancing. It signifies that she is a
virgin.'*

The bridal parties once again face the groom's parties at the
kraal – in this case the dancing-ground prepared in the open veld,
to accommodate the unusual gathering. For the first time the
fathers of the brides appear. 'They each address the bridegroom's
party in the following words: "Here is my child, treat her well
for me. If she takes ill let me know. If you cannot agree with her
and you are tired of her, return her to me. If she troubles you rebuke her as you would your own child; if she errs, report her to
me. Her only ailments that I know of are these ... (naming
them)."' There follows a prayer that the bride may be fruitful
and then the father runs into the open and *giyas*, that is, he goes
through the motions of fighting an imaginary foe.*

Then all the girls begin singing the *inkondlo*, the wedding
song, and the bride and bridesmaids start evolutions similar to the
'Lancers', threading in and out in dancing lines, with voluptuous
movements of hips and thighs. Some older women dance in and
out of the figure, carrying a maize cob stuck on an assegai, which
they flourish for luck and prosperity.* Finally the lullaby which
the bride's mother composed for her when she was a baby is sung
for the last time. After an interval and more dances the bride
goes to her mother-in-law and kneeling by her side says: 'Keep
me as your child, do not get tired of me, do not be quick-tempered
when I trouble you, do not get tired of me when I am ill. I request you to spare me.' She asks to be taught her duties as a
wife and for her faults to be pointed out, and concludes: 'If you

*Dr E. J. Krige, *op. cit.*

treat me well I shall do the same to you. If you treat me badly I shall do likewise to you.'

On the following day the bride is entitled to receive a goat, called *umeke* (from *mekezisa*, to deflower), if she can indicate her transition from girlhood to womanhood by pointing down the small assegai she carried at the first bridal dance. Prior to this the assegai is carried pointing upwards. Shaka had decreed that to punish Mgobozi for his greed – for to marry more than one bride at a time was unheard of – he should pay a goat for each day each marriage remained unconsummated. And the Zulus say that Mgobozi, with his twenty brides, would have been ruined had not Shaka paid the fines out of the Royal flocks.

The news of Shaka's liberality to a soldier of fortune belonging to a clan beyond his domain spread far and wide and gained in legends as it travelled. This resulted in an immediate increase in the flow of adventurous warriors to his army. Many of these volunteers became the best fighters he had; and Shaka needed warriors, and still more warriors, with the emphasis on quality rather than quantity. Only with a strong and efficient army could he carry out his plans, nay even survive, as he had many powerful neighbours who were envious of his growing strength.

It is said that Shaka had as yet not touched any of his harem girls or 'sisters' and this in spite of the fact that even as a young warrior his immense size and magnificent appearance, allied to his prowess, had made him the cynosure of all women's eyes. But he was determined not to dissipate his strength or thoughts on women until he had established his power.

All the girls in the seraglio liked Pampata. Her kindly disposition and solicitous care for all of them endeared her to all. Shaka was too practical to keep them idle, and when the lands needed tilling, all except the daughters of chiefs had to give a hand, but their hours were light, and the food good and plentiful enough to make them value their privileged position. Their envious sighs at the sight of Pampata were subdued when the latter assured them that their time would come.

At about this time an urgent message arrived one day at noon to inform Shaka that his old foster-father, Mbiya, was dying seventy miles away at the coast. Within the hour Shaka had handed over the affairs of State to Mdlaka, Nzobo and his council of headmen including Mgobozi, and with an escort of 200 picked Fasimba he was on his way to Mbiya. Well before noon next day the journey was accomplished, and having sent messengers to Ngomane that he had arrived, Shaka entered the hut of the dying man. Mbiya was frail and old, but his intelligence was unimpaired. He was pathetically pleased to see Shaka, who, during all his absence had kept the old man well supplied with all his needs, and had sent him frequent messages of good cheer. Shaka still had some of his cattle quartered here, and he immediately had an ox sacrificed for the old man's recovery. In spite of the exhausting march of seventy miles in less than twenty-four hours Shaka showed no signs of fatigue, but most of the Fasimba were tired out and slept before they touched any food. All the afternoon and part of the evening Shaka stayed with Mbiya and greatly cheered him.

Next morning the old man was much improved, and Shaka set off with Ngomane to pay his respects to his suzerain lord, Dingiswayo, at his O-Yengweni kraal eighteen miles away. The Fasimba warriors remained at Mbiya's, except for about a score who accompanied Shaka.

Dingiswayo, who had been notified of Shaka's impending visit, gave his favourite a great welcome. Beer and meat were plentiful, but as usual Shaka partook only sparingly of the repast laid before him. Dingiswayo, Shaka and Ngomane then retired to the Council Hut and discussed affairs of State until late in the night. Dingiswayo warmly congratulated Shaka on the rapid expansion of his power in the most exposed bastion of the empire, but mildly criticized the severity of the Butelezi campaign. He agreed that it had been a salutary lesson to all the other tribes, but hoped that such drastic methods could be avoided in any future campaigns. He then disclosed that he wished to bring Matiwane, the chief of the powerful Ngwane tribe, within the orbit of his suzerainty. This tribe dwelt in and around Tabankulu – the present-day Vryheid – and their territory bordered on the north-western confines of Zwide's domain.

The details of the forthcoming campaign against Matiwane were fully discussed, and it was agreed that Shaka should join the expedition with half his forces when the time was ripe, that is, the beginning of the winter season in the year 1817. It was now about autumn, which in the Southern Hemisphere begins in March.

Next morning Shaka returned with Ngomane to Mbiya's kraal. When he arrived there he found that the condition of the old man had deteriorated rapidly and he was obviously dying.

'My son, I am glad you have come, for very soon now I will *goduka* (go home). The *amadlozi* (ancestral spirits) have given me a clear vision, and I can see you as a mighty tree which, with its branches, will cover the whole country which we know, and many moons' journey beyond. Your name will *sabeka* (frighten with respect) all who hear it and all the people and tribes will shiver like reeds in the wind when your name is mentioned. You will be a Chief such as no one has ever seen before, and no one will ever see again. But listen carefully to these words, my son. You drink but little of our beer, and the hemp-horn of strength you smoke not at all. Why? Because you know that overmuch beer dulls the mind, and the hemp-horn turns it into a mad bull with much strength but no judgement. The strongest drink or smoke of all, however, is power. Be careful, then, to mix it well with mercy, and the reasoning of your councillors and friends, lest it overwhelm you and you become like a mad bull, who, having killed all his opponents, starts goring his defenceless cows and calves and finally charges against the walls of his own kraal and senselessly breaks his neck instead of walking through the open gate of reason.'

There was a long silence, which was presently broken by Shaka. 'Leave us not, my Father, for we will be as lost calves without you, and there will be no one to tell us the wishes of the ancestral spirits.'

'Nay, my son, grieve not, for my time has come, and I can no more stop it than I could prevent myself from leaving my mother's womb when her time had come to deliver me. I am now like an old and withered tree, but for a season I was able to give shade and protection to a younger tree which will outgrow all others, and in that lies my great happiness today. Although you did not spring from my loins, you have been a far better son to me than my very own – good as they have been.'

Shaka was visibly moved and his eyes were wet. 'Again I say you must not grieve, my son,' Mbiya consoled him. 'The spirits are kind to an old man who has outlived his usefulness. As a mother weans her child by putting bitter aloes on her breast, so the spirits make one thing after the other distasteful to us in this life, until nothing is left to hold us here and we are glad to go. For many a season I have stayed on to see you grow, and now that you are strong and great I would leave before my head becomes silly and childish again. Then as a spirit I can, per-chance, visit you in your dreams, and guide you as I tried to guide you when you were young. Now let us say farewell and let me leave you through *isango elihle*.'*

Having said farewell, Mbiya expressed a desire to sleep and Shaka left him with streaming eyes. That night Mbiya died.

Shaka made all the funeral arrangements next morning, but did not stay for the funeral itself, as this would have meant, ac-cording to custom, that he would have to remain for a month after the burial to observe all the necessary ceremonies. Long before noon he was on his way back to Bulawayo with his escort. The return march was more leisurely, and he did not reach his capital before late the following afternoon.

* A nice gate – 'to leave through a nice gate' is a Zulu metaphor for parting as friends.

CHAPTER 10

The struggle with the witch-doctors

ON his return to Bulawayo there was evil news for Shaka. Firstly a *tekwane* (hammerkop or hammerhead heron) had flown over the kraal; then a porcupine had wandered in. This had been followed by a crow perching on the kraal fence and uttering human words. Lastly two cows were killed by lightning at the kraal gate. Quite obviously witchcraft had been practised and the evil-doer, or doers, must be 'smelt out'.

Nobela, the renowned woman *isangoma,* or witch-finder, was immediately sent for, and after 'throwing the bones' she ordained a general 'smelling out'.

Three days later nearly all the adult males within Shaka's domain were marshalled at Bulawayo, including all the regiments. They were drawn up on the parade ground in lines, with wide avenues between them, and formed a rough horseshoe with the opening facing Shaka, who was seated on a large man-made clay mound with his councillors around him, commanding a good view of all the gathering.

A hush of fearful expectancy hung over all the motionless assemblage. The silence was broken by eerie high-pitched shrieks and yells which came from a group of five grotesquely dressed female forms which approached from behind the clay mound, crouching and leaping as they headed for the opening of the horseshoe.

Nobela was the leader of the group. Her face was an evil mask streaked with white clay paint, which also covered her arms and legs. An assortment of dried and inflated bladders and snakeskins adorned her head and arms. Claws and teeth of leopards and hyaenas, and goats' horns hung from her neck, and over her shrunken breasts grinned the skulls of two baboons. A kilt of softened cowhide hung from her hips to above her knees. In her hand she carried the tail of a gnu, or wildebeest, which resembles that of a horse. Her four companions were similarly dressed.

The five *isangomas*, or witch-finders, arrived in front of Shaka and the gathering in an undulating and creeping line led by Nobela. They then formed a circle, which began to turn slowly whilst they kept up a constant, low, sibilant hissing, which increased in volume as the tempo of the turning increased. The witch-finders' eyes began to roll, and their bodies to pirouette whilst they still kept up the circling movement. Gradually they lashed themselves into a frenzy of gyrating, madly jumping, fiendishly grimacing and demoniacal creatures, emitting the most ghoulish, blood-curdling and cackling cries.

The horror-stricken people were paralysed with fear as they gazed on the *isangomas*. No one except the chief was safe from 'smelling out' immediately followed by a brutally cruel death. The most atrocious feature of these 'smellings-out' was that all the inmates of the condemned man's kraal – if he were a kraal-head, which he usually was – would also be slain, albeit mercifully with the assegai whereas the condemned man suffered death by torture. His kraal was surrounded and every human being in it butchered, the huts set on fire, and all the stock driven off to augment the herds of the chief, who suitably rewarded the witch-finders and the slayers with a portion of the booty.

This was the immemorial custom of all the Nguni and kindred races and its justice was never questioned, for it was held that even a totally innocent person could nevertheless be the unwitting medium of some wizard, and therefore a source of evil to the whole community, who must be destroyed with all his kith and kin. There was no appeal to the chief, for witchcraft was an occult and invisible force which could only be interpreted and understood by witch-doctors. If, however, a condemned man could escape from the slayers attending the witch-finders – an extremely unlikely event – and reach the feet of his chief, he could claim and receive sanctuary and all further proceedings were stayed.

When the screams, howls and gymnastics had reached their

climax, Nobela and her evil brood stopped dead-still with dramatic suddenness and in a group faced Shaka. Then with leering eyes each one started to sniff like a dog and Nobela commenced to chant: 'There are evil-minded people in the land,' and she paused whilst her four helpers repeated the sentence in unison. 'We can smell their thoughts,' continued Nobela, sniffing the air, and sentence by sentence the four repeated her words, with sniffs. 'They would harm the chief by witchcraft, but we can smell their evil machinations.' ... 'Yes, we can smell them in the smoke of their kraals and in the morning mist.' ... 'We can smell them in the air and on the ground and in the earth.' ... 'We can smell them in the rain and the running waters of the land.' ... 'They cannot hide from us anywhere' ... 'We are the dogs of the chief' ... sniff, sniff, sniff ... 'And we will find them everywhere.'

At the last words they jumped high in the air and with a turning movement landed on their feet facing the opposite way, that is, with their backs to Shaka; then shading their eyes with their left hands, they glowered at the spellbound gathering whilst assuming the crouching position of a beast of prey about to spring on its victim.

Then Nobela shrieked: 'Chant ye people all, chant, so that we may smell the sweet breath of those who are innocent, and the foul odour of those tainted with witchcraft.'

The customary low chant rose from all those present, including all the councillors around Shaka, who alone, as chief, was not supposed to join in.

Led by Nobela the five *isangomas* darted off swiftly through the middle of the horseshoe formation until they reached the arch, some 200 yards away, where every line showed a gap, expressly left open for the ghouls, to enable them to reach all the other lines. As they ran they jumped at every ten steps or so, emitting frenzied shrieks and howls, and with madly rolling eyes. Sometimes the witch-finders would crawl on all fours, continuously sniffing the ground and the feet of the unhappy people. Sometimes they would move in a crouching position. Always they sniffed, and always their eyes would dart around, and with grimacing faces and leers petrify their beholders, who would almost choke with fear as they valiantly tried to keep up the chant. Then like scenting dogs they would sometimes return on their trail, questing and sniffing for a lost scent, and then partly raising the deadly gnu-tail, as if about to strike a person with it, to indicate that he had been 'smelt out' as a wizard.

With half a dozen slayers solemnly walking behind each of the two witch-finding parties, the agony of suspense became almost unbearable at times, but the five witch-finders knew that this was the hour of their power, and not lightly would they relax their grip on the minds of the people, by too speedy a judgement. They gloated in the agony they beheld all around them, and to their utmost they prolonged it. Only in the second round of sniffing each line would the gnu-tails strike the fore-doomed and fore-chosen victims.

It was noticeable, whenever the divining ghouls approached an individual who for some reason or other was considered a possible culprit, perhaps because he was unpopular, the chanting of the people would unconsciously grow louder, and this invariably guided the diviners to make a popular choice, quite apart from those whom they might have on their own list. Similarly when they approached a man who was universally popular the chant died down to almost nothing.

Mdlaka, the commander of the Fasimba, who was second to none in bravery, quaked inwardly when Nobela sniffed at him and almost thrust her evil face into his, and then deliberately returned twice, but each time the chant sank to a diminuendo, and as far as the warriors were concerned, it fell to an almost in-audible undertone, for next to Mgobozi he was one of the most popular people in the country. Nobela, however, disliked him and Mgobozi, as she disliked all clever people, especially if their coun-sels were moderate and they failed to woo her power.

Shaka frowned, for he felt that even his own power was cur-tailed when the witch-doctors held the stage, for the moment they struck their victim with the gnu-tail the slayers immediately marched him off to his grisly doom without any command from the chief.

Having completed the first preliminary round of all the lines,

Nobela and her associates now directed their attention to the councillors surrounding Shaka. They approached in a line, with their bodies almost bent double, silent except for the sniffing, but with the most frightening grimaces and rolling of the eyes imaginable. Even Shaka, immune though he was, felt the hypnotic spell of the witch-finders. As they passed along the line of paralysed and perspiring councillors he remembered Mbiya's words, and with a deep hoarse growl muttered: 'Seek not witchcraft among my tried friends. Leave them alone.'

With her face distorted with rage, but looking at no one in particular, Nobela gave her answer in a low chant. 'Those closest and dearest are ever the most potent mediums of the wizard, even though they know not that they are being used. Take heed, Oh Chief, for our eyes can see what you cannot see, and our noses can smell the taint of evil as surely as a dog follows the scent of a buck which is imperceptible to man.'

Shaka felt uncomfortable, for he still had a high respect for witch-doctors, ingrained in him through custom, although his innate intelligence made him suspect that a goodly percentage of their practices were based on fraud or self-interest, and some of them were certainly altogether humbugs.

'I hear you, Mother of Fear, but what if your choice is against the popular will?' said Shaka in a low undertone.

Nobela continued to give a chanting reply. 'There is too much interference already. Shall the children teach the mother?'

'Carry on with your hunting, but take care not to thrust your face into a hornets' nest,' Shaka replied with a low but ominous growl.

With a malignant look of triumph Nobela now advanced on Mgobozi and pointedly hovered around him like a veritable angel of death, continuing to torment him with suspense, while the slayers behind her fingered the bundles of twelve-inch wooden skewers, each slightly thicker than a pencil. If he were found guilty he would be led away and these skewers would be driven into his rectum, and he would be left to die a lingering death in the veld, and of course all his brides would be massacred.

Led by Nobela the quintette formed into a winding file heading for the horseshoe opening for the final and decisive 'smelling out'. By this time the whole multitude was in a state of stupor. The dreadful suspense was broken for the first time when Shaka slowly rose to his full height and bellowed: 'Ho! Mdlaka there! collect me a company of the best Fasimba lads and come and stand guard here around my person.' Like a man awakened from a horrible nightmare, Mdlaka rubbed his eyes and with hope and joy in his heart carried out the order with smooth efficiency.

The strangling grip of Nobela was broken – at least for a time – and no one knew it better than she did. With a venomous intensity she now whipped up all the terror she could, and prancing along the outer line where she had commenced the 'smelling out' earlier in the day, she hovered around a luckless ring-headed man of some fifty-five years, who was obviously a well-to-do kraal-head. His eyes bulged with terror as she played with his feelings, now raising his hopes by leaving him and then tiptoeing back again. At last, with a diabolical shriek, she jumped shoulder high and struck him in the face with the fatal gnu-tail.

Almost immediately two slayers closed in on him and led him into the centre of the horseshoe, where he stood in a state of stoical stupor. Here they guarded him and presently he was joined by another wretch. This went on till there were four. This apparently completed the 'harvest' in the outer, and less important, lines of people, for Nobela and her colleagues now came running and vaulting into the central arena, where they pointed accusatory fingers at the victims and shrieked the manner of their doom at them.

'Look at them, ye people. These are the *abatagati* (wizards) who would bewitch our chief and his people, but we have smelt them out, as we will smell out a great many more in this inner circle which stinks of witchcraft. Away with them, ye slayers, and see to it that they suffer before they die. Report their names to the military council so that the warriors may wipe out their kraals before their contaminated inmates can get any warning.'

During the five minutes or so whilst the first pair were being skewered the other two condemned men looked on in a state of stupor. The victims of a 'smelling out' were usually so overwhelmed with superstitious dread, and the enormity of being unconscious mediums of witchcraft, that they became mentally and physically paralysed, and it was exceedingly rare for any one of them ever to make even an attempt to escape. In any case they knew their families were doomed even if they should escape, unless they could reach the sanctuary at the chief's feet. Otherwise, forsaken and shunned by all as polluted malefactors, and bringers of evil to the tribe, they would now die a lingering and horrible death, with their minds racked as cruelly as their bodies.

By the time the slayers returned to the central arena Nobela had another batch of four hapless wretches awaiting execution. They were all dignified and prosperous kraal-heads. One had opposed the Shaka régime. Another one was unpopular on account of his frugal hospitality, through which he had grown exceedingly rich. The third one believed in putting cattle-manure on his lands rather than pay Nobela for charms to grow his crops. When his crops were, therefore, outstandingly more abundant than those of his neighbours doctored by Nobela a whispering campaign by her agents soon convinced everyone that he must be employing witchcraft to obtain such exceptional results. When Nobela therefore approached him the chant rose, and reached its highest pitch when the gnu-tail struck him, thus indicating that the choice was a popular one.

The fourth man was unlucky, inasmuch that good luck had always trailed him in his efforts at stock-breeding. He selected the best breeding bulls and exercised every care to avoid stock losses, but the most uncanny feature was the prodigious growth of his herds through the fortuitous and phenomenal number of heifer-calves which were born. Envious neighbours began to mutter, and when predatory beasts like lions chose to break into their less-palisaded kraals instead of the rich man's better-protected ones, it became apparent to all that he must be relying on witchcraft.

These four men were now hustled off to their terrible death, and presently were joined by another three who were also 'smelt out' in the inner circle. With eleven thus disposed of, Nobela now turned her final attention to the councillors and guards surrounding Shaka. This would provide the climax of the day. She would strike hard with the authority of tribal law, sanctified by immemorial custom. The chief himself must submit to this, and new chiefs, especially if they were headstrong, must always be shown that witch-doctors and diviners are indispensable. She was determined to get rid of Mdlaka and Mgobozi, for those two honest warriors never took any trouble to hide their dislike of her, and when Mgobozi was 'driving goats' (Zulu euphemism for a person who is drunk) he had even spat at the mention of her name, and referred to her as *umdidi we Mpisi* (hyaena's anus). Such an insult to the head of the diviners' profession could not be tolerated, and must be punished with death.

It was one thing for Nobela to act within the limits of Shaka's wishes: let her confine her efforts to genuine witch-finding; but if she went beyond that for her own ends, then she became a menace to his power, for she could do a great deal with the assistance of tribal law, and could not be denied if she was within her rights. Shaka had, therefore, some time previously, instructed both Mdlaka and Mgobozi to sit close to his feet, and in a low undertone had told them to apply for sanctuary if Nobela should 'smell them out'. Their position was thus screened by the company of Fasimba which Mdlaka had been told to bring up.

When Nobela passed this screen, quivering with the excitement of her prospective catches, she took in the situation at a glance, and in order to gain time she first 'smelt' along the lines of the Fasimba, closely followed by the slayers, to whose leader she conveyed some instruction in a low chant.

Then the five diviners formed into a line facing Mdlaka and Mgobozi and began to crawl on all fours towards them, with the slow, halting gait of chameleons and with rolling eyes and sniffing nostrils. Nobela in the middle, and slightly leading, with two assistants on each side. Eight slayers almost stepped on their heels. It was a picture of slow, creeping horror.

Mgobozi and Mdlaka, sitting side by side about two feet apart, were perspiring profusely. They remembered that, owing to the steepness of the mound and Shaka's command to sit low enough to be out of view behind the Fasimba company, they were some three yards away from the feet of their chief.

With a hideous cackle, imitating the hyaena's demoniacal laugh, all five jumped up simultaneously. With lightning speed Nobela struck right and left with her gnu-tail and jumped over Mdlaka's and Mgobozi's shoulders, whilst each of her immediate assistants also struck the man in front of her and vaulted high over his head. The two diviners on the flanks ran each around her man, striking him as she passed, and joined the other three, who now formed a compact line between the 'smelt out' men and Shaka. No sooner had the three central diviners jumped over Mgobozi and Mdlaka than the slayers had bounded forward and seized them – four pairs of hands to each victim – and, violently jerking them to their feet, dragged them away from Shaka and their sanctuary. All this happened in three or four seconds and Shaka, according to tribal custom, could not interfere and order a rescue. He and the two warriors had been neatly out-manoeuvred by Nobela, and he was shaking with suppressed rage, especially as that creature and her four harridans were now cackling in triumph.

Mgobozi and Mdlaka had been paralysed by a combination of hypnotic stupor and the suddenness of the events. Mgobozi recovered his wits first and brought his knee with crushing force into the nearest slayer's crutch. He let go his hold with a howl of pain. Like a mad bull Mgobozi drove his head into the solar plexus of the next one, and then, with his gigantic strength, broke loose from the other two. In an instant he picked up the first slayer's heavy club and jabbed it in the face of the third, and a second later cracked and crushed the skull of the fourth. He was now fighting mad, and like a whirlwind he descended on the captors of his friend. In a matter of moments they were all on the ground with cracked skulls or broken limbs. He and Mdlaka now helped themselves to more clubs, and then ran to the foot of Shaka's mound, where both greeted him with 'Bayete! Nkosi.'

Shaka addressed the two: 'You claim sanctuary?'

'Yes, my Father,' they both replied. Then Mgobozi went on,

'If my father will, however, shield my back, I would much sooner fight the lot and die like a warrior with a good mat of corpses to sleep on. That evil woman there kills those she dislikes, and not because they are your enemies.' And Mgobozi ostentatiously spat in Nobela's direction, one of the heavy clubs twitching in his fingers.

Shaka laughed, and turning to Nobela he said: 'You heard Mgobozi's words. Goad him not for his temper is short, and I see nobody about who could prevent him from cracking your skull. I certainly would not intervene, for I warned you not to poke your head into a hornets' nest. Have you anything more to say before we close the day's proceedings?'

'No, O Chief,' Nobela replied in a subdued tone.

'You agree that these two have secured rightful sanctuary according to the laws of the land?'

'Yes, O Chief.'

'Do you wish me to subject them to the *Moave* bark (poison) ordeal, to be administered by a witch-doctor of my choice?'

'No, O Chief.'

'Why not?'

Nobela hesitated, and while she was apparently thinking how to formulate a reply, Shaka continued: 'It seems to me that you wrongly accused Mgobozi and Mdlaka. How much of your "smelling out" was due to personal spite, especially after your informers had reported to you that when Mgobozi was "driving goats" he spat at the mention of your name, and likened you to an unsavoury part of a hyaena's body?'

'Nay, O Chief, it was thus. These two were the innocent, and therefore most dangerous mediums of an evil wizard, but the spirits came to their aid, and so enabled them to throw out the witchcraft from their bodies, else had they not the power to overwhelm the many slayers.'

'Your fraternity ever speak with a split tongue, and as a hammerkop (hammerhead heron) always has four doors in his nest to enable him to have a lee loophole in any wind, so you always leave a door to escape by, no matter from which side the wind blows. The truth is you have made two bad mistakes, and

two of you must die for that. Smell each other out now
and find the guilty two, or, if you prefer it, throw the divining
bones.'

There was consternation amongst the five witch-doctors, but
Nobela recovered her wits first and said it was out of the question
to smell each other out, as none of them was tainted with witchcraft, but if an error of judgement had been made the bones would
show which one had been at fault. Nobela hoped to escape by
getting her two juniors to divine each other first, and then she
and the two senior assistants would find both the juniors guilty
and so secure a majority.

Shaka, however, ordained that Nobela, as senior, must throw
the bones first, and reveal the guilty one, each diviner having one
vote of death only. Two votes were to constitute a death sentence,
but unless two diviners were voted to death with a minimum of
two votes each, in one round, a fresh throw must be made. The
five diviners now formed a semicircle facing Shaka at the left
below the dais. Nobela was in a cleft stick. Not all her wriggling
could get her out of the first throw, and the junior assistant she
thereupon indicated became her implacable opponent. The second
in seniority threw her bones against the junior, too, thus quali-
fying her for death, provided one other got two votes for death in
this round. The junior shrieked and jabbered that there was cheating and a mis-direction of the bones, but Nobela glared at her and
asked 'Since when could the pupil teach the master?'

'I will teach you, and today, too, you wicked old *matanazana*'
(barren female baboon who acts as 'free for all' to the males of the
troop, who are otherwise savagely restrained by the leader from
touching any other normal females, which are his sole perquisite
until a stronger rival beats him in battle and the whole troop then
expels him, never to return). 'Before I die today I will tell the
chief how you make us lie and cheat for your own evil purposes,
and maybe he will order me to be clubbed before they put the
skewers into us, but you will get a double dose of them.'

'*Tulani umsindo!*' ('Stop the noise!') Shaka commanded the
women, who were babbling among themselves to the accompaniment of the hysterical outbursts and accusations of the condemned

one. 'Any more noise and I will have your mouths stuffed with
cow-dung, and then we can finish this business without any inter-
ruptions.'

The third senior diviner threw the bones and indicated Nobela.
With a scream of rage and fear the latter denounced the throw as
blatant trickery and gibbered imprecations at the thrower until
Shaka boomed out the single word *'Bulongwe!'* ('Cow-dung!'),
whereupon she subsided into a venomous silence.

It was now the turn of the second junior to make her throw –
the fourth in the round. Nobela had fixed her with a hard, hypnotic stare and a confused and vacant look came over her face. She
handled the bones like a somnambulist, and was a long time in
throwing them. Shaka looked on with intense interest. At last
the bones were thrown, and the thrower looked at them in a
dreamy way and said: 'Why, they point all ways, and at no one
in particular.' Here the third senior shook her vigorously and told
her to wake up. It was 'no throw', she declared, and must be done
over again.

'It was a correct throw,' yelled Nobela, 'and she can't have
another one.'

Shaka then declared that it was indeed 'no throw' and that the
second junior must throw again, but with her back to Nobela.

Once more the second junior threw the bones, and in a clear
and emphatic voice declared that the bones pointed to Nobela, as
all could see.

With the agility of a baboon Nobela dashed to, and up, the
clay mound and reached Shaka's feet, and a second later the
junior diviner was alongside her.

'Sanctuary, O Chief! Sanctuary,' they both wailed. 'We have
ever been the true servants and loyal dogs of your house and your
father's.'

Everyone was completely taken by surprise at the dramatic
turn and swiftness of these events. Shaka now sternly turned to
the two pleading women. 'Sanctuary is only granted to those who
escape after being "smelt out" for witchcraft. You were not
charged with witchcraft, but with cheating for your own ends,
and your own colleagues have found you guilty. It is merely a

question of how you are to die now as ordinary evil-doers, unless'
... and here Shaka paused, 'you voluntarily confess that it was
witchcraft, and not cheating you were guilty of. In that case, as
an act of special clemency, you may claim sanctuary, for,' he
added with a knowing look, 'you also may have been the innocent mediums of a more powerful wizard. Nevertheless, cheat me
no more, for on that day you will fail to find sanctuary anywhere.'

Shaka having thoroughly exposed, chastened and humiliated
Nobela was not disposed to turn her into carrion, for he recognized her cleverness, and she still had her uses in certain State
affairs, especially now that her wings had been clipped and dissen-
sion had arisen between her and her colleagues.

Nobela and the junior diviner acknowledged their guilt as
innocent mediums of witchcraft and Shaka accorded them sanctuary, and told their colleagues to agree to waive the trial by
poison ordeal. Then he lined up all the diviners below his dais and
told them to face towards the gathering, and underline all he had
to say. The slayers who had been killed or injured by Mgobozi had
by now been removed to the rear. The Fasimba company still
acted as a screen in front of Shaka's dais for all but Shaka on his
high seat. The company was now ordered to divide and each half
to wheel around for all the world like two swing doors, to reveal
to the populace the full stage once more of the councillors seated
below and around Shaka, and the five diviners facing the audience in the open horseshoe.

Then Shaka arose and told the gathering that much good work
had been done that day, inasmuch that the indiscriminate use of
power by diviners for their own purposes had been stopped, and
that in future every death sentence for a 'smelling out' would
have to be confirmed by him or his duly appointed deputy.
Henceforth all people could live in security under his protecting
shadow, provided they carried out his dictates, but woe betide
anyone who tried to thwart him either by actions or passive
evasions.

The melodious Zulu language, in which every syllable and
word ends in a full vowel sound, lends itself to a deep, far-carrying,

and rolling intonation and the measured and dignified delivery has the euphonious rhythm of poetry.

Shaka's words therefore clearly reached every person present. Addressing the army, he said that in future no warrior serving in it should be 'smelt out', and so long as the warriors did their duty they had nothing to fear. That day evil influences had been at work to try to implicate Mgobozi and Mdlaka – members of distant clans – but he had taken them under his arm-pits and exposed their accusers. This would show that no matter where a warrior came from he found a secure refuge under the chief of the Heavens (Ama Zulu). Shaka paused, and received a tumultuous ovation from the army.

Continuing, Shaka now referred to the eleven people who had been 'smelt out' and skewered that day. 'The first one from the inner circle was evilly disposed towards me and therefore deserved his fate, and his whole family will likewise be eaten up. The others were mostly rich men who were envied by their neighbours and generally disliked for their meanness. This meanness of the rich and well-to-do is a very serious thing, for they should liberally support the chief, who with his army alone is the shield under which they are able to grow rich. The army needs cattle and grain, and who alone can supply them but the people who grow fat under its protection, for without the protection of the army you would all have nothing. Look at me. I am far thinner than any man of my age. Do I eat your cattle and drink your beer? No, but I need these things for the army and if property owners will not give me what the army needs, they are useless to me and the tribe, and will go to feed the birds. Therefore I say if a man has ten head of cattle he can afford to give one to his chief and tribe, and even two or more in times of stress, for I warn you we have powerful neighbours on many sides who will eat you up and all you have, unless the army stops them, and I am the army. Why? Because it is the master's eye which makes the cow grow fat, and it is my eye alone which has given our Heaven-land (Zulu-land) an army which can hold its own.

'I now refer to the punishment of those others who were "smelt out" today. I see no sense in wiping out their families, for they were not guilty of true witchcraft. They shall therefore live, but half of their cattle will be confiscated and the other half, which they are to retain, will be made good to me by Nobela and her assistants, as a fine for their wrongful findings. The skewered men are past all help and I have therefore ordered the slayers to speed all of them on their way by smashing their skulls. Nobela will now confirm that all my findings have been correct and within the law.' Nobela now got up and screeched: '*I-Zulu li duma iqiniso*' ('Heaven thunders the truth !').

'It thunders the truth,' echoed her assistants.

'*Li zo shaya aba-tagati*' (It – the Heaven – will strike the wizards, i.e. evil-doers) roared the whole gathering.

'*Indaba ipelile*' ('The affair is closed') boomed Shaka.

'*Ba-ye te! Nkosi!*' thundered the crowd in an ovation such as Zululand had never heard before.

CHAPTER 11

Zwide – The tribal migrations

THE unprecedented rebuff Shaka had given to the divining profession within his domain had many repercussions. The fact that the army had been lifted completely above its reach, coupled with promises that warriors would be still more liberally treated with gifts of cattle, raised as a protective insurance from their owners, made the Zulu army the cynosure of all eyes far beyond Shaka's domain. The cattle owners too did not mind this imposition much, as it removed the dread and perpetual fear of being 'smelt out'. Many of the most intelligent people beyond Shaka's boundaries who were above military age moved with their whole kraals into Zululand, which now indeed lived up to its name of 'Heaven-land'. Because of their superior intelligence they realized that they too would some day be 'smelt out', merely because their sharper wits brought them more prosperity than their neighbours. In the same way that the Huguenots and Pilgrim Fathers had been attracted to countries with more liberal ideas, so Zululand – as yet an embryonic State – became the mecca of thinking people beyond its boundaries, and an asylum for all the oppressed.

In return for all this Shaka had, however, incurred the deadly hatred of the whole divining fraternity, which knew no tribal boundaries. Considering the times he lived in, when superstitious dread of witchcraft held all the Nguni race in thrall, it is difficult to assess the extraordinary courage and intelligence he needed to fight against this curse of his race: especially, too, since he had not long been chief and was still a young man, surrounded by powerful tribes seeking his destruction.

Nobela was brooding revenge on Shaka who, however, further checked her power by offering large rewards to young male members of her profession to come to Bulawayo, men like Mqalane who became his permanent war doctor and trusted friend. Mgobozi, meanwhile, urged that Nobela should be killed for she would always be dangerous. To this Shaka is said to have answered him: 'Snake-bite remedy is composed of the bodies of snakes.' He kept Nobela, confident as he was that he could control her, to serve him when dealing with other exponents of witchcraft.

Meanwhile Shaka was completing his arrangements, including the doctoring of the army, for the forthcoming campaign ordered by Dingiswayo against Matiwane of the Ngwanes. He planned to take 1000 men made up of contingents from all his regiments, leaving Mgobozi in charge of the home garrison, while Mdlaka guarded the southern frontier, and watched the Qwabes, with the remaining 1500 men of the Zulu forces.

Dingiswayo was leaving 2000 men to contain Zwide and the Ndwandwes, and proceeding with 2500 against Matiwane. The Ntshalini and other tributary clans would provide a composite contingent of another 1000 men, bringing the total to approximately 4500.

Dingiswayo and his army duly arrived. It was now about the beginning of the southern winter, June 1817. Joined by Shaka's forces the whole host crossed the White Umfolozi river a little to the west of Nhlazatshe mountain and into the Ntshalini territory where the last reinforcing contingent was picked up.

Matiwane, chief of the Ngwanes, was a fierce and proud man of short, broad build and with a pronounced stoop. He had a head and a heart of whose martial genius and latent ferocity the world was as yet entirely unaware. Wrapped in his customary cloak of black-and-white calf-skin he gazed southwards, sensing danger, restlessly vigilant. His intelligence department had kept him fully advised of the gradually approaching and ever triumphant invasions of Dingiswayo and Shaka. What, therefore, could be the purpose of the present universal mobilization of which report now reached him? Able captain as he was, he prepared for the gathering storm. He petitioned Mtimkulu, the neighbouring Hlubi chief on his western boundary, begging cover for his herds of cattle in the mountains, around present-day Utrecht, which lay within Mtimkulu's territory. The petition was granted and all the Ngwane cattle were safely deposited in the land of the Hlubis.

Despite Shaka's efforts to persuade Dingiswayo to make this campaign one of total war, Dingiswayo refused. Shaka's Zulus were now, of course, equipped with the stabbing assegai, went barefoot into battle, and were drilled to fight in regiments, in order, and under rigid discipline. They were, moreover, far better supplied than any other part of the army, since Shaka had en-rolled boys of fourteen and fifteen in a corps of *u-dibi*, mat-carriers or orderlies, one for every three fighting men : these boys carried sleeping-mats, light covers, dry fuel and food for the troops, so that while other tribes passed nights in discomfort and cold, and fared very poorly while on active service, Shaka's troops were warm, well fed and, therefore, their morale was high. But still Dingiswayo would not allow Shaka to make proper use of his new military instrument, allowing that chief only to frighten Matiwane into a quick surrender, followed by submission and the incorporation, in all but name, of Matiwane's territory into the commonwealth of tribes under Dingiswayo's paramountcy.

Before departing Dingiswayo gave Matiwane a lecture. He laid down the law and announced his firm resolve to maintain order among the quarrelsome Nguni clans, and to raise them into a great and good nation under his own paternal supremacy.

Dingiswayo's intention was no doubt a noble one, but it was utterly without avail, as will presently be seen.

Shaka was more than annoyed, and did not fail to express frankly his views to Dingiswayo, pointing out that he was merely making enemies and no friends at all, and that presently he would be overwhelmed by these enemies, who were daily grow-ing stronger and more war-like, like the Ndwandwes.

The whole expedition then returned homewards.

A diversion is necessary here to give a picture of the times before Shaka started his major contests.

By no conceivable stretch of the imagination can Shaka be

blamed for the devastations about to be described, and yet the
calumny persists that he was the author of them. The subsequent
carnage and destruction in the remainder of Natal and elsewhere
has also been laid at his door, but when the facts are later revealed
in their chronological order, this too will be seen to be an absurdity. The truth is that Shaka destroyed only in order to rebuild.
He was an empire-builder, whereas most of the leaders of the
destructive tribal hordes were desperadoes, intent solely on self-
preservation.

No sooner had Dingiswayo left than Matiwane sent a request
to Mtimkulu to return his cattle, and the latter raised objections.
Mtimkulu's tribe – the Hlubis – was big and powerful, and enjoyed Dingiswayo's special favour, as he had himself found refuge
with it for many years under Mtimkulu's father, Bungane. Matiwane, refused his cattle, obtained some of Mtimkulu's cut hair,
with a view to establishing magic power over the other Chief.
But meanwhile another invader suddenly attacked him, one less
merciful than Dingiswayo.

Zwide, the Ndwande king, swept down on the Ngwanes and
drove them in panic before him, killing all in his path. 'With the
Ngwanes already deprived of their wealth, and now driven from
their homes and country, Matiwane decided there and then to
seek a new home.'

It was, therefore, Zwide – and not Shaka – who inaugurated the
terrible tribal migrations about to be related.

With his army in the van, and all the women and children of
the tribe at its heels, Matiwane fell without warning on the
Hlubi capital, and razed the whole place, annihilating everyone
in it, including Mtimkulu. Before the tribe could organize any
resistance he burned and butchered everyone within his reach,
driving the cattle he could get before him, including his own,
which he had recovered. However, a large proportion of the
Hlubis did escape westwards and, gathered into a formidable
horde of refugees by Mpangazita, the slain chief's brother, they
crossed the Drakensberg and in their turn telescoped violently
into the Sutu domain – the present-day Orange Free State. Here
they came into murderous conflict with the Batlokwa tribe, then

under the regency of Mantatisi, mother of Sikonyela, who was then a minor.

This Mantatisi became one of the most renowned military leaders of the time – a veritable Boadicea. After her collision with Mpangazita and his Hlubis, she struck south-westward down the Caledon river, spreading death and destruction all around her, whilst Mpangazita, with the cattle of her tribe in his possession, moved in a north-westerly direction, leaving the same devastation in his track. Between them they spread misery, death and destruction over the whole of western Basutoland and the greater part of the Orange Free State.

So successful was the ferocious Mantatisi, that within a year or two she had scattered the Ba-Fukeng, frightened the Ba-Kwena out of her way, plundered the Ma-Khwakhwa, and even beaten Mshweshwe (Moshesh) himself, at Butabute in the war of the pots – so called because in the fight Mantatisi got all her tribal crockery broken.

Throughout these widespread depredations, without their knowing it, Mantatisi and Mpangazita were gravitating towards each other in two semicircles, and at Mabolela they ran up against each other again. After a savage battle Mantatisi was able to retire over the Caledon, below Kolonyama, and there she kept Mpangazita at bay. Through all the following grim years the doughty chieftainess managed to preserve her tribe from destruction, but at fearful cost to other tribes. The ruses and stratagems she employed, allied with her deathless courage, would alone form a complete narrative.

Mpangazita, on the other hand, after successfully fighting innumerable battles and ruining an untold number of clans, ultimately clashed once more with Matiwane in 1825 near Mabolela, when the latter was putting all the distance he could between himself and Shaka. For five days Matiwane and his Ngwanes fought a battle of annihiliation with Mpangazita and his Hlubis.

After Matiwane's first clash with the Hlubis in their original homeland he did not follow them when they crossed the Drakensberg mountains. Instead, he ravaged the whole of the northern, central and western portion of the present-day Klip-river country in Natal. He annihilated the Bele tribe, who were first cousins of the Hlubis, and mercilessly hacked his way south, burning and butchering infants and females, aged and sick alike. Whenever a fallen chief could be found he plucked the gall-bladder from the corpse and greedily drank its contents, believing, thereby, that he would add his fallen enemy's courage and ferocity to his own. After crossing the Upper Tugela river he settled in the present-day Bergville district under the shadow of the Drakensberg, where it rises to its greatest height of nearly 12,000 feet. Here he found peace, but for four years only, when Mdlaka, Shaka's general, drove him and his tribe helter-skelter over the Berg and into the Free State with the loss of all his cattle.

A second wave of devastation now swept over north-western Basutoland and the eastern Free State, and the remnants of tribes which were trying to re-establish themselves after the blood-tide of Mpangazita and Mantatisi had submerged them, were now broken up and dispersed, their granaries pillaged, and their remaining cattle driven off by the hungry Ngwane horde.

The pitiless cruelty and unspeakable brutality of these inter-tribal wars of annihilation baffle description, and whether they were perpetrated by the followers of Matiwane, Mpangazita or Mantatisi they all bore the same pattern.*

Matiwane's defeat by Colonel Somerset at the head of 1000 Europeans, supported by 18,000 Xozas and Tembus, took place on 26 August 1828, near Mount Baziya, in the Eastern Province of the Cape Colony. Actually the expedition was directed against Shaka, whose armies had penetrated to that neighbourhood but by clever manoeuvres had got away with much booty. Counting the more or less direct distance from point to point along Matiwane's route, and excluding the countless zigzag perambulations, he had covered the best part of 1000 miles through new territory, since he left his ancestral home, and converted his tribe into

* There must have been some basic cause of these movements. Peoples practising agriculture by essartage and stock-raising are often driven into movement by temporary soil exhaustion. This is a possible cause.

Nomads of Wrath, whom he skilfully guided through countless dangers and appalling vicissitudes, only to be broken at last by the White man's guns and horses, allied to an overwhelming horde of Nguni warriors. By constantly absorbing fugitives from everywhere, this able captain had gathered a striking force far more formidable than anything with which he had started. These Nomads of Wrath were guilty of most atrocious barbarities, but ultimately they died with reckless bravery even in the face of the new terror of thunder, smoke and death.

With a handful of followers Matiwane escaped from the holocaust, with the intention of throwing himself on the mercy of Shaka. On the way he passed once more the Mountain of the Night (Ntaba Bosiu) and the Sutu people he had so barbarously afflicted for years. 'There Mshweshwe (Moshesh) with a heart as noble and magnanimous as ever nature bred, forgiving and forgetting all, compassionately invited him to dwell with him in peace. But Matiwane, leaving in his care one of his wives and sons, himself broken of heart and sick for home, passed on his way.'*

Matiwane finally reached Zululand to find that Shaka was no more, and Dingane on the throne. The latter accommodated him at his Royal kraal for a time, and then summoned him to appear. Suspecting the worst, Matiwane solemnly removed his brass armring and handed it to his fourteen-year-old son, Zikali, whom he instructed to remain at home.

'Where are your people?' asked Dingane. 'Here they are, all that are left of them,' was the reply. 'Then take them all away,' Dingane ordered. Thereupon they were led away and each Ngwane had his neck broken by a violent twist of the head; but Matiwane they tortured to death.

So ended Matiwane, one of the most redoubtable and resourceful of the Nguni conquistadores. Perhaps, given better opportunities, and without the constant necessity of wolfing his way for mere survival, he might have established as great a Nguni kingdom as did Mzilikazi of the Matabele, some years later. The direction he chose was unlucky; had he gone north-west instead

* Bryant, op. cit.

of south-west he would have anticipated Mzilikazi by four years, and had the free run of Africa without coming into collision with the Whites or other Nguni tribesmen.

It is not expected that the reader will have been able to follow these tribal movements and clashes closely, nor is that necessary. The object of describing them, albeit briefly and sketchily, has been twofold: to show that not Shaka, but Zwide, set off this chain reaction of misery and bloodshed, or, ultimately, and with the best intentions, Dingiswayo. And to give some idea of the disorder upon which Shaka was to impose the Zulu *Pax*. Not only did he not start the disastrous tribal wars of Natal, Free State and Basutoland, he checked them and, during his imperium, maintained an increasingly vast area within which, whatever was happening outside, law was respected, and peace and prosperity reigned.

CHAPTER 12

Death of Dingiswayo – The First
Zulu-Ndwandwe War

DINGISWAYO was disappointed and angry: his policy of clemency and conciliation towards Zwide had proved a failure. Three times he had subjugated, captured and magnanimously released him, and every time Zwide had promised to acknowledge his supremacy and to refrain from attacking his neighbours, unless he had a just cause approved of by Dingiswayo.

Zwide had for some time been intimidating his eastern and northern neighbours into alliances with himself, and now to cap it all he had without any cause whatsoever struck a devastating blow at Matiwane and his Ngwanes, driving them headlong out of their country, ruthlessly killing all men, women and children in his path, and burning all their kraals. Zwide thus inaugurated the devastating tribal migrations, recorded in the previous chapter. Dingiswayo sent peremptory messages to Zwide asking for explanation and redress. That wily chief advanced the ingenious and plausible excuse that he feared the Ngwanes might have attacked Dingiswayo's old friends, the Hlubis, over the cattle question, and their subsequent treatment of that tribe proved that his fears had been well founded.

When this hypocrisy was laid bare Zwide sent his sister, Ntombazana – daughter of the notorious Ntombazi of the skull museum – to be his ambassador and to try to win the love of Dingiswayo. She was accompanied by an attractive-looking cousin, the daughter of Malusi. In addition to placating Dingiswayo, the real object of the mission was to procure some particle of Dingiswayo's person for the purpose of working magical ascendancy over him – and the more intimately personal the object might be the more powerful the results; for after his late success over Matiwane, Zwide had become inordinately ambitious, and was now aiming at securing the Nguni paramountcy by overcoming Dingiswayo. This he felt he could only do with the assistance of magic. Before the girls left he therefore instructed Ntombazana that she was to obtain and bring back some of the King's semen. The pair then went their way; Ntombazana succeeded, and in due course returned, carrying 'him' (Dingiswayo) about her person.

Arrived in Ndwandwe-land the tribal medicine man took possession of the smuggled substance and busied himself with the manufacture of the charm.

Through skilful negotiations and with the aid of presents, Zwide kept Dingiswayo inactive. Then the planting season, weeding and finally the harvest festival became his fortuitous allies. Eventually he was quite ready to try his luck, magic and arms against Dingiswayo. It was now very early in the year 1818. To create a *casus belli* he had Malusi (who was married to Dingiswayo's sister Nomatuli) killed. His widow, being Dingiswayo's sister, would naturally inflame the King against Zwide. Dingiswayo certainly was inflamed, and in view of Zwide's unsatisfactory attitude in the past, he immediately prepared for action. He mobilized his Nyelezi brigade and instructed his vassal, Shaka, to do likewise, both armies to invade Ndwandwe-land simultaneously.

The Mtetwa army passed through the Mkwanazi location and along the ridges until it reached a point near the present-day Nongoma-Somkele road, a few miles east of the Nongoma magistracy. Here they awaited the arrival of Shaka, having in their precipitate action neglected to keep in touch with him, and so outraged the maxims of good generalship by exposing their available forces in detail to the enemy. No doubt Dingiswayo's original concept was sound and anticipated von Moltke's dictum 'March separately; strike together'. But the execution of the plan was deplorable.

Dingiswayo had halted in the neighbourhood of Zwide's Kwa-Dlovunga kraal whence he was being assailed with the most deadly of magic spells. These were effective: Dingiswayo, apparently taking leave of his senses, decided to advance, accompanied only by some girls as a bodyguard, leaving his army, and stating neither reason nor destination. At Mbuzi hill he walked into a Ndwandwe patrol and was taken to Kwa-Dlovunga. There he was treated with royal honours and courtesy. A beast was killed in his honour, a meal served and beer drunk.

Meanwhile Ntombazi, the sorceress, mother of Zwide, was urging her son not to weaken now that the King was in his hands. Zwide needed no such urging. He sent to Dingiswayo: 'Zwide, the Chief, summoneth thee.' To which Dingiswayo angrily returned: 'Is, then, a King summoned?'

Angry words followed, and when Zwide's armed messengers tried to force an entrance into the hut where the Mtetwa chief was sitting, a scuffle ensued, with the King's Amazons blocking the doorway. Zwide, after having kept his Royal visitor imprisoned in the kraal for several days, at last, yielding to his mother, ordered the King's death, and Dingiswayo was led away to his execution.

With royal dignity he walked to his doom, and when his women made frenzied attempts to rescue him from the armed guard in whose midst he walked, unfettered, and with a firm step, he told them in a kindly way to desist, and not to try the impossible and grieve him by incurring more hurts in a lost cause.

Arrived outside the kraal, Dingiswayo stood with folded arms and with quiet command in his voice told his executioner to drive his blade well and true under his left arm-pit, into his heart.

With one swift stroke the tragic deed was done.

The faithful maidens were then ordered to return to their home: but they resolutely refused to go without their lord. They formed in a circle around his body, on which their tears fell. They chanted their lament in low tones and as the last note died away they each drew out a toy bridal-spear or knife, secreted in the bags in which they had carried their master's food. Then with one accord they plunged the weapons into their hearts, and collapsed dying on the body of the man they had loved, thus loyally accompanying him right to the end.

'Dingiswayo himself – or, rather, that which remained of him after his head had gone to adorn Ntombazi's hut, and divers bits of his person had been cut away and stewed in a pot for their fat, and his head-ring carefully scraped of its mystical dirt – was granted a ceremonious burial under the direction of a specially deputed *umtakati* (he who had done the cutting-up and stewing) previously fortified against all possible evil consequences. A number of slaughtered oxen, buried in a separate grave close by, furnished the Royal traveller with agreeable provisions on his long journey to the Elysian Fields.'*

Thus in or about the year 1818, died Dingiswayo, the most enlightened chief of his race. His humane and tolerant methods might have succeeded with the less war-like and more easy-going Sutu clans, as was shown, indeed, by the success of Mshweshwe (Moshesh), but the turbulent Nguni chiefs and their fierce fighting clans needed the master-hand and ruthless genius of Shaka to weld them into a homogeneous nation, after first smashing them, in many cases, well-nigh out of recognition. Even Mshweshwe might not have succeeded had the invading Nguni hordes of Mpangazita, Matiwane and Mzilikazi not first created chaos amongst the Sutus and enabled Mshweshwe to gather up the pieces, and cement them together with the common interest of self-preservation.

By whatever standard we measure Dingiswayo, however, he stands forth as a great man, and all the greater for subduing the minds of men with reason rather than with the all too common method of ordinary conquerors, who only attain their ends through fear preceded by bloodshed.

Meanwhile Dingiswayo's army, alarmed at the strange disappearance of its king, remained inactive and disconsolate in its camp. But when at last the Ndwandwe hosts were seen swarming over the hills, the Mtetwas' officers knew that the worst had happened, and the all-conquering Mtetwa army became for the first time apprehensive and unnerved. Yet it stuck manfully to its duty, succumbing neither to cowardice nor panic, and with a half-hearted effort to save the position, beat an orderly retreat, fighting effectively along the homeward path. On its hard-pressed

* Bryant, *op. cit.*

retreat it was met and joined by Nqoboka and his Sokulus, who, like Shaka, had not been given time to complete his arrangements for joining this ill-starred, precipitate and badly timed expedition.

Meanwhile Shaka and his troops had reached the Ama-Yiwane Neck ('esi-kaleni sama Yiwane' – a low ridge at the head of the Ama-Yiwane stream, two or three miles south of the present Ma-Hlabatini Magistracy). There word reached him from Donda, one of the Kumalo chiefs, also on the way to join the badly arranged rendezvous with the Mtetwa army, asking, 'Whither are you going? Dingiswayo is already killed and the Mtetwa army is in full retreat.'

Then Shaka returned homewards.

Although Shaka did not participate in the hostilities of this campaign, the fact that he had a powerful force on Zwide's flank prevented the latter from exploiting his success over the Mtetwa army and overrunning their country. For with Shaka's army intact, the Ndwandwes had to keep in a compact body, which prevented them from doing much looting of cattle or burning huts. Zwide's army therefore retraced its steps and returned home practically empty-handed.

In the meantime Ngomane, the late Dingiswayo's headman, with the whole of the 2nd Izi-cwe regiment, joined Shaka, an example which was followed by great numbers of individual Mtetwas. Nqoboka, chief of the Sokulus, Shaka's early warrior friend, also stood by with his own force, strongly augmented by leaderless Mtetwas. These additions, plus the steady stream of recruits Shaka had received since putting Nobela in her place, now gave him an effective fighting force of close on 5000 men, who were daily drilled with the utmost rigour.

Shaka's position was, however, precarious, situated as he was between the powerful and ambitious Zwide in the north, the formidable Qwabe clan in the south, who looked with envy and suspicion on the rapidly growing power of the Zulu junior brother-clan, and finally Ngoza, of the equally strong Tembus, in the west.

Zwide was trying to inveigle the Qwabes and the Tembus into joint action against the centrally situated Zulus, holding out as a bait the partition of Zululand between them. Conversely Shaka was trying to get the Qwabes and the Tembus into a joint alliance against Zwide – 'The Eater-up of Chiefs'.

Whilst these diplomatic manoeuvres were going on, Zwide, having heard that Donda of the Kumalos, whose territory lay between his and Shaka's, had warned Shaka when he was hurrying to Dingiswayo's aid, and had so saved him from putting his head in the noose, decided to eliminate Donda and his tribe by treachery. He therefore suggested to Donda that they arrange in his domain an *inqina yom Senge* (a short informal hunt), followed by the usual *ijadu* (love dance), which the girls attended bearing *umsenge* (cabbage tree) branches. Zwide told Donda not to be alarmed if he saw his men coming armed for war and numerous, as he had to be on his guard for any surprises from Shaka. On the appointed day the trusting Donda and his Kumalo men were surrounded and treacherously massacred to a man, as they were only armed with light hunting-spears and carried no shields. The girls were carried off as booty and so was Donda's head to augment Ntombazi's collection.

Farther north dwelt another section of the Kumalos under Chief Mashobane, the father of the subsequently famous Mzilikazi, founder and king of the conquering Matabele nation. Mashobane, although the son-in-law of Zwide, and a large section of his clan were also killed by treachery, immediately after Donda had been eliminated, and his head too went into Ntombazi's collection. Mzilikazi for a time became a vassal of Zwide's but not long afterwards joined Shaka, in whose service he rapidly rose to the position of a general.

These treacherous massacres, which hitherto were an unheard-of enormity among the Nguni race, caused Zwide to be generally hated and distrusted by all the surrounding tribes, and lent point to Shaka's warning against him, and his suggestion to the Qwabes and Tembus to form a joint protective alliance. As Shaka's territory lay between them and Zwide as a buffer, they were not, however, inclined to pay any heed to his warning.

In the meantime Zwide was rapidly extending his power through the coercive alliances in the north, east and west, and he now felt that the time had come to eliminate Shaka – the only remaining obstacle in his way to securing the Nguni paramountcy.

In order to have a just cause for war in the eyes of his allies and other chiefs, Zwide now remembered that Senzangakona, Shaka's father, had promised him three selected Zulu maidens if he would give him support against the Butelezis, who in those days were his principal oppressors. The fact that Zwide had given no aid made no difference to his claim, nor that the commitment, if any, had been incurred by the late Senzangakona, for according to Nguni law an heir inherited not only the estate but also its debts – and it was remarkable how many debts suddenly cropped up after a wealthy man's death. Zwide now demanded from Shaka the immediate delivery of the maidens.

'What impudence !' said Shaka. 'Never shall a sister of mine wed that dried-up old hide ("*lolo'luGagada oludala*") who has already devoured half the chiefs in the land. Let him come and fetch them.'

The infuriated Zwide came, guided more by rage than reason, for his preparations might have been more thorough had he been less precipitate.

Shaka was ready, and not only with his army, for he had mobilized the whole tribe and all the cattle, and these were dispatched to the southern boundary near the Umhlatuzi river, so that if need be they would have a good start to retire into the fastnesses of the Nkandla forest, a day's march beyond his frontier. A *levée en masse* (*ukukulela ngoqo*) of all males above and below military age who were capable of bearing arms had been ordained some time before, and they had been drilled into some semblance of discipline by the indefatigable Mgobozi. Most of the *Nkomendala*, as these conscripts were called – 'toothless old cattle' – but the name became as honourable as 'the Old Contemptibles' – and a strong contingent of regular warriors would have to be detached to guard the women, children and cattle evacuated southward. This would leave Shaka with well under

4000 men to meet Zwide's host, now grown to far more than double that number, and greater still, if he fully completed the mobilization of all his northern allies.

Nqoboka of the Sokulus, who with Mgobozi had been Shaka's great warrior friend when he was still a private in Dingiswayo's army, was of great value to Shaka, and took command of the allied contingents of the Dlaminis, Sibiyas and others who had responded to the call *inkomo ibajiwe* (the cow is stuck), i.e. in the mud.*

It was about the beginning of April 1818 when Zwide's host descended on Shaka. Reaching the White Umfolozi river, at that time the northern boundary of the little Zulu kingdom, Zwide's army found the river still running high – though not in spate – due to the late rains and a recent unusual downpour. It could, therefore, only be forded in a very few places, and these were guarded by strong detachments of Zulus; whilst Shaka's main force was concentrated on the summit of Qokli hill, a little south of the White Umfolozi river. Here Shaka had drawn up his regiments in a complete circle some five or six lines deep, with a tactical or strategic reserve hidden on the central plateau. In this centre he had collected an ample supply of water in earthenware pots, gourds and beer bags, a quantity of *kota* ('lick' – maize roasted on the cob and then shelled and ground to meal) and some slaughter-oxen and firewood.

For some distance around Qokli hill there was no water, and for a considerable radius every scrap of food had been removed.

Knowing from his accurate intelligence service that he was very heavily outnumbered by the Ndwandwes, and their numerous allies and auxiliaries, Shaka felt he could not risk an open battle in

---

* This appeal is frequently made by Zulus and, as everyone is expected to, and does help spontaneously when a cow is stuck in the mud, so an appeal framed in these words will invariably be acceded to with jovial good humour, and without any thought of recompense. For instance, if an automobile is stuck in a sandy patch, or a load is too difficult to lift, one has but to say to any by-standers, 'Wo! *madoda, inkomo ibajiwe'.* – Wo! men, the cow is stuck, i.e. in the mud – and with cheerful smiles they will all give a hand.

lines which could be overwhelmed on their exposed flanks, as there were no natural obstacles on which he could securely rest them.

Drawn up in a circle his army could and would be surrounded, but it would have no loose lines which could be rolled up in detail. It would have a solid, unbroken front even when the losses mounted, as these would be counteracted by drawing in his lines into smaller circles. He knew that this dangerous manoeuvre of allowing himself to be completely surrounded could only be attempted with well-trained and steady warriors, and he had absolute confidence in the iron discipline of his Zulus, and the well-tried courage and steadiness of his auxiliaries. Unconsciously he was adopting the famous British square tactics of the Duke of Wellington at Waterloo, but modified by the Nguni conception of orderliness into a battle circle, thus avoiding dangerously exposed corners and the grave risk Wellington was faced with, when his depleted squares had to be re-formed into triangles in the face of heavy enemy pressure.

Shaka was confident that he would be able to last out the day under any circumstances, and that his men would be comparatively fresh with their supplies of food – and especially water – whereas the Ndwandwes would, after a time, be tormented with thirst, for fighting was the thirstiest work in the world, and the early April days were still very hot. This would lead to frequent and considerable diversions of their strength. In his commanding position on top of the hill, in the centre of his army, and with the reserves standing by all the time, he could view the whole battlefield and every disposition of the enemy, and the moment his adversary made a mistake he could strike hard in any direction, as he had the advantage of the shorter inner lines. Shaka never believed in a defensive action or war except as a temporary means to lure his opponents into making a false move, or exposing some weakness, at which he would strike like a thunderbolt.

If perchance by the end of the day he should have received too hard a gruelling, he would, after nightfall, form his warriors into a solid phalanx and if necessary hack his way through the enemy,

and retire with his whole tribe into the Nkandla forest. It was
more likely, however, that the thirsty Ndwandwes would break
off the battle to quench their thirst, away back on the Umfolozi
river in the north or the equidistant Umkumbane river in the
west.

Zwide's heir, Nomahlanjana, commanded the Ndwandwes. He
was a young man of about Shaka's age and was accompanied by
nearly all the sons of Zwide, who had reached manhood, and all of
them served in the famous Ama-Nkayiya regiment or brigade.
Zwide, who was now about fifty years of age, never accompanied
his army.

Finding the ford immediately in front of him held by an apparently weak force, Nomahlanjana immediately tried to force it.
The current was swift and in places ran shoulder high. Immediately below the ford there was a treacherous series of rapids. The
Ndwandwes waded into the river in files, five or six abreast. The
natural causeway would not admit of any more. Each warrior
held his shield and assegais high in one hand, whilst holding on
to the shoulder of the man in front with the other. In this way
they formed a chain which was particularly effective in the deeper
places.

Nqoboka commanded the Sokulus and Zulus who guarded the
central ford, and was ably assisted by the newly arrived Ndlela,*
and that remarkable warrior Njikiza Ngcolosi, the wielder of an
oversize club, with which he worked such prodigious execution
that ever afterwards the club was known as 'Nohlola-Mazibuko'
(The Watcher of the Ford), which name was also conferred on the
owner as a praise name.

Standing waist deep in the shallower water near the bank, the
defenders had an enormous advantage over the attackers, who at
this point had to cross a steep depression which put them shoulder
deep in the water. It was here that the iron-spiked and long-
handled club did great damage to the Ndwandwes, crashing down
on shield and head and sending warrior after warrior down the

* This Ntuli cannibal recruit rose to be a general under Shaka and
at last Dingane's Prime Minister.

100-yard wide river into the rapids, and if not already dead, to meet death through drowning. Nqoboka and Ndlela were also in the van, and having secured some of the long throwing spears which were flung at them under difficulties, they used them for underwater jabs into the unprotected bodies of the Ndwandwes, who had no chance whatsoever of warding them off, as it was all they could do to keep their footing on the slippery rock-floor in the strong current.

It was about this time that Shaka arrived with 500 of his swiftest Fasimba for a personal reconnaissance. The main army he left to the trusty Mdlaka, who was now second-in-command to Shaka. The irrepressible Mgobozi accompanied Shaka. He was to have stayed behind with the strategic reserve, safely tucked away within the army circle on Qokli hill. Shaka always appreciated Mgobozi's shrewd advice on State matters and general strategy, but when he got within sight of the enemy the old war-dog became intoxicated with but one idea, and that was to get to personal grips with the foe regardless of odds, and contemptuous of tactics.

When Mgobozi heard that fighting had commenced at the ford, he implored Shaka to be allowed to join in. 'My Father, must we, then, sit here like a lot of vultures on top of the hill waiting for our people to be killed, or are we going to be men and join in the fight?'

'Mgobozi, it is impossible to argue against you! You may accompany us, but mark you, for once I expect you to control yourself!'

'*Bayete Baba!*' Mgobozi acclaimed his chief and then with sparkling eyes he told the warriors around him: 'It seems to me there is still a chance of avoiding death from old age like an old cow in a kraal.'

When Shaka arrived at the ford the action was at its height, for the Ndwandwes thought that by holding Nqoboka here they could, unperceived, cross at a lower and a higher ford and then fall on his back. But these crossings, they soon found out, were equally well guarded.

Shaka was delighted to see and hear the blows of 'The Watcher of the Ford', and the extraordinary ability of Ndlela the ex-cannibal, and the excellent generalship of Nqoboka.

Well before noon Nomahlanjana realized the hopelessness of trying to effect a crossing, no matter where he tried, so he broke off the action. He had lost several hundred men killed or drowned, whereas Shaka had only a few dozen casualties, very few of which were fatal. In the afternoon the river began to drop rapidly and Shaka told Nqoboka to retire to the main body as soon as the river dropped to a level which would make the fords redundant.

Shaka then rejoined the main body with his escort, having throughout the greater part of the day carefully studied the enemy dispositions across the river. Before nightfall he had seen to it that all the receptacles on Qokli hill had been replenished with water. The army had a substantial meal of grilled meat and *kota*. Guards, pickets and patrols were sent out and touch was kept with Nqoboka. After a council of war attended by all the commanders and senior officers, including Mdlaka, Nzobo, Ngomane and Mgobozi, Shaka lay down to sleep with Mgobozi close to him. The latter was soon 'dragging dry hides' (polite Zulu figure of speech for snoring) and sleeping as happily as a child on the eve of a great holiday.

Long before dawn Nqoboka arrived with his contingents from the ford, and was posted to the central strategic reserve on Qokli hill. When he came to report he found Shaka seated on a large stone on the edge of the flat summit or plateau, facing north-wards towards the White Umfolozi river and the Ndwandwes. He was alone and in deep thought, with orderly lines of sleeping warriors all around him.

Nqoboka greeted him with a low '*Bayete! Baba*', and Shaka responded with a hearty '*Sakubona Nqoboka, my old friend*'. A quick and soldier-like report followed, to the effect that the river had dropped rapidly and was easily fordable in many places, and the only obstructions were now the deep, long pools. Observation pickets had been left all along the river and would keep the enemy in view and report at intervals to Shaka. Mdlaka, Nzobo and Mgobozi now arrived and heard Nqoboka's further report that the

Ndwandwes had received considerable reinforcements during the night and were at least three times as strong as the Zulus.

Shaka then revealed to Nqoboka his plan for decoying a portion of the Ndwandwe army from the main fighting. At daylight the Ndwandwes would see one in every four of the Zulu cattle being driven over the Tonjaneni Heights (six or seven miles to the south). They were guarded by 500 *Nkomendala* reserves and 200 Fasimba as a selected rearguard. When the Ndwandwes found that they had surrounded the Zulu force at Qokli hill, and thinking that all the Zulu cattle were being driven southwards out of their reach, they would assuredly detach a large force to go after the cattle. By the time they caught up with them they would be twice the distance, or more, from Qokli as that lying between there and the Tonjaneni Heights, as the running fight which would ensue would also tend to delay the enemy. Before the pursuing Ndwandwe force could be back again, encumbered with many cattle, the main decision would have been reached at Qokli.

In order still further to deceive the Ndwandwes and their young and inexperienced commander, Nomahlanjana, most of the Zulus would be concentrated around the central reserve, and out of sight, on the summit or plateau of Qokli hill. This would give the impression that there were but 1500 Zulus on the hill whereas actually they would be over 3500 strong. The commander of the force covering the Zulu cattle would also resort to various subterfuges of deployment, disappearance and reappearance, so that his 700 men would in the distance look like a force several times that number. This would make the Ndwandwes think that the Zulu army was divided into two almost equal bodies.

A blood-red dawn heralded the day. At this moment a picket appeared escorting a file of girls carrying pots of beer on their heads. Leading them was Pampata. Shaka was amazed and exclaimed, 'Whence come you at such a time?'

'The *Ndlovukazi* (She-Elephant — courtesy title of Nandi, Shaka's mother) sent us with this good cheer for you and a message,' answered Pampata. 'We left the E-Langeni yesterday afternoon and these warriors escorted us through the night.'

'You should have stayed at home,' said Shaka brusquely.

'Pampata, did my mother really send you, or was it your idea?'

'My Lord, I entreated her to send me, for this day will be the mother of much death and I would be near you. See how red and ominous is the dawn.'

'Indeed it is, and before the sun sinks this hill will be redder still, and much of its colour will come from the best blood in Zululand. You speak truly, for this day will give birth to much death (*li zo zala ukufa*), especially for the Ndwandwes. Pampata, are you not afraid?'

'For myself, not at all. For you, my Lord, very much. I beseech you not to forget in the heat of battle that you must not join in. For what is the use of a body without a head? Direct the fighting only and, this day, besides death, will be born the greatest captain of war.'

Pampata relaxed into silence, but fidgeting nervously she looked at Shaka shyly.

'What is troubling you, Pampata?' asked Shaka very gently. 'Speak up, and do not be afraid.'

'My Lord, the Ndwandwes are many and they fight well, yet we all know how Nowawa – Zwide's half-mother – stopped the war against Zangendaba of the Ncwangeni clan by disrobing in the cattle-kraal before the gathered army. This was an *umhlolo* (evil omen) and so frightened them all that there was no war. I therefore have in mind that if we could arrange an evil omen, even it were but a lesser one, there being no cattle-kraal here – it would make them uneasy, and they would soon loose heart in the battle.'

Shaka stared in wide-eyed astonishment, but in the gentlest of tones he asked: 'What have you in mind?'

'My Lord, as you know I am an unmarried woman and still dressed as a maiden. I have, however, procured a married woman's kilt, and by combing my hair I can make myself look like one. With your permission, thus dressed then as a married woman,* I propose to go out alone in front of the Ndwandwe

* As maidens wore very little their nudity would not be apparent at a distance. In any case it would not be the heinous offence presented by a married woman discarding her kilt.

142

army as it assembles before battle in front of this hill. Thereupon
I will disrobe before them, and saying nothing I will slowly des-
cend the hill and advance towards them with upraised arms pointing in their direction. My silence and slow advance will dismay
them, and they will call it an *um-hlolo*, as such a sight has never
before been witnessed, and they will be smitten with fear. Even
when they have killed me, they will feel uneasy, and their blood
will turn into water, and not much fighting will be needed to
make them run. That is all, my Lord, except this little parting
gift of stringed beads, the words of which you understand,' and
she unfastened from her neck and handed to him the intricately
woven pattern of white, red and black beads, which were the
silent messengers of her love and devotion.

Shaka always admired courage, but this outstanding example,
coupled with such love and devotion, moved him so deeply that
he merely held in his hand the little gift – so small, yet signifying
so much. At last, after a long silence, during which his eyes,
says the chronicler, were moist, he spoke.

'Thank you, Pampata. It is but small, and yet it speaks louder
than all the voices in Zululand. Tell me, that bundle yonder,
does it contain the kilt you would don for the first and last time
before you go forth naked, as the bride of Death?'

'Yes, my Lord, but in my heart I will feel that you are my
bridegroom, and the army there our children, most of whom will
be saved from the harvest of death which now faces our Zululand. Thus, then, my Lord, I will be the proudest and happiest
bride, as I walk to my death, and in my heart I sing the farewell
ihubu' – a bride's swan song on leaving her home – 'and then
give thanks for the honour you have conferred on me.'

'Pampata, you are the finest but strangest woman in the world.
But where is the Zulu who would ever again hold up his head if
we sheltered like cowards, and worse, behind the defenceless and
naked body of a brave and beautiful young woman? All the same
I thank you for your offer, and will always treasure it in my
heart.'

The sun had just arisen and the Ndwandwes were reported to
have started the crossing of the river two miles away, by two of

the fords. It would still be a long time before they were all over. Shaka's warriors were having their breakfast of grilled meat and *kota*, and Shaka with the reassembled council was doing likewise. Covering the distant Tonjaneni Heights were many cattle, apparently the rearguard of others which had crossed before. Behind them were lines of warriors, their spears flashing in the rising sun. 'Splendid!' said Shaka. 'The Ndwandwes will think that most of the Zulus have gone with the cattle.'

Shaka, accompanied by his commanders, now addressed the quarter circle of his warriors on the northern slope of the hill, facing the coming approach of the enemy. He emphasized the necessity for absolute obedience and discipline. To maintain their formations and keep their ranks closed. To keep their ears open to the commands of their leaders. Above all to beware of any simulated flight by the Ndwandwes, and even in the final chase no formation to out-distance by more than half a spear's throw, the formation on either side. Any man or group who ventured to get more than half a spear's throw ahead of the others, no matter how heroic, would, if still alive after the battle, forfeit their lives.

Shaka then made the same address to the three other quarter circles, and finally to the strategic reserve who were drawn up in a close circle many lines deep, and well away from the edges of the plateau, so as to be completely out of sight when the enemy enveloped the hill. The reserve was told to sit down and keep still until they were called. The other warriors on the hillside were told to 'sit on their spears'.

From time to time Shaka stopped and spoke to individual warriors by name, recalling some incident in the past. His astonishing memory for names and faces made them all feel that he took an interest in every individual. Thus with encouraging words, allied with his confident and authoritative manner, he imbued every warrior with his own dauntless spirit.

CHAPTER 13

The battle of Qokli hill

As Shaka had foreseen, Nomahlanjana detached four regiments, a third of his forces, in pursuit of the Zulu cattle and their escort over the Tonjaneni Heights, while the rest of his Ndwandwes crossed the White Umfolozi and formed up eight thousand strong on the north-eastern base of Qokli hill, in a semicircle. Nomahlanjana took the northern wing of his army, with four guards regiments, the veteran Ama-Nkayiya.

Shaka had so arranged his forces that a little under half of each regiment was in open view just under the crest of the hill, whilst the rest were immediately opposite in the rear, but completely hidden from view. His total fighting strength on Qokli hill was approximately 3600 men, of whom little more than 1600 were visible to his enemies. They were drawn up in five lines, each man on a front of approximately two short paces in order to have sufficient elbow room.

Nomahlanjana's scouts had reported to him that the hill was thinly held, an illusion which was deliberately heightened by Shaka, who, prior to the Ndwandwes' approach, had ordered the four rear lines to pack closely behind the leading one, and as all were seated closely behind each other, and on their shields, they gave the impression that he had no depth of formation. Nor could his regiments be identified, with their shields out of view. Nomahlanjana therefore felt more than confident that he would have no difficulty in over-running the Zulus, who would be swamped by his overwhelming numbers. To him the Zulu dispositions appeared to be stupid and suicidal. 'It will be like slaughtering a lot of cattle in a kraal,' he remarked to his staff.

An order to advance within two spears' throw of the Zulus was shouted by Nomahlanjana and with an exultant shout the whole

Ndwandwe host closed in, but as the circle narrowed the warriors were jammed ever closer together, until the lines buckled and a great confusion arose everywhere. The Ndwandwes, from the very beginning in an over-close formation, had overlooked the fact that, starting in a circle with a diameter of some 550 yards and a circumference of over 1700, they were in their first advance shrinking the diameter of the circle by 200 yards and thus reducing the circumference to 1100 yards. After much shouting and abuse from the captains of hundreds and leaders of platoons, they finally drew up in badly dovetailed formations, two spears' throw (100 yards) from the Zulus.

The Zulus were still sitting in absolute silence, many of them nonchalantly snuffing tobacco, the grim, dour looks of the warriors in the older regiments contrasting strangely with the eager look of the young Fasimba and Izi-cwe.

The Ndwandwes now hurled the customary abuse at the Zulus. The Zulus were grimly silent; but when the Ndwandwes called them toothless dogs and baboons perched on a hill, there was an ominous growl and movement, and Shaka's voice roared to them to sit down. The order was repeated by Mdlaka and Nzobo, and then by the regimental commanders, echoed by the captains of hundreds, and quietly emphasized by the platoon leaders.

'Where are your champions?' yelled the Ndwandwes.

'Here,' called out Manyosi, the son of Dlekezele, as he stepped out of the Izim-Pohlo front, and advanced – with Shaka's permission – half a spear's throw. A Ndwandwe warrior now likewise stepped forward, and at a quarter spear's throw hurled his throwing assegai at Manyosi, whose shield it transfixed. Approaching nearer still, the Ndwandwe made a feint as if to throw his second spear, halted the throw, as Manyosi ducked behind his shield, and then waited for Manyosi's face to reappear, which he narrowly missed from transfixing. The next instant Manyosi had closed with him, and he gave a death bellow as the broad blade went in under the left arm-pit, and Manyosi gave his exultant *Nga-dla!* (I have eaten!).

There was a roar of applause from the watching Zulus. 'Are

we, then, as toothless as you thought?' they shouted. A yell of rage came back from the Ndwandwes.

'Who comes next?' challenged Manyosi, and another Ndwandwe stepped forward. No sooner had he thrown his first missile than Manyosi rushed at him. There was a clash of shields and then the Zulu hooked his shield round his opponent's, and with a wrench to the left exposed the Ndwandwe's left side. There was another triumphant *Nga-dla*. After Manyosi had disposed of a third enemy champion, there were no further offers to fight him and he returned to his line.

Stung by the jeers of the Zulus, the whole Ndwandwe army advanced to give battle. It was now about nine o'clock – 'the sun was midway between noon and sunrise'.

'*Ayi hlome!*' ('To arms!') commanded Shaka, and as before the order was shouted from brigade to regimental commanders, and through the captains to the platoon leaders. With that incredible timing of mass-movement which has ever been such an outstanding characteristic of the Zulus, the 1500 warriors seated around the hill brow rose like one man. Then with a crash 1500 feet – only the right foot is used for this demonstration – struck the ground as one unit and made the hill vibrate, and there followed a rolling rattle and drumming as every spear shaft was beaten in rapid succession against a corresponding shield for a few seconds. The four lines packed closely behind the front one now moved backwards to allow for a space of three or four paces between lines.

Mgobozi, seated in the middle of the strategic reserve out of sight in the plateau, groaned. He had heard that single vibrating thud, and knew what it meant. 'I cannot even see them and what is coming, and here I must sit as useless as a broody hen on a lot of addled eggs.'

'Nay, Mgobozi,' remarked a staff *induna* (headman), who had just then arrived with a message, 'the "Great Elephant" is but teaching you what to teach to your "boys". He asks you now to come and see them. You are to stay by his side, but to do no fighting till he gives you the word. Your work is to watch the warriors fighting and to see where improvements can be made.'

With a glint of hope in his eye Mgobozi hurried to Shaka's side. He was standing on the northern brim of the plateau, with Mdlaka and a few *indunas* by his side. Nzobo, commander of the Bachelors' Brigade, and his *indunas* occupied a similar position on the southern brim. Nqoboka and Ngomane were likewise placed respectively on the eastern and western fronts. Between all four commanders there was a perfect liaison. Shaka kept himself free, to enable him periodically to inspect all the fronts, and within two minutes he could make a complete round and get a true picture of everything that was going on, and not a single move of the enemy could be kept hidden from him.

Far otherwise was the position of Nomahlanjana. Seated in the shade of a mimosa tree at the northern base of the hill, he could only see his immediate front, and could only gather through runners what was taking place on the other three sides of the hill. He was an able and ambitious man, but as the heir of Zwide he could not be bothered with too much personal exertion, or any attention to detail. In any case it would be a walk-over, and a calabash or two of beer in the shade of the tree was more to his liking.

The Ndwandwe army made its final advance into battle very slowly and cautiously, for when the Zulu lines jumped up and 'showed their shields', they looked a very different proposition from the seated rows.

Again the shrinking of the circle caused an ever-growing congestion in the Ndwandwe lines, and by the time they halted twenty-five long paces from the Zulus, preparatory to hurling their spears, they were in an indescribable state of confusion and congestion, for the length of their lines had again shrunk from 1100 yards to 600.

Shaka, with sparkling eyes, saw his opportunity, and like a thunderbolt he launched his leading line at them, closely supported by the second. '*Si-gī-di!*' roared the charging Zulus and then the war-cry became an ominous, sibilant hiss. Like an avalanche they struck the densely packed Ndwandwes, who were jammed together so tightly that they could not even throw their spears, and the Zulus commenced a fearful slaughter.

Shaka watched with grim pleasure, but he was not content

with the view of one section only of the battlefield, and with rapid strides he made a round of the three other commands or sections, but everywhere he found the same successful progress.

After the first two minutes the carnage slowed down, as the Ndwandwe company commanders and their regimental commanders ordered a general movement backwards, which, with the casualties in front, at last gave the enemy warriors a fair fighting space. With the traditional bravery of the whole of the Nguni race, the Ndwandwes now fought back vigorously, but they lacked the iron discipline, the training and the broad, short, stabbing blade of the Zulus.

After the whole action had lasted less than ten minutes the customary lull took place – both sides falling back a little as if obeying a command. Thereupon Nomahlanjana ordered the withdrawal of all his regiments to the foot of the hill, in order to consider this phenomenon of congestion, and the grievous losses it had caused. Shaka then ordered his two front lines to rejoin the others but to form up behind them, so that the third line now became the front one. First, however, all Ndwandwe spears were collected, and then the badly wounded Zulus were helped up the hill. Those who were past any hope of recovery were mercifully dispatched, as their Spartan logic demanded a quick end to their agony. If a comrade could still speak they would ask, and invariably receive, his consent. If he was past speaking, his silence was accepted as consent. The enemy wounded were all killed and disembowelled as a matter of course.

The seriously wounded Zulus were all gathered in the centre of the plateau, next to the water supplies, where they were tended by the *u-dibi* boys. The lesser wounded stayed in their ranks, and they and those warriors who had been in the battle now received a welcome drink of water, for apart from the physical exertion of the intense footwork, the psychic tension of fighting creates a terrible thirst.

When Nomahlanjana saw the havoc the Zulus had caused amongst his warriors – for there were well over 1000 dead – it was decided that half the army should remain in its present position at the foot of the hill, and the other half should attack, with big intervals between the lines and the warriors well spaced within them.

Shaka made another careful round of inspection of the battle lines. All the warriors had to turn about and face him as he strode along the higher ground inside the lines. The majestic splendour of his immense athletic form was heightened to the onlookers below, through their relative positions. From time to time he spoke encouraging words to the lightly wounded in the ranks, and noted with satisfaction that their flesh wounds on arms and thighs were bound up with bark over a dressing of *u-joye* (*Datura stramonium*) leaves, which his forethought had ordered the *u-dibi* to bring. For Shaka knew he needed every warrior, and he did everything he could to avoid wastage in the army. Several of the wounded whom he considered too seriously hurt he ordered back to the central depot for those grievously injured. A badly bandaged wound called for instant censure, and remedial measures. So did any defect in armament.

Mgobozi followed behind his chief, and between the lines of warriors and with a mixture of praise and good-humoured banter, the beloved drill-instructor left a warm glow in the hearts of all his men. But woe betide the luckless warrior whose shield fastenings were not exactly as they should be, or whose stabbing blade showed the slightest blemish.

Once more the Ndwandwes advanced, but this time they were appropriately spaced. Again they halted within half a spear's throw from the Zulus, who had been instructed to crouch low behind their five-foot-long shields. A 'shelf'* of spears came hurtling amongst them, but the damage they did was negligible. Presently the leading rank of Ndwandwes had but one spear left to each warrior, which they must retain for hand-to-hand fighting. What now? For these strange Zulus did not throw back the spears, they merely confiscated them. Again the Ndwandwes looked 'like cows before a new gate'.

Shaka was in a gleeful mood. Turning to Mgobozi and his staff, he said: 'As I pointed out in the very beginning this form of

* So called because a volley of spears looks like a shelf.

warfare is stupid, when warriors have to throw away their weapons.'

When the second Ndwandwe rank had also spent their missiles, Shaka gave the order for his two front lines to charge, and with their war-cry of *Si-gī-di!* they threw themselves at the Ndwandwes twenty-five yards below them. The battle now resolved itself into hundreds of single combats all round the hill. These duels might last from a few seconds to many minutes and were very strenuous, involving a great deal of footwork and all manner of acrobatics. The end was usually fatal for one of the protagonists and often for both. The fighting was chivalrous, a third warrior would not intervene to help one of his own side against an enemy.

When the Zulus and Ndwandwes paused after about five minutes of savage fighting, and drew a little apart, it was obvious that at least three Ndwandwes had died for every Zulu. One-third of the leading line of Zulus was dead or mortally wounded, and another third wounded, but still fit to fight. The whole first line of the Ndwandwes was down and the equivalent of another line wounded.

During most of the battle Shaka occupied the northern brim of the hill where he could concentrate his attention on Nomahlanjana under the shade tree, and observe that part of the semicircle where the veteran Ama-Nkayiya were attacking. Members of his staff kept running to the other fronts, and reports were pouring in all the time. Even so he left nothing to chance, and during an engagement he would go bounding to the other side of the plateau – a matter of 100 yards – to see with his own eyes.

After the engagement had lasted somewhat longer than the preceding one, both sides again fell apart. In assessing the casualties (which both parties invariably did) the superiority of the Zulus became more evident than ever.

Nomahlanjana again broke off the battle by withdrawing his fighting lines to the foot of the hill, and after another council of war he moved the fresh rear half of his army through the mauled ranks of the front half. These were now harangued for a considerable time by their fighting *indunas* or officers and given a discourse on new tactics. They were to advance right up to the

Zulus without any spear-throwing, and then they were to rush them, and whilst the front line was engaged, the second line were to throw their spears through the gaps in the first, at any exposed portion of the Zulu warriors busily fighting in the front rank.

Shaka welcomed these delays, for with the gathering dry heat his principal ally – *thirst* – was inexorably marching to his aid. By early afternoon the heat would be great, and all the still-combatant or lightly wounded enemy warriors would be looking for water two miles away. Many of these would be accompanied by unwounded, thirst-goaded warriors, who would slip away with them. Then, too, the Ndwandwe discipline was slack, and in no way to be compared with that of the Zulus. Thus Shaka would strike at a depleted and parched enemy with his fresh and well-nourished reserves, and even his lightly wounded would be comparatively fit as a reserve, well provided as they were with water and bark bandages.

Shaka had arranged for a series of smoke signals which would keep him fairly well advised of the movements of the Ndwandwe regiments who had gone in pursuit of the cattle. The smoke columns on the far left flank indicated the advance, and were to be liberated as soon as the Ndwandwes came abreast of the spot. When they started to appear on the right it would indicate their return. So far they were all on the left.

As the Ndwandwes advanced again, their plans were upset by Shaka, for as they approached within half a spear's throw he sent his two leading lines crashing into them. The impact hurled the first enemy rank into the second, and they were now too close to each other to enable the third rank to throw their spears between the contemplated intervals, which had disappeared through the merging of the two leading lines. Again there was a ferocious encounter, and the Zulus, who had in the interval been instructed to press forward with the preponderant weight which their downward progress gave them, vaulted at the Ndwandwes with their shields. In this way they ensured the congestion of the enemy ranks, whilst the second line of Zulus was in such close support of the first echelon as it were, between the leading files, that they were in a position to effect thrusts past their leading comrades, by holding their stabbing blades near the shaft ends to give them the necessary reach. In the meantime Shaka sent in his third line, leaving himself with but one line in reserve, which consisted solely of more or less lightly wounded warriors. The strategic reserve on the plateau, however, was as yet untouched.

By the time the usual pause set in, the savage aggressiveness of the Zulus had driven the Ndwandwes back some two dozen paces or so.

Again the contending forces fell away from each other, and again Nomahlanjana withdrew his regiments to the foot of the hill. He was intensely annoyed at the repeated repulses he had suffered, and summoning his commanders and most of the captains he gave them a scathing talk on their incompetence.

Then once again he sent them into action, but again they failed to break the Zulu lines. It was now past noon, the heat was great, and many of the Ndwandwe wounded, but still able-bodied, warriors were drifting away northwards and to the west to look for water.

There was another consultation among the Ndwandwe leaders. Two of the five Zulu lines had vanished through attrition and many of their warriors in the remaining lines were wounded. But the havoc among the Ndwandwes was great, and their relative strength was less than in the beginning. If only the formation of those unshakeable Zulus could be broken, thought Nomahlanjana. He therefore instructed his commanders to pass along the word quietly that in the next attack, after a short clash, all the warriors were to simulate a panic flight, until they had reached the bottom of the hill, and then, as they contacted their reserves, they were to turn on the Zulus, who were sure to follow them in the heat of the action.

Once more the Ndwandwes advanced to attack, and as they drew near, the Zulus, as before, rushed at them. After a brief clash a cry arose from the rear ranks of the Ndwandwes, and they turned and ran away, with their shields held behind their backs.

Rank after rank did the same, but before the front fighting rank (of the Ndwandwes) could do so, Shaka had roared out orders that it was a trap, and that his warriors must not pursue the enemy more than one spear's throw. Even so the exultant Zulus, mad with battle-lust and the sanguinary opportunities of the chase, became deaf to all commands. They inflicted a fearful toll on the fleeing enemy, whom they so easily outstripped, encumbered as they were with sandals. In vain the company commanders shouted orders to break off the pursuit after the spear's-throw line had been crossed, for most of the platoon leaders had caught the prevailing fever, and were vying with their warriors in the glorious and gory pursuit.

Shaka was furious, but could not help noting the appalling execution his warriors were inflicting on the running enemy. He was thinking furiously too, for a column of smoke was visible on the *right* flank of the Ndwandwe force, which had been sent after the cattle. That meant that they were now returning and would be able to participate in the battle, if it were not finished shortly after the sun had sunk a little past midway, between noon and sunset. Was this the opportunity of hurling his hidden reserve at the enemy, and so turning a simulated panic into a real one, especially after the punishment his warriors were now dealing out? He reflected, however, that if the enemy were now put to flight he would fan out and scatter, and too many would escape the encirclement which he ultimately hoped to effect. Moreover, he thought he still had enough time to annihilate the Ndwandwes before the four cattle-collecting regiments returned. He noted with satisfaction that although his warriors had taken the bit in their teeth they still retained their superb formation, and were not out-running each other, as he had expressly forbidden them to do on pain of death. When the Ndwandwes turned at the foot of the hill a number of Zulus cut straight into them, and many nearly got right through before they were all killed.

The majority of the Zulus, however, came to their senses when they realized their desperate position, and now their iron discipline and superior speed came to their aid. 'Back to the top of the hill with your shields behind you,' came the reiterated command. 'Run as fast as you can, but keep your formations.' The captains, platoon leaders and many warriors kept shouting this order.

The Zulus again had no difficulty in outdistancing their foes, who presently found themselves faced by two solid lines of their enemies in their original positions encircling the hill-top. Such were the fruits of discipline and speed.*

After a desultory clash the Ndwandwes fell back, and once more were recalled to the foot of the hill. A further conference then took place.

The heat of the day had now reached its climax, and the Ndwandwe wounded were streaming away, accompanied by very large numbers of unwounded, but thirsty, warriors. Nomahlanjana and his staff took no account of this deadly thirst, as they were well provided for with beer and water, but the rest of the army were suffering badly.

All Shaka's warriors, on the other hand, had been well served with water by the indefatigable *u-dibi*, whose enthusiasm grew as the day wore on, and some of them had got into mischief by joining in the recent pursuit, and actually bagged several fleeing Ndwandwes with well-aimed assegais, which they had collected on the battlefield.

Whilst the Ndwandwes were in conference Shaka strode along the lines of his warriors as stern as death and roaring invective against them, for he was angry 'as a lion in a net'. In vibrating accents he denounced their disobedience, and like Thor he hurled his thunderbolts of death. In each platoon he condemned one man to die as an example to the others. There would be no senseless killing of Zulus by Zulus in face of the enemy. Instead, they would be granted the privilege of dying like warriors with full battle honours; this, because, although they were guilty of the worst crime a warrior could commit, namely disobedience, they had fought like heroes. Nevertheless discipline must be maintained. Those who were to die would be chosen by their captains, who would see to it that the guilty platoon leaders contributed their quota. The manner of their death would be that they each

*On this subject cf. Sir Reginald Coupland, *Zulu Battle Piece.*

proceed one spear's throw in front of their respective platoons, and there remain and fight alone till they were killed by the enemy in his next attack.

The warriors selected to die went without demur to their allotted places. Arrived there these outposts of death spontaneously turned round, and with upraised spears for the last time gave the Royal salute *Ba-ye-te*! Then facing the enemy they gave the right foot stamp, and bellowed '*A-yi-ze*' ('Let it' – the enemy army – 'come!').

Shaka, ever on the alert, now noticed a most unusual manoeuvre on the part of the Ndwandwes. Whilst leaving the southern semicircle of their warriors in the position they occupied at the base of the hill, they withdrew the northern one, and massed it around Nomahlanjana's tree. The latter had begun the battle with eight, more or less, full regiments – say about 7500 warriors. One-third were dead or mortally wounded. One-third had gone in search of water, and more than half of these were wounded in varying degrees, but still fit for fighting. That the percentage of these was not higher was due to the wounded going into action again and then being killed or mortally wounded. Nomahlanjana, therefore, only had some 2500 effectives at his immediate disposal. As far as he could see he had only two lines of Zulus to deal with – say 600 men – of whom one-half or more were wounded and no longer as good as they had been. He would now crush the Zulus with one overwhelming blow. It was annoying that so many of his warriors had absented themselves, but even so he had enough to deal with the remaining enemy.

An ominous quiet pervaded the whole hill. The smell of blood, entrails, fresh corpses and those beginning to putrefy hung over everything. The heat was oppressive. High overhead circled a multitude of vultures, their ever increasing number being reflected by the multiplying lines of shadows which swept the battlefield. The only sound to penetrate the stillness was the occasional raucous cry of the white-necked carrion crows which from time to time flew across the hill-top.

Shaka was intently watching Nomahlanjana massing, especially when he saw a proportion of the warriors from the southern circle joining him. He sensed that there was something new in the wind. The columns of smoke on the right were ominously advancing, but still beyond the Tonjaneni Heights, so there was yet time, but not overmuch. The crisis of the battle was at hand.

The Ndwandwe plan now took shape. From the massed formation poured out a column of warriors twenty abreast with intervals of three paces between the ranks. They were heading for the centre of the northern arc, where Shaka was sitting on the brow of the hill. Rank after rank came on, until the head of the column reached the foot of the hill – seventy-five ranks in a column 200 yards along. Nomahlanjana was using a battering ram against two lines of Zulus, whom he expected to drive against the open maw of the southern semicircle.

Shaka's eyes glowed: the approaching column was 1500 strong; he had 2000 fresh reserves. He would fling 1500 of them at the enemy in enveloping lines. He would keep 500 on the hill to face the head of the column with a 'chest' and as a central reserve for emergencies, against the southern semicircle of the enemy, which now contained but 1000 warriors. He would not disturb his two-line circle round the brow of the hill.

Nomahlanjana was amazed to see pouring over the hill-brow the head of a column to meet his own. Then he saw the appalling phenomenon of two parallel columns, eight warriors abreast, tearing down the hill at tremendous speed, on either flank of his column, and a little over a spear's throw removed from it. He had hardly time to realize that his battering ram was being enveloped before the Fasimba regiment, on Shaka's right, and the Izi-cwe regiment on the left, had almost reached the tail of his column, and that his life was in jeopardy. With a rush he and his following dived for safety into the rear of his column, and very soon thereafter the 'horns' of the Zulus closed around his force like the arms of a grizzly bear.

Behind the Fasimba streamed the auxiliaries led by Nqoboka and behind the Izi-cwe came the U-Dlambedlu. The veteran Ama-Wombe wrapped themselves around the head of the Ndwandwe column. They were all half regiments, but perfectly fresh and tumultuously eager for the fray. The Jubingqwanga were in reserve behind the centre of the southern semicircle, the two lines of which were now likewise heavily attacked by the Ndwandwes, in the manner of all the previous attacks. All the doomed outposts on this front also died gallantly. Some of them went berserk and cut right through the six or seven Ndwandwe lines, and then turned and drove into them from the rear, till they finally collapsed dead in the midst of the enemy. These incidents caused the surviving Ndwandwes to originate the legend that you must not only kill a Zulu, but you must also push him over to make the corpse lie down.

Shaka had at last allowed Mgobozi to go. He put him at the head of the Fasimba regiment but surrounded him with a special bodyguard of selected veteran Ama-Wombe, including Njikiza, 'The Watcher of the Ford', who would be less impulsive than the younger Fasimba, and act as a restraining influence.

'See that the gate of my kraal is closed properly and let none of Zwide's young bulls escape,' Shaka adjured Mgobozi, 'and pay more attention to this than to the fighting.'

No sooner had the 'horns' met behind the Ndwandwes, than Mgobozi, having 'closed the gate', felt himself absolved from all irksome duties, and free to indulge in a little blood-letting by way of hacking his way through the Ndwandwes till he had killed all their princes.

The most bloody battle in the history of Zululand up to that date was now reaching its climax. Incessant *Nga-dlas* arose all around the Ndwandwes, but although they knew they were doomed, the veteran Ama-Nkayiya regiment fought back with dauntless courage and were taking their toll. The gaping wounds caused by the broad Zulu blades practically drained the Ndwandwe corpses of their blood, which, with the Zulu quota, was now flowing or in pools in the confined area of the fighting, and its odour intoxicated the fighters. On both sides warriors with blood-spurting wounds and red frothing mouths would pluck bunches of hair or feathers from their heads and stuff them into the wounds if they had a few free seconds to spare.

After Mgobozi had received his first flesh wound, he went

berserk, and with the murderous agility of a leopard he became a raging flail. Time and again, however, he himself escaped death only through the alertness of 'The Watcher of the Ford', who, at Shaka's command, kept close behind him, and with his long-handled club, wielded from his towering height, staved off many a deadly thrust aimed at the stocky Mgobozi, by cracking the enemy warriors' skulls, or jabbing the spiked point of the club into their faces. Ndlela, the ex-cannibal and future Prime Minister, guarded Mgobozi on the right, and performed incredible deeds of destruction which were almost equalled by Nkayishana Kuzwayo on the left, but Mgobozi excelled them all.

Nomahlanjana now made a desperate bid to try to break out of his trap. His commander on the southern front was totally oblivious of the tragic predicament of his commander-in-chief, so no help could be expected from that quarter. Nomahlanjana therefore told his halted column to move northwards, away from that hill of surprises, in the forlorn hope that they might be able to break through homewards and save some lives. He and his brother princes were no cowards, and being near the rear of the column, which now, through reversing, became the head, they soon came into personal conflict with Mgobozi's phalanx, and royally acquitted themselves. But they were no match for Mgobozi and his warriors. Fighting with the utmost bravery, Nomahlanjana and all his four brothers, Nombengula, Mpepa, Sixoloba and Dayingubo, rapidly fell. It was a black day of sorrow for Zwide, as these five sons were the pride of his heart. The enraged Ama-Nkayiya veterans now surged towards the killers, oblivious to everything but revenge.

Quick-witted Ndlela knew it was time to give way, but in vain he and the bodyguard tried to get Mgobozi away from the coming avalanche, for that berserk warrior was past all reasoning. They had turned for but a moment to await reinforcements, but when they looked round again they saw Mgobozi lying motionless under his shield between the princes, with the 'Watcher' silently dealing death and destruction to a group of dazed and bewildered Ndwandwes.

'They have killed Mgobozi-of-the-Hill' shouted his bodyguard, and the grief-stricken army took up the poignant cry. Then with a yell of rage the Zulus all seemed to go berserk. They were met with equal fury by the Ndwandwes.

Soon it was all over, and the whole Ndwandwe column of 1500 men were dead. They had not died alone, though, for 500 Zulus lay beside them. Two thousand corpses, or nearly dead, in the space of 4000 square yards, with an ominous hummock of them over the bodies of the princes where brave Mgobozi lay.

Shaka noted with grim satisfaction the rapid extinction of Nomahlanjana and his column. Already the returning Ndwandwe regiments had been sweeping down the Tonjaneni Heights in the south for some time, with the cattle which they had succeeded in capturing. This was a serious loss, but he hoped it was only a temporary one.

He must hasten now to sweep up the scattered parties of Ndwandwe warriors who had gone in search of water, and who were now streaming back, and annihilate the southern semicircle.

He therefore issued prompt orders that the 1000 warriors who remained after destroying the Ndwandwe column were to hunt down the watering parties in the north and west. Then withdrawing his northern two-line semicircle, except the outposts of death on their front, and bidding them form the right and left 'horns' on the flanks of the southern semicircle, he made ready to hurl at the remaining Ndwandwes still before him every warrior he had at his disposal, except some 200 of the less seriously wounded Zulus who were to guard the hill.

Just before this the wondering commander of the southern Ndwandwe semicircle had been apprised by his scouts of the appalling tragedy in the north, and having also seen the Ndwandwe regiments returning with the Zulu cattle, he immediately ordered a rapid retreat in their direction. He had a 200-yard start and a great proportion of the pursuing Zulus were stiff or otherwise handicapped with wounds. Nevertheless they very soon caught up with him, but by skilful manoeuvring through constricted valleys and gullies and along narrow ridges, and by sacrificing his slower-moving wounded warriors in a series of delaying rearguard actions in these confined spaces, he was able to avoid a battle until he reached the more open ground three miles away. Here help was already near in the shape of the vanguards of the four returning regiments. He only just escaped annihilation, but nevertheless suffered grievous losses before the weight of the returning Ndwandwes forced Shaka, who had joined the pursuit, to break off the action, and in his turn to beat a slow fighting retreat. He led them in a north-westerly direction towards his Bulawayo kraal, where he had arranged for the Belebele brigade, after completing their mopping-up operations, to come to his aid, or alternatively to catch the enemy in a pincers movement.

The cattle-rustling Ndwandwes had by no means had an easy time, for the Nkomendala and the 200 Fasimba had made many a stubborn stand, and time and again had fallen on and destroyed numerous Ndwandwe platoons which had been so ill-advised as to outdistance their regiments, in the eagerness of the chase. Young and old, the barefooted Nkomendala easily outran the clumsily shod Ndwandwes. The original strength of the Zulu cattle guards had shrunk from 700 to 400, but they had accounted for nearly twice as many Ndwandwes, and their shrunken numbers still hung grimly to the Ndwandwes' tail trying to recover their lost cattle.

Arrived outside Bulawayo kraal Shaka determined to make a stand before it, as he was averse to having it burnt down. He had upwards of 1000 men at his immediate disposal, and had diverted the Nkomendala to the rear of the force attacking him, and their harassing guerilla tactics would tie down a considerable number of Ndwandwes. He had information, too, that the Belebele brigade, having completed the mopping up of most of the water-seeking parties, was now hurrying to his aid on his left front, and nearly athwart the Ndwandwe line of retreat.

The 3000 fresh Ndwandwes pressed Shaka sorely whilst the 500-odd who had escaped from Qokli held off the Nkomendala. The Jubingqwanga bore the brunt of the fighting, as most of the other Zulus in this reconstituted Isi-Klebe or Izim-Pohlo brigade had been wounded at Qokli and were no longer first-line troops. Manyosi, the pre-battle champion, who had distinguished himself earlier in the day, fought like a lion. But gradually his wing of the brigade folded back on the Royal kraal, and Manyosi made a final stand before the door of the Royal hut itself, where he was grievously wounded by a throwing spear.

The issue was beginning to look ominous, but Shaka remained cool, and with a selected reserve raced from point to point, wherever the threat appeared greatest. Nor did he hesitate to throw himself into the battle, and with many a timely joke and cheering word he kept up the confidence of his warriors.

Then the Belebele brigade arrived on the enemy's right flank, and instantly the situation was changed. To avoid encirclement the Ndwandwes immediately tried to break off the battle, but now the 'Shorn Head-rings' hung on to them on the west, the Nkomendala partly barred the south, and the Belebele completely barred the north, and were rapidly threatening the only exit in the east.

Less than 1000 Ndwandwes escaped encirclement and death, and this last action paid a dividend to Shaka equal to, if not greater than, the destruction of Nomahlanjana's column.

All the enemy wounded, as well as the hopeless Zulu cases, were dispatched. The seriously but not fatally wounded Zulus were accommodated at Bulawayo and were given an adequate guard.

And now all the fleetest warriors were sent after the cattle, and the others, chiefly the lightly wounded, after a good long drink at the Mhodi stream, returned with Shaka to bloodstained Qokli hill, where they arrived as the sun was setting – as blood-red as when it had arisen on that fateful day.

Arrived at the hill of death Shaka grimly surveyed its toll. The Zulu army had fought its first real battle and it had gloriously proved itself, but the cost was great – exactly how great he would only learn on the morrow when the depleted regiments paraded for the roll-call.

He looked over the northern semicircle and saw the 'outposts of death' still standing at their allotted places, except the one who had been engulfed by the column, and far down at the foot of the hill stood 'The Watcher of the Ford', his towering form leaning on the long shaft of his prodigious club, still guarding the mound of corpses under which Mgobozi and the princes lay. Shaka's stern face relaxed and he ordered the Outposts to parade before him.

Addressing them he said: 'The Spirits have been kind to you, for all your comrades on the southern arc were caught up by death, and only one on your side. I promised you that you would not be killed by Zulus, and as the enemy has failed to do so, I can but let you go. Rest now with the others on the hill-top, and on the morrow rejoin your regiments.'

With a grateful *Bayete* ! the Outposts went to do his bidding.

Shaka was now rejoined by his staff and the military council, including Mdlaka, Ngomane and Nqoboka. Nzobo and Ndlela were away leading the chase after the cattle. Shaka attended to all the requirements of the military situation. He decided to bivouac on the hill, as he still had enough water and food for the diminished numbers around him, especially as the *u-dibi* had fetched more water after the battle, and a few stray Zulu cattle had been recovered from the Ndwandwes. Caution also pointed to the hill as the safest place, as there were still some 2500 Ndwandwes at large, and the force remaining with Shaka was weak.

It was near the full moon, and the council were sitting in its light in a semicircle around Shaka, who was seated on a big rock. Everyone was sad at the loss of Mgobozi and the warriors around the fires some distance away, where the *u-dibi* were roasting meat, discussed him in mournful undertones.

Nqoboka, who with Mgobozi and Shaka had formed the original triple pact, was particularly distressed at Mgobozi's death, and asked for details. Shaka told him of the bodyguard and that the Watcher was still on duty at the mound of corpses, and now proposed they should proceed there, view the bodies, and get the Watcher's report.

A strong odour pervaded the whole battlefield as they proceeded down the hill to carry out Shaka's suggestion. All around could be heard the mournful howl of hyaenas with an occasional demoniacal laugh – the cackle of the hyaena in the presence of much food. It is the most eerie sound of the wild. Jackals joined the chorus, and in the distance could be heard the rising cadences of a lion roaring.

The Watcher stood like a statue in the moonlight, leaning languidly on his club, but as Shaka approached him he stood sharply to attention.

'Where is Mgobozi?' Shaka demanded.

'He sleeps with Zwide's sons beneath this mound of corpses.'

'What? Beneath all that heap of death?' inquired Shaka with great concern. 'I entrusted his life to you.'

'In the last extremity I carried out the "Great Elephant's" command. Hark, my Father.'

'*Dadewetu!* Someone is "dragging dry hides" (snoring) beneath those corpses,' exclaimed Shaka joyously. 'I know that sound well, for did it not keep me awake last night when Mgobozi slept near by! Is he hurt much?'

''Tis but flesh wounds, my Father, though he is well bled, and of course he received the little extra which came on him from Heaven (Zulu). 'Tis the corpses which keep him in his place, and out of further mischief, for he has been stirring restlessly and will soon be awake.'

Shaka approached the mound. 'Mgobozi!' he roared. 'Mgobozi! Mgobozi!'

At the third call a deep, sepulchral voice came from the depths of the corpses, '*Yebo, Baba.*'

'What are you doing in there?'

'I don't know, my Father, but the hill has collapsed on top of me (*ngi dilikelwe intaba*).'

Shaka's attendants, having recovered from their fright of the supposedly supernatural, now eagerly pulled away the corpses which held down their beloved Mgobozi.

When the last body had been removed from him, the old wardog sat up. In his right hand he still held his trusty blade. He placed it across his knees and rubbed his eyes. Then he gazed all around him at the mound of corpses, and with a snort he exclaimed 'Hau! It looks as if there has been some fighting here.'

The battered old war-dog was visibly affected by the many spontaneous manifestations of joy at his 'miraculous' return, and the bloodthirsty, leonine grandeur of his rugged features relaxed into a smile, which gave a glimpse of that hidden charm which captivated all who knew him.

When Mgobozi then gave a characteristic reply there was a deafening shout of applause. '*Yebo madoda, ngi buyile. Beseni zo hlutshwa ngo bani?*' ('Yes, men, I have returned! Who otherwise would have continued to plague you?')

The evacuation of the hill began next morning for the Esi-Klebeni military kraal. The seriously wounded were assisted or carried between the locked arms of two warriors. As they passed through the ring of disembowelled corpses which lay around the hill, the practical object of this process became apparent, when presently down in the plain they came to a group of corpses, the remains of some of the Ndwandwes who had gone in search of water. In the heat of the chase these had not been disembowelled, and their gas-distended bellies looked grotesque, and gave point to the Nguni superstition that it was due to the inability of the spirit to escape. Moreover, the stench was infinitely greater than that which emanated from the opened and dehydrated bodies on the hill, as the putrefactive process had been hastened in the unopened bodies. The humane side of this grisly disembowelling was also forcibly illustrated. For one wretched Ndwandwe warrior was still alive and moaning from the tortures of thirst and his hopeless wound. He was quickly dispatched and ripped open – the most humane and merciful thing that could be done for him.

During the day the pursuing regiments returned to the Esi-Klebeni kraal with most of the cattle the Ndwandwes had captured. Nevertheless the Ndwandwes had got away with much cattle under cover of the darkness, and this was tantamount to losing the honours of battle.

When the decimated regiments paraded Shaka found that he had lost upwards of 1500 killed, 500 seriously wounded and most of the rest with slight wounds. He had started with approximately 4300 men, including the cattle guards.

As Shaka strode along the depleted lines, and noticed the ominous absence of so many familiar faces, the tears streamed down his face – his last silent tribute to those who had gone. Then with the army facing him in a semicircle he thanked all the warriors for their effort, which had never been equalled before.

The Ndwandwes had lost about 7500 killed. This was a signal achievement, for it would take Zwide some time to recover, although he could always count on reinforcements from his northern cousins. Nevertheless Shaka had received a severe mauling, and his strongest intact force now consisted of the 1500-odd warriors who were guarding the women, children and cattle on his southern border facing the Qwabes. These were all now recalled to their kraals, and were grateful that the non-combatants at least had been spared the horrors of war, through the magnificent fighting ability of the Zulu army.

Pampata was the first to break the detailed news of the victory to Nandi.

CHAPTER 14

Dingiswayo's heir

DINGISWAYO'S death had left the Mtetwa hegemony without a head. Great though Shaka's reputation had already become and formidable though the Zulus were known to be, before the battle of Qokli hill Shaka was not great enough for the confederation – the word is used loosely – to re-form about the nucleus of Bulawayo. But after that battle the case was different: Shaka and his Zulus had defeated the greatest power in Zululand and the most able chief after Dingiswayo. Almost automatically, then, all those who had looked for leadership to Dingiswayo now turned towards Shaka, the Zulu and Mtetwa peoples grew together, Mlandela, an old friend of Shaka, became Mtetwa chief, while the Mtetwa Ngomane became Zulu prime minister. As the young Zulu State grew, its magnetic power increased, and by peaceful means drew within its orbit the small states of Sikakane, Mpungose and Ndlovu.

It was about this time that a young petty chief, Mzilikazi Kumalo, the future founder and king of the conquering Matabele nation, entered the service of Shaka. His father, Mashobane, in spite of being the son-in-law of Zwide, had been treacherously killed by the latter, and his skull had as usual gone to adorn the museum of the notorious Ntombazi. For a time Mzilikazi had submitted to the vassalage of his grandfather, Zwide, but after the battle of Qokli hill this shrewd, ambitious and able young man decided to throw in his fortune with Shaka.

Shaka, a born general, discerned character at a glance, and when Mzilikazi appeared before him, he instantly recognized his merits and took immediate liking to him. Although Mzilikazi was some eight years Shaka's junior, and therefore approximately twenty-three years of age, he was immediately given a responsible post in the Zulu army. Mzilikazi brought with him only a limited number of his clansmen, the northern Kumalos. But presently the southern Kumalos, the Mabasos, and the kindred clans of the Kozas, Magubane and Ncubeni, who inhabited the area between Babanango and Nqutu, became allies or were peacefully incorporated with the now rapidly growing Zulu State.

With these additions, on top of Dingiswayo's estate, Shaka could now muster an army of eight full regiments, each 1000 strong, in spite of the losses he had incurred at the battle of Qokli. He also formed the first regiment of maidens, which was known as the *Vutwamini* (Those who ripen at noon – the name of a luscious wild fruit).

Mgobozi, who had recovered quickly from his wounds, therefore had his hands full as chief drill instructor of the army. Until a regiment was able to keep an almost perfectly straight line at the double, over rough ground, Mgobozi relentlessly drilled them. He was an absolute martinet on perfecting the system of rapid transmission of orders from the commander to the ranks, the pause for one deep breath, and then the simultaneous right foot crash which was the signal for executing the order.

Training included very rapid and complex evolutions in rigid order, the technique of close in-fighting devised by Shaka, and war-games and manoeuvres with blunted weapons. If Mgobozi was feared for his driving and his bitter tongue-lashings, he was also loved for his care for the men's well-being: 'Do I want to see you eaten by vultures and hyaenas after the next battle, merely because you were too stupid or lazy to understand that what I am trying to teach you today will save you tomorrow?'

After the regiments had passed through Mgobozi's fiery ordeal, their strenuous field training began under Shaka and Mdlaka. Fifty or sixty miles a day in route marches mostly at a jog-trot, culminating in battle manoeuvres, were the order of the day. In these route marches, any warrior who fell out without just and sufficient reason was instantly killed with his own spear by the rearguard, induna or headman, who was specially deputed to do so in every regiment. Thus was born the Zulu Army, which had either to conquer or to die.

Zwide too was very busy making good his losses. He had an almost inexhaustible reservoir amongst his northern relatives, the Swazis. He appointed Soshangane as his commander-in-chief. He was a member of the junior Ndwandwe Royal House, the son of Zikode, son of Gaza, son of Manukuza. This Soshangane subsequently became famous as one of the three great conquistadores – the other two being Mzilikazi and Zwangendaba – who each formed great nations from 500 to 2000 miles beyond the borders of Zululand proper. He formed the Gaza or Shangana Empire, which extended from just north of Delagoa Bay, up the East Coast, as far as the Zambezi. In his victorious progress he annihilated or drove into the sea all the Portuguese in his path, and it was he who destroyed van Rensburg's party of Voortrekkers on the south bank of the Limpopo.

Zwangendaba, the third of the trio of successful conquistadores who emanated from Zululand, or its borders, now also took a leading part in Zwide's army under Soshangane. He was the son of Hlatshwayo, and the head of the tiny Jele or Gumbi clanlet, which, itself, was an offshoot of the Ncwangeni (or Mfekane) clan.

With such redoubtable personalities and generals now in his army, including Nxaba of the Msane clan (the same as Mgobozi's), who almost equalled Soshangane's exploits, and many other distinguished warriors, and fed from the northern, eastern and western reservoirs of manpower, Zwide's army was also growing with alarming strides, in this race for the Nguni paramountcy. Moreover, Zwide's northern friends and relatives had preached so effectively against the 'Zulu upstart who had killed Zwide's sons', that a regular crusade was in process of inauguration against Shaka.

Shaka, who above all valued correct and timely information of his enemy's plans, had succeeded in getting into his pay a highly placed secret counsellor of Zwide's named Noluju (The Honey Man). He therefore knew precisely everything that was going on in Zwide's camp, and soon he realized that a tidal wave of invasion was being prepared against him.

Once more he appealed to Pakatwayo, chief of the Qwabes –

the senior Zulu brother-clan – to join forces with him. He sent Ncozana, son of Moni, as his ambassador. The latter told Pakatwayo that the only grievance Zwide could have against Shaka was that the latter had called him a 'dried-up old cowhide'. Whereupon Pakatwayo replied: 'Go and say to the king, why did you do this thing, and hurl insulting epithets at your elder? If now you want assistance go and seek it of the Sutus' (a clan 200 miles away).

When Shaka received this unsympathetic message he swore by his sister, Nomcoba, and said to his ambassador: 'Return and say to the Chief, "*A-ka-pisele-ke*"' ('Let him get the blades in their hafts').

When this ominous message was delivered, naming, moreover, the day and place where the armies should meet, Pakatwayo was dumbfounded, and could find no better way of expressing his feelings than saying '*Wo! madoda, ngi hudelwe yi hubulu*' ('*Wo!* my men, I have been voided on by a raven – flying over-head!') a Zulu idiom to describe a totally unexpected misfortune: out of the blue, as it were.

Knowing through his spy Noluju that Zwide was far too pre-occupied in the task of strengthening his army and mourning his sons to contemplate immediate military adventures, Shaka felt confident that there would be no interference from the north on the day he set out for the battle on his southern frontier. The armies met – midwinter 1818 – and Shaka gained a quick and easy victory by brilliant manoeuvring and the early capture of the Qwabe chief by the Nxumalos. He gave immediate orders for all hostilities to cease, and instructed that every enemy warrior could safely return to his home.

The shock of his utter defeat had caused Pakatwayo to have a fit and convulsions. He died during the night. Shaka accused his brothers of neglect and possibly worse, and sent them into exile, and whatever Royal cattle they had hoped to inherit he confiscated, as well as the whole harem.

The conquest and incorporation of the great Qwabe clan with the minimum of bloodshed and with no destruction of property was a signal achievement, and Shaka felt that his southern frontier, which was now the Tugela river, had been completely secured.

Beginning with 100 square miles of territory, Shaka had in two and a half years extended his rule over 7000 square miles, from the White Umfolozi in the north to the Tugela river in the south, and from the sea to the great Nkandla forest – the roof of Zululand – in the west. Thirty chiefs and their clans, including the two large ones of the Mtetwas and the Qwabes, had been consolidated into a single political and military unit, which paid homage to Shaka as supreme chief and absolute ruler over the whole realm. Shaka indeed was now a King. Whilst the training of the army was carried on with unabated energy, the shield-makers and smiths were kept busy throughout the land providing uniform-coloured shields for the different regiments and the standardized stabbing blade for the warriors.

Agriculture was intensified, and a vast number of grass-woven grain bags were manufactured throughout the land, for a purpose known to Shaka only. Stock raising was rationalized by the castration of all scrub bulls, and the selection of the best for stud purposes. The Royal herds were grouped in uniform colours, and Shaka's special milk-white herd was increased, and only the bulls of proven white strain were allowed to run with this herd.

Although Shaka had administered a sharp rebuff to the witch-doctors or diviners, the extraordinary success of Zwide's magic over Dingiswayo could not be gainsaid, and with such an advertisement the occult 'profession' received an extraordinary impetus which was not without its effect on Shaka himself.

Never a believer in chance, and knowing that Zwide would bombard him with magic if he could but gain some personal objects of Shaka, the latter took every precaution against this. He deemed himself less vulnerable as he had not (as yet) associated with any of his harem, and only his closest friends were allowed access to his hut. He also got his trusty war-doctor, Mqalane of the Nzuza clan, to surround him with a cordon of repellent magic. Shaka, however, never believed in defensive methods only, and now carried the magic war into the enemy's camp. He therefore arranged with Noluju, Zwide's treacherous counsellor, to furnish him with regular consignments of every variety of Zwide's 'body matter' – doorway-grass (*amakotamo*), hair-shavings, nail clippings, shreds of raiment and the like – as were required by the Zulu war-doctor to furnish the base essential for his deadly charms. With these he started a counter-bombardment.

Moreover, he perfected his Dlamini newscarrier service to such an extent that whatever happened in Ndwandwe-land was known to him in less than twenty-four hours. These Dlaminis were close relatives of the Ndwandwes, whom they hated, and formed a tiny State immediately on the north of Shaka's boundary, and whilst professing to be allies of Zwide, were aiding and abetting every effort for his overthrow.

Shaka had been kept so busy since he became the chief of the original small Zulu clan that he had never had time to hold a great *Umkosi* or harvest festival. He had, of course, held the annual little *Umkosi*, or first-fruits festival, as otherwise no one would have been permitted to eat any of the products of agriculture. The little *Umkosi* had been held as usual at the full moon about Christmas (1818), and now with the next approaching full moon the great *Umkosi* was about to be held. All Zulu festivals were held only at the full of the moon.

This annual first-fruits festival was essentially an agricultural ceremony, and as the King was held responsible for all the crops in the land, as well as the general well-being of the nation, it was necessary that the King and the instrument of his power – the army – should be strengthened at this season with specially prepared medicines administered with prescribed ceremonies.

At the same time this was the occasion for the full-dress review of the whole army, the promulgation of new laws, and the abrogation of old ones. The whole adult male population of the nation, and all the marriageable girls, and most of the matrons, assembled for the great *Umkosi*, whilst the little *Umkosi*, as its name implies, was a minor affair, although otherwise in every respect more or less similar to the great *Umkosi*. Both festivals are occasion for general rejoicing, dancing and singing of new songs, and no executions took place at this time. Moreover, at the review of the army a remarkable feature was that considerable freedom of speech was allowed, and the King could be cross-examined by any warrior with impunity, and was bound to reply. His acts could be denounced in the presence of all, obliging him to explain, and the reasoning in his answer could be dissected and destroyed.*

At the new moon after the little *Umkosi* the regiments began to arrive at the Royal Bulawayo Kraal to hoe the King's gardens. They brought along their warrior's full-dress outfits, and their leaders had to see that they were turned out spick-and-span. From their respective military kraals they brought the necessary number of slaughter cattle. At some distance from the Royal Kraal each regiment erected its own temporary shelters, known as *amadlangala*, and well away from any other regiments. This was necessary because of the intense rivalry that existed between the different regiments. This might have precipitated a fight between the various units, if they camped too close together for any length of time.

The Vutwamini Maidens' regiment was now mobilized for the first time and allotted a select piece of ground whereon to erect their shelters, which were strictly out of bounds to all males. Numerically they were the strongest regiment, numbering some 3000.

Next to them, on either side, Shaka barracked two regiments of cadets – another of his innovations. They were lads above the age of puberty, but below that of a warrior, and consisted of the age-groups from sixteen to nineteen years inclusive. Their shields were wholly black, whereas the warriors in the junior regiments always had a little white showing on their black shields. As the regiments became more battle experienced so they were given shields with increased white markings, until finally the veteran guards regiments carried pure-white shields, with, at the most, a tiny spot of black. Shields which were red, or had red markings, were not favoured by the Zulus in the days of Shaka.

Three days before the full moon the fiercest and strongest black bull procurable was driven into the cattle-kraal and with

*Krige, op. cit.

bare hands had to be captured, thrown and strangled by the youngest regiment. This feat invariably resulted in the goring of a number of warriors and one or more fatalities, particularly in the case of the bull that was killed for making war 'medicine'.

Parts of this 'medicine' were used for strengthening the whole army and other portions were used for the special strong brew of 'black' medicine which Shaka had to take to fortify himself. This 'black' medicine contained many ingredients – herbal, animal and human fats – and was considered to be so strong that no ordinary mortal could drink it and live.

As the well-being of the whole nation was intimately inter-woven with that of its ruler, a strong king meant a strong nation – simple but irrefutable logic !

Shaka had to stay in the seclusion of his 'great' hut for two days and nights. In the day-time he was attended by the doctors, who administered the medicines with the necessary ceremonies of purification and fortification, known as *uku-qunga*. At night-time he was allowed to be attended by one selected maiden,* and he naturally chose Pampata. According to Njengabantu Emab-omvini, the girl, in the course of conversation, told the King an allegorical story.

'Behold the fig tree, my Lord. It grows speedily, and with its young, massive body and mighty branches it gives shade and security to many people and cattle; but then the branches con-tinue to grow till they are a burden to the trunk, and there comes a day when they become too heavy and snap, tearing a big rent in the body which gave them life, and causing death and destruc-tion to those who have sheltered underneath. Thereafter such a tree is shunned by all thinking people, for they know it can and will happen again, until the tree is a bare and rotting stump, or at best but a mangled image of its former glory.'

'And all this because the tree, or body, was not strong enough to support the branches, Pampata?'

'Not at all, my Lord, for no matter how strong the tree, if the branches keep on spreading a time must come when they will snap through their own weight, and where they are broken the

* Krige, *op. cit.*

174

rot will set in, until it reaches the parent body, and it too sickens and decays. These things I learnt from our "father", Mbiya. As a woman it would come easier to my tongue to mention our old proverb, which tells us to measure the size of our fields by our capacity to hoe them and keep out the weeds.'

And Shaka, says the chronicler, replied:

'Well spoken, Pampata. No other woman or man could have put it better than you have done, and withal so sweetly. Have no fear – at any rate as yet – of my outgrowing my power. With that ogre in the north seeking my destruction day and night we might yet have to eke out an existence on roots and berries in the Nkandla forest.'

We are also told that although Shaka observed custom and drank the medicines prepared for him, he was aware and told Pampata that their beneficial effect was 'psychological' and had nothing to do with their constitution. And Pampata agreed with him, thus:

'My thoughts run side by side with yours, my lord, for when I got my herbs mixed up by mistake I cured my headaches just as well with the stomach specifics, until I discovered my error. Then they ceased to work.'

Towards sunset of the second day Shaka had to perform the ceremony of *uku-kwifa*, that is, squirting or spitting out (*chintsa*) of the medicine at the setting sun.

All the warriors – and the rest of the adult male population – were drawn up in ranks when Shaka emerged from the hut, and was greeted by the Royal salute, '*Bayete!*', which was given thrice.

Pointing his assegai and the Royal stick at the setting sun, Shaka squirted the medicine from his mouth in the direction he was pointing, whilst the warriors shouted: 'It stabs, it with the red tail.'* This squirting and shouting was repeated twice. Then Shaka returned to his hut, and all the adult males were issued with beer and meat and sang and danced through the night.

At dawn the warriors, singing, approached Shaka's hut and kept up shouting: '*Woza ke, woza lapa!*' ('Come forth, come

* Krige, *op. cit.*

hither!'). Shaka delayed his appearance, according to custom, till the Royal women joined in the song. He was decorated with corn ears and leaves, various herbs and beads and bangles. He strode past the massed ranks of his warriors until he reached the gate of the cattle-kraal, and there awaited the rising sun.

As soon as its first rays streamed over the horizon, the King repeated the squirting ceremony. Thereafter he broke an *uselwa* gourd by dashing it to pieces on the ground. Hereafter some wormwood was set on fire, and the King repeatedly squirted medicine on it till the fire consumed the wood.* Each time he squirted the warriors shouted 'U! U! U!' The purpose of this was to exorcize all pestilences, evil spirits, and diseases from the nation.*

Cattle were now slaughtered as a sacrifice to the ancestral spirits, and the praises of the King and his forefathers were recited. Thereafter the regiments visited the sacred burial ground *Emakosini* – where Shaka's ancestors were interred. From a respectful distance an appeal was made to the spirits to come out, with shouts of 'Come therefore, come hither'.* After prayers had been addressed to the ancestors, general feasting, drinking, singing and dancing became the order of the day.

About noon Shaka appeared in full war-dress, and this was the signal for the Vutwamini to appear in its almost nude and natural glory – three lines of them, each 1000 strong. They wore the regulation dress of a maiden of that period. This consisted of the underskin of *Ubendle* (fig) leaves twisted into strings and browned, and formed a fringed girdle four inches wide, suspended around the hips with a slightly forward tilt. A bracelet or two, and sometimes a string of beads around the neck was the sum total of their attire.

The daughters of chiefs, headmen and wealthy fathers dispensed with the string girdle, and replaced it with a bead token-dress consisting of a patch of beads three inches long, and two inches wide – for beads then were rare and expensive – which was suspended from a string around the hips, and acted as an apron rather than a dress.

*Krige, *op. cit.*

On top of the nine-foot-high clay mound, which was the Royal dais overlooking the parade ground, Shaka seated his mother Nandi, on the rolled-up rush mats. On her right was his sister Nomcoba, and on her left Nomzintlanga, his half-sister, the Princess Royal of the Zulus. At Nandi's feet sat Pampata and all around her the Zulu Royal ladies.

Shaka stood below his mother in front of the dais, but high enough to overlook the whole field.

The regiments of warriors, each about 1000 strong, were paraded on his right, whilst facing them on the left were the three lines of the Maidens' regiment. The opposing lines were about 200 yards apart when they started slowly towards each other, singing and dancing, but keeping almost perfectly straight lines. The warriors presented a magnificent sight in their full war-dress, and with the uniform colour of the shields of each regiment. The sea of tossing white shields, and waving ostrich plumes of the veteran regiments, followed by the black-and-white shields of the younger regiments and the flashing of all the spears, formed a picture of sinister military beauty and efficiency. The rhythmic stamping of 10,000 feet made the earth shake – an ominous display of power which was heightened by the deep, sonorous chant of the warriors.

When the lines of warriors and maidens were but a few paces apart, they receded a little as slowly as they had advanced, but only to come forward again. This was repeated several times. Then the lines opened out once more, and now Shaka strode midway between them, and gave them the new songs which he had composed for the new year. They were taken up by song leaders who had been previously coached, and the whole assembled multitude took them up in the form of community singing.

Thereafter a dense semicircle was formed in front of the dais, and Shaka entered the arena to give a performance of dancing and singing, intermingled with the release of his latest puns, which were greeted with thunderous applause. These puns were put in the form of questions. Thus: 'A coward (*i-gwala*) is an object of contempt, but a double coward is held in esteem. What is it?' Answer: '*i-gwala-gwala*' (the red loury whose striking red

feathers are the insignia of outstanding bravery given to distinguished warriors).

After Shaka had given his displays, the warriors and maidens
danced and performed in groups of 500 each, and then, swinging
into companies, advanced to the foot of the dais to acclaim Shaka
and the Queen Mother – Ndlovukazi (Great She Elephant) to
whom special homage was paid as the first and greatest Lady
in the land.

Shaka standing beside his seated mother – an unheard-of
Nguni precedent – said: 'Look! Mother, all these people are
yours, and I spoke no empty words when I swore to you, during
the years of our poverty, that some day you would be the greatest
Queen.'

'Yes, my child, your power now is almost terrifying, and far
beyond my dreams already. As it grows I see less and less of you.'

'True, my Mother, but unless my power continues to grow
quicker than that of my enemies you will all have to live on
berries in remote forests.'

Early the next morning the great military review took place.
Each regiment competed in various military evolutions and
manoeuvres, ending in the march-past of the regiments in companies or *ama-gaba*. Thereafter the whole army formed up in a
dense circle around Shaka and the remarkable 'Freedom of
Speech' ceremony began. Each regiment sent one or more spokes-
men, who now began to criticize various acts or omissions of the
King.

Stepping up to Shaka the first spokeman fearlessly demanded,
'Why are outsiders promoted over the heads of the Zulus?'

Shaka replied, 'Any man who joins the Zulu Army becomes a
Zulu. Thereafter his promotion is purely a question of merit,
irrespective of the road (*ndlela*) he came by.' There was a roar
of applause at this pun, or double meaning, for Ndlela, the
ex-cannibal, was the most outstanding example of promotion,
regardless of antecedents, and, as Shaka shrewdly guessed, the
probable cause of the question.

The second questioner asked: 'Why were the Qwabes let off
so lightly?'

Shaka replied: 'Brother does not eat brother, and two brothers are stronger than one.' There was another deafening shout of applause.

The third questioner asked: 'Why not strike the Ndwandwes now before they get too strong?'

Shaka: 'A shrewd question. But tell me, does the hand tell the stomach when it is time to eat, or is it the other way about?' More shouts of applause and jeers at the discomfited questioner.

Fourth Questioner: 'Why did you not kill Nobela? She sent many innocent people to a painful death, and she deceived you, and you found her guilty.'

Shaka: 'She reached and claimed sanctuary and was entitled to it according to the laws of the country, as soon as she confessed to the graver crime of witchcraft.'

Questioner: 'Yes, but you could have executed her on the lesser charge of deceit, for which there is no sanctuary. Instead of that you bargained with her. What for?' There was loud and general applause for the questioner.

Shaka, somewhat nettled, replied: 'Do the fingers know what the head intends the feet to do?'

'That is no answer,' shouted the questioner amid great applause. 'Tell us why you bargained with her, and let this evil thing loose on us.'

'Because I needed her as you need an up-wind fire to save yourself from a greater one bearing down on you with the wind.'

'That is a reasonable answer, but still it is a pity you let her go,' replied the questioner and withdrew.

Fifth Questioner: 'Why does the King not marry and beget heirs?'

Shaka: 'A bull has perfect peace until the young bulls – his progeny – begin to dispute his supremacy.'

Questioner: 'Then why do you allow Dingane' (Shaka's younger half-brother) 'to roam about as a potential threat?'

Shaka: 'Must I, then, kill the son of my father?'

Questioner: 'Nay, Great Elephant, but hearken to my words,

and trust him not. Those who love you have seen a wicked gleam in his eyes when he looks at you. Carry a shield on your back, my Father.'

Sixth Questioner: 'When will the warriors be allowed to marry?'

Shaka: 'Marriage for young warriors is a folly. Their first and last duty is to protect the nation from its enemies. This they cannot do efficiently if they have family ties. When they reach a mature age, and have also proved their worth, I am prepared to consider individual cases, and even whole regiments, if they have shown exceptional merit. But, until the nation has been made secure against all external enemies, the marriage ban will be strictly enforced on all warriors, saving only in quite exceptional cases.'

Questioner: 'Must then all these beautiful maidens languish and be wasted as potential mothers?'

Shaka: 'A mature woman produces better children than an immature one. Fewer, well-spaced children are better than too many.'

Questioner: 'Must they then later be wasted on a few old men who have survived the wars through greater caution, whilst the bravest have gone to their deaths?'

Shaka: 'Look at Mgobozi. One such man will produce better fighting stock than twenty untried young warriors who are allowed to marry indiscriminately. Do we not now select the bulls of our herds? Should we then be less careful in selecting the right fathers for the future children of Zululand? I tell you all, in future a man will have to prove his worth to be a father, before he receives permission to marry. I will not tolerate the propagation of our race by untried men, who may be undesirable fathers. Finally, look at me, all you who are my age-mates and below. Although I am the King and have all power, I have not taken a wife. I have told you the true reason but, apart from that, there is too much fighting ahead to allow me to dally with women, and you all know that I have not touched a single one of the um-dlunkulu women – as yet. None of you can therefore complain that I ask you to step where I do not step, any more than I did when I led you on to the field of thorns, and showed you how to stamp them down before I asked you to do so.'

A storm of tumultuous applause broke out from all the massed ranks. 'He is indeed a chief of chiefs,' yelled the warriors, 'for he never asks us to do anything which he himself does not do first. Who is there who is like him? Lead us, Father, and we will follow until we eat earth. Say but the word, son of Heaven, and it shall be done. *Bayete!*' and 10,000 feet crashed down and shook the earth. '*Bayete!*' they roared again, and then once more, '*Bayete!*'

In the afternoon the final great assembly took place, which all adult males attended. Shaka then promulgated all the new laws for the year, and abrogated some old ones. His commands were repeated by criers all along the lines, and it is remarkable what a word-perfect repetition they gave.

Thereafter the assemblage broke up to continue the feasting and drinking, and the discussion of all the happenings.

On the morrow the multitude dispersed to their homes, and the regiments to their military kraals.

CHAPTER 15

The Second Ndwandwe War

SHAKA'S capital, Bulawayo, was situated only five miles away from his northern boundary – the White Umfolozi river – and on a more or less direct line between the capital and the river lay the Esi-Klebeni and the Belebele military kraals, which were three miles and one mile respectively away from the boundary.

Across the river towards Zwide's territory lived the friendly Dlaminis, and the neutral Zungus a little downstream. The two little States were the only buffers remaining between Shaka and Zwide.

Manzini, the young, inexperienced chief of the Zungus, possessed a small 'regiment' of idle youths whom he named the *Amankentshana* (Wild Dogs). Shaka, ever on the look-out for means of strengthening his forces, made the novel offer to Manzini of twenty oxen, plus a heifer apiece, for every warrior in this 'regiment', which was probably only 200 strong. Manzini jumped at the offer, and Shaka, with the aid of Mgobozi, soon had them moulded into a high-spirited and disciplined warrior band.* The purchased Zungu warriors behaved as their Zulu counterparts when it came to shedding their blood; and, indeed, the Zulu army finally consisted of parts of 300 different Nguni clans; racially and linguistically they belonged as much to a single nation as do the numerous clans of the Scots.

Soon after this transaction between Shaka and Manzini had been completed, the latter received another tempting offer – this time from the mighty Zwide in the north – who told Manzini that he wished to dispose of his superfluous girls and suggested the holding of an *ijadu* (love-dance) to enable the Zungus to make

* Cf. the British purchase of Hessian troops for £5 apiece during the eighteenth century.

their choice. The unsuspecting Manzini agreed, and again the joyful love-dance was transformed into a blood-bath by the treacherous Zwide, although Manzini was able to escape with his life, as did also many of his tribe, by swimming across the swollen White Umfolozi. On reaching the southern bank they found refuge under Shaka's protecting wing.

Immediately after the grain harvest, in May 1819, Shaka ordered all the inhabitants living in a forty-mile-wide belt, from his northern boundary to the Tugela river in the south, to carry their grain in the bags he had provided, and to store it in the remote caves and fastnesses of the Nkandla forest. The rest of the nation were to hide their grain wherever they could conveniently do so. Only sufficient food for present needs was to be kept at every kraal.

Noluju, Zwide's trusted counsellor, was equally busy manoeuvring his master into the trap. On the plea of making secret service observations in the enemy's camp, he paid a visit to Shaka and while there made final arrangements for starving and wearing out the Ndwandwe army by leading it in an endless chase on an empty stomach. Leaving Shaka thus perfectly prepared, he hastened back to Zwide to report on what he led him to believe was a golden opportunity to 'catch the Zulus asleep'. Accordingly Zwide mobilized his whole Ndwandwe confederation, and with three days' supply of millet bread his army started on the southward march.

Shaka's secret service was so well organized that a day before the Ndwandwes marched from their capital, he had evacuated to the Nkandla forest every living thing in the forty-mile-wide corridor, down which he proposed to lead the enemy. In the rest of the territory all women, children and stock were also evacuated from their kraals and went into hiding in various forests, such as the Edlinza at Eshowe, the Duku-Duku and others.

The Ndwandwe army was led by the redoubtable Soshangane, of future fame, and one of his eighteen regiments by Zwangendaba, who later led his own conquering Nguni legions up to the shores of Lake Victoria Nyanza – 2000 miles away.

Soshangane had learned much from the Ndwandwe defeat at

Qokli hill, some fourteen months before, and his warriors now were mostly armed with some kind of heavy and short spear for close-in fighting, as well as two light throwing spears. However, they still retained their sandals, which so greatly reduced their speed when compared with the Zulus. Their manual drill and discipline had been greatly improved, too.

The Ndwandwes, 18,000 strong, again crossed the White Umfolozi into Zululand where they had entered before. They passed by Qokli hill, with its litter of white bones, but no Zulus were massed there to meet them. Instead, they encountered only scouts, and here and there strong patrols. As they moved onwards they saw the first regiment of Zulus slowly moving southwards over the Tonjaneni Heights.

At the end of the first day the Ndwandwes camped on the bleak Melmoth highlands which, now that winter had arrived, were very cold and frosty. Without fuel, they spent the night in shivering misery, a condition which was heightened by the alarms they were subjected to. Whole companies of Zulus made frequent sham attacks on their camp, making the night hideous with their war cries.

The Ndwandwes had left with three days' provisions thinking that their replenishments would come from the full granaries of the Zulus, but they were amazed to discover that these were absolutely bare. Not a handful of grain was obtainable anywhere, and the total absence of any kind of life at the Zulu kraals had an eerie and depressing effect.

When they left the Melmoth highlands in the morning to continue the southward march, after the phantom Zulu regiment which always preceded them, they had very little millet bread left, for they had spent the best part of two days in reaching the Zulu border, and the Royal capital and military kraals, where they had expected to find so much food.

On the second day's march in the enemy's country, and the fourth day since they left their capital, the Ndwandwes made a fatal blunder, as the 100 oxen or so they had brought with them for food had tailed out too much in the rear of the army, and a complete Zulu regiment had appeared out of the earth, as it were, overpowered the weak guard and whisked most of the oxen away. They had timed their attack for the late afternoon and, making use of the defiles and broken country in the west, which they utilized for running rearguard actions, they held back the enemy till darkness put an end to all pursuit.

That night the Ndwandwes camped on the south bank of the Umhlatuze – cold, hungry, and mostly sleepless because of the night alarms of the Zulus, whose main army was camped in the relative warmth of an eastern outrunner of the Nkandla forest.

Shaka's chief worry now was that the hungry Ndwandwes might turn back, so in the night he had a large troop of his commissariat oxen driven to a point some two miles south of the Ndwandwes, and, sprinkling a quantity of fresh ox-blood amongst them, he started them on their usual bellowing, a reaction which the scent of bovine blood always had on cattle.

The hungry Ndwandwes sat up and took notice, for in the clear wintry air the oxen sounded nearer than they actually were. A clamour arose to go after the 'meat', but Soshangane was far too prudent, for he scented a trap, and insisted on sending out his scouts first. They were purposely not molested by the Zulus, who pretended to take fright and yelled to each other to drive on the cattle as the Ndwandwes were coming. They also shouted much gratuitous information at each other, which was intended to mislead the Ndwandwes into believing that all the Zulu nation, with their cattle, had either crossed or were still crossing the Tugela opposite Ntunjambili (Kranskop) on a southward flight.

On getting the reports of his scouts Soshangane decided to wait for daylight, and then to follow in hot pursuit. At daybreak the Ndwandwes saw, seven miles away, troops of cattle and Zulus disappearing over the eastern ridges of Sungulweni hill, which lay immediately east of the Nkandla forest, and the hungry regiments set off after them.

By this trick the Zulus led their enemies on a thirty-five-mile dance – to the Tugela, snatching the cattle lure across the river and there standing to receive the Ndwandwe attack. Their stand, at some of the fords, was, however, so suspiciously feeble that

Soshangane would not allow his now ravenous troops to continue the pursuit. He was supported by Zwangendaba and Nxaba, who were unhappy about the inability of the Ndwandwes to pin down the Zulus. It was, therefore, decided to begin an apparent retreat, and then to vanish into the eastern outrunners of the Nkandla forest – there to await the next move of the Zulu weasel. Simultaneously, foraging parties were to be sent eastwards to try by every means to bring in cattle for food, as the last few remaining oxen had been killed, and even on quarter rations the meat was now finished. Not much game had been encountered on the rolling grasslands, or open bush country, for the Zulus had seen to that. In the dense Nkandla forest hunting would be more profitable, but surprise attacks by the enemy were also likely. Again, all Ngunis had an intense dislike of these gloomy, primeval forests in enemy country, however much they favoured them as a refuge in their own land.

Whilst these talks were going on Shaka and his staff were looking from the Nkandla heights, at the back of the Ndwandwe army, and surveying the numerous camp fires glowing in the night on the river bank many miles below. With him were Mzilikazi, the future King of the Matabele, and Mdlaka, who now held the highest rank in the army next to Shaka. The latter had as usual been indefatigable all day observing every move of the enemy with his own eyes. He was in high spirits, and remarked: 'A crocodile in the water is dangerous. Lure him on to the dry land and he is easy meat. The Ndwandwes are hungry, unhappy, and far from home. I hope they cross the river, but even if they do not they will be sufficiently softened for us to attack them soon.'

Next morning Soshangane recalled his two forces which had crossed the Tugela, and began his retreat up the steep northern slopes of the river. By late afternoon his whole army had vanished, according to plan, in an eastern outrunner of the Nkandla forest. The manoeuvre was carried out with great skill behind dense screens of scouts, but before darkness set in Shaka knew exactly what had taken place. His own force was camped within the deep, gloomy recesses of the main forest, only some three miles westward of the Ndwandwe host. On innumerable small fires ample rations of meat were being grilled and orders had been given to cook enough for the morrow, too.

With the exception of Mdlaka, not a single soul besides the Zulu King knew what the future plans were. This was Shaka's invariable method until the time came to strike. Later in his life, when he no longer accompanied the very distant forays of his army, he only entrusted the commander-in-chief and his next in command with the strategy of the expedition. This secrecy avoided all leakages of news to the enemy, and accounted for the remarkable fact that the Zulu army almost invariably achieved surprise, no matter how distant the objective.

On this night, in July 1819, was presented an eerie sight of savage majesty, with 10,000 Zulu warriors camped under the canopy of the great yellowwood trees, the underside of whose leaves reflected the glow of a thousand fires and the uniform-coloured shields of the different regiments and the scintillating assegais beside them. Savages at war – yet what extraordinary order and discipline everywhere!

Shaka the King sat with his back to the bole of a 1500-year-old forest giant. Some distance in front of him there was a bright fire. On his left was young Mzilikazi, future King of the Matabele, and on his right the brooding Dingane, his twenty-two-year-old half-brother and future King of the Zulus. Another half-brother, fifteen-year-old Mpande, an *u-dibi* now, but later a king who ruled the Zulus for thirty-two years, was serving meat and beer to his brothers. Also present as an *u-dibi* was Chief Sigananda Cube.* On the enemy side were three men whose future was to be quite as august. The forest, that night, contained the destiny of half Africa.

Shaka now unfolded his plan for the first offensive action against the Ndwandwes. He had during the day formed a specially selected composite force of 500 men, who were stealthily to approach the sleeping Ndwandwes from the eastern, or farther side, in the guise of returning friendly foraging parties. As both

* He died in 1906 at the age of 96, and was the author's one living link with Shaka and his great captains.

sides spoke the same language and wore similar war-dress, it would be impossible to distinguish friend from foe in the darkness, except by a prearranged counter-sign. The Zulus would have all the advantage of surprise and preparedness on their side. They would infiltrate into the enemy lines in numerous files, and would be guided by the glowing embers of the nearly dead Ndwandwe fires.

Shaka's object was to create a panic among the Ndwandwes, in which many would kill each other in the darkness and confusion; to rob them of a night's sleep, and to break down their nerves generally. Actually, he was anticipating by over a century a Commando raid.

The raiding party was now drawn up before Shaka in a forest clearing, in which there was burning a big fire to light up the very dark night. Shaka gave them the counter-signs by which they were to identify each other in case of doubt. This consisted of the doubtful one saying to the one whom he accosted, 'Ndwandwe!' The reply would be 'Qobolwayo!', failing which the accosted one would be stabbed. If the reply 'Qobolwayo' was forthcoming, the first speaker would clinch matters by also saying 'Qobolwayo'. This word means 'Its very essence' and coupled with 'Ndwandwe' was meant to convey, 'I am a real Ndwandwe', which would tend to heighten the confusion of the unprepared enemy, who, if questioned, would at most affirm 'I am a Ndwandwe', and not 'I am a real Ndwandwe'.

Shaka gave these instructions to each platoon in a low voice, as he said that forests had ears, especially at night. 'When all their fires are reduced to embers and all are asleep,' he whispered to his trusty veterans, 'you will creep along like snakes among them' (*niti kisi kisi kisi*) 'stabbing them as they lie; and see you cease not nor return before the approach of dawn.'

Meanwhile, Soshangane was sitting at a fire in the midst of the Ndwandwe host only three miles away, in an outrunner of the forest. They were all greatly worried by the lack of food, as the few head of game they had killed had not gone far in spite of their altruistic Nguni habit of sharing everything equally. The foraging parties had not returned, and indeed few of the Ndwandwe scouts ever did. The Zulu army behaved like a will-o'-the-wisp, but it had teeth and claws, as evidenced by the destruction of the Ndwandwe patrols and outposts. It was all very uncanny and quite unlike any other campaign. It had, therefore, been decided to return home on the morrow and, after securing ample grain rations and slaughter oxen, to return to Zululand to plan a new and better prepared campaign. As the forest bivouac was relatively warm compared with the three previous camps on the open, wind-swept highlands and chilly river banks, the exhausted Ndwandwes made an early night of it and were soon fast asleep.

The Ndwandwe camp fires had hardly died down to glowing embers, when ghostly forms flitted in and threaded their way through the whole encampment, guided by the pin-points of the fires. To a few sleepy questions from Ndwandwes nodding before the warmth of the embers, the 'Angels of Death' gave a curt, low reply, 'Returning patrol', or 'Returning foraging party', and passed on. The leading Zulu slayers penetrated right through the bivouac, before they lay down next to the sleeping Ndwandwes and then, as arranged, waited for a time.

Presently a piercing yell awoke the forest, followed by similar yells everywhere, as the Zulu slayers began their deadly work. In a moment pandemonium broke loose, and hundreds of hand-to-hand encounters took place, principally among the Ndwandwes themselves. The Zulus had practically each got his man and had then evaded action by a pretence of death, lying beside each corpse, and only occasionally mixing with the standing Ndwandwes. After the first sharp tumult was over a general truce automatically succeeded it, in which each Ndwandwe sat down and suspiciously regarded his neighbour, whom at the best he could but dimly see.

This tense situation had continued for a time when inquiries were shouted from Soshangane's headquarters and relayed by further shouts to the confines of the encampment. Confused reports came back in the same way, which only heightened the bewilderment of all ranks, as well as headquarters. All agreed that there had been no general or organized attack, and yet death had smitten them from amidst their own ranks. Some evil sorcery was abroad, for friend had killed friend.

Soshangane gave orders that twigs and branches should be collected and piled on the glowing embers to light up the forest. No sooner had the Ndwandwes moved to carry out this command, when death yells arose again everywhere, and the fuel collecting ceased abruptly. The Ndwandwes were petrified with fear by these indistinguishable death dealers. Never afraid of the normal, they were completely cowed by the abnormal. The dark, eerie forest made them feel uneasy even in the daytime, as there were only a few of such primeval areas throughout the whole country, and not one of them as extensive as the Nkandla forest. Such a complete arboreal canopy was unknown to most of them, who only felt at home in the open, park-like bush country, or the highland grasslands. Their imagination needed little stimulus to conjure up every kind of witchcraft as having its abode in this damp and gloomy place!

Soshangane was a brave and resourceful man. He ordered all the Ndwandwes forthwith to concentrate and mass around his own headquarters, and to keep as close together as the trees and undergrowth would permit.

A general movement on these lines now began, but presently in the rear of the outermost groups the horrible death-cries arose again. The Zulu killers mostly attached themselves to the tail end of the innumerable Ndwandwe groups and, as the groans and yells of the mortally stricken increased, a general rush began for the headquarters rendezvous. Soon it became a case of everyone for himself, and the Devil take the hindmost! Stentorian shouts from headquarters indicated its locality, and with a large fire there whose glow was visible for 200 yards.

When the Ndwandwes were all drawn fairly close together around Soshangane's headquarters, he bade them face outwards and sit down, and called the regimental and many company commanders together for a report. Most of the evidence favoured a supernatural agency, which, through vivid dreams or otherwise, had started a panic that had resulted in a fratricidal stabbing match. There were some level-headed leaders, however, who felt fairly certain that the stabbing had been started by Zulu scouts who had penetrated into their midst. With these latter Soshangane agreed. The question now was how to discover and ferret them out, presuming that there were still some amongst the concentrated Ndwandwes. The forest was excessively dark, as the young moon had set, and the bright starlight could not penetrate the thick canopy of foliage. Dry fuel was scarce in that damp forest, so it would be impossible to make any useful number of effective fires for identification purposes.

Soshangane, therefore, decided that they must wait till daylight. He then gave a bracing talk to his army, which was relayed by the captains, sentence by sentence.

The Ndwandwes lay down and tried to sleep, but this was no easy matter after their recent alarming experience. Among them lay Nombanga, a champion Zulu warrior, very much alert, and wondering how he would get out again before daylight brought his discovery.

After a period when he judged the time to be ripe for action, Nombanga carefully studied the dim outline of a warrior's body lying beside him and then sat up and delivered a mighty thrust into his chest. There was a gurgling scream from the stricken man, and an instant commotion among the Ndwandwes which Nombanga heightened by shouting that he, too, had been stabbed by a sorcerer riding on a hyaena. This dread supernatural combination was firmly believed in by all Ngunis, and Nombanga's announcement caused consternation. This spread when death cries began to arise all over as the other Zulus got busy. Another panic arose and many Ndwandwes stabbed their comrades.

When Nombanga arrived at Shaka's headquarters at dawn, two-thirds of the expeditionary force, which had wisely avoided being trapped in the Ndwandwe crush, were parading before the Zulu King. He had been posted missing, much to Shaka's regret, for he was a renowned warrior with many *izibongi* or praises – the Zulu equivalent of a medal or clasp. Nombanga, therefore, received a warm greeting and, when he had finished giving his report, with some embellishments, Shaka bestowed another 'praise' distinction on him by calling him the 'Widow bird –

(from the feathers he wore) – which got lost among the Cockroaches' (Ama Pela, the name of a Ndwandwe Division).

The Ndwandwes lost no time in getting out of the gloom of that, to them, accursed forest, and into the open grasslands on the way home. Their losses, chiefly self-inflicted, had been grievous, as Shaka noted with satisfaction when he inspected the scene soon after the Ndwandwes had evacuated it. Nearly half a score of enemies were dead for every Zulu slain. But, more important still, the Ndwandwes had lost a night's sleep and their morale had been lowered.

Shaka, therefore, decided to strike that very day. At the head of his whole army he set off in hot pursuit of the Ndwandwes. With their superior mobility the Zulus came up with their rearguard about mid-morning, eastwards of the Sungulweni hill. Both armies now formed up in battle array. Shaka knew that the Ndwandwe army had been thoroughly reorganized by Soshangane and almost completely rearmed with numerous types of heavy stabbing blades. Moreover, they were commanded by a very able general who had many first-class officers. The principal advantages of the Zulus now lay in their iron discipline, superior spear-drill, and their great mobility. The advantage of numbers was wholly on the Ndwandwe side, who still mustered 16,000 against Shaka's 10,000. On the other hand the Zulus were well fed, whereas the Ndwandwes were half-starved. Still the disparity was so great that it could only be made good by better tactics and strategy – no easy matter with Soshangane at the helm – and, finally, by the unequalled morale of the Zulu warriors.

The two armies were about half a mile apart. Shaka selected certain of the younger regiments of the Belebele brigade, namely, the *Izin-Tenjana* (Plovers) and the *U-Kangela* (Look Out), to open the attack. Its nature was most unusual and rather puzzled Soshangane. The recognized method of attack by a regiment was to spread out on a front of some 300 yards, and several lines deep. Shaka, however, formed the two regiments into two columns of five men abreast, which now proceeded to outflank both

Soshangane's wings. Thereupon the latter extended his front to prevent the Zulus from getting behind him. The two columns responded by veering ever more to the right and left respectively, until Soshangane realized that his front would be dangerously attenuated in the face of the solid phalanx of the main Zulu army before him. He therefore detached the outermost regiment on each of his wings, to keep the outflanking columns of the Zulus covered, and the rest he ordered back into their original positions. That was exactly what Shaka wanted – two detached Ndwandwe regiments. He now made what looked like a general attack on the Ndwandwe position but halted two spears' throw away from them except at the extreme flanks, where he bit into them in a sharp five-minute clash. Whilst this was going on two regiments streamed out in column from behind these fighting flanks of the Zulus and sped straight after the two detached Ndwandwe regiments.

Soshangane instantly became aware of their peril but, with his flanks held and with no means of communication beyond runners, he was reduced to the rôle of an impotent spectator of the fast-moving doom approaching these regiments from behind. True, he could have orders shouted along the line, like a *feu de joie*, but to detach regiments from it now, with the mass of the Zulus in close proximity, would leave dangerous gaps and cause confusion, which might leave fatal openings for that Zulu weasel, who never seemed to run short of stratagems and surprises. Soshangane could now only hope that his doomed regiments would give a good account of themselves, and rectify matters by attrition, instead of giving way to panic when they were caught between the Zulu grinding-stones.

The isolated Ndwandwes soon knew that they had seen their last day. They realized they had no hope in flight, so they formed up in lines facing either way. Had they learnt the lesson of the battle of Qokli hill they would have formed a battle circle, which would have enabled them at least to hold out longer than they did, and inflict far greater losses on the Zulus.

The 'Plovers' regiment of Zulus were partnered by the Fasimba regiment. By a half-turn they changed their columns of five into five battle lines of some 200 men each, with a front of about 300 yards. Then began the sonorous Zulu war-chant, as the two regiments converged towards the Ndwandwes in the ccntre. The incredibly fast run of the Fasimba slowed down to an easy jog-trot, for their quarry had been cornered, and it is not good to start a battle when you are short of breath. The 'Plovers' marked time in order that both Zulu regiments should strike simultaneously. In almost perfect lines they came on. At one spear's throw the terrible Zulu war-cry rang out, finishing with a sibilant hiss, which sounded as ominous as thousands of angry serpents about to strike. This was the signal to charge. Then there was a clash of hundreds of shields, and the flash of spears. The momentum of the two Zulu regiments which crashed into the Ndwandwes from opposite sides threw the latter backwards and sandwiched them far too tightly for effective footwork. Nevertheless, the Ndwandwes fought with a stubborn ferocity which surprised the Zulus, including Shaka. The other Ndwandwe regiment died in a similar way. The destruction of the two regiments cost Shaka nearly the equivalent of one of his own in dead or disabled.

As soon as the destruction of these two isolated Ndwandwe regiments became a certainty, Shaka broke off the pinning action on the two extreme flanks of Soshangane's army. When the latter then essayed to attack on the whole front, Shaka refused action and retired, but only sufficiently to keep a distance of two spears' throw between his army and the enemy. This tantalizing interval he kept up, and demonstrated the superb discipline of his regiments, who kept their formations as perfectly as if they were on a parade. All the taunts and insults of the following Ndwandwes failed to shake them.

After half a mile of this retreat Soshangane realized the futility of it, and how completely Shaka's swift-moving army retained the initiative. He therefore turned and headed homewards again, in battle formation, on a single-line regimental front, which would be about 1500 to 2000 yards. His sixteen regiments would, therefore, give him a depth of as many lines. The main Zulu army now followed again – six regiments – but in compact separate bodies.

In front of Soshangane's path hovered the other four Zulu

regiments which had destroyed the two Ndwandwe regiments. They were reduced by about one-quarter in their fighting strength.

So long as the Ndwandwes moved in open or undulating country their formation was a good and safe one, but when they presently came to broken terrain their lines became disorganized, resulting in big gaps and corresponding jams. It was here that the following Zulus cut off many a straggling tail protruding from valleys through which the main bodies of Ndwandwes were crushing their way, their orderly lines having been changed into disorganized columns by the nature of the country.

In front, too, the Zulus had the disconcerting ability of vanishing into thin air and then reappearing, as if out of the ground, at the most awkward time for the Ndwandwes. Soshangane's scouts and patrols were of little use to him, as they were almost invariably destroyed by Zulu platoons who pounced on them like panthers from well-concealed positions.

Having emerged into more open country, Soshangane again concentrated his hungry and dispirited army for the night's bivouac. As the locality was open and exposed to a biting wind, he withdrew overnight into the Umhlatuze valley near the confluence with the Mvuzane, where there was shelter and plenty of fuel.

At dawn the Zulu army appeared half a mile away, on a ridge overlooking the Ndwandwe position. They were in the highest spirits, and so elated with the previous day's fighting that they were straining at the leash. But Shaka bade them sit on their shields. Soshangane would have welcomed a battle there and then, but confronted with the sudden uncanny immobility of the Zulus, and knowing that with his famished army he could not afford to wait at all, whereas his enemies could, he decided there was nothing to be gained by postponing his retreat. So with his sixteen regiments reduced to an effective strength of about 12,000 men he began to cross the river over a ford which permitted about twenty men abreast.

Shaka stood on a prominence of the ridge opposite the ford; this day he must gain a crushing victory in order to do away with the Ndwandwe menace once and for all, and to be ready to face the coming Tembu-Cunu coalition in the west. A semi-pyrrhic victory like Qokli would not do. The Ndwandwes must be utterly destroyed. But with their predominant numbers, under the able generalship of Soshangane, this appeared almost impossible.

Yet, here before his eyes there was unfolding what appeared to be a totally unlooked-for chance – something outside the frame of his calculations. 'A partridge was about to settle in his yard.' Soshangane, careful general that he was, had detached a Guards regiment to cover the crossing in a dense formation. Behind this he was withdrawing his regiments, which were strung out on a 2000-yard front parallel with the river, in the extended single-line formation in which the regiments had reached it during the previous night. What Soshangane failed to observe was that his front was not being shortened to make up for the lines he was withdrawing, and so preserving the density of his formation. This blunder can only be explained by the fact that his position, low down in the valley, precluded his seeing what was happening.

Shaka's ten regiments had an effective strength of about 8500 spears. When about half the Ndwandwes had crossed the Umhla-tuze river, and the rest were still strung out on their 2000-yard front, except the regiment of Guards covering the ford, Shaka knew that the hour had struck. He gave a sharp command, which was immediately echoed by the commanders and captains all along the Zulu lines. A few moments later there poured over the ridge as if by magic the hitherto invisible half of the Zulu army, who formed up behind their comrades in front of the ridge.

Keeping but one regiment in reserve, Shaka hurled the other nine at the enemy, bidding them: 'Up! Children of Zulu, your day has come. Up! and destroy them all.'

Over 7000 Zulus sprang to their feet. '*Bayete!*' they roared. Down crashed 7000 right feet, making the earth shake. Then the human tidal wave swept down in uncanny silence, on a 2000-yard front, in seven perfect lines of 1000 men each, the lines spaced about ten yards beyond each other.

At four spears' throw the deep, majestic Zulu war-chant rolled like rumbling thunder across the valley. With the beginning of the chant the speed of the warriors slowed down to the rhythmic measured jog-trot of a death dance, and at every tenth step there was an earth-shaking stamp of the right foot, carried out with perfect unison by all. At one spear's throw the chant ceased abruptly. There was a deadly silence for the time required to take a deep breath. Then the fearful Zulu war-cry crashed out: '*Si-gī-di!*' and the Zulus charged.

Within a very short space it was all over. The Ndwandwes who had not been killed had been pushed into or had taken to the river, except only the Guards regiment which covered the ford in a compact body. Fighting furiously, this regiment now began to retire across the ford in good order, under terrific pressure from the Jubingqwanga (Shorn Head-ring) regiment.

Shaka could barely restrain his glee when he assessed the losses of the Ndwandwes in that initial clash. Half of them had been killed on the river bank, and the other half had lost their spears and shields in swimming across the river to safety. As they swam a great number of these again were transfixed with the throwing spears which the Zulus picked up on the bank from the fallen Ndwandwes. Soshangane's fighting strength was therefore now limited to that half of the army which had forded the river before the battle began, and such warriors of his Guards regiment whom he might be able to withdraw over the ford. All the swimming survivors were useless to him without shields and spears, and might as well be dead for any practical value they retained for this battle. This stupendous achievement had cost Shaka less than 1000 men.

The Ndwandwe Guards managed to withdraw across the ford, but not without heavy losses, as they had to fight desperately all the way. The Zulus could, however, secure no permanent footing on the opposite bank, and the Ndwandwes counter-attacked with such ferocity that they were thrown back into the ford.

After this repulse Shaka tried to effect a crossing at some of the shallow stretches above and below the proper ford, but the Ndwandwes were now desperately defending the river bank on a broad front; under the able direction of Soshangane, and his lieutenants Zwangendaba and Nxaba, the fight swayed to and fro amidstream in the shallows, till the water of the Umhlatuze ran reddened with blood. Even the veteran Ama-Wombe regiment was unable to make any headway. It was here that Ndlela, ex-cannibal and future Prime Minister, and Hlati, the brother of Mdlaka, Shaka's second-in-command, were severely wounded.

At this stage Shaka sent in his reserve regiment, the Fasimba, downstream to effect a crossing there over the Mvuzane, and then over the Umhlatuze to take the enemy on his left flank. The Izi-cwe regiment and another which he had unobtrusively sent to the rear after the first clash, carried out a similar turning movement upstream.

So secretly did the two forces carry out their wide outflanking movement, that the Ndwandwes did not become aware of them till they fell on their flanks from the rear, and then proceeded to roll them up towards the centre. This new attack very soon reduced the resistance of the enemy at the ford-head and the shallows, and the veteran 'Ama-Wombe' succeeded in gaining, and retaining, the farther bank. Other units similarly forced the shallows, and soon the whole Zulu army was across.

In a short time the whole of Soshangane's remaining army disintegrated into little groups of fugitives, savagely pursued by the Zulus, and what was worse for the Ndwandwes, heading them off in an easterly direction, instead of homewards to the north.

Shaka's relentless pursuit of the beaten enemy contributed as much to his decisive victory as did the battle itself. When night put an end to the slaughter Shaka dispatched his fleetest and freshest regiments, the Mbonambi and Isi-Pezi, hotfoot to Zwide's Royal kraal to secure the person of the king and his evil mother, Ntombazi, owner of the infamous museum of skulls, before any of the fugitives arrived there. By next nightfall they had covered the seventy miles there, and, as instructed, approached the Royal kraal singing the Ndwandwe national song. All the inmates were deceived, and thinking that their army was returning victoriously, they hurried out to greet them, except Zwide and Ntombazi, who remained in the kraal. The Zulus then prematurely started to kill the surprised and terror-stricken women and children, and Zwide, being apprised of his mortal danger, managed to escape by way of a near-by reed-bed. Ntombazi, however, was captured.

By next dawn the rest of the Zulu army was sweeping through Ndwandwe-land, destroying without mercy every human being and dog, and capturing all the cattle, sheep and goats, and thereafter burning every hut.

Whilst this destruction was proceeding, Zwide, with his sons Sikunyana and Somapunga, escaped north-westwards through present-day Vryheid, and thence due north over the Pongola river, leaving Swaziland on his right, and did not stop until he had crossed the upper waters of the Inkomati river, where he settled down with such remnants of his tribe as had managed to escape. He thus put 200 miles between himself and his original homeland, which now fell to the Zulus as an ownerless estate with vast numbers of cattle.

Soshangane, with Zwangendaba and Nxaba, had managed to escape from the great battle with a small composite force made up of remnants of the army. They were saved from complete destruction by the covering wings of night.

This decisive and crushing victory for Shaka had the most far-reaching consequences imaginable. In one smashing blow he gained the Nguni paramountcy in so absolute and so predominant a degree that no one hereafter challenged his supremacy again, though they defended themselves against his wars of aggression. Except only once, when many years later, Sikunyana, the son of Zwide, led a forlorn crusade against him.

At one stroke Shaka became the supreme overlord of the fighting core of the Nguni homeland, Dingiswayo's heir but of a greater empire more absolutely ruled. From the Tugela in the south to the Pongola river in the north, and from the Buffalo river in the west to the sea – 11,500 square miles – now formed the greater Zululand, which in its turn was rapidly to become but the heart of a vastly greater empire.

When the ten Zulu regiments paraded at Zwide's kraal, their warriors were but enough to fill little more than five full-strength regiments.

Shaka thanked them all, and stressed that there was no necessity to search for cowards as they had all fought like lions. This should be a day of rest and rejoicing, of rewards and feasting.*

Shaka's first award was a startling novelty in Nguni history. Pointing to the thinned ranks, he said: 'Those who are not here are eating earth that we might live. Are we to forget the sorrowing mothers who bore them, and let their younger brothers and sisters go in want, because they gave their lives for our Zululand? Have we not a saying that a grieving mother's heart is soothed by a stomach full of meat? Well then, let us give to the bereaved the reward which the departed warriors would have received had they lived, and let us give a double measure, with both hands, to take the taste of bitter aloes from the mouths of the sorrowing ones.'

The warriors almost gaped in incredulous astonishment. Almost all of them had lost near relatives, but for all that, no one's imagination had ever risen to the heights of expecting a posthumous honour or reward for dying. Then the sky was split with a roar of applause – a thunderous 'Bayete!' such as Shaka had never heard before.

Shaka then announced the rewards to all the living, namely, a flat rate to all the warriors, plus a bonus for every enemy killed, or other outstanding act of merit. Platoon leaders received double the rewards of ordinary warriors. Captains twice as much again. Regimental commanders received very liberal rewards, according to merit, and the same applied to other high-ranking officers. Mzilikazi, Mdlaka and Mgobozi, for instance, received round about 500 head of cattle each.

Shaka personally attended to every detail of the selection and distribution of the cattle for rewards.

First of all he selected the very best for the Royal herds. This was not a selfish action, for they were essentially national property – the wealth of the nation, on which it could fall back in

* In spite of this the stupid legend persists amongst some authors that Shaka ordered the execution of half the 'Umkandhlu' regiment for retreating in the face of the enemy – a regiment which no Zulu has ever heard of, and of which no mention is made in the reliable regimental lists of A. T. Bryant and E. J. Krige.

times of need. Then in a truly democratic way he selected the best cattle for the common warriors first, then for the platoon commanders, and so on upwards. As the most senior officers received the scrubbiest, but by far the greatest number of cattle by this unique method of distribution, Shaka laughingly told them that there was consolation in numbers, and that the very special breeding-bulls he would give them from the national herds would soon eliminate the defects, and that he would in addition, out of the kindness of his heart, add some of the choicest breeding-cows. In this way he satisfied the seniors, whilst the common warriors worshipped the man, and King, who so justly looked after the interests of the lowly.

CHAPTER 16

The trial of Ntombazi

WHEN Shaka arrived at Zwide's kraal he ordered that a live hyaena be caught and brought to him uninjured. Zwide had escaped but Ntombazi had been kept captive in her great hut, in which she kept about thirty skulls belonging to former chiefs, including Dingiswayo.

Shaka established his headquarters in a temporary shelter outside the kraal as it was taboo to live in another's kraal when it had been deserted or conquered in war. But on the day set for Ntombazi's trial he entered the Royal kraal and sat in Zwide's place of judgement, where Ntombazi was brought before him.

Although over seventy years old she looked barely fifty and retained the vigour and carriage of a woman in early middle age. She had what the Zulus call a 'shadow' – that is, personality, character to a marked degree, and her fierce, proud eyes betrayed her ruthless spirit. A helpless prisoner, her dreams of conquest shattered, she retained a savage majesty and did not hesitate to abuse the Zulus and vilify Shaka. When he ordered her to be silent, she answered him derisively :

'Give the judgement first and then go on with the mockery of the trial.'

'True, you are judged, but I wish to hear your side and see if you can advance a single mitigating circumstance which may influence me in passing a sentence different from the one I have in mind.' Shaka then proceeded to give a list of some thirty chiefs whose heads Ntombazi had mounted in her hut, but as yet he did not mention those of Donda his friend, Mashobane, the father of Mzilikazi and Ntombazi's son's son-in-law, nor did he say anything about Dingiswayo, his great friend and benefactor.

'Why did you have all these chiefs killed after securing most of them through treachery?' inquired Shaka.

'To gain power as you are doing now,' said Ntombazi defiantly.

'To gain power is a good reason, but why did you resort to treachery, and so make the good name of the Nguni people stink? Our laws of hospitality have never sanctioned such an evil thing.'

'Power goes to the head and recks not what means it employs, as you too will soon know,' Ntombazi replied quietly.

'Why did you cut off those heads and mount them in your hut? It is an abomination according to all true Nguni customs. Only those who practise witchcraft resort to that.'

'I did it to gain the power of all those chiefs. If a chief is above the ordinary laws applying to witchcraft, how much more so am I, a Queen, above them? How, then, can I be accused of witch-craft?'

Shaka, who never missed a chance to advertise his increasingly rational point of view, is said to have replied to the witch:

'Your answers are shrewd, but tell me of what avail was all this witchcraft of yours against my better trained and better led army? Had Zwide relied more on training and equipment, especially in our first war, you and he would not now be where you are. Witchcraft may help the weak to have faith in themselves, but beyond that it is useless against a stronger opponent.'

'How then did we secure the mighty Dingiswayo?' returned Ntombazi with a sly smirk.

'You are ill-advised to boast of that foul deed. The downfall of that great good king was due to his kindly heart and misplaced trustfulness. Often did I warn him that his generosity to Zwide and yourself would not, and could not, beget gratitude, any more than he could expect that from a wounded hyaena which he had nursed back to strength. Why did you urge Zwide to kill him and return evil for good?'

'To gain power. To secure the Nguni paramountcy.'

'Did you also have to desecrate his body by removing the head?'

'Yes, to gain all the power which lived in him.'

'And your son's son-in-law Mashobane, and my other friend

Donda, whom you invited to a love-dance and then treacherously killed and beheaded?'

'Also for power, and more power, which their heads would give me.'

'And where is all your power now?'

Ntombazi pointed to her hut and to her head with an evil smile.

'Those of you who practise witchcraft make use of hyaenas as your mediums. Is that true?'

'Indeed it is,' said Ntombazi, hoping to instil the fear of the occult into Shaka.

'And you have complete power over these beasts?'

'Absolute power,' replied Ntombazi with emphasis.

'That is good,' said Shaka; then speaking in a gentle but ominous tone of voice he continued: 'You may return to your hut – your centre of power – and gaze on the heads of your victims. Perhaps you may even meditate on the reward for treachery when your thirty silent witnesses bear testimony against you. Lest you be lonely I will provide you with a like-minded companion to help you to while away the time. No hurt will come to you through my warriors, who will merely constrain you to remain in your hut. Food and drink will be provided for you only, but your companion will have to fend for himself.'

Ntombazi stirred uneasily. 'What, then, is the nature of my punishment?' she exclaimed.

'That you will learn in due course,' Shaka quietly replied.

'Have you captured my son Zwide? Is he to be my companion?'

'Nay, it is a nearer relative than that. Go now and partake of a good meal which will be given to you whilst your hut is prepared for you and your companion.'

Ntombazi was puzzled and ill at ease, but her dignity forbade her to show any sign of it. As she arose to go she said: 'I thank you, O Chief!'

'Thank me not before you know the end,' Shaka sternly replied.

The interior of a Nguni hut is almost pitch black in broad daylight when the door is closed and there is no fire in the hut.

There are no windows. The ventilation is by way of the grass covering which is supported by a strong lattice-work of laths in the form of a beehive. Rays of light filter through the chinks between the hut and the door posts, and between the latter and the door, and this again lets through a little light between the transverse poles forming it, for at this time planks were unknown.

When the door closed behind Ntombazi she could at first see nothing until her eyes became accustomed to the gloom. However, she at once became aware of a strong animal odour, and brave though she was, the fear of the lurking unknown clutched at her heart. The silence was as awful as the gloom. If only she could see what was waiting for her. Minute after minute the tension of suspense increased as she stood rooted at the doorway. Gradually her eyes became accustomed to the gloom and then at the farther end of the hut, some twenty feet away, she became aware of two dimly glowing eyes staring at her.

Ntombazi, the woman, shrieked and for a time forgot she was a queen. The guards pulled apart a little of the grass covering on the outside of the hut and asked why she shouted, and she gibbered to them, imploring them to tell her what the unknown was. They pleaded ignorance.

With more light coming in through the apertures made by the guards, the glow of the eyes increased and took on a terrifying intensity. Gradually Ntombazi discerned the outline of massive carnivorous jaws below the fiery eyes – jaws which began to move and slaver and revealed the most powerful teeth in existence – those of an outsize dog-hyaena, which can crack the thigh bone of an ox with ease.

Again Ntombazi screamed, as the full horror of her impending doom dawned in her fear-numbed brain. The loathsome, cowardly, but powerful scavenger would probably not dare to touch her for a long time, but goaded on by hunger, he would acquire the courage of desperation, and in any unguarded moment those fearful rending jaws would rip a lump of living flesh out of her. Ntombazi screamed again as she came to a full realization of her position. This again brought the guards to the apertures in the side of the hut.

'More light, more light,' called Ntombazi in answer to their inquiries.

'As the Inkosikazi (queen) commands,' replied the guards respectfully, and proceeded to make more apertures in the straw. Each of these was limited by the lattice-work to openings measuring some four inches by four. With nearly one dozen of these, Ntombazi was at last able to see quite clearly nature's undertaker who would dispose of her body partly alive, and partly dead, but altogether very thoroughly.

Ntombazi was a brave and resourceful woman, and not for nothing was she the mother and driving force of the redoubtable Zwide, who so nearly acquired the Nguni paramountcy. If she could but lay her hands on any of the dead chief's spears, which had been thrust into the sides of the hut, she would there and then attack the beast, and if she did not kill it, in spite of her seventy-odd years, at least she would die fighting like the paramount chieftainess she was. But on the floor of the hut there were but two large pots of water – one for the hyaena and one for herself near the door, with a dipping gourd, and she discovered to her dismay that the walls were stripped bare of all but those thirty skulls, and more, which now appeared to grin at her in malevolent derision.

There was good-natured and trusting, but somewhat brainless, Donda, whom she and her son Zwide had invited to a love-dance. How smilingly punctilious he had been on observing the etiquette due to a chief at his execution. And how absolutely hearty and free of malice or rancour had been his farewell!

Dingiswayo's skull occupied the place of honour, higher by many heads than all the others. How she had gloated when she had mounted it and felt assured that the paramountcy was now hers, and it would have been, she reflected bitterly, but for that Zulu upstart. If she had him in her power she would know how to make his death anything but easy.

Towards nightfall a strong guard was placed around Ntombazi's hut. Grilled meat in moderate portions was offered to her through the apertures, and small ladles of the best beer in unlimited quantities. She dreaded the oncoming night and asked for fire, but this was politely refused.

Animated by a sudden hope Ntombazi threw the first piece of meat to the hyaena, which it voraciously snapped up, with a metallic clicking of the jaws which made Ntombazi shudder.

When she tried to repeat the manoeuvre the guard deferentially remonstrated with her: 'Nay, mother, we have no meat to spare except for you, and we must see you eat it before we are allowed to pass you any more.'

Baffled, but determined to keep up her strength, Ntombazi had perforce to eat her portions with the guards watching. Of beer she first partook generously until to her dismay she remembered it would make her sleepy, and to sleep with that hungry monster in the hut was to court immediate disaster. For again in Ntombazi's fevered imagination arose that blossom of hope, that if she held out, that unpredictable Zulu upstart might reprieve her. Then free once more and amongst her northern relatives, she would preach a crusade against him, and humble him into her present position, from which she would never let him escape.

So Ntombazi resolved to keep alert all night, but she dreaded the impenetrable darkness which would presently settle in and over the hut.

Knowing that hyaenas will for long periods subsist on bones only, Ntombazi decided just before the darkness set in to detach several of the skulls of the lesser chiefs and feed them to the hungry beast. When the first skull rattled at its feet the hyaena cowered away, but presently Ntombazi was gratified to hear an ominous crunch as the starved scavenger sank its powerful jaws into the mouldy scalp and bones. The gruesome crunching continued in the dark, and the hyaena needed no second invitation when Ntombazi presently threw it another skull.

Ntombazi had an imagination, and in the impenetrable gloom, as hour after hour slipped past in absolute silence, her nerves began to break down. Her tortured mind began to detect stealthy stalking footsteps creeping nearer and ever nearer.

'Go away,' she shrieked. 'Don't touch me, you evil beast,'

and then she laughed the laugh of the hysterical, which in crescendo waves rose to the laugh of the insane.

Presently the horrible, and indescribably terrifying, demoniacal laugh of a hyaena in the presence of much, but inaccessible, meat broke the silence, and even the guards outside felt their hair rising in sheer horror – and these were men of Shaka's guard who dreaded nothing in the world, if we except their chief.

Demented with fear, and paroxysms of rage, Ntombazi decided to end everything by hurling herself at the unseen monster with which she was caged. With shrieks of laughter she rushed at it in the dark, but with its stomach partly filled with bones its natural timidity had returned, and it cowered and scurried away from her with snapping jaws.

Sanity returned to Ntombazi once more. If this cowardly creature avoided her thus, she would be reasonably safe until the morning – provided she kept awake, and perhaps shouted at it from time to time. With the morning hope would revive, and perchance new plans could be made. Thus in trembling hope Ntombazi spent a fearsome night. Except for lapping up water towards dawn the hyaena had kept an unnerving silence.

Daylight came at last and showed the hyaena lying down with its head on its paws, intently watching Ntombazi with an air of sinister patience. Again the circle of skulls became fully visible and now they appeared to be stern judges about to pronounce sentence. Ntombazi wailed. Then, desperately sleepy, she dozed fitfully in a sitting position, but awakened frequently with starts of terror.

At the time of the first Zulu meal – about eleven o'clock – the guards called respectfully to Ntombazi that her food and beer were ready for delivery through the apertures, and she arose drowsily to receive the measured portions handed to her. The guards gave Ntombazi as much food, and of the very best, as she wanted, provided always that she completely finished before their eyes every portion handed to her, or returned any uneaten food to be exchanged for anything else she demanded.

Ntombazi in spite of her age was a robust and hardy woman. She ate and drank generously, for she was determined to keep up her strength. When the hyaena sniffed hungrily as she ate large portions of savoury grilled meat, the redoubtable old Amazon picked from the wall some more skulls of the lesser chiefs and bombarded the questing beast with them, and as the beer took effect she chased it round and round the hut several times with high-pitched yells, which she felt would intimidate it, and establish her supremacy. Then she settled down for a real sleep when she heard the hyaena presently crunching the skulls, to which her grill-smeared hands had intentionally imparted a pleasant flavour.

At sunset the guards called her once more for the evening meal, and she awoke from a heavy sleep with a start. This time she ate sparingly and merely took a sip of beer. Then she placed a few more skulls beside her for throwing at the hyaena during the night and sat down in patience to pass through the hours of darkness as best she could. At intervals she shouted at the invisible and silent beast, and when she threw another skull at it she welcomed the sound of crunching bones, as it indicated its whereabouts. And so passed another night of dreadful suspense and Ntombazi did not dare to relax into a doze until full daylight had set in, but not before she had again shouted, stamped, and raved at the beast which she drove cowering against the farther wall of the hut.

When Shaka heard of her dauntless courage he could not repress the admiration which he always had for the brave. 'Hau! the old witch has a liver (courage). Almost am I minded to pass her a spear; but if she wins what am I to do with her, for I have sentenced her to be constrained to her hut only, and sooner or later the venomous old serpent would strike back at me.'

To which, says the chronicler, Mgobozi replied:

'Burn down the whole evil place now, and be done with it. I like not this infliction of many deaths on one person, even though she deserves it.'

'Nay, that I cannot do whilst she lives,' replied Shaka, 'for then I would eat my words, which said that no harm would come to her from my warriors.' And there the matter rested.

This new day passed much like the previous one for Ntombazi.

She ate and drank more at the morning meal and slept more deeply-after it in a fully recumbent position. Thus she lay at sunset in the growing gloom inside. Presently, she slept, but not for long: there was a sudden savage snap of jaws, a piercing scream of agony, a rending and a tearing of flesh and bone, and the hyaena retired with the front half of one of Ntombazi's feet.

Presently the game and redoubtable Ntombazi recovered her composure, and called to the guard, who immediately responded from the aperture. She asked for a bark bandage, a ball of spider's web and 'joye' leaves. The guard replied that he only had orders to supply food and drink, but that he would refer the matter immediately to the King. Very shortly he returned and told her that her request had been granted, and over and above that Shaka sent her a spear as a token of respect for her courage. Thereupon fresh hope surged through the indomitable old Queen's heart. Methodically she bandaged her amputated and lacerated foot. By now it was getting quite dark and she asked for a bright fire to be lit at least outside the hut. The request was transmitted to Shaka and was granted. More of the thatch cover was removed from the side of the hut and now at least she could see a little, even if it revealed those glowing, gloating eyes. Then with royal assurance the old Queen called for beer and meat. Grimly she ate and recklessly she drank. At first in silence, and then with imprecations and curses at the waiting beast, at which she shook the spear which had been given to her. Presently she plied the guards with questions as to the mood of Shaka, and then under the influence of the beer she became talkative and elaborated on her experiences in the hut, which she interlarded with grim bits of irony and humour. 'I am going to kill that monster, but if I don't, at least I will know that mine will not be the only chiefs' bones in its stomach.'

And so the grim vigil continued during the greater part of the night, with the light from the fires outside gradually failing. Racked with pain and apprehension Ntombazi nevertheless became drowsy, whereas the ever vigilant beast having tasted fresh meat and smelling fresh blood, was now savagely eager for more, yet wary of running into danger.

Ntombazi must have dozed, for again she felt those clashing jaws close on the stump of her foot and an instant later a mouthful was ripped from the calf of her leg before she made the first ineffective lunge with her spear, to an accompaniment of terrified shouts. In the pervading darkness she could see nothing and yelled to the guards to stir up the fires. This they did. It enabled Ntombazi to see the grievous fresh injuries inflicted on her. Again with amazing courage she bound and staunched her wounds. Then she tried to tackle the hyaena by crawling towards the shadowy form, but as yet it evaded her, and once more she settled down with her back against the wall of the hut. Presently the hyaena approached and commenced to lick up some of the blood which had flowed from her and had formed a little pool which had congealed. Then it eyed her, keeping just beyond her reach. It was becoming bolder now. Once more it began its ghastly laugh, with low chuckles which rose to an eerie crescendo, dropped and rose again. It was too much for Ntombazi. She screamed and laughed in a rising flood of demented hysteria.

The captain of the guard peered in through one of the many apertures which had now been made. With the blazing fires at his back he beheld the awesome sight of a woman and hyaena sitting and facing each other at a distance of two paces apart – the luminous eyes of the hungry brute, with slavering, drooling mouth open to emit its dreadful laugh of anticipation – the horror-stricken eyes of the demented woman who was laughing in return.

Then without any warning the hyaena made a lightning snap at the woman's foot; she countered with a thrust of her spear which the brute evaded, and then caught the blade sideways in its powerful jaws, and with a backward leap jerked the weapon out of the woman's hand.

Ntombazi knew she had lost, and with the fatalism of her race she regained her regal dignity. Addressing the guards in her old queenly manner, she said: 'This beast will now eat me up piece by piece. Tell the King I thank him for the spear, but I received it too late. Ask him to have this hut burnt down speedily, so that once more I will be able to laugh, as I see my last enemy perishing in the flames with me.'

Before the messenger returned from Shaka, some little time elapsed, during which the hyaena became even bolder and finally worked its will on its rapidly weakening victim. When Shaka's consent to the burning arrived most of Ntombazi's legs had gone, but with arms flailing she had kept the brute away from her more vital parts – nevertheless she was dying from the loss of blood.

As the crackling flames seïzed on the dry grass-covering of the sides and roof of the hut the hyaena rushed about with terror-stricken whimpers. Ntombazi, with her back still supported by the wall of the hut, gave a shout of savage triumph and hurled abuse at her tormentor. Then the interior of the hut became as light as it had never been before, and the remaining skulls on the wall grinned down on their stricken murderer.

Kneeling in the centre of the hut and looking upwards at the skulls, Ntombazi called out 'Dingiswayo!' and then she fell prone a moment before the burning roof collapsed and enveloped her and the hyaena in roaring flames.

When her death was reported to Shaka his comment was, 'She was an evil woman, but she was brave and died like a Queen.'

CHAPTER 17

Carnival of victory - The royal lover - The great hunt

AFTER the great victory at the Umhlatuze river Shaka sent his regiments of young women to the Nkandla forest to bring back the hidden grain. Vast supplies of grain were also available in the granaries of the Ndwandwes, who, like all the Nguni tribes, made them in the form of domed pits dug deep into the cattle-kraals; these pits were lined with clay and then fired to give a brick-hard inner shell; the opening on top was sealed with a large flat stone which was let into the earth so that the top was level with the ground floor of the kraal. Over this rested a six-inch or thicker accumulation of dry cattle-dung which was capable of absorbing a great deal of rain before the ground underneath got wet, and in dry weather the evaporation, assisted by the churning hooves of the cattle, was rapid. Grain preserved in these pits has been known to keep fresh for up to seven years and free from weevils. The pits do, however fill with carbon monoxide gas when they are nearly empty and after exceptional rains.

In addition to carrying grain the maidens' regiments had a less onerous and more pleasant duty to perform. The 5000 surviving warriors obviously had more than that number of 'axes to wipe' and Shaka could not afford to let them roam far afield in search of unknown maidens to assist them in this congenial task. He therefore marshalled the male and female regiments into inner and outer horseshoe formations respectively and told them that since there were thousands among them due to 'wipe the axe' and that even this limited sexual indulgence was illicit before the warriors were disbanded, that all regiments of both sexes would disband for two nights and one full day and attend to the purifying ceremonies, necessary before the victory celebration, by indulging in *ama hlay endlela*.

According to Njengabantu Ema-Bomvini, there was universal agreement that Shaka was now the supreme overlord of all greater Zululand from the Pongola river to the Tugela, and from the Buffalo river to the sea, and that he had no rivals beyond his borders who could even hope to challenge his position. Within a little more than three years, after succeeding to the petty chieftainship of the small Zulu clan, he had built up a Nguni kingdom such as had never existed before.

'My Father, you are the greatest and the only Elephant now,' Mgobozi told him with emphatic fervour, 'and there is nothing beyond your borders which can stand against the Zulu Army.'

'Forget not the Tembus beyond the Buffalo,' said the ever-cautious Mdlaka. 'If they form a coalition with the Cunus, and maybe the Ngwanes, farther back along the Kahlamba (Drakensberg) they may yet give us all the fighting we want. The tribes are no longer what they were, and under their able leaders they are rapidly learning the new methods of fighting.'

To this Shaka said, 'Well spoken, Mdlaka! Although we will celebrate our victory in a manner and on a scale never attempted before, we must not relax our vigilance till every tribe from the Kahlamba mountains to the sea owes absolute allegiance to us, or is exterminated.'

'And what about the Swazis and the tribes still farther north?' put in Mzilikazi.

'You will get your fill in that direction, young cockerel, but all in good time,' replied Shaka with good humour, looking at his young favourite. 'It is well,' replied Mzilikazi with a disarming smile which masked the ambitious plans which had been rapidly germinating ever since the overthrow of the Ndwandwes – plans and dreams which were ultimately to make him the head of a great new nation.

On the second sunrise all the regiments of both sexes reassembled in full strength. All the maidens looked subdued, and the warriors somewhat morose. After gazing at them for some time in intense silence, Shaka's face broke into a sardonic smile. '*Dade-wetu!*' (By our Sister) 'You all look like a collection of wet finches during a long drizzling rain.'

Shaka thereupon issued instructions for the triumphal march back to Bulawayo – his capital – some fifty miles away. Owing to the great number of captured cattle – some 60,000 – they did not arrive there until mid-morning of the third day.

In the van came the Royal cattle all marshalled according to colour into separate herds.

Behind the cattle came the army, headed by Shaka and his headmen, and, finally, the maidens' regiments. For two miles in front of the Royal kraal the route was lined with women, who received each contingent with shrill ululations and praises. Around the parade ground of the kraal stood the cadet regiments with their black shields. On the high clay mound on which Shaka used to sit to watch the parades was seated Nandi, with Pampata at her feet amidst all the feminine members of the Zulu Royal Family, including Shaka's aunts Mkabayi, Mmama and Mawa, who each ruled over a military kraal.

Shaka marched straight up to where his mother was seated on the mound and gave her a hearty personal greeting before he extended it in a general way to the others, at the same time giving Pampata a friendly glance. Then he mounted the mound and seated himself on the large roll of rush mats which constituted his throne. Whilst he was in friendly converse with his mother and the other Royal women, the regiments and populace were drawn up in dense lines to receive the King's address.

When all were assembled Shaka rose and briefly reported the results of the campaign, and then gave the glad tidings that he wished the whole nation to celebrate on a grand scale. There would be all the meat and food they could eat, plenty of beer, dancing and singing, and, finally, a review of the captured cattle.

Temporary shelters (*amadlangala*) had been built within a radius of two miles of the Royal kraal; the military kraals Isi-Klebe and Belebele lay within three and five miles respectively, and there was consequently sufficient accommodation for all during the sharp winter nights. The beer and food were evenly distributed everywhere, with large reserves under guard at the capital and military kraals. The meat was supplied by many hundreds of choice fat oxen which were killed in scores, as the demand arose. A spirit of joyful carnival was manifest everywhere. Shaka himself led in many of the dances and songs. Mgobozi was there, too, with all his wives except three who were not 'walking cases'. Only half the remainder carried babies on their backs; it is recorded that Shaka turned to him in mock surprise: 'Where, then, are the rest of your children?'

'My Father, they are still coming,' replied the embarrassed Mgobozi.

On the second day Shaka issued a proclamation that all the veteran warriors who had proved their worth were to be granted the right to put on the head-ring, or, in other words, received permission to marry, the 'lobola' or dowry of cattle for their wives to be given by the King. Deafening applause greeted this decision. The selected warriors – over 1000 – were given permission to choose their wives from the senior girls of the Vutwamini maidens' regiment. The warriors were released from active service, but were transferred into the reserve, which would only be called upon in a national emergency.

The head-ring, distinguishing a married man, was made from a plastic fungoid growth obtained from trees, and the circle was about five inches in diameter, whilst the body of the ring was about three-quarters of an inch thick and rounded. It was fixed around the head whilst still plastic, and in a short time became fairly hard. It was polished and assumed a glossy black colour, and was regarded with respect as a badge of honour and dignity.

During all this time, Shaka was in a very affable mood and spent much time in friendly conversation with his mother and the other Royal ladies. To his aunts and 'half-brothers', who ruled over military kraals, he gave 500 head of cattle each, and to the other 'half-mothers' a generous portion. To Nandi he gave a herd of thousands and initiated steps for the building of her own great Royal kraal at Emkindini, half-way between present-day Melmoth and the Umhlatuze river not far from the Mfule.

Nandi said of her son: 'All the things my *Umlilwane* promised me as a herd-boy have come true. In those days only Pampata believed in them, and I, for my part, was hoping for but one substantial kraal for all of us.' She now deemed the time propitious again to broach the subject of marriage to Shaka; but, as usual, he evaded the issue in a bantering way, fearing to hurt her by telling her the blunt truth, that he had definitely decided against marriage. Nandi was very hurt, and then became angry and rebuked Shaka, especially as he had hinted that the time had now come for him to enter his harem. 'So you will only have concubines and no real wives, and none of your children will have any legal rights to succeed you.'

'Nay, *Mame*,' (my mother) 'there will be no children,' mildly countered Shaka.

But she wished Shaka to marry and, when he evaded this question, she was distressed and angry, and reproached him.

Mkabi, Senzangakona's first wife and mother of Nomzintlanga, the Zulu Princess Royal, was present for the celebrations. She and Langazana, the fourth wife, were in charge of the Isi-Klebe military kraal.*

The Zulu Royal women played an important part in the councils and actual administration of the country, and in Shaka's days ranked much higher than his younger brothers or any other Royal males in the realm.

Njengabantu Ema-Bomvini was told by his father that when the maidens' regiments appeared with their smart little shields

* The former lived till the collapse of the Zulu power after the battle of Ulundi in 1879, when she called her people together and said that she, who had seen the glory of the Zulus, could not tolerate the idea that the last Zulu king, Cetewayo, was a hunted fugitive, and, therefore, she would end her life. Thereupon the dour old centenarian severed her throat in front of all her people. Langazana lived till 1884. To the very end she retained a clear memory and was the richest living repository of Zulu history from before the rise of that nation's power to its zenith and final collapse. She was particularly versed in all the events of Shaka's life, from his birth to his death. Nqakamatshe Ntombela passed on some of this to the author. Leslie the hunter describes her in 1866 (when she was forty-seven years older) as 'a remarkably jolly old lady and the biggest woman I have ever seen, weighing at least 350 lbs. She was then ruling over a large tract of country, and consequently had her hands full of cases to try every day.'

and sticks in orderly lines, high-stepping on to the parade ground, in their all but nude state, they presented a grand sight of military precision wedded to natural feminine glory. A murmur of admiration greeted them from all the spectators, but was instantly hushed in order not to interfere with the girls' singing. Shaka was most agreeably impressed and his eyes danced with pleasure. This display seemed to fill the measure of his success, and he felt a King indeed. He was in a generous mood and he felt that his warriors should be rewarded for their great effort by a relaxation – a very temporary one – of the stern military and moral code. In a puckish spirit he arose and strode in front of the massed warriors, who were eyeing the maidens hungrily, and addressed them as follows:

'Because as you have all fought well, and, in the kindness of my heart, I am minded to make a concession to you to mark this great festival of victory. The whole of the '*Izimpohlo*' (Bachelors') division will be disbanded for three days and three nights. Thereafter they will resume duty, and then it will be the turn for the *Belebele*,(Everlasting Worries) to be likewise disbanded. All the maidens' regiments will be relieved of military duty for six days. During this period of disbandment the code will be relaxed. The warriors may all go and "*soma*"* (have full sexual intercourse) with the maidens of their choice, but I expect them, nevertheless, to exercise restraint. In every case of deflowering, the guilty warrior will pay two head of cattle to the maiden's father as damages, and in a case of pregnancy he will pay three cows, so that she and the child will be provided for; but this fine will under no circumstances be classed as part of the

---

* Bryant in *Olden Times in Zululand and Natal*, p. 641, says this order only applied to the Izimpohlo Division, and for one night only, and after they had gone the Belebele Division were ordered to impound all their cattle. According to Bryant, too, the order was casually shouted by Shaka over the royal enclosure and apropos of nothing. This seems quite illogical and does not harmonize with the detailed account of Njengabantu Ema-Bomvini and Nqakamatshe Ntombela whose version is given above. The latter had it from Langazana, Senzangakona's fourth wife.

dowry should the warrior subsequently be allowed to marry. These fines are to be regarded as punishment for a lack of restraint. Moreover, as soon as the period of this concession has ended, the old stringent law will be in full force again, and any infringement will, as before, be punished with the death of both the erring parties. The Bachelors' Division and all the girls' regiments are dismissed forthwith. I have spoken.'

'*Bayete!*' roared five thousand joyful warriors. The Bachelors' Division melted away with uncanny speed to get rid of their military accoutrements, nor were the maidens found lagging in dropping their shields and sticks in their cantonments, which was indeed about all they could drop as the rest of their 'outfit' could easily be held in one closed hand without showing anything.

So superb was the discipline and self-control of the Zulu army even in this hazardous and delicate operation, and so perfect was the sexual technique of the Nguni people, that there were few casualties amongst the maidens. These were ascertained at the monthly routine examinations* and the prescribed fines were duly paid.

For the first time since his boyhood days Shaka felt that he could afford to relax. He had acquired the Nguni paramountcy and his position was unassailable. His *Um-Dlunkulu* girls numbered several hundred and were as yet untouched. He invariably referred to them as his 'sisters', which euphemism he kept up to the end of his days. The time he felt was now ripe to enter his harem. He had set a good example of celibacy to his warriors and, having allowed them to have their fling, his nature demanded that he should lead and surpass them in the field of Venus as he had done in that of Mars.

Pampata invariably supported and encouraged every reasonable ambition manifested by Shaka and in this way maintained her guiding influence over him. When, in this instance, he asked her: 'Will you not be jealous, Pampata?' she replied: 'Nay, my lord. Your pleasure is my pleasure.' And, it is said, provided the aphrodisiac ointment scented with aromatic 'mpepo' leaves, to maintain his strength.

*See Appendix.

Shaka's 'nuptial' palace was the great Royal hut shaped like a beehive, some thirty feet in diameter, and about twenty feet high at the dome. The roof was supported by a dozen stout poles which reinforced the strong lattice-work; to this was fastened the thatchgrass covering, which was about four inches thick at the sides of the hut and reached its greatest depth of about one foot at the top of the domed roof. Shaka selected fifty of the maidens he fancied most and with those he entered the hut. He knew every one of them by name and who they were. He had apprised them in the morning that their mass honeymoon would begin that evening, and those who were paying their routine tribute to the moon were replaced by others.

Shaka entered the hut first and took his seat on several layers of karosses (fur blankets) which had been spread on the floor on the right-centre perimeter of the hut. Then fifty maidens filed in after him and seated themselves in a double semicircle on the left perimeter of the hut. Shaka's position was directly opposite the open arch of the semicircle and about halfway between the door and the back of the hut, and close enough to the wall to have his head near it if he took a recumbent position, with his feet in the direction of the small fire in the centre of the hut.

Plying them with beer, and humorous talk and puns, Shaka soon had them all in a gay and expectant mood, for nobody could be more genial than he when he wanted to be. Then Shaka made his first choice. It was 'Gijima' which means 'run' or 'hasten', and she belonged to the Sibiya clan. When Shaka then bade 'Run' to run to his couch, both the pun and the honour conferred were received with general acclamation by the others.

Ngunis do not kiss, or did not before they came in contact with European civilization. They had, however, a profound knowledge of the female physiology which was imparted to them during and after the ceremonies connected with puberty, and they were past masters in the delicate art of pre-coition excitation or love-play.* Nguni husbands provided each wife with her own hut, in the privacy of which he would visit his wives in rotation – more or less. Chiefs sometimes dispensed with this and

*See Appendix.

ordered their wives to visit them in the great council hut, and sometimes several of them would be present at the same time. The concubines, who had no status beyond that of being jealously guarded royal property, and no huts for their individual use, were invariably summoned to the chief's hut, singly or in parties. They were later given in marriage to deserving subjects, and brought with them the halo of association with Royalty as compensation for their somewhat seasoned virginity.

Shaka's *Um-Dlunkulu* (Great House) maidens were treated with the utmost respect by everyone, for were they not Royal property and his 'sisters'? Actually they were his concubines, and ultimately he had approximately 1200. Even so, they were regarded as maids of honour and as aristocrats, ranking immediately after the Royal ladies – or wives, if the King had any – and took precedence over councillors and even the Prime Minister himself.

As a chief or king could do no wrong there was no impropriety in the fact that Shaka was making love to Gijima in the very dim and uncertain light where his kaross was spread, but otherwise not screened from the other harem girls.

Presently, Shaka announced that he was about to select another maiden and the animated chatter ceased while an air of excited expectancy hung over all. Another flare of *uqungu* grass was lit and Shaka with teasing words kept the maidens on tenterhooks as his eyes roved hither and thither, whilst he extolled the perfections of many, whom he mentioned by name; and in order to put the others at their ease, he told them that they were all so desirable that his one difficulty was to know which to choose. For, with all his power, he nevertheless knew the value of a psychological approach, and, in the case of women, he often publicly affirmed that you could do nothing with them in any sphere if they were unwilling. Moreover, it was one of his ambitions that all his women should spontaneously acclaim him as the greatest lover of all times. With generous gifts, hearty talk, beer, food and song, as the allies of his carefully preserved virility and masterful but delicate technique, he felt as assured of success in love as in war.

Although Shaka imparted full satisfaction to all his partners by means of Nguni 'love-play' he was only able to deflower a reasonable number; according to Langazana they numbered 'less than the fingers of two hands' in the first three hectic days of his sexual marathon. This was a sore point with Shaka, which, however, was retrieved for him by the resourcefulness of Pampata.

When the night was far advanced Shaka ordered an interval and everyone trooped outside. Thereafter, everyone lay down to sleep – the maidens on their mats with well-brayed skins as blankets and Shaka on the more luxurious karosses. Activity was not resumed till dawn, and early in the morning all the maidens were temporarily dismissed. Shaka then breakfasted and, before attending to urgent State business, had his daily public bath in front of all the people present. No sooner was the short court session concluded than Shaka repaired to his great hut and sent for Pampata.

She perceived at once that he was moody and even peevish. She divined the cause, and when Shaka said 'Speak!' almost abruptly, she immediately replied. 'All the maidens you honoured with your embraces last night say that you are the most marvellous man, and as outstanding in love as you are in battle. Not one of them you lay with remains an *Intombi ese yonke* (literally a 'complete maiden', meaning virgin) 'and your strength is fearful. Like a fire driven by a high wind through dry grass these praises of the maidens are running through the country. All the other maidens you have not as yet honoured are eating out their hearts waiting for their turn to come.'

Shaka was visibly pleased but tried to look stern as he asked, 'And where did the cattle come from to bribe the maidens as I bribed Mgobozi's wives to admit what was not true?'

'There was no bribing, my Lord. I have had a few words with the maidens who all come to me for advice. All I did was to appeal to their vanity. I said that if I were one of the maidens who had perchance not been deflowered, I would not proclaim it, for those who had been would laugh at me and declare that I had not received the same favour as they had.'

'Your words are comforting, but already I am tired of them all, and yet will I have to continue for another two days for the sake of my reputation, when I would much sooner enjoy your company and your words.'

Shaka certainly enjoyed a little diversion with his harem, but he was never a sensualist like his half-brother and successor Dingane. Almost invariably it was the women with brains who appealed to Shaka, but he was also attracted to those in whom he was able to arouse an unusual degree of sexual excitement, and particularly to that tornado of passionate reactions, Mbuzikazi of the Cele clan, who, in spite of her name, also possessed intelligence, wit and a tongue as sharp as a razor. In spite of every precaution which Shaka took to avoid pregnancies, this young woman ultimately managed to break down his iron self-control at least once, and ensnared him in a joint amorous ecstasy which resulted in her pregnancy.

Shortly after the great carnival of victory Shaka decided on a further relaxation from State affairs by indulging in a great Royal hunt on a scale never before attempted. He chose the empty Ndwandwe domain and made use of most of the standing army, carrying *isipapa* hunting assegais, all the cadets, and a large proportion of the senior *u-dibi*.

The hunt was as carefully planned as a military expedition and aimed at encircling the country lying between the White and Black Umfolozi rivers, from their confluence upwards for twenty miles. The direction of the drive was down the rivers into the *cul-de-sac* formed by their junction. Here ready egress was barred by many long and deep pools, and fordable places were heavily guarded by hunters, as they were also all along the two rivers up to where the driving line was thrown across country from river to river. This line would advance in skirmishing order, at ten- to twenty-pace intervals between the warriors, and drive all the game into the narrowing apex of the converging rivers, and the gradual shortening of the line would decrease the intervals between the driving warriors till they formed almost a solid line. The far banks of the rivers were lightly guarded all along except at possible fords, where they were doubled.

Shaka with his bodyguard of the Fasimba regiment and a strong force of selected hunters, was to take up his position on the right bank of the White Umfolozi, near its junction with the Black Umfolozi, on the morning before the drive. This would place the river between Shaka and the driving line.

Igebe, or deep big-game pits, had been dug at all promising places on this right bank and were, moreover, connected with an elaborate *isengqelo* fence made of thorn trees and branches. Unlike the *iveku* pits, these *igebe* had no sharpened stakes in them. They were about nine feet deep with sheer sides, six feet wide and approximately twelve to fifteen feet long. They were cleverly covered up with branches, reeds and grass, and appeared to be solid causeways leading to and through the formidable thorn fences which blocked every crossing place between the long pools. These fences were built in zigzag lines in order to form funnels leading to the concealed pits. Beyond these, and farther away from the river, a second but lighter fence had been erected parallel to the first.

This was intended to screen the hunters who would man it, but it also had its funnels or runways, which, starting with a wide mouth, would narrow into a fairly long passage. Behind the branches forming its walls the hunters would be so placed that any game passing through these passages would have to run the gauntlet of many spears. Any animals which got through these two fences would finally have to negotiate a very steep ridge lining the river. The several natural cuttings or causeways over this ridge were flanked with heavy obscuring fences which, however, had many screened openings in them; through these agile hunters were intended to make darting attacks at passing elephants labouring up the declivities, and to hack through with axes the tendons of their hind legs.

Thus was the setting for the great hunt. The time – about August 1819. The month was well chosen, for north-westerly winds prevailed then and would move with the driving line against the receiving line; thus the latter could not be detected by scent. The weather was still cold and lent itself to preserving large quantities of meat by *benga*-ing it, i.e. cutting it into strips and drying it over fires, which would also partly scorch it on the surface.

Shaka was particularly interested in the methods adopted in hunting elephants, and more especially how to hamstring them. This was a dangerous method which generally appealed to him. He disliked the idea of hunting them with the *impingo*. This was a small barbed and grooved blade which was thickly coated with poison, and loosely fixed to a shaft which broke away soon after impact. The poison was a mixture of atropine, derived from the seeds of *Datura stramonium*, and septic poisons obtained from specially decomposed cadavers. An elephant seldom received enough of the former to cause death, which would be fairly quick, but more often succumbed to the latter, many days later, after an acute attack of septicaemia. It was a form of hunting alien to the Zulu nature and, without a doubt, imported from the Bushmen, but never put to much use. Certainly Shaka would not hear of it and regarded it as unmanly.

At dawn Shaka and his hunters manned all posts, as did also all the men who were detailed to guard the river banks up to the position occupied by Shaka's receiving line, which would be the only stretch in which game would be allowed to cross. The driving line, twenty miles above the confluence, stretching from river to river, had also been occupied the previous evening, and started the drive downwards towards Shaka at the first break of dawn, with a following wind. This line, marching through open bush country at ten- to twenty-pace intervals between the men, soon undulated, but was corrected from time to time by headmen when the line swept over low-lying hills and ridges, which enabled observers from there to give directions. As the rivers converged, the intervals between files shortened. All the time this driving or beating line made as much noise as possible.

It was quite a considerable time after sunrise before the first faint dust clouds in the distance indicated the approach of stampeding game. The first animals to come into view were elephants, which travel far and fast once they are fully alarmed. They formed the vanguard and were followed by a few giraffe. That is all that could be seen at first. Some dust clouds led to the rivers higher up, but could be seen to recoil inland as the animals were frightened away by the guards posted there to prevent any premature crossings.

Most of the elephants zigzagged from river to river, uncertain which direction to take, but one troop came on straight towards the waiting hunters. Leading it was a tuskless old cow followed by younger ones with calves in all stages of development, whilst the young and mature bulls formed a mixed rearguard. They all halted for a brief drink in the river and then crossed over to the first and massive fence. The old cow leader regarded this new structure suspiciously and tried to find a way around it, but in vain. She sniffed at one of the apparent causeways with extended trunk and drew back in alarm. Then she walked along the fence, and finding a less massive-looking section, she tore away some of the trees and branches forming it, and then walked through followed by the rest of the troop.

Shaka on the top of the ridge expressed his admiration for the sagacity of the leader. 'Mamo! The old granny has the brains of a man and has at least saved one of her children.' After questing along the second or light screening fence the leader showed a marked dislike for the inviting runways, and suddenly crashed through the fence away from these and headed for the ridge, thus by-passing the hunters who guarded the passageways. As soon as it became evident which causeway over the ridge she was heading for, Shaka and his hunters raced there to intercept the troop. The elephants, now having got the scent of the hunters who were screened by the second fence, moved in fast alarm, trumpeting as they went. It is suicidal to try to cut into a line of elephants retreating in close single file. It is, however, a reasonable hazard to attack the last one in the line as it labours up a steep declivity. Some extra bold, if not foolhardy, hunters will try to rush in for a cut if the next following elephant is a spear's throw (fifty yards) behind. Even then he must be very agile to get in a hamstring blow on the elephant just passing him, and jump to safety before the following one is within reach of him with its trunk.

Shaka and his hunters reached the causeway just ahead of the leading cow and took cover behind the flanking fence near the

many openings left for attack and escape. From here they observed
the great animals laboriously lumbering past up the steep declivity almost within touching distance. As the last elephant – a big
bull – entered the defile at a speed now regulated by the slow-
moving leading files, it was immediately set upon from both sides
as its hindquarters came abreast of the lurking hunters. They
darted in with their tomahawk-like axes and inflicted deep gashes
at the knee and heel tendons and succeeded in severing these.
The bull was brought to a halt, trumpeting with rage, and staggered around to get at its assailants with its trunk lashing its sides
like a death-flail. The handicapped elephant was now, however, no
match for its nimble adversaries, who darted about inflicting gash
after gash into its hind legs, whilst an observer kept watch to
warn them of the approach of any other elephant from behind.

No sooner had the first elephant, that is, the last one in the line,
been incapacitated, than the one immediately preceding it was
likewise attacked from the ambush of the flanking fence. And so
the same manoeuvre was repeated all along the line. But things did
not always run as smoothly as this; for quite frequently the elephant preceding the one which was attacked would swing around
to the rescue of its comrade on hearing the agonized and angry
trumpeting, and it was a waste of time to hurl even the heaviest
spears at its sides, for all the effect this would have within any
useful time.

When it was Shaka's turn to try his luck on the rearmost
unwounded elephant – also a big bull – he bounded in with
savage glee and, with a rather heavier axe than those ordinarily
used, inflicted a terrific and crippling blow on the most vulnerable
spot on the hind leg. His companions had been instructed to
stand by, but not to join in except in case of an emergency. The
big bull trumpeted and, squealing with rage, turned quicker than
might have been expected, lashing from side to side with its
trunk. Shaka nimbly stuck to its heels and, with another mighty
blow, severed the tendon of the other leg and brought the elephant to its haunches. With demoniacal fury it tore at the branches of the fence on either side of it and, using one of them as a
flail, only just failed from striking Shaka a mortal blow with it.

As he staggered away from the sweeping brush he had received from the light ends of the branch, death swept down silently on him in the shape of the bull immediately in front of the one he had attacked, and which now came bearing down to the assistance of its stricken mate. A charging African elephant is an awe-inspiring sight. With the enormous ears held at right-angles to the body it presents a tip-to-toe frontal span of nine to ten feet and, with its upraised trunk towering over the twelve-foot-high body and sweeping tusks, it is a living engine of death and destruction.

It was in this moment of his direst need that two hunter warriors unflinchingly stepped into the path of the oncoming death with the characteristic and amazing loyalty of the Zulu to his chief. From the right and, from the left, just in the nick of time, they challenged the storming monster with upraised axes. They each inflicted a deep but totally ineffective gash, before one was knocked down and mortally crushed; the other was lifted on high with an encircling trunk around his waist, and then violently hurled to the ground as the elephant came to a stop. This gave Shaka sufficient time to get clear and, as the bull proceeded to trample the prostrate hunter into the ground, Shaka and another rushed on it from behind and hacked through its tendons, reducing it to the same state as its mate which it had valiantly tried to rescue.

Some five or six of the last elephants in the line had thus been hamstrung and left to their fate by the rest of the troop. No attempt as yet was made to kill the crippled giants, as this involved much work, and their trumpeting was needed to attract the more bellicose single, or outcast bulls, which would presently be driven along. These single bulls were the biggest tuskers and, therefore, the most desirable. The hunters, therefore, resumed their stand behind the fence flanking the defile, after first removing the remains of the two men who had sacrificed their lives. As Shaka looked at the mangled bodies he exclaimed sorrowfully: 'They were the bravest of the brave to throw themselves into the path of that running mountain. But for them I would be just such a shapeless thing now. I can but reward their kraals now and give a sacrifice to the spirits of their ancestors and mine.'

Several times again Shaka joined in the fray when a great lone tusker tried to pass through one or other of the two main defiles. It exhilarated him to join battle with these monsters, but as they were at the disadvantage of labouring up a thirty-degree incline they were almost invariably hamstrung.

Once again Shaka nearly lost his life. A vicious rhino was signalled. When it was lumbering up the steepest part of the defile Shaka rushed through one of the apertures in the flanking fence and delivered a blow at its heel tendon and the huge animal subsided on its haunches with an angry squeal. Shaka was exultant, but failed to take into account that the rhino was slowly slewing around; suddenly it catapulted itself down-hill, and at him. Only his panther-like agility saved him from destruction as the mass of vengeance swept past him down the defile, to receive one heavy *isipapa* hurling spear after the other from those hunters armed with that weapon. Bleeding profusely from lung and liver wounds inflicted by half a dozen heavy blades, the rhino finally collapsed.

Some 200 buffalo splashed through the river led by the big bulls. The younger bulls, mixed with cows and calves of various ages, followed. Arriving at the first fence, the leaders stopped and regarded it with suspicion, whilst the rest of the herd formed up on either side, horn to horn, into a single rank with a broad front. With heads thrown high in a challenging gesture their statuesque immobility presented an imposing sight. Some of the hunters, who guarded the river bank above and below the crossing, now crept forward along the edge of the reeds lining the river. As the buffalo caught their scent coming down-wind from behind, they became uneasy, whereupon the hunters raised a mighty shout and stampeded the whole herd, which went crashing through the passages, through any openings they could find in the first and then the second fence. The waiting spearmen, who were more or less safely posted behind the fences lining the passages and runways, hurled their heavy *isipapa* spears into the sides of the passing animals over embrasures or large loop-holes in the lining fences. Separated as they were by the width of the fences only from the running animals, the spears were very effective at such a close range. Many buffalo went headlong into the game pits situated in the passages of the first heavy fence. Sometimes two of them would be trapped in one pit before their bodies provided a causeway for the following ones.

The casualties were not all on one side, however. Many wounded buffalo became fierce and, if a waiting spearman betrayed his presence through incautious movements at the openings in the branches, an infuriated animal would turn and crash through to get at him. Unless the spearman could instantly dive under the cover of massive branches which might be fortuitously available, nothing would save him from being knocked down, albeit with his shield covering him. Even so, he would be fortunate to escape goring, and generally only did so if his comrades could quickly come to his aid and stab the buffalo through the heart, or divert the attack on to themselves, until one of them succeeded in inflicting a mortal injury.

It was dangerous and exciting, and entirely after Shaka's own heart. In vain the master of the hunt and Mgobozi pleaded with him to keep out of it. Shaka took up his position at a favoured spot behind a flanking fence forming one side of a narrow passage or corridor and, after several full or partial successes, he must have relaxed his care, for when another bull was about to pass he betrayed his position by some slight movement, and instantly the great bulk swung around and thrust its head through the fence at him. For one second or so they stared at each other, almost face against face, each spellbound by the other's apparition. In that time Mgobozi thrust his shield between the two, and the Watcher, with his club ever at the ready, delivered a mighty stroke on the bull's head. It dropped silently on its knees and Shaka jumped away sideways. Then, in spite of another blow of the club on its shoulder, the bull rose and charged at the Fasimba spear carriers, hurling Mgobozi, shield and all, sideways. The buffalo knocked them over like ninepins – the brunt of the blow being usually caught on the shield, under which the warriors fell. One warrior it caught low and tossed him into a thorn tree.

All frontal thrusts with spears were useless, as the charging animal's head, with the horn-plated forehead, was held too low to allow of any thrusts into its chest. As it turned to gore a warrior lying under his shield, Shaka, Mgobozi and other warriors transfixed it from both sides, whilst the Watcher broke one of its hind legs with his long-handled club. Even then, with impaired mobility, and with vitality ebbing from spurting lung wounds, it took some killing. Two Fasimba warriors were dead or dying, and others battered about and bruised.

'Hau! That was a bull,' said Shaka admiringly in an undertone as he wiped the sweat from his forehead. 'What a fight!'

'It has cost two of my "boys",' replied Mgobozi, *sotto voce*. 'If they want to fight animals, why not tackle lions and leopards, which are our natural enemies?'

'Lions it shall be, Mgobozi, and plenty of them,' exclaimed Shaka gleefully.

The game now passing were mostly the great antelopes. The huge, good-natured eland were speared without any resistance. The wildebeest showed fight, and the sable and roan antelopes were not to be trifled with. Giraffe, aptly known as *Indlulamiti* (Those who exceed the trees), were scarce even at that time and only a couple were bagged – one in a game pit, and one by spears. Zebra contributed a heavy toll, but only if they could be driven through the runways or passages or through the defiles. Their only defence lay in speed. Innumerable koodoo and waterbuck fell; only the males possess horns, and even so do not fight against man.

Hundreds of lesser antelopes, such as impala and bushbuck, were slain. The wild pig refused to be driven across the river and broke back from the reed-covered banks through the lines of the driving hunters, inflicting casualties as they did so. Here they met the parties in charge of the dogs which were held in reserve for the specific purpose of rounding up wounded game which had got away with one or more valuable spears or spearheads. These dog-parties had some tough battles with doughty old boars which had doubled back, or equally fierce sows defending their young.

The lions and leopards were amongst the last arrivals, being preceded by single jackals, wild or hunting dogs in packs, and lone hyaenas. The three latter species ran the gauntlet at a heavy price.

The leopards came singly, in silent, sullen resentment. Few escaped, but neither did the hunters remain scatheless, for repeatedly a wounded leopard would turn and fly at its assailants over the breast-high embrasures. At other times they would succeed in clearing the passages, only to be met by a semicircle of hunters armed with an assortment of throwing spears and protective shields.

Once a leopard decided on its victim nothing but death would divert it from the object of its attack. In this way it differs from a charging lion, which can be diverted. Finally the claw-work of a leopard is horribly swift and efficient, and unless the wounds are immediately treated, the victim almost invariably succumbs to acute septicaemia within a few days. This is due to the cadaver poisons (staphylococcus and streptococcus) which are always present in a virulent form on the inner sides of the retractable claws of leopards and lions, which, contrary to popular opinion, will eat the most decomposed cadavers if no fresh kill is available.

Then came the lions. Three prides of them. They were annoyed and restless. Half a dozen times and more that day they had been forced to make an undignified retreat before the advancing driving line, and loss of dignity is resented by all cats.

Shaka, with his group, which was now augmented by some specially chosen hunters, manned the outside wall of one of the runways leading from the first fence into the big enclosure formed by this and the second fence. A lookout posted above Shaka in a tree kept the group advised of all movements. Shaka watched his chance opposite one of the embrasures and presently a large male came stalking through the runway. Shaka with spear poised and partly thrust through the leafy branch covering the breast-high embrasure, waited until it was opposite him, only a few feet away, and then sped his heavy weapon into the lion a few inches behind the shoulder blade. It was a mortal wound, but with a low grunt the lion bounded forward, clearing the exit of the runway and, partly turning round, collapsed with a moan.

Other lions passed through the runways, many of them more or less wounded, and still others took cover in the funnels and refused to proceed until hunters of the beating line drove them through with shouts. The net result was that the large open space between the first and second fences presently contained a number of wounded and unwounded lions, as the runways of the second fence had been manned by hunters to prevent all egress. All the lions were virtually kraaled (corralled) and a series of fights started similar to those in a Roman arena, but with this big difference that there were no spectators sitting around in gloating safety, and the Zulu Caesar was in the arena himself to share all the dangers of the forthcoming combats.

The dogs were now brought up to follow all the wounded game which had escaped with spears in their bodies. The hamstrung elephants had been dispatched before this, by having the arteries of their hind legs opened, as any attempts to kill them with thrusts into the heart would have courted the death-dealing danger of their trunks. The elephants in the pits were treated in the same way. All other game in the pits were killed with spears.

It may be here mentioned that some eight years later Henry Francis Fynn recorded the killing of forty-eight elephants in a single hunt by Shaka and his warriors in a great national drive organized by the Zulu King. Massed spearing attacks by regiments were then apparently made after the elephants were surrounded.

Then the cutting up began, and the drying of the strips of meat on a framework over a low fire, in order to preserve and lighten it for transport. More than three-quarters of the hunters were engaged in this task, whilst at the same time toasting on spits of wood the livers and hearts of the game. So great a number had been killed that the customary distribution was dispensed with, and all the meat was pooled and afterwards distributed on the basis of carrying capacity. The honours of the killing were, however, correctly distributed by the master of the hunt and his deputies, and, naturally, any claims which the successful killers made for special tit-bits from the game they had bagged were duly honoured. Shaka maintained, however, that the driving and cornering parties had to be equally considered, and that everything should therefore be pooled.

The elephant tusks were all claimed by Shaka as King, in compensation of which he paid out in cattle. Leopard skins could never be claimed by commoners, as these were the tribute of the chief, but an ox or cow had to be given as compensation to the one who had secured the skin.

Hippopotami were not hunted by the Zulus in Shaka's days as they did not eat the meat; they likened it to pork, which they also eschewed. The exception was if these animals interfered with their fields, when they were destroyed but not eaten.

Next day after a night of feasting, Shaka returned to the Royal residence at Bulawayo and covered the forty-five miles there by the afternoon.

Nandi gave him an especially warm welcome as she said her spirit had been greatly worried, and she was thankful for his safe return. Shaka chaffed her affectionately and likened her to an anxious hen constantly worrying that a hawk might fly away with its chicken, even though it was now fully grown.

'Yes, you have outgrown all the other chickens, and are a veritable ostrich now.'

'And still, my mother, you fear a hawk will get me?'

'I like not your new Induna (Major-domo) of the Royal kraal. He is too polite and smooth and slippery, and reminds me of a poisonous snake, the way he glides about noiselessly. Some day he will strike you in the back when you least expect it. And Pampata thinks as I do.'

'Hau! Mame, what makes you dislike Mbopa, son of Sitayi, of the Gazini (Blood) clan? He is a most efficient personal councillor, and administrator of the kraal, and a man of interesting conversation.'

'His clan name is "Blood", and I see blood, and it is not his, but yours. Kill him now, this very moment.'

But although Pampata shared Nandi's fears and said so, Shaka laughed at them.

CHAPTER 18

The Tembu War - The new Bulawayo - Shaka's testudo - Order restored in Natal - Mzilikazi's treachery

IN the winter of 1820 Shaka sent envoys west of the Buffalo river to Ngoza, paramount chief of the Tembus, conqueror of the Kuzes, Mbatas, Sitoles, Ntuli, Bele and others, saying: 'Let us, the mighty ones, unite our forces and rule the world in peace.' Ngoza summoned to him one Sigwegwe, a very bold man, and ordered him, 'Go to Shaka and tell him to make ready his spears. And as a sign take a reed and set it up before him.'

The purport of this sign was that even the bending reed could stand up before the King of the Zulus; it was an insulting declaration of war.

Shaka ordered that the messenger be supplied with all the beer he could consume and three fat oxen; one for immediate food and two as a present to take home. Then he told Sigwegwe: 'Go back to Ngoza and tell him to await me on the new moon. "He-who-calls-and-expects-response" invited him, but he spurned the offer. When, therefore, the new moon is visible, let him understand it is not the moon he sees, but – Shaka.'

When Sigwegwe got back to Ngoza he said: 'Here I am bearing him (the enemy) on my back,' which metaphor was as unmistakable to Ngoza as was the reed challenge to Shaka. So he sent an urgent message to the Cunu chief, Macingwane, bidding him to guard the lower fords of the Buffalo river while he (Ngoza) barred the way above, at Mount Hlazakazi. All the tribal cattle, with the women and children, were sent into hiding in the bush on the right bank of the Lower Buffalo river in the Cunu area.

The Zulu army appears to have been divided into two divisions so as to tackle Ngoza's Tembus on both their flanks. One division took the lower route and passed through the Cunu country. The Cunus, who had undertaken to guard the fords, beating a corresponding retreat as the Zulus advanced, until at last they found themselves well beyond the Tugela river and out of the Zulus' present range of action. For the first time Shaka remained an interested spectator on one of the spurs of the towering Qudeni Range, probably in order to be able the better to follow the progress of the two divisions.

The object aimed at by this division of the Zulu army was no doubt to prevent the escape of Ngoza by any back door in case of rout. Strategically the plan had its risks as well as gains. It chanced to bring the lower division straight on to the whole unguarded multitude of Tembu women, children and stock, carefully concealed within the Buffalo river bush. The great mass of these were either killed or captured. It left the other or upper division, which had taken the route by the Esipezi mountain and crossed the Buffalo at Hlazakazi hill, to confront alone the whole combined Tembu and allied forces. The result of this was that although the Zulus succeeded in forcing the Buffalo river, in the stand-up fight which ensued about the Tembu capital, they were heavily repulsed and forced back again across the Buffalo river. Only the superb discipline of the Zulus and the cool generalship of Mdlaka averted complete disaster.

Meanwhile Shaka, from his high position on the Qudeni Range, eagerly scanned the deep, wide and rugged valley of the Buffalo river at his feet. In places it was covered with dense thorn-scrub and in others dotted with mimosa trees. His look swept to the right in the direction of the Tembu capital beyond the western heights of the valley, and to the left, where the other division was operating fully twenty miles away from the first.

Whilst sitting thus, attended only by a small staff, there arrived Jobe, the chief of the Sitoles, and the ally of Ngoza, for his country bordered on the Qudeni Range. He was accompanied by a strong retinue, but neither he nor Shaka, by their dress, indicated a status higher than that of prosperous headmen, and Shaka's stature was not revealed because of the fact that he was squatting on the ground.

After mutual greetings, each, according to invariable Nguni custom, stated whence he hailed and what his purpose. What the two parties declared themselves to be has not been recorded. They sat there on the hill-top for the greater part of the day discussing current events and exchanging candid opinions concerning the recently risen Zulu upstart Shaka, and their hopes and expectations in the present conflict, the while they anxiously peered at the western horizon.

And while they thus conversed, there came to Shaka, in breathless haste and excitement, a messenger saying, 'O King, our army has been beaten from the field and it is even now in full retreat.'

Shaka arose in a towering rage – 'as angry as a lion in a net' – and roared to his attendants to 'kill the babbling fool' – the ill-starred messenger who had at once betrayed his deceit and his disgrace. The unfortunate man stood rooted to the ground and with horror-stricken eyes looked mutely at Shaka as the executioner approached and crushed his skull with a heavy club. Shaka then strode away majestically towards the Buffalo river ford, followed by his attendants. He did not even deign to cast an eye at Jobe, much less to bid him farewell.

'And Jobe's eyes were opened and he knew him; and for the rest of his days he ceased not to praise those protecting ancestral spirits who had saved him from "putting his foot in it".' But Jobe who, with Shaka in his grasp, had suffered his escape, was cursed by Tembu friends evermore; but all his days remained in Shaka's graces.'*

From a considerable distance Shaka could see that violent fighting was in full swing at the ford where Mdlaka had halted the victorious progress of Ngoza's forces. He was in a furious mood, all the more so because the ever cautious Mdlaka had counselled against the dividing of the army into two widely separated divisions. If the lower division drew a blank his gamble would have failed and the results of the day would be humiliating.

* Bryant, op. cit.

Messengers then arrived from the lower division to announce that this division, commanded by Nzobo (Dambuza) assisted by Ndlela, had been entirely successful in capturing and getting away with all the Tembu cattle, and had killed or secured most of their women and children. Shaka was considerably mollified, for it justified the losses which Mdlaka's upper division had suffered, especially as the latter now appeared to be holding its own on the narrow front presented by the ford.

In the late afternoon Ngoza broke off the battle and retired to his capital, and the Zulus too fell back to effect a reunion with the lower division, and thus to safeguard the booty the latter had captured. This reunion took place near the Etaleni (Flat Top) hill in the present Nkandla Magistracy. It was here next morning that Shaka ordered the ferreting out and trial of all shirkers and cowards. Any warrior who could not produce a fallen enemy's assegai immediately became suspect and had to bring forth evidence to prove that he had not shirked.

Ultimately some fifty luckless warriors were found guilty and ordered to be executed in full view of the whole army.*

The captured Tembu women and children were now led past in a review. Shaka knew that, with the women and cattle in his possession, many of their menfolk would presently follow them, and if not he would find them husbands. In this way they would be absorbed by the rapidly growing nation he was creating, and the Tembus were especially valuable to him, as they, like the Zulus, were true Ntungwa Ngunis.

The booty in cattle was great, but not to be compared with that obtained from the Ndwandwes in the previous year.

Ngoza's costly victory did not deceive him, and knowing that he would not be so fortunate in a second encounter with Shaka, he decided to emigrate. The movements of the Tembus, Mbatas and Kuzes were accompanied by the atrocities associated with such migrations.

As Ngoza and his Tembus had migrated, there was no cause for Shaka to renew hostilities against a rapidly receding foe. He therefore decided to build a new capital more in keeping with the

* Cf. Caesar's decimation of certain legions.

King of Greater Zululand. He chose a place on the southern slopes of the lower Umhlatuze valley, and in this broad expanse of undulating parklands dotted with mimosa (acacia) trees the new capital was built, and like the first was also named Bulawayo (The Place of Killing).

'The new capital might well be likened to a gigantic platter, resting on a broad and gentle slope (to the right of the present Eshowe-Empangeni road, some seventeen miles distant from the former, and with an umkiwane (wild fig) tree near where the entrance used to be) – an inclined, circular plain a mile in width, surrounded by a palisade and dotted within with 1500 dwellings (huts), themselves encompassing a central open cattlefold encircled by another palisade. The upper segment of the circle was further hedged around to form the private quarters sacred to the King and his multitude of serving girls. The huts along each flank were garrisoned by a couple of thousand of celibate warriors; the chief entrance to the whole being a broad opening at the lowest end of the outer palisade, through which passed in and out both men and cattle. There were also two small private exits in the King's sacred section, each guarded by a sentry. One was for the sole use of the King and the other for his girls. The King also had a private entrance into the upper arch of the inner palisade which enclosed the cattle kraal. This entrance was directly opposite the great council hut. The large main entrance was always guarded by a company of guards with several officers in attendance. Mbopa was the major-domo over the whole establishment, within which reigned stringent rules of etiquette and order.'*

There were no sanitary arrangements: scrub areas were specially reserved for this purpose, one for the men and another for the women. These areas were always situated well below the springs and rivulets from which drinking water was drawn. The purpose of toilet paper was served by bunches or pads of soft leaves. At night-time hundreds of hyaenas and jackals would 'clean up' the area and as they roamed far afield to find shelter in the day-time their own droppings were widely distributed, and in turn were dealt with by dung beetles, scavenger ants and the

* Bryant, op. cit.

fierce African sun assisted by wind and rain. In the day-time the carrion crows had the first pick.

The huge cattle-kraal in the heart of the town might have been thought to be insanitary, but was nothing of the kind. With cattle feeding solely on grass, the dung is merely a pulp which is practically odourless and soon dries out, and a cattle-kraal is sweeter than the average horse stable. The dung of cattle fed on the European model with concentrates, turnips, kale and such is a totally different thing and can be very objectionable. This point is specially stressed because Europeans – even most of those living in South Africa – cannot understand why cow-dung is used, even at the present day, to smear frequently the earth-floors of huts and rustic houses, schools and churches. Moreover, where wooden fuel is scarce on the high-veld, cow-dung is made into flat cakes which, when still wet, are slapped on to the stones of stone-wall kraals to dry them quickly. The resulting fires are exactly like those made with peat.

Finally the cattle-kraal acted as a gigantic fly trap, for the flies would lay their eggs in the fresh cow-dung which would be churned into the inches-deep dry manure by countless hooves before the maggots had a chance to develop into flies.

As soon as the new Bulawayo was completed Shaka built a similar kraal, but of much lesser dimensions, for his mother, Nandi. It was situated on the broad, flat summit of a hill three miles south-west of the new Bulawayo. It was almost encircled by the Emateku and Embuzane streams, with the Empongo hill to the east. It was called the Emkindini (Girdle) kraal after the name of her earlier one, which was situated between the Mfule river and present-day Melmoth. This earlier Emkindini was now presided over by her unmarried daughter Nomcoba, Shaka's full sister. It is well to memorize the topography of the new Emkindini kraal, for it was here that, six years later, one of the greatest tragedies recorded in history took place.

For the rest of the year 1820 and up to the first half of 1821, Shaka undertook no military ventures but concentrated on organizing his realm, encouraging settlers or colonists into the empty Ndwandwe country, and other thinly populated areas. During this time he in no way molested any of his neighbours, yet immediately after the 1821 harvest, about May or June, the powerful Cunu tribe, the defaulting allies of the Tembus, decided to migrate *en masse*, drawing another broad trail (the third), of blood and ruin and inexpressible miseries, across the whole face of Natal from the Tugela river in the north to the Umzimkulu river in the south.

In view of the disturbances caused in Natal by the Cunus, Shaka made a reconnaissance in force along his southern boundary. Crossing the Tugela river, he penetrated a few miles into Natal and skirted the right bank of the river, meeting no opposition until he reached the stronghold of the Pepeta clan, which was situated on the summit of the Opisweni mountain. Solitary and of conspicuous height, its top was formed by a circular, perpendicular escarpment. This was the clan's safe and impregnable retreat whence their chief, Mshika (alias Mapinda), son of Kondlwane, hurled defiance and rocks at every comer. The rocky cliff was scaled by means of a ladder, up which the baskets of foodstuffs were passed and stored on top. With everybody and everything at the top, up went the ladder too. There was a natural supply of water. Shaka looked up at this natural castle and the 'baboons' peering and jeering at him from the top, with considerable interest.

Mdlaka advised him to leave well alone. Mgobozi snorted his contempt of the cliff-dwellers and asked why the Zulu army should take to hunting baboons on inaccessible cliffs. All the commanders were unanimous that the place was impregnable even without defenders. This merely irritated Shaka, until Mgobozi remarked morosely : 'It is rock-rabbits and baboons you need, my Father, and not warriors.' Shaka persisted, and after circling the mountain for the second time found a solution. His discerning eye had discovered the vulnerable point in the ramparts and he forthwith repaired to the camp to carry out the necessary preparations.

Several oxen were slaughtered, but not so much for their meat as their hides, which were immediately cut into long thongs by means of a circular cut starting on the perimeter of the skin and finishing in the centre. This gave a very long thong, an inch wide, which was cut into fifty-foot lengths, and being raw, they were pliable. By means of a stone tied to the end of a thong certain selected warriors were told to practise throwing them over the branches of the highest trees available. Other selected warriors were now ordered to climb up the thongs with their shield and stabbing assegai fixed on their backs. The resulting antics caused much good-natured chaff, especially when Mgobozi remarked that those recruits whom he had likened to baboons now had a chance of showing their merits. The best climbers were selected into a composite force. These, and others, were now formed into dense columns of five, with the shields of the inner files held over their heads and overlapping in Caesar's best *testudo* (tortoise) style; the warriors on the flanks held their shields on their exposed sides, whilst the leading rank held theirs in front – the heads of all being covered by the shields of the three inner files. When they had perfected their drill they were dismissed for the time being.

Lastly, Shaka selected a number of senior *u-dibi* and told them to show the warriors what they could do in the way of climbing trees with and without long thongs, and to practise pulling up the latter by means of light strings. The *u-dibi* entered into this with enthusiasm and excelled themselves.

At dawn next day Shaka made a number of sham, or diversionary, attacks at many different points of the stronghold, especially on the side where the Pepetas were wont to climb up with the aid of their ladder.

In the meantime the real attacking column had long before daylight disappeared from view in the thick bush at the bottom end of a gully which ran from the summit to the base of Opisweni mountain. A sheer drop in the gully, at the level of the cliff which encircled the mountain, appeared to bar any attempt at scaling the stronghold from this side, but well-spaced bushes and trees grew out of one of the precipitous sides of the gully where it formed what would be a waterfall after a heavy rain. The agile *u-dibi* scaled this side under great difficulties, and many a section was only negotiated by throwing weighted strings over branches and trees above, and then pulling up light ropes on these, and finally the substantial rawhide thongs. The overhanging vegetation, and in places the outjutting ledges, screened them completely from all observers on the summit. Ultimately they have several stout thongs securely fixed, and the special climbing-cum-tortoise column, about three companies strong, slowly but surely scaled the almost perpendicular wall and assembled under cover of the bush above. This took time, and the morning was well advanced before they were all up; the while Shaka was distracting the Pepetas elsewhere, and accumulating all the insults the joint ingenuity of the tribe could think of, in addition to the rocks they rolled on the pseudo scaling parties.

The scaling column left the *u-dibi* and a platoon of warriors to guard the thongs in their positions, in case reinforcements should be needed. They now emerged into an open, canyon-like gully, with sheer sides about forty to fifty feet high. The bottom of the canyon was about as wide, and did not rise steeply enough to be used for rolling rocks down it. From side to side the bottom lay on an even plane, which also precluded the rolling of rocks from either side. It was, in fact, an inclined trough with a more or less even bottom. Heavy rocks pushed over the top would fall straight down and remain there without injuring a column advancing up the centre. Throwing stones and javelins could, however, turn the canyon into a death-trap.

No sooner did the Zulu column clear the little bush which obscured it in the lower canyon, than it was observed by some Pepeta women perched on top. The alarm was instantly given and Mshika, the Pepeta chief, rushed his warriors, and every woman and child capable of throwing stones, to the brow of the cliffs on either side of the canyon. The Zulus, some 300 strong, immediately formed their *testudo*, or tortoise, exactly as they had been shown on the previous day, and stolidly moved forward covered by their shields, looking like a squared-off armadillo rather than a tortoise. The Zulus, however, called it *Isongololo lika Shaka* (Shaka's millipede).

A hail of throwing spears, clubs and stones – the latter varying from the size of a fist to half a brick – descended on the 'milli-pede', whose 600 feet, however, moved forward with a stoical rhythm. Soon, however, the feet became less, as one warrior after another was disabled and left lying on the ground, where he would be finished off in the open without any protection, by stoning from the cliffs in the old Biblical way. For a fallen war-rior's shield had to be picked up by the nearest file and held on high, to avoid any gaps in the roof and the walls formed by the shields.

Every one of the Pepeta tribe, male and female, who could throw a stone joined in the fray from both sides of the canyon cliffs. As the tribe mustered about 1000 souls the effective throw-ing strength must have been well over 700. Nothing but this *testudo* formation would have permitted the Zulu column to pass through this ordeal in strength. On swept the millipede at a steady walking pace, regardless of the showers of the variegated missiles. It reached the top end of the canyon with a loss of about one-sixth of its strength, and there it was met by some 200 Pepeta warriors, drawn up many lines deep from one wall to the other. The Zulu column pushed its way through them slowly, but surely, like a slow-motion battering-ram, and as they burst through to the open summit the Pepeta ranks were split in twain. Their desperate valour did not offset their poor training and lack of experience, and as the Zulus also had an advantage in numbers, organized resistance was soon at an end. A general *sauve qui peut* ensued, but whither? The great majority fled in terror-stricken blindness in every direction, pursued by the enraged Zulus, for most of them had received some kind of knock. But every direction on this summit ended in a 200-foot drop.

'There they come,' said Shaka with a sardonic smile, as scream-ing women and children arrived at the top of the cliff facing him, with the pursuing Zulus close behind them. Some faced the blood-dripping spears, but the majority jumped and went hurtling to their doom, shrieking all the way down, till a sickening thud brought a sudden silence.

The conquest of the Opisweni stronghold added immensely to the prestige of Shaka, and nothing hereafter appeared impossible to the Zulu arms. But the fact that hundreds of men, women and children met their deaths by jumping over the precipices of this mountain, rather than face the Zulu assegais, originated the prevalent myth that Shaka habitually killed people, and indeed whole tribes in this way. Here lies the origin of the fantastic tales one hears about nearly every precipice and waterfall in Zululand and the greater part of Natal and Pondoland. It is even stated that Shaka frequently used this method of execution at his three residential Royal kraals – the old and the new Bulawayo, and Dukazu. A study of the topography surrounding these old sites will reveal that the execution parties, and the supposedly gloating Shaka, would have been compelled to march from fifteen to twenty-five miles to find any cliff or waterfall which could have been used for such a purpose. There is not the slightest evidence that Shaka ever had a single individual executed by precipitation over a cliff or waterfall.

Shaka did not penetrate any farther into Natal in this year 1821, but returned to Zululand to continue the consolidation of his country and the expansion of the army, whilst Ngoza and Macingwane continued their dreadful devastations in the south.

In the meantime bloody trails of destruction had been inaugurated beyond the northern boundaries of Zululand too by Soshangane, the former generalissimo of the Ndwandwes, Zwangendaba his second in command, and Nxaba, a more junior officer. After the total defeat of the Ndwandwes each of these men had gathered a band of freebooters around him, which was daily augmented by freelances and survivors of clans which had been broken up by this trio. In the west, the present-day Free State was being ravaged by the hordes of Mpangazita's Hlubis, and Mantatisi's Batlokwas. The only tranquil island enjoying the benefits of ordered government in a sea of unrest or chaos, was Shaka's Greater Zululand. For from the Limpopo river in the north to the Orange and St Johns rivers in the south, and from the Kalahari desert in the west to the Indian Ocean in the east, there was no peace and security except in Shaka's domain.

By the end of 1821 Shaka had completed the unification and consolidation of the Zulu homeland, from the Pongola river in the north to the Tugela river in the south, from the Indian Ocean in the east to the Buffalo river in the west – in all, about 11,500 square miles of territory. It was this central core of Zululand which was to enable him, between 1822 and 1826, to extend his actual power over territory twenty times as extensive and to cast his 'shadow' far beyond even those limits. His rise to power had been more rapid than Napoleon's, an advantage due less to superior genius than to the absence of interference; he had, no doubt, ambitious generals to bridle, but no treacherous politicians.

In the early winter of 1822 he decided to end the chaotic conditions prevailing in Natal as a result of the devastations caused by Ngoza's Tembus, and Macingwane's Cunus, and to bring to book Matiwane, the chief of the Ngwanes. The latter, it will be remembered, had pioneered the first grisly devastation through northern Natal in 1818, and had firmly established himself as a robber-baron under the shadow of the Drakensberg at the headwaters of the Tugela river, in the present Bergville district.

The Zulu army now numbered about 20,000, due to Shaka's colonization methods, and the constant influx of refugees and displaced persons who streamed into Zululand from the welter of chaos prevailing outside its borders.

So to Mdlaka Shaka gave a division numbering some seven regiments, of approximately 7,000 men, with instructions to restore order in Natal.

Simultaneously he gave Mzilikazi his first independent command of two composite regiments, made up largely from Mzilikazi's own Kumalos, and other kindred clans. With these he enjoined him to win his spurs by conducting a cattle-raising raid, and generally showing the Zulu power in the north. 'The objective was the Sutu clan ruled by Ranisi, near the Zulu border in the Transvaal.' The Sutu clans spoke a language quite different from that of the Zulus, and were never considered by them as likely material for incorporation, although Mzilikazi by force of circumstances was later compelled to adopt them. Only a few individual Sutus were ever settled in Zululand. Before leaving on this expedition Shaka invited Mzilikazi to share some beer and snuff with him. Addressing him, he said:

'Son of Mashobane, you are a man after my own mind and I will miss you when you are away, for always our talks have given me a sweet heart. You have proved yourself to be a capable general under my own command, but the time has arrived when you must act on your own initiative, of which you have plenty. This is necessary in order that you may win your own renown, and by conquering the north become my right hand there, and a great chief whose glory will not lessen, but add to mine. Still, I shall miss you sorely, my son.' Mzilikazi responded: 'I thank you, my Father, for your words, which sweeten my heart and put a stone into my stomach' (Zulu saying which means to give strength and courage).

Shaka then gave him a new war-dress almost as resplendent as Shaka's own, but instead of the single blue crane's feather, eighteen inches long, which Shaka wore with a circlet of scarlet feathers from the red loury, Mzilikazi was given an imposing plume of white ostrich feathers; this contrasted strongly with Shaka's simple headgear, and helped to offset the difference in stature between them, for although Mzilikazi was rather tall, he was inches shorter than the Zulu king.

They both now repaired to the parade ground, where Mzilikazi's two regiments were drawn up. Mbopa followed them, carrying a war-shield, an axe and an assegai. Addressing the warriors, Shaka bade them look well after their commander. 'Be you his shield like this new one I now present him with, and his spear like this bright and sharp weapon which goes with it,' and Shaka took the shield and spear Mbopa was carrying and handed them to Mzilikazi. They were magnificent specimens – the shield a glossy white with a single black spot in the middle; it differed only from Shaka's in the larger size of the spot, and in being slightly shorter to conform with the rule that a war-shield must measure from the mouth to the toes of the owner. The spear was an extra large stabbing assegai, which glinted ominously.

'*Bayete! Ndabezita!*' ('Thy will be done, Illustrious Sir!') acknowledged Mzilikazi, and the regiments echoed his thanks with a thundering '*Bayete!*'

Then Shaka took from Mbopa the ivory-handled axe which

had been well burnished and polished and glittered in the sun. It was the smaller of the two which Shaka had taken from the Mad Giant after slaying him in the renowned single combat.*

Holding the axe on high, Shaka told the regiments: 'Behold this axe. It is one of my most cherished possessions. I present it now to my "Child", as a token of my love for him, and as an emblem of his authority.'

'*Bayete! Ndabezita!*' responded Mzilikazi, and again the regiments roared '*Bayete!*', for Mzilikazi was very popular.

And so Mzilikazi, 'The Great Trail', left Shaka 'through a pleasant gate'. His future career became indeed a great trail. His name does not signify 'A trail of Blood' as is erroneously supposed: it would then have been spelt *Mziligazi*, with the soft 'g' in place of the hard 'k'.

Meanwhile Mdlaka had crossed the Tugela river with his division and headed south through the Natal midlands, questing after the Cunus led by Macingwane. His final raid had taken him down into the fertile plain of Kwa Cekdane (Dronkvlei), rich in the corn and cattle of the Nxasane. And it was here, after a massacre of the Nxasane, that Mdlaka caught Macingwane. Abandoning his conquest and loot, that chief retreated to the forested Ntsikeni hill country, where the Zulu general caught up with him, massacred his troops, and killed or captured the women and children. A number of men escaped, including Macingwane and his sons, Mfusi and Pakade. But no way was now open to these fugitives who decided to return in their tracks and rely upon Shaka's justice while hoping for his mercy. On the way, however, the defeated chief vanished.

Mdlaka, having meted out justice in the south of Natal, collected all the waifs and strays he could lay his hands on, and sent them under a strong guard to Zululand. He then turned northwards along the foot of the Drakensberg, his objective being

*It is now to be seen in the museum of that other Bulawayo, which was founded by Mzilikazi in memory of Shaka, 1000 miles from Zululand, and is the present capital of the province of Matabeleland in Southern Rhodesia.

Matiwane and his Ngwanes, who four years earlier had settled in the present district of Bergville, with their rear and flanks securely guarded by the towering, and now in winter, snow-clad mountains.

Their front was fairly well protected by the Tugela and Lambonja rivers, from which side alone they expected an attack, and in an emergency felt that they could escape via the Umhlwazini and Ndidimeni rivers, over the Drakensberg into present-day Basutoland. Here there were narrow passes which could easily be held by a resolute rearguard, whilst the women, children and stock were taken to safety. No doubt Matiwane made an excellent choice, but he overlooked the possibility that the Zulus would come by a very circuitous route from the extreme south of Natal.

The Zulu army had travelled via Tabamhlope (White Mountain) and Emangweni, and behind Arthur's Seat. Worse still, one arm had travelled even closer to the little Drakensberg, and had crossed over the long rising ridge which leads up to the Esiqotsheni (Rockery), and was even now streaming into the upper Magangangozi valley, to head off any retreat up the Lambonja river to the pass over the main Drakensberg.

With only their bare lives did the Ngwanes escape. Their subsequent wanderings and fate have already been described in the gruesome events related in Chapter 11.

Mdlaka having accomplished his mission returned to Zululand by the direct route (via Bergville, Ladysmith and Pomeroy). He brought back a multitude of cattle, and many captured women and children, who were settled throughout the realm and given more cattle to make a fresh start in life. As they were later joined by their menfolk, or found husbands, they settled down to a life of peace, which for a score of years was denied to most living outside the confines of Zululand.

Meanwhile, Shaka's other general, Mzilikazi, had marched to his own Royal kraal, for he had been reinstated in the chieftaincy of the Kumalos, of which he had been robbed by Zwide. This kraal, in the direct line of his route, lay in the upper Sikwebezi valley, on the borders of the present magisterial districts of

Nongoma and Vryheid, and within his territory lay the great natural stronghold of the afforested hill known as the Entubeni (the Pass), and the great Ngome forest. Arriving at his kraal in command of two regiments greatly added to his prestige. After attending to his personal affairs for a day, Mzilikazi continued on his northward march. Nobody knew the objective except he himself, and his chief of staff, a lesson which he had thoroughly learnt from Shaka. 'Consequently his whole campaign proved eminently successful and the loot was great. So great, indeed, was it that Mzilikazi felt he could retain a goodly quantum of the proceeds without his Royal master being one whit the wiser. This was a most disastrous error of judgement; for never yet had anyone caught the Zulu King sleeping. Shaka's intelligence department was supremely efficient, and soon laid all the facts before him.'

Shaka was taken aback, but showed no anger, an extraordinary manifestation of his liking and indulgence towards Mzilikazi. For to raise Satan in a Zulu King's breast one had but to tamper with the King's cattle, and all looted cattle were his and had to be accounted for.

Shaka took the lenient course of sending his messengers to Mzilikazi to demand the handing over of the missing cattle. 'To this Mzilikazi replied by impudently cutting off the plumes that waved so proudly above their heads, and sending them back home with no other message than the one which could be implied.'

'Wo!' said Shaka sorrowfully when he saw their shorn plumes, 'Wangi hudela umtwana wami." ('Wo! my child has voided its diarrhoea on me!') Shaka's councillors were amazed that he took this insult so quietly, for ordinarily he would have been in a great rage. They were even more astonished when he dispatched the punitive force – the Izimpohlo Brigade – with the injunction to bring Mzilikazi to him unharmed.

Mzilikazi awaited the Izimpohlo in his forest-mountain stronghold and repulsed them severely with rock-rolling and other means, and they had to report back to Shaka empty-handed. The whole affair appears to have been as half-hearted as Shaka's order, and instead of looking for cowards he appeared to be almost pleased, and told the Izimpohlo that it served them right, and they deserved the drubbing they had received. Still more astonishing is the fact that Shaka let the matter rest there, until early in 1823, when public opinion became inflamed at Mzilikazi's persistent and open flouting of the King's authority, and the Council of State compelled Shaka to act.

'The Young Cockerel is getting over-bold and must have his comb clipped. Let the Belebele Brigade deal with him,' Shaka ordered.

These old veterans would brook no nonsense, especially from a youngster like Mzilikazi. They made a determined assault on the Entubeni stronghold, but with no better results than their predecessors had achieved. So they sat down and besieged Mzilikazi, meanwhile thinking out other methods. They were saved the trouble of much thought, however, by a certain Kumalo, Nzeni by name, who harboured an old grudge against Mzilikazi and betrayed the stronghold to the Zulus. They were able to surprise the rebel from the rear; a bloody engagement followed and only Mzilikazi and about 300 of his young men escaped, together with many women and children. They were joined by other members of their tribe who had been hiding in the Ngome forest and were left unmolested by the Belebele, whose commanding officer apparently had orders to extend clemency where it was possible. Mzilikazi led the remnant of his people northward without interference from the Zulus, and began upon his career of conquering inner Africa and building there a new Empire, that of the Matabele.

Mzilikazi's first act on his northward flight was to fall on the small Nyoka clan, which, as a tributary to the Zulus, had sought to detain him. He annihilated or scattered them, and taking all their cattle headed steadily north. Next he passed through the territory of the Sutu clans in the Eastern Transvaal, capturing their women, impressing their young men into his own service, leaving nothing behind him but a long, black and bloody trail of conflagration, massacre and desolation. At first he therefore did not differ from the southern bloodthirsty freebooters.

It would fill a book of its own to recount adequately the subsequent history of Mzilikazi, and only a very brief summary can be given here. Suffice it to say that next to Shaka he became the most powerful Nguni potentate and extended his sway over an area even greater than that of his Zulu counterpart; for he left no tribe unconquered between the Vaal river and the Zambezi, between Lake Ngami and Portuguese East Africa – an area covering nearly 500,000 square miles.

As soon as Mzilikazi had established his power he applied Shaka's methods of nation and empire building and ceased to be a blind destroyer. His Kumalos and other Nguni clans closely related to the Zulus, formed the aristocracy and hard core of his Matabele nation, known as the *Abenzansi* or 'Those from the South'. Around them he built up selected members of the conquered tribes of Sutus, Chuanas, Kalangas and others who all, more or less, learned the Zulu language of their conquerors. These were known as the *Abenhla*, or 'Those from the North', and formed the second grade of the Matabele society. A third grade, or class, were known as the *Amahole*, and as the helots of the nation represented the lowest social rung.

After moving his capital to the central, and then to the western, Transvaal, Mzilikazi finally settled in present-day Southern Rhodesia, where he built his last capital and named it, like Shaka's, Bulawayo.

CHAPTER 19

Shaka's Court of Justice at the new Bulawayo

SHAKA certainly felt keenly the defection of Mzilikazi. 'My heart is sore, for was he not my son?' He would recount the excellencies of Mzilikazi, and then like Saul fall into a brooding mood, which brooked ill for other transgressors, but, unlike Saul, he did not hurl his spears at his favourite. For Shaka would not hear of any punitive measures, and indeed issued instructions that all the Kumalos (Mzilikazi's clan) living in Zululand should be treated well, and not hindered if they wished to follow their young chief. On the other hand, he tightened up all his measures by centralizing his authority, and proceeded to weld Greater Zululand into a single, homogeneous nation whose members would proudly call themselves Zulus first, and derogate their clan-name into second place, as a surname or *Isibongo*.

The clans naturally still retained their chieftains, but their power was largely curtailed in favour of the one central authority – Shaka.*

In trying cases, Shaka at this time still conformed with the old Nguni custom in which the chief was the judge, but was assisted by his councillors as assessors. His overpowering personality had, however, secured such dominance over them that they were virtually reduced to a chorus of 'Yes men', who would applaud his every act, even before he asked their opinion, which formality he soon also dispensed with. It was only at military councils that he really still gave a full ear to all the regimental commanders and generals, who jealously guarded this privilege of the army.

Excessive adulation, an obsequious approach, and crawling servility to Shaka were now fostered by Mbopa, his induna or major-domo of the Royal kraal. Two *imbongi*, or court praisers,

* Cf. the unification of Scottish clans by Robert Bruce.

were always present. They frequently shouted a string of praises recounting Shaka's prowess. These were a factual recountal of all his deeds, and how he earned the praise names '*Nodumehlezi*' (Sitting Thunder) and '*Sigidi*' (One Thousand – He who is equal to 1000 warriors).

At the new Bulawayo Shaka's court was held under a huge, spreading fig tree situated in the five-acre yard in front of his Great Council hut. Immediately below this yard was the great inner enclosure, or cattle-kraal, of the new capital, which measured fully half a mile in diameter, and was surrounded by 1500 huts enclosed by the outer palisade, which was a mile in diameter. Great national gatherings, which could not be accommodated in the courtyard, were therefore held in the cattle-kraal, whose upper segment, abutting on the Royal yard, was reserved for Shaka and important guests, who from this higher position commanded a good view of the whole kraal. Here, too, there was a large fig tree which provided shade for the King and his Court on hot days. In the winter Shaka and his councillors sat in the open sunshine a little aside from either of these trees.

Shaka's Court opened early every morning, shortly after sunrise and before breakfast, for he was now a very busy monarch, who held every portfolio in the realm besides being its Chief Justice and *Pontifex Maximus*. These early sessions had the advantage, too, of avoiding the frequent heavy thunderstorms in summer, which generally occurred in the afternoon. On rainy days the outside courts were suspended, and only important cases were tried within the council hut. The agenda for the day was usually arranged by Mbopa assisted by other councillors.

A typical day at the new Bulawayo; the time, late summer. By sunrise a crowd of litigants had collected in the courtyard in front of the big fig tree. There were others closely guarded by warriors. The councillors were already seated underneath the tree in a semicircle around the Royal throne, which consisted of a rolled-up bundle of *induli* rush mats. Beyond them, on either side, stood a group of slayers, or executioners, with massive clubs.

Presently, Shaka, followed by Mbopa, issued from the Great Council hut and with measured, dignified steps approached his 'throne'. A complete hush fell on all the assembly. Shaka was dressed in his resplendent warrior-chief's panoply, but, instead of his big war shield and stabbing assegai, he only carried a little spear with a short handle of dark-red wood made from a freak-coloured *umsimbiti* or iron-wood (*Milletia caffre*). Others say it was made of the *um-ncaka* or chiefs' tree, but that is light red in colour. As Shaka reached an unmarked spot, about midway between his hut and the tree, all the assembled people, without a word of command, rose like one man, with a timing so perfect that they might have been propelled by some centrally controlled mechanism. Then with upraised right hand and in perfect unison, sharp and precise as an explosion, the Royal salute split the morning air. Just that one 'Bayete!' followed by complete immobility till Shaka was seated. Then the assembled people squatted on their haunches and the *imbongi* shouted out strings of praises such as these:

'The Great Elephant who stamped his enemies flat, the Lion of Lions who ate Zwide's sons. Shaka! who cooked Ntombazi in the pot she intended for him. The calf which climbed on top of Ntombazi's hut. The Heaven (Zulu) which struck the Ndwandwes from they knew not whence. Heaven's thunder smote them, and they hear the lowing of their kine no more, for now they low at our Bulawayo only. Shaka! whose millipede ate the Pepetas at Opisweni. The mighty bull who stopped the lowing of a multitude of yearning heifers, and made them chew the cud of contentment. Sigidi! (One Thousand). Nodumehlezi! (Sitting Thunder).'

Mbopa held up his hand, and the *imbongi* ceased. One of the indunas now brought forward the first litigants. They were two Royal herdsmen, each in charge of a large herd in a depopulated area in Natal. Each accused the other of encroaching on his grazing lands, and because of this serious faction fights had occurred amongst their respective herdsmen. Shaka told each of them to delineate the boundaries of his section, and found that there was indeed a considerable overlap in the rival herdsmen's claims. He asked the first one to affirm on oath that justice would be done if his, the herdsman's, boundary award for his own section were granted. The herdsmen solemnly affirmed by his sister (*dadewetu*). Then turning to the other chief herdsman, Shaka received a similar affirmation.

'Good!' said Shaka. 'You will now, each of you, with all your herdsmen and cattle, exchange sections. On your own showing that will leave you both with a considerable empty space between you, and if any members of either party encroach on this they will eat earth. "*Ngitshilo!*" ' ('I have spoken!')

'Heaven thunders wisdom,' acclaimed the councillors in chorus. 'Give your thanks to it!'

'*Baba! Nkosi!*' responded the two litigants with upraised right hand, and withdrew with a dubious look as they puzzled out the implications of this Solomon-like judgement.

The next case was called for by Mbopa. A young married woman and a bachelor were brought up. This was apparent to all, for she was wearing a kilt and the top knot of hair, whilst the man lacked the head-ring which proclaimed the Benedict. These two had been taken in adultery.

'Do you admit your guilt?' Shaka asked them. There was no response.

'Your silence convicts you. You know that death is the penalty. Have you anything to say?'

'What can we say, Baba?' answered the man in a low voice.

'*Nitshilo!*' ('You have said it!') 'Take them away and twist their necks.'

'*Izulu li duma umteto*' (Heaven thunders the law) acclaimed the councillors. With a look of mute resignation the condemned pair were led away to their doom by the slayers, who escorted them beyond the outer palisade of the town to a near-by eminence, and there executed them by breaking their necks, and then crushed their skulls with a blow of the heavy clubs.

A young man was brought up next. It was obvious by his markings that he was a novice in the profession of witch-doctors. Owing to the number of these men who were trying to avoid military service by apprenticing themselves to witch-doctors, Shaka had promulgated a law that all such male apprentices, or novices, must prove their manliness by sleeping outside the shelter of any kraal, and preferably in country badly infested with lions, during the period of their apprenticeship.

When the young man stood before Shaka and was charged with sleeping within the kraal of the witch-doctor he was apprenticed to, which he did not deny, the King's first question was directed to his councillors. 'Where is the witch-doctor who harboured him? Why was he not jointly charged? Am I to be the fool who strikes the tail of a snake instead of its head?'

There was an uneasy shuffling amongst the councillors, and then the boldest one replied. 'Ndabazimbi (Bad Things) is a great and fearful witch-doctor. He eluded the apprehending party by putting them all to sleep.'

'How?'

'Just by looking at them, and surrounding them with smoke.'

'And how did this apprentice come to stay?'

'Ndabazimbi commanded him to surrender himself.'

'So the old hyaena thought it would save its life by sacrificing its tail?'

'Who knows the ways of witch-doctors, my Father!' was the cautious answer.

'I know them,' was the fierce reply, 'and I will not tolerate this defiance of my laws, nor those who fumble in carrying them out. Dispatch this instant the two fleetest companies of warriors "to eat up" Ndabazimbi and his whole kraal, man, woman, child and dog, yea, even the rats in the thatch, and let them rest not, nor come back, till this order is fully carried out. And let no other person leave the Royal kraal till the slayers are well on their way. Kill the novice and bring hither the arresting party which failed in their duty.'

A platoon commander and some half-dozen warriors stepped forward with their shields, but in place of assegais they carried sticks, as it was against the rules of etiquette to carry sharp arms in the Royal presence.

'You received my orders?' Shaka inquired in that low tone which presaged doom.

'Yes, my Father,' the platoon leader replied as spokesman for them all.

'You know the penalty of failure?'

'Yes, O King.'

'Three of your men bear the decorations for slaying in battle. Let them step aside. They will not eat earth today, but will be sent on a hazardous mission from which they will probably not return. But you, the leader, who failed me, and these others, are of no further use to me, and will this day eat earth. You will be granted a warrior's death, for you failed only in the face of witchcraft. I have spoken.'

All the warriors, condemned and semi-reprieved, drew themselves up proudly, and with upraised right hands gave the Royal salute as firmly as if they had received a decoration instead of their doom. '*Bayete!*' (Thy will be done!) And so with firm, martial step, with never a complaint or murmur, they were led away to their respective fates.

Next to appear before the Royal judge was a man accused of disloyalty by another man. The accuser stated his case and the accused was thereupon allowed to cross-examine him and his witnesses and to bring forward his own. Shaka listened to both sides intently, and frequently put questions to the various witnesses. Then, telling both parties to withdraw out of earshot, he held a consultation with his councillors in a low tone. Thereupon the two parties were again summoned before the Royal presence.

Addressing the accuser, Shaka said: 'If this man is indeed guilty of disloyalty he will die. Do you agree?'

'Yes, great Elephant, devourer of your enemies.'

'Who will gain by his death?' Shaka snapped at him like lightning.

The accuser looked about uneasily, but failed to respond.

'I will tell you,' said the King in his softest voice. 'You, and you only. For your own advancement you have concocted this slander against a man who has proved his loyalty to me again and again, especially at a time when I was still eating bones' (living in austerity). 'Then you were not so solicitous about the loyalties of others towards me, and thought more of your own belly, which was fat even then. This pit you dug for the accused has been very cleverly covered up – so cleverly, indeed, that you have walked into it yourself. People who falsely accuse others are an abomination, and the sooner they are eaten by the birds, the better for the country. Take him away.' (Synonym for 'Kill him'.) 'One of every two of his cattle shall be confiscated, and one of every ten of these will go to the man who was falsely accused.'

'*Liya duma!*' ('It (the Heaven) thunders!') chorused the councillors. '*Li duma iqiniso!*' ('It thunders the truth!').

Civil actions followed. Claims which originated between the fathers and grandfathers of the litigants, and although the original contracting parties had been dead for a generation or two, were still valid, for in Nguni law death cancels no obligations, as these are inherited by the heirs. The maze of tangled evidence which had to be dealt with was truly remarkable. Shaka only dealt with the very big cases, or sat as an appeal judge. All lesser cases were handled by sub-chiefs and the district headmen, or the Royal ladies in charge of the military kraals, although the latter were given very much wider powers, including the trial of criminal cases which involved the death penalty. This power was also given to the chiefs of such powerful tribes as the Qwabes and the Abambo, who enjoyed almost complete autonomy under the suzerainty of the Zulu King.

When the sun had travelled about two-thirds of the way to the zenith – approximately ten o'clock – the Court was adjourned and Shaka had his usual daily bath in front of all the people. Thereupon he had his breakfast, during which absolute silence had nowadays to be observed – 'for the "lion" is eating now'. The breakfast consisted of boiled and grilled meat presented on a wooden platter. The King cut off pieces to suit his taste, and these he transferred to his mouth with his fingers. Spinach was eaten out of a dish with a spoon, and so was porridge sweetened with honey. The whole meal was washed down with sour milk, or beer, or both.

After the meal the Court was resumed and continued till mid-afternoon, when it was interrupted by a thunderstorm and closed for the day. Matters of State were then attended to in the Great

Council hut, whence directives were issued for the smooth and orderly running of the whole kingdom.

Like other great dictator-reformers, Shaka was much concerned to check the power of the 'spiritual arm' – in this case, the order of witch-doctors. It seemed to him, as he told the Induna Mbopa, that the witch-doctors and diviners had forgotten the lesson he had taught them, and that even Nobela was becoming bold again. The old witch was gathering information of Court secrets in the course of her traffic in drugs and medicines. And Ndabazimbi had defied the government by hypnotizing a military patrol sent to arrest his novice. Shaka therefore planned to expose the principal practitioners of sorcery as frauds, for it was necessary to have the support of the people against them, and to avoid shocking religious sensibilities. In his preparations Shaka made use of Mbopa.

On a certain night Mbopa had so manipulated the setting of the Royal night guards, that there was not a single one of them around the Great Council hut, or even near it. Pampata had been sent with a message to Nandi, three miles away, so that even she was not aware of the plot.

About bed-time Mbopa appeared in the Great Council hut, carrying what appeared to be a pot of beer. This he handed to his Royal master, together with an ox-tail cut short and resembling a brush. Leaving Mbopa in the hut, Shaka proceeded outside with the pot and the tail-brush. Dipping the latter into the pot, the King now began to sprinkle the sides of his own hut liberally with the contents of the pot, until the whole circumference had been treated. Then he repeated the same thing on the yard floor right round the hut. Having completed his task, Shaka re-entered the hut, and gave both pot and tail to Mbopa, with instructions to burn the latter on the hearth fire within the hut, and to clean out the residues left in the former. Mbopa then carefully examined Shaka to make sure that no tell-tale marks remained on him. Then Mbopa was bidden to leave with the pot, and to rinse and wash it well within his own hut, and to fill it with beer and put it away. Thereafter he was to see that the different reliefs of the guards took up their posts again.

On the following morning, immediately it became light enough to see, the guards then on duty were struck with consternation, when on their rounds they beheld that the Royal hut was spattered with blood, and the yard around it smeared with the same substance. Who could have perpetrated this horrible sacrilege in the heart of the sacrosanct Royal enclosure?

The matter was immediately reported to Mbopa, who, appearing to be petrified with horror, made no move until he had hurriedly called together the councillors and the officers of the outer and inner guards. In a body they now moved to the Royal hut, and when they beheld the awful desecration they raised a loud lament. Then Mbopa approached the door and in anguished accents inquired if his Royal master were still alive after the perpetration of so heinous a deed.

Shaka growled from within and peremptorily demanded to know the cause of all the hubbub. On being told, he immediately came out in undress, with a thunderous look on his face. All those who beheld him quailed and even Mbopa did not have to simulate his agitation!

As he gazed at the blood-spattered hut and yard, Shaka roared in majestic anger, 'Who has committed this vile deed against the house of Zulu? Who had the criminal audacity to insult me thus? Blood calls for blood. What were the guards doing? What say they?'

Mbopa replied: 'Great Crushing Elephant, the Royal hut is but lightly guarded according to the instructions which you, who fear nothing, have issued. Moreover, the guards are enjoined to keep an eye on the women's huts rather than on yours. The night was dark, and perchance as they were at the far end the evil perpetrator sneaked in and did the foul deed, for the guards saw nothing. This *umhlolo* (bad happening) reeks of witchcraft, and should be smelt out by the diviners, who will soon find the sorcerer who did this evil thing.'

'You have said it,' bellowed Shaka. 'I will have such a smelling out as the land of Zulu has never seen before. Summon this instant all the diviners and witch-doctors in the land, and tell them to be here on the seventh rising of the sun. Let them all prepare their medicines, and smell from where the sun rises, to where it sets; and from the south to the north, for the vultures are hungry for the great harvest of evil-doers which is due. Summon, too, the whole adult male population to be assembled here on the seventh day, so that they may present a fitting field for the "smellers out". Blood calls for blood, and blood I will have.'

The smelling-out parade was arranged to take place in the great cattle-kraal, whose 130-odd acres would provide ample room for the 30,000 or so people who would be present. Shortly after dawn the people began to arrive and took up the positions appointed for them by the officers in charge of the marshalling of the populace. They formed them into lines similar to those at the great smelling out which Nobela had carried out half a dozen years earlier at the old Bulawayo. Again they were drawn up in horseshoe lines, and the openings facing the upper end of the kraal where Shaka would presently be seated with his councillors, and from where he would have a commanding view of all the gathered people. There was another opening at the arches of the horseshoes at the lower end of the kraal facing the main cattle entrance.

Shortly after sunrise the Royal Family and the councillors took up their positions in front of a company of guards, and not long afterwards the King arrived with Mbopa, Mgobozi, Nqoboka – the Sokulu chief and Shaka's old comrade-in-arms – and the military chiefs, including Mdlaka, Nzobo and Ndlela, who had recently been promoted. As Shaka passed through the small upper gateway into the kraal the whole multitude burst into a spontaneous '*Bayete!*' Then the King advanced and took a seat on a roll of rush mats, with Mgobozi and Mdlaka immediately at his feet, whilst Mbopa took his seat some little distance away, among the other councillors, who were squatting on the ground to the right and left of the King.

There now arose an eerie wailing and caterwauling from outside the cattle-kraal palisades, and through a side gate near the head of the kraal there poured a gibbering, crouching, vaulting and seemingly endless line of witch-doctors – male and female – led by Nobela, more grotesquely dressed than ever. The line of diviners cut across the openings of the horseshoes and in front of the councillors, and then doubled back like a snake, till the head formed by Nobela came opposite Shaka, and then, again serpent-like, turned to face him. All the heads of the profession were grouped around her, grimacing, gesticulating, pirouetting and emitting the most ghoulish noises imaginable.

Shaka rose and commanded silence. Then he told them to smell out the perpetrators of the outrage, but as the diviners were many, and the business must be finished by sundown, they were to divine in groups of ten. As there were 152 of them, it would mean some fifteen teams. They must work swiftly but efficiently. Those who were 'smelt out' would sit in groups under guard on his right front. Those who had smelt them out would sit in corresponding groups on his left front. Then, at the end of the day, there would be one great killing of all the guilty ones. 'Now divide into groups of ten and begin the day's work, and waste no time on preliminary antics, or double-rounds of "smelling out",' concluded Shaka.

This peremptory command put the witch-doctors out of countenance, for in the first place it meant a hurried making-up of teams which might not be too well assorted, and lacked the necessary training for passing the ball of duplicity and guile from one member to the other. True, they were there in their trained co-operating teams of threes, and fives and more, but these had to be amalgamated, or broken up and re-formed, in order to comply with Shaka's behest that they must form teams of ten.

Another weighty disadvantage was that they were now to a large extent deprived of the privilege of using their horrible methods of calculated suspense, which reduced the people into a state of helpless agony. Nevertheless, the fifteen separate combings the people would be subjected to on this day would benefit each succeeding group of witch-doctors, as this long-drawn-out ordeal would reduce the assemblage to a state of petrified fear.

Quick-witted Nobela, however, instantly rose to the occasion by augmenting her team of two with rapid invitations to other small teams and individuals, and soon had her quota of ten complete. The leading witch-doctors were not long in following her example, and soon there were fifteen teams of ten each, with two lone witch-doctors left over, namely Songqoza, son of Ntsense of the Magwaza clan, and Nqiwane of the Dlamini. These two Shaka decreed could finish off the day's proceedings as independent diviners or as a fragmentary team.

Then, with Nobela's cry of 'Chant, ye people, chant,' there began that process of terrorization which has been described in an earlier chapter. The familiar of the witch-doctors was said to be a python and Nobela, as chief pythoness, had the skin of a great snake wound round her body, the stuffed, open-jawed head mounted on her head and reaching forward.

All the councillors, and even Mbopa, Mgobozi and Mdlaka, felt a hypnotic terror stealing over them as the undulating horror came creeping nearer, and even nearer. Drops of sweat began to form and roll over the brows of the beholders. Mgobozi interrupted his chant to mutter to Mdlaka: 'The old bitch-hyaena is after us again, but this time in the form of a python which will hold and crush us.'

When Nobela reached Mbopa, whom she had never yet seen, her eyes gloated in unholy triumph. She chuckled, and cackled, and her mouth drooled saliva like a hungry hyaena's. She sniffed at his right ear, she sniffed at the left, and she sniffed at his mouth.

At an almost imperceptible signal four of Nobela's assistants formed up ahead of her, and the other five closed in on her, leaving her in the centre, facing Mbopa. In a high-pitched falsetto Nobela now screeched, 'Do you smell what I smell, my sisters?'

'We smell what you smell,' came the sing-song chorus from her assistants.

'Have we dreamed correctly, my sisters?'

'What we dreamed in the night we see in the day,' answered the chorus.

'*Igazi li puma egazini*' ('Blood comes from blood!'). Mbopa's clan name was Egazini, signifying 'from the blood'.

'Blood calls for blood,' came the chorus. Then, with a shriek, Nobela vaulted high in the air, and as she came down, struck Mbopa with the wildebeest tail across the head; then she pirouetted backwards with explosions of derisive, triumphant and malignant laughter, an example which was followed by all her disciples.

As Nobela struck, Shaka muttered: 'Very near. She couldn't have struck nearer. The old python will yet upset all my plans.'

When the last diviner had struck Mbopa, the slayers pounced on him, according to custom, and marched him off; but contrary to custom, not to immediate and painful death, but to the place which Shaka had ordained. Mbopa, though buoyed up by his secret knowledge, felt and looked shattered by the tenfold public denunciation, and uncomfortable realization of the uncanny powers which Nobela wielded.

Nobela and her evil brood now advanced boldly to within a dozen places of the Royal throne, and formed into a line before it, with Nobela in the centre and directly facing Shaka. She was going to strike against the high ones – the very highest in the land, and after her former humiliating experience, she was taking no chances, which the exercise of prudence might avoid. She would therefore divine by the wonted and more cautious manner of self-evident ambiguity, which closely paralleled the famous Oracle of Delphi.

'What is sometimes said of a person travelling? What is he called?' shouted Nobela for all the councillors and important persons to hear. At which Shaka whispered, 'She means Nqoboka' (his friend, the Sokulu chief, from the Zulu word 'Coboka', to be exhausted by a journey). Shaka glowered, and Nqoboka, who was seated close to him, on his left, stirred uneasily, as he felt the gaze of all directed towards him. Thus Nobela had, through an innuendo understood by all, cleverly passed the onus of taking action on to Shaka. If he failed to take action, he risked public criticism unless the person indicated was very popular. Nqoboka was, however, not well known at the Zulu capital, but he was one of Shaka's best friends, who with Mgobozi and Shaka, as ordinary warriors, had vowed to protect each other's backs. The slayers moved towards Nqoboka in anticipation of the Royal order to remove him. Here was a dilemma for Shaka. The councillors looked expectantly at him, for every person 'smelt out' increased the chances of the rest. Only Shaka – and Mbopa sitting lonely under the shadow of death – knew on what a volcano the diviners were standing, or sitting! If Shaka shielded Nqoboka prematurely, Nobela's uncanny reasoning powers might detect the truth, if indeed she had not already done so. Mbopa needed some heartening companionship at this stage too. Shaka therefore decided to send Nqoboka to him, but he would give his old comrade-in-arms a cabalistic message which would reassure him. As Nobela looked like forcing matters, the more prominent the people she condemned, the more devastating would be the popular reaction against the diviners in the final act.

'Nqoboka!' said Shaka addressing him, 'You must go, but as a chief, and without an escort of slayers. For this you must thank the day you threw away your sandals, which later cost you five of your best cows, and now this road.' Nqoboka at once understood the implication of the nebulous message, but it went above the head of Mgobozi and the crowd, who knew nothing of that little private cattle transaction. Nqoboka arose, and giving the Royal salute, '*Bayete!*' he strode away to join Mbopa.

This was more than Mgobozi could stand, for had he and Shaka not long ago promised Nqoboka, and each the other, that they would be each other's shield, and if need be, eat earth together? Rising and turning, Mgobozi faced the King, with a resonant, '*Bayete!* my Father, have me killed too; for I go to join Nqoboka, and eat earth with him. In any case it will save time and trouble, as that old strumpet of the baboons will not rest till she has killed all your best friends. She stinks of witchcraft herself, and her odour exceeds that of a mangy hyaena seven days dead; and as the maggots come out of this, so the lies pour out of her evil mouth. I will be silent now, my Father and King, lest I say something unseemly about her before I die. *Bayete!*'

Shaka had difficulty in restraining a smile at this honest outburst, and touching loyalty to a friend, and the veiled rebuke to himself, for the blunt old warrior lacked that discerning finesse to understand that Shaka was playing a deep game – moreover, one which the continued presence of Mgobozi might now jeopardize. In any case Mgobozi merited at least a sharp rebuke for speaking out of his turn. In fact, it was a case of *lèse-majesté*, and in itself sufficient to earn the death sentence. The King, therefore, rejoined sharply: 'Go, then, you fool. Join Nqoboka, and find a premature death with him.'

'*Bayete!*' saluted Mgobozi, with upraised hand, and with proud step he marched to where Mbopa and Nqoboka were squatting.

A low moan of anguish arose from the whole assembled multitude. Starting from the councillors and the Royal Family, it ran like a *feu de joie* to the farthest ends of the crowd, and then came rolling back again. Nandi was dreadfully upset and on the point of intervening, when she was pacified and restrained by Pampata, who sat beside her. For Pampata's amazing intuition had begun to grasp the whole situation. The manifest distress of all the people showed the immense popularity of Mgobozi, and provided a striking contrast to the venomously gloating divining fraternity, who, as a whole, felt the heroic fool had indeed spoken the truth when he said that his act would save them time and trouble.

'Greetings, Nqoboka and Mbopa,' Mgobozi said grimly, as he joined the other two. 'Now there are three of us in the pot of that old witch, and plenty more are coming.'

'She may overfill it,' was the quiet and cryptic reply of Mbopa.

Whilst these conversations were taking place Nobela had resumed her oracular divination.

'A sticky thing that grows on trees; do you recognize it?' she called to the councillors. None dared reply till Shaka guessed: 'She means *ntlaka*' (the Zulu word for gum). This obviously indicated Mdlaka, the generalissimo of the army, who was sitting at Shaka's feet.

'I hear you, Nobela,' interposed Shaka, 'but the army is not to be touched. I alone deal with it. That was my word long ago, when you thrust your face into a hornets' nest.' A sigh of relief swept over the officers and guards near by, and like a telepathic wave rolled onwards through all the tense regiments drawn up in the great kraal.

Again Nobela asked, 'When a person is in want, what is it that is said of him?' Perfect silence reigned till Shaka broke it – 'She means "Udingani" ' – an obvious reference to his half-brother Dingane, who scowled and cast a murderous look at Nobela.

Shaka frowned as he replied. 'Again I hear you, Nobela, but leave my father's son alone.'

Once more Nobela propounded a riddle. 'What is it which grows on the banks of rivers and swamps with a flower like a plume: when it is but a small plant, what do you call it?' She obviously meant a reed, the Zulu word for which is *umhlanga*, and its diminutive *umblangana*. It could indicate none other but Shaka's half-brother Mhlangana.

'Cease your animosity against my father's house, O bird of evil omen, and get done with your business.'

'I hear you, O King,' replied Nobela, 'but on the day you see the blood dripping from the blade of the little red-handled assegai you now hold in your hand it is then, O King, you will hear my words again, and bitterly regret that you heeded them not in time. For then it will be too late. I have said my say and I go to make room for these other diviners.' Nobela then walked upright at the head of her line of assistants to the place which Shaka had indicated – each team of diviners to sit opposite those whom they had condemned.

As the two teams headed for the multitude the chant of the people dropped almost to nothing, and thereupon all the twelve waiting teams of diviners struck up a grisly song 'Tonight the hyaenas will sleep with their stomachs full, and tomorrow the vultures will have their fill. Weep with your skins, and weep with your eyes, you evil-doers, for justice is threading your way. Though you may think you are innocent, you are the unwitting tools of the evil ones, who would corrupt the nation through you. Laugh with us, you righteous ones, laugh at the plight of the wicked, for soon they will taste the impalement sticks. Laugh, laugh, laugh.' A cacophony of horrible, derisive, and demoniacal laughter floated over the air, and chilled the hearts of all who saw the two lines of doom coiling their way towards them – with the slayers trailing in their wake.

The wildebeest tails began to strike frequently now and, by

the time the two teams passed each other at the arch or farther end
of the horseshoe, well over a score of unhappy victims had been
hustled away to the central depot of the doomed by the slayers,
who then returned for more.

Thus the melancholy day wore on and, as the heat and strain
increased, it not infrequently happened that some of the more
sensitive or delicate people collapsed in a faint. This was regarded
by the witch-doctors as conclusive evidence that they had been
justly overwhelmed by the evil sorcery within them and, without
any other formality, these unfortunates were dragged away by the
slayers.

The sun had sunk to a 'little beyond half-way between the
zenith and the horizon' before the last teams had finished their
merciless work and rejoined the satisfied throng of witch-doctors
who were gazing with unconcealed exultation at their harvest –
well over 300 innocent people mutely suffering an agony of apprehension, not only on account of their own approaching hideous death, but that of all their helpless dependants, for by
immemorial law and custom these, too, were doomed the moment
the head of the family had been 'smelt out'. Most of them were
well-nigh insane with grief to think that they were the unwitting,
and therefore the most dangerous sources, of contamination and
corruption to their neighbours, and consequently to their chief,
and the State as a whole. Had Mgobozi tried to lead them in a
revolt against the witch-doctors he would not have succeeded, for,
with few exceptions, they felt utterly crushed and hopelessly
unclean. Only another witch-doctor, or the head of the State,
could now reverse the awful verdict of the witch-doctors.

There were now left but the two witch-doctors, Songqoza and
Nqiwane, who had not yet divined. All that day they had sat
apart and aloof from the other diviners.

They now approached the Royal throne with the step of warriors, and none of the usual antics of a witch-doctor. They gave the
Royal salute, which was also unusual.

Shaka looked at them as stern as death and, as they were silent,
he told them abruptly to begin.

'Does the King wish to hear the truth?' asked Songqoza.

'What else have I asked you all here for? Speak, and speak quickly,' returned Shaka.

'O! King! I divine the Heaven (Zulu).'

'It, and It only, did it.' This meant Shaka himself, whose clan name was Zulu. There was a pregnant silence. Then, noting Shaka's approving smile, Nqiwane, not to be outdone, instantly chimed in, '*I-Zulu nempela*' ('The Heaven and none other').

'*Nitshilo!* ye have said it,' roared Shaka as he rose to his full majestic height.

'You, and you alone, have spoken the truth. Listen, my people. I, and I alone, did the deed. I spattered blood with my own hands on the walls of my hut, and smeared it on the yard outside. I did it, that I might find out who were the true diviners and who the false.

'Look, all, and see. In the whole land there are but two true witch-doctors – these young men – and the rest are false. See, there they sit, the evil brood, who but now rejoiced at the plight of all those innocent people they would have sent to a painful and dishonourable death. They have ceased to rejoice, for now they know the wrath of Heaven is about to strike them. See how they tremble, for they know that real justice is near. Now, I ask you, my people, what shall be done to these false accusers?'

The silence of death hung over all the assembled people like a pall. It was like the hush of nature before a great tropical storm – the hush which is the prelude to the first shattering stroke of lightning, which opens the sluice-gates of heaven.

Then a great roar went up from all the multitude – the instantaneous release of the pent-up feelings of thrice 10,000 hearts. 'Kill them! Kill them! Let them die, through the impalement skewers they intended for us.'

'Ye have said it,' Shaka thundered back, 'and let those whom they falsely condemned be their executioners.'

A whimpering wail arose from all the false diviners which rapidly rose to a great lament. So sudden had been this totally unexpected and horrible catastrophe which had overwhelmed them, out of the blue heaven as it were, and in the very moment of their greatest triumph, that they were at first completely numbed.

They knew the ghastly doom which was now about to fall on them in the shape of their intended victims, who would now, with merciless zeal, do to the diviners what they had enjoined the slayers to do unto them.

These slayers were now giving bundles of skewers to the reprieved, and rage-maddened people. The reaction, due to the sudden reversal of fortunes, had made them into vengeful blood-thirsty leopards with but one idea – to rend and tear those who had so grievously tortured them. Mbopa assumed the leadership of this infuriated mob.

Nobela had preserved a wonderful calm and dignity, and when she saw that everything was irretrievably lost she unobtrusively emptied into her hand the contents of a little gourd which resembled a snuff container. Half a handful of this she slipped into her mouth. She knew the effects of the ground-up seeds of *Datura stramonium*, of which she had taken a sufficient quantity to provide a manifold lethal dose of atropine. It would take a little time, however, before her stomach extracted enough of the deadly alkaloid to put her beyond the reach of all human vengeance.

Then Mbopa and the mob poured amongst the now screaming diviners, each 'smelt-out' person looking for the one who had indicated him. Mbopa, as a high councillor, had the authority to invoke the aid of the slayers, and with them cordoned off the whole of Nobela's team, for neither Mgobozi nor Nqoboka, blood-thirsty warriors though they were, showed any inclination to participate, though they stood and watched the proceedings. When Mbopa told the slayers that Nobela would be reserved for the last to enable her to see what would happen to her in an intensified degree, a gleam of triumph flashed from her eyes, whose pupils were already beginning to dilate, and in this early stage of atropine poisoning, gave them a starry brilliance. While the people were killing the diviners in the prescribed horrible fashion, she turned to the gloating Mbopa in the hearing of Mgobozi and Nqoboka, and said: 'Henceforth you will live in fear, and you will die in fear. True, you will be one of the slayers of the "Great Elephant", but remember you will only be making room for another "Elephant", and they like not the slayers of their own kind.'

Mbopa cursed her and told her he would soon make her retract every one of her lying words with the extra tortures he would devise for her.

The pupils of Nobela's eyes had by now dilated to the full extent of the iris, which made her look truly terrible. Only four of her assistants remained unskewered. She leaned heavily on the two immediately beside her. Then she made her supreme effort and in a far-carrying and commanding voice cried out: 'O foolish people. You imagine you will kill us with these skewers, not knowing that our magic can remove them again, and then we will return to plague you more than ever before,' and she laughed derisively at them. Then a mysterious voice arose from among the mob, 'Crush their skulls, and finish them off for good.' A similar voice echoed the same words from another part. Then the mob took up the cry and, seizing the clubs they had been given by the slayers for the purpose of hitting the protruding heads of the skewers out of sight into their victims' bodies, they fell on the writhing diviners. With true unthinking mob-violence, they now started on an orgy of skull-smashing, which extended even to those diviners who had not yet been skewered. Mbopo tried to stop them, but only succeeded in guarding Nobela's team and then only through the strenuous efforts of his cordon of slayers.

Nobela was sitting now with her head upon her knees. The open jaws of the stuffed python's head still looked menacing. Two more of her assistants were receiving the skewers and screaming dreadfully. Mbopa was relentless. Presently the last two assistants were held down, and Mbopa specially prolonged the proceedings till they became unconscious.

Then, with all the irony at his command, Mbopa approached the immobile Nobela, and in honeyed accents said: 'It is your turn now.' Nobela did not respond.

'Did you hear me, mother of evil? or must I prod you with one of these pleasant little sticks?' Again there was no response.

'*Dadewetu!*' (By my sister!) 'the old python is fast asleep, but

I will soon prod her into wakefulness. Give me one of those skewers,' Mbopa commanded a slayer. Thereupon he gave a vicious jab into Nobela's side, and without a sound she toppled over limply. Nobela was dead.

CHAPTER 20

The English – The Little Umkosi – The eclipse

AT about the time of Nobela's death in March 1824, Lieutenant F. G. Farewell, R.N., chartered the two brigs *Julia* and *Ann* at Table Bay to proceed with some forty persons to Port Natal (Durban). Henry Francis Fynn headed that portion of the trading party which was on board the *Julia* and made a quick voyage to Port Natal, where the vessel arrived towards the end of March.

Fynn, whose object was trade, sent native messengers ahead to seek audience with the Zulu King, but Shaka, who had never set eyes on so uncanny a being as a White man, refused 'until a more suitable reception could be prepared', and sent a gift of cattle and ivory.

Fynn is thus described by his subsequent associate Isaacs:

'In stature somewhat tall, with a prepossessing countenance: from necessity his face was disfigured with hair, not having had an opportunity of shaving himself for a considerable time. His head was partly covered with a crownless straw hat, and a tattered blanket, fastened round his neck by means of strips of hide, served to cover his body, while his hands performed the office of keeping it round his "nether man"; his shoes he had discarded for some months, whilst every other habiliment had imperceptibly worn away, so "that there was nothing of a piece about him". He was highly loved by the natives, who looked up to him with more than ordinary veneration, for he had often been instrumental in saving their lives and, in moments of pain and sickness, had administered to their relief. About 100 had attached themselves to him (1825, one year after arrival), so much so that they were inseparable.'

Fynn, this time accompanied by the rest of the party, now made a second attempt to see Shaka, his whole party first improving their attire, Farewell in cocked hat and epaulettes, and all mounted on horses with improvised saddles and bridles. Their progress through Natal was watched by Mhlope, Shaka's spy, who built himself a kraal above the White man's camp on the Berea rise and came down to move among them. He reported to the King that the White men were friendly and tame, had a wealth of extraordinary property and a beverage fit for kings.

Shaka responded with dispatch. He summoned his most tactful and imposing diplomat, Mbikwane (the new Mtetwa chief), earliest of friends in the days of youth, and appointed him ambassador plenipotentiary to the White man's camp, bearing a cordial invitation that they honour him with a visit. This Mbikwane was by nature an amiable soul who had won the love of all his people. He gained at once the confidence of the solitary and helpless Whites, and proved throughout his life their protector and their friend.

Guided by Mbikwane, the English, on their horses, took the coastal path, fording the rivers at or near their mouths then, over the Tugela into Zululand and across the Amatikulu river, they traversed the broad Inyezane plain, past the great military kraal of Entonteleni on the northern slope of the Obanjeni ridge.

Here they first saw the imposing might of the Zulu King in the form of a regiment of warriors in all their panoply of war. The commander received them with regal dignity, acting as deputy for the King's maiden aunt Mawa, who was in charge of the kraal. Food, beer, and shelter were provided, but the warriors and all unauthorized persons kept at a respectful distance, apparently on orders from the highest authority.

Recording their progress through Zululand, Fynn writes: 'We were struck with astonishment at the order and discipline maintained in the country through which we travelled. The regimental kraals, especially the upper parts thereof, also the kraals of chiefs, showed that cleanliness was a prevailing custom, and this not only inside their huts, but outside, for there were considerable spaces where neither dirt nor ashes were to be seen.'

The next day the cavalcade continued over the middle Mlalazi and up the Ngoye hills, into the crisp air of these semi-highlands, whose southern and eastern slopes were covered with 100-foot-high primeval forests, the dense growth of which afforded a striking contrast to the acacia savannahs which predominated the country they had traversed so far. As they emerged on the northern side of the hills the broad panorama of the Umhlatuze valley, with its expanse of mimosa-clad hill and vale, lay spread before them down below, the great Bulawayo kraal – the Royal capital, at the centre.

'On arriving within a mile of the King's residence', writes Fynn, 'we were directed to wait under a large tree till the arrival of the messengers who were to call Mr Farewell and myself and the rest of the party.

'At the time of our entering the gates of the inner kraal it was lined by about 12,000 men in their war attire. We were then desired to gallop round the kraal several times, and returning, bring the remainder of our party. When we came again we were directed to gallop four times more round the kraal – then to stand at a distance of twenty yards from a tree at the head of the kraal. Mbikwane, who had accompanied us, made a long speech to the king, who was so surrounded by his chiefs that we could not distinguish him. One of the chiefs spoke in reply to Mbikwane, to whom he stood opposite. His speech concluded, he brought an elephant's tusk as a present to Mr Farewell. Mbikwane again spoke, urging us frequently to exclaim "*Yebo*" – meaning "Yes" – but what we were assenting to we did not know. Shaka then sprang up from among the chiefs, striking the shield of the chief on either side of him. The whole body then ran to the lower end of the kraal, leaving us alone, with the exception of one man who had been in the crowd.'

To the intense surprise of Farewell this uniquely favoured individual turned out to be none other than his own ex-interpreter, Jacob Msimbiti, former cattle thief and convict on Robben Island, the penal settlement at the Cape. As he was a Xoza and, therefore, spoke a dialect closely related to Zulu, and had acquired a smattering of Dutch and English, he had been given to Captain W. Owen, R.N., by the Cape Government, the understanding being that if Jacob behaved he would secure his release. Captain Owen had lent him to Farewell in the previous year when the latter was making an exploratory cruise up the East Coast.

In trying to effect a landing at St Lucia Bay the boat with the landing-party had capsized in the surf, four of its inmates being drowned; but the principals, Thompson and Farewell, managed to reach the shore, the latter by the strong arm of the native Jacob, who had proved to be an expert swimmer. But the native had been immediately rewarded with a cruel clout by the irate Thompson. Mortally offended, Jacob had there and then left the Whites and marched off inland, and in this way had arrived at Shaka's Court. Shaka had received the wanderer at first with some suspicion; but later on, recognizing his abilities, had showered his favours upon him and had decorated him for his valour with the praise-name of *Hlambamanzi* (The Swimmer), and had now raised him to the dignity of Royal interpreter and intermediary with the Whites.

Jacob's association with the English not having been of the best, he had naturally tended to paint anything but a pleasant picture of them to Shaka. In this he had been ably supported by a half-caste Portuguese trader who had arrived at Bulawayo soon afterwards. It is to the everlasting credit of Shaka, and a tribute to his fairness, that he heavily discounted all the tales as coming from people who, for one reason or another, had a personal grievance against the English: he remained a steadfast friend of the English to the end of his days, and always strove to have an alliance with his Britannic Majesty.

Farewell recovered quickly from his surprise but could not escape the realization that he and Fynn were at a permanent disadvantage now with Jacob as court interpreter. However, the latter did play fair, for Shaka had given him a very compelling reason by intimating that any misinterpretation would be as good as a signal to the executioners.

Shaka's dignified geniality soon put his guests at their ease and, after a few searching questions as to the purport of their coming to his domains, he invited them to come farther under the big spreading fig tree. There he took his seat on a roll of rush mats, and motioned his visitors to squat on reed mats which had previously been laid on the ground before his own seat as a special mark of honour to the Whites. Farewell and Fynn occupied the two front mats to conform with their dignity as leaders. Their European followers sat or squatted immediately behind them. Fynn's Hottentot servants and the other natives squatted in the background out of earshot beyond the tree in the open kraal. Jacob squatted on the bare ground slightly in front of Shaka's right. Thus, then, was the setting for the first Royal audience. Not a councillor or guard or slayer within 100 yards. Such was the nature of Shaka that he never took any precautions for his own personal safety and was quite content to be left alone and within the power of these mysterious newcomers. For he was aflame with curiosity to learn from them, nor did he want any of his councillors or subjects, save only the necessary interpreter, to be privy to his talks.

Although it was in July, the early afternoon sun was warm and the shade of the tree welcome. Shako almost immediately motioned to one of the page-boys hovering in the distance behind him to have a supply of beer brought. Then he inquired after the welfare of the travellers and what kind of a journey they had had. Jacob interpreted slowly and haltingly into English, but communicated the answers in Zulu more rapidly to his King. It was somewhat heavy going, especially at first.

Presently the beer arrived in charge of Pampata, who knelt before the King and, taking a sip from the one-gallon pot, handed it to him. Shaka took a draught and then handed l ack the vessel to Pampata who passed it on to Farewell. The pot circulated among the Whites.

The King told his visitors about the glories of his realm. His vast wealth in cattle of which they would get an idea on the morrow and the following days. His regiments which were the terror of all his enemies. The magnificence of his capital, Bulawayo. Then he very pointedly asked if Farewell and his companion had ever seen a more orderly governed State than his Zululand, or subjects who were more moral and law-abiding. For in his Kingdom anyone could leave his property anywhere without fear of it being stolen, nor need any man be apprehensive that his wives or daughters would be dishonoured. To all of which the visitors frequently responded '*Yebo*' (Yes) or '*Yebo, Baba*' (Yes, Father).

Thereafter he made many inquiries about King George, the size of his army, the nature of his government and country, the size of his capital and the number of his cattle and wives. He applauded the wisdom of his 'brother' King in having only one wife. 'That accounts for his advanced age; but he would have been wiser still to have none at all like myself', and here he chuckled heavily. He told them that he had had a special kraal of their own built for them on the outskirts of his capital, and that they would presently be conducted there and would find a repast laid out for them. But first he would call his councillors together and issue a Royal command that all the Whites were to be looked upon and treated as hereditary chiefs, and no one must regard himself as their equal.

Shaka then bade his visitors a temporary farewell and Mbikwane escorted them to their special State quarters. There they found a royal banquet awaiting them, namely, an ox, a sheep, baskets of ground corn, native potatoes, groundnuts and honey. As it was winter-time there were no vegetables. Lastly there were many three-gallon pots of the choicest beer. The English were greatly elated, not only on account of all the fare laid before them, but for the most friendly nature of their reception. They therefore sent a supply of beads and other trinkets to the King, and presently fired a salute of eight guns, and Shaka listened intently but without apprehension to the ominous reverberation of so many firearms. That night they shot up four sky-rockets which had been expressly brought in order to impress the King and his nation, and this they certainly did.

On the following morning, upon invitation by special messenger, the visitors mounted their steeds and sped to the Royal Court. They found the King having his bath. While bathing, Shaka chatted gaily with those around him; then, suddenly turning about, perfunctorily ordered one of them off to instant execution, 'for what reason we could not learn', writes Fynn, who with his companions was rather shaken at this abrupt termination of life. The victim had his neck twisted whilst still in the full view of the Whites.

Fynn goes on to say that Shaka, at that time, was still in the prime of manhood, some thirty-eight years of age, over six feet in height, of sleek but stalwart frame, and still unmarried. He wore neither head-ring nor, as they could see, had he been circumcised.

'The "savage" potentate entertained his distinguished visitors with all the pomp and festival usually accounted the distinctive monopoly of cultured monarchs. All the might and opulence of the Zulu nation were brought forth and displayed.' Regiment after regiment of warriors marched past, each with its distinctive shields and plumes, the court praisers calling out the name and battle honours of each. Fifteen regiments swept past and then gave massed war dances which made the earth shake.

Fynn records: 'It was a most exciting scene, surprising to us, who could not have imagined that a nation termed "savages" could be so disciplined and kept in order.'

Then came the cattle in herds of approximately 5000 each, every herd of uniform colour, and some 60,000 in all.

The choicest displays of all were reserved for the last: 'Regiments of girls,' says Fynn, 'headed by officers of their own sex, then entered the centre of the arena (kraal) to the number of 8000 to 10,000, each holding a slight staff in her hand. They joined in the dance which lasted about two hours.'

Lastly there was a dance of the younger Royal Ladies followed by more than 500 of the 'Great House' girls – the harem lilies, or, as Shaka called them, 'his sisters'. The King joined in these dances accompanied by many of his men. Each dance usually concluded with a short speech by Shaka. In these speeches Fynn writes, 'He desires his people to look at us, to see the wonder of White men, and to consider his own greatness ... His own forefathers and theirs were cowards, who would not have dared to admit a White man to their presence ... He would expect his nation to look on us and pay us the respect due to Kings, and not consider us their equals.' Then he repeated in public some of the questions he had put to the English in private, for instance: 'He desired to

know from us if ever we had seen such order in any other State ...
He assured us that he was the greatest King in existence; that his
people were as numerous as the stars, and his cattle innumerable.'

Fynn records a number of conversations he had with Shaka.
'He said that the forefathers of the Europeans had bestowed on us
many gifts, by giving us all the knowledge of arts and manu-
factures. He then asked what use was made of the hides of oxen
slaughtered in our country. When I told him they were made into
shoes, and other articles I could not distinctly explain, he exclaimed that this was another proof of the unkindness of our
forefathers, who had obliged us to protect our feet with hides, for
which there was no necessity – whilst he had shown the natives
that the hide should be used as a more handsome and serviceable
article, a shield.

'Then he changed the conversation to the superiority of their
arms, which, he said, were in many ways more advantageous than
our muskets. The shields, he argued, if dipped into water previous
to an attack, would be sufficient to prevent the effect of a ball
fired whilst they were at a distance, and in the interval of loading
they would come up to us at close quarters; we, having no shields,
would then drop our guns and attempt to run; and, as we could
not run as fast as his soldiers, we must all inevitably fall into their
hands. I found it impossible to confute his arguments, as I had no
acquaintance with his language, and his interpreter, on whom I
had to depend, would not have dared to use strong arguments in
opposition to the King. I was obliged, therefore, to accept all his
decisions ... He placed the worst construction on everything,
and did this in the presence of his subjects, ridiculing all our manners and customs, though he did this in perfect good humour.

'He (Shaka) would listen with the greatest attention when
none of his people were with us, and then could not help acknowledging our superiority. He expressed, however, his aversion to
our mode of punishing for some crimes by imprisonment, which
he thought must be the most horrid pain that man could endure.
If he were guilty why not punish the deed with death? If suspicion only attached to the individual, let him go free; his arrest
would be a sufficient warning for the future. This argument had

arisen from the circumstance of his interpreter having been taken prisoner and sent to Robben Island, and, through him, therefore, it was out of my power to explain how wishful we are to save the lives of the innocent, and in how few instances life was despised by its possessor. I had to give way as before ... Our explanation of the laws of our country called forth some very unpleasant observations from him.'

When the State festivities in their honour were over, Farewell and his companions returned to Port Natal, except Fynn, who remained behind for another month and records the following startling experience:

'Having spent the afternoon in reading, I was induced to take another peep at the dancers. As it was dark when I came, the King ordered a number of people to hold up bundles of dried reeds, kept burning, to give light to the scene. I had not been there many minutes when I heard a shriek; and lights were immediately extinguished. Then followed a general bustle and cry ... I found at length that Shaka, while dancing, had been stabbed. I immediately turned away to call Michael (one of Fynn's Hottentot servants) whom I found at no great distance, shouting and giving the hurrah, mistaking the confusion for some merriment. I immediately told him what I had heard, and sent him to prepare a lamp, and to bring some camomile, the only medicine I had by me ... Jacob (the interpreter), in the general uproar, fell down in a fit, so that now I could ask no questions or gain information as to where Shaka was. I attempted to gain admittance to his hut. There was a crowd round it. My lamp was put out. The women of the seraglio pulled me, some one way some another; they were in a state of madness. The throng, still increasing, and the uproar, with shrieks and cries, becoming dreadful, my situation was awkward and unpleasant in the extreme. Just as I was making another attempt to enter the hut in which I supposed the King to be, a man carrying some lighted reeds attempted to drag me away and, on my refusal to accompany him, he made a second effort to pull me along, and was then assisted by another. I thought it best to see the result and, if anything were intended against myself, to make the best of it. I walked with them for about five minutes, and my fears and suspicions were then relieved, for I saw the King in a kraal immediately near. I at once washed the wound with camomile-tea and bound it up with linen. He had been stabbed with an assegai through the left arm, and the blade had passed through the ribs under the left breast. It must have been due to mere accident that the wound had not penetrated the lungs, but it made the King spit blood. His own doctor, who appeared to have a good knowledge in wounds, gave him a vomit, and afterwards repeated doses of purging medicine, and continually washed the wound with decoctions of cooling roots. He also probed the wound to ascertain whether any poison had been used on the assegai. Shaka declined nearly the whole night, expecting that only fateful consequences would ensue. The crowd had now increased so much that the noise of their shrieks was unbearable.

'Morning showed a horrid sight in a clear light. I am satisfied that I cannot describe the scene in any words that would be of force to convey an impression to any reader sufficiently distinct of that hideous scene. Immense crowds of people were constantly arriving, and began their shouts when they came in sight of the kraal, running and exerting their utmost powers of voice as they entered it. They joined those already there, pulling one another about, throwing themselves down, without heeding how they fell, men and women indiscriminately. Many fainted from over-exertion and excessive heat.

'All this time I had been so busily employed as not to see the most sickening part of the tragic scene. They had begun to kill one another. Some were put to death because they did not weep, others for putting spittle in their eyes, others for sitting down to cry, although strength and tears, after such continuous exertion and mourning, were wholly exhausted.

'We then understood that six men had been wounded by the same assassins who had wounded Shaka. From the road they took it was supposed that they had been sent by Zuedi (Zwide), King of the Endwandwe (Ndwandwe), who was Shaka's only powerful enemy.* Accordingly two regiments were sent at once in search of the aggressors.

'In the meanwhile the medicines which Mr Farewell had promised to send had been received. They came very opportunely, and Shaka was much gratified. I now washed his wound frequently and gave him mild purgatives. I dressed his wounds with ointment. The King, however, was hopeless for four days. During all that time people were flocking in from the outskirts of the country, joining in the general tumult. It was not till the fourth day that cattle were killed for the sustenance of the multitude. Many had died in the interval, and many had been killed for not mourning, or for having gone to their kraals for food. On the fifth day there were symptoms of improvement in the King's health and wounds, and the favourite indications were even more noticeable on the day following. At noon, the party sent out in search of the malefactors returned, bringing with them the dead bodies of three men whom they had killed in the bush (jungle). These were the supposed murderers. The bodies were laid on the ground at a distance of about a mile from the kraal. The ears having been cut off from the right side of the heads, the two regiments sat down on either side of the road. Then all the people who had collected at the kraal passed up the road crying and screaming. Each one coming up to the bodies struck them several blows with a stick, which was then dropped on the spot; so that before half the number had come to the bodies, nothing more of these was to be seen: only an immense pile of sticks remained, but the formal ceremony still went on. The whole body now collecting, and three men walking in advance with sticks on which were the ears of the dead men, the procession moved up to Shaka's kraal. The King now made his appearance. The national mourning song was now chanted and, a fire being made in the centre of the kraal, the ears were burned to ashes.

'From the moment that Shaka had been stabbed, there had been

*It seems likely that Zwide, the Ndwandwe king, may have died about this time, and that this attempted assassination of Shaka was part of the *i-hlambo*, or cleansing ceremony, inaugurated by Zwide's son and heir, Sikunyana.

a prohibition to wear ornaments, to wash the body or to shave; and no man whose wife was pregnant had been allowed to come into the King's presence. All transgressions of these regulations being punishable with death, several human beings had been put to death . . .

'The restoration of the King's health made some great changes. The tumult gradually ceased. A force of a thousand men was sent to attack the hostile tribe, and returned in a few days, having destroyed several kraals, and taken 800 head of cattle.

'Mr Farewell and Mr Isaacs,* having received a letter from me stating particulars of the recent occurrence, came to visit Shaka, and had not been seated many minutes, when a man, who had, in defiance or neglect of the prohibition, shaved his head, was put to death. After this the privilege of shaving was again conceded.'

In the matter of the first land-concession transaction between Shaka and the British, it has been considered best to quote the account given by Dr A. T. Bryant. This transaction seems to have been so discreditable to the Whites, that if the authority for it were not given in full, it would hardly be credited. Bryant says :

'Farewell, however, arriving at this very opportune moment when Shaka was in the generous mood, expressed himself as thoroughly satisfied if conceded the minor privilege, not of shaving but of merely fleecing none other than the wily monarch himself. And the wily monarch – at least so we are told – amiably allowed himself to be fleeced.

'The unctuous sense of self-righteousness which invariably wells up in an Englishman's soul whenever he is engaged annexing the property of others – and notably so when it be the land of the primitives – is to the unbiased observer, sometimes as astounding as amusing. At the very moment when Fynn was feeling real resentment at (as he thought) Shaka's unfair "ridicule of our manners, and customs" and his disapproval of some of the "laws

* Isaacs, it may be remarked, was at that time still in St Helena, not reaching Port Natal till the following year, on 1 October 1825.

of our country" there is little room for doubt that he was privy to the mean trick which even then, under the sanction of those laws and customs, Farewell was playing on the unsuspecting savage.

'With the obvious purpose of defrauding the natives, under the guise of a legal document, of their natural birthright, Farewell had drafted the following deed of cession (which none but himself could read or fully grasp the force), in which he gratuitously declared that "I, Inguos (Nkosi, meaning chief) Shaka, King of the Zulus and of the Country of Natal, as well as the whole of the land from Natal to Delagoes Bay, which I have inherited from my father" – as a matter of fact, Shaka's father had never heard of, much less ever owned or bequeathed, any land of Natal or Delagoes Bay; – "do hereby ... of my own free will and in consideration of divers goods received" – what precisely these latter were, was unstated, but there is every probability that they were of not more than a few shillings' worth – "grant, make over and sell to F. G. Farewell and Company the entire and full possession in perpetuity ... of the Port or Harbour of Natal ... and the surrounding country as herein described, viz.: the whole of the neck of land or peninsula on the south-west entrance" – this was the Bluff – "and all the country ten miles to the southern side of Port Natal, as pointed out" – apparently as far as the Em-Bokodweni river – "and extending along the sea-coast to the northward and eastward as far as the river known by the native name, 'Gumgelote' " – presumably the Umdloti – "being about twenty five miles of sea-coast to the north-east of Port Natal, together with all the country inland as far as the nation called by the Zulus 'Gowagnewkos' " – Kwanogqaza or Howick – "extending about one hundred miles backward from the seashore, with all rights to the rivers, woods, mines and articles of all denominations contained therein ... In witness whereof I have placed my hand, being fully aware that the doing so is intended to bind me to all the articles and conditions" – we cannot unravel the confused verbal jumble here ensuing – "of my own free will and consent do hereby ... before the said F. G. Farewell, whom I hereby acknowledge as chief of the said country with full power and authority over such natives that like to remain there ... promising to supply him with cattle and corn" presumably owned or grown by those selfsame natives ! – "as a reward for his kind attention to me in my illness from my wound".

'To all this Farewell on 8 August, 1824, requested the untutored barbarian to subscribe his sign manual, and, as a matter of courtesy to a trusted friend, the unsuspecting barbarian did so, and on Farewell's request, directed Mbikwane, Msika, Mhlope, and Hlambamanzi to witness the fact.

'Of course, it goes without saying that Shaka had not the slightest intention of perpetrating any of the absurdities contained in this egregious document. No sable monarch, so astute and jealous as he, would ever have entertained the idea for one moment of delivering over his country and sacrificing his sovereign rights to a rank stranger, and least of all to a "mean White"; for, as Isaacs attests, while externally friendly and polite, "whenever the natives spoke of us, it was always with reproach. They called us 'Silguaner' (*I-Silwane*) or beasts of the sea, and whenever they pronounced this term, it was accompanied with a gesture of opprobrium that could not be mistaken for kindness." Anyway the fraud deluded Farewell right enough, and he went home pressing to his bosom a bogus concession of one-seventh of the country of Natal.'

So far then Dr A. T. Bryant with his facts and opinions. The former cannot be gainsaid, but the latter appear to be rather harsh. Isaacs erred too, for the term '*I-Silwane*' (Silguaner) is not one of opprobrium but one of awe and was frequently used of a great chief to show his might. The term does not specifically mean, 'beast of the sea', but any powerful and dangerous animal with the stress on 'powerful'. Indeed the kindred Matabele specifically use this term for a lion. Under no circumstances could *I-Silwane* ever be used to denote anything mean. In that case *Isi-Lokazana* would have been used, which means anything which is creepy-crawly or low.

One outstanding fact, however, emerges and stands forth like a shining beacon above the haze of time and controversy, and that is that the White men had some dominant quality even when in

rags which compelled the black men to regard them as their
superior. Shaka not only recognized this but had it proclaimed
to all his nation. It had nothing to do with sky-rockets or horses
or firearms, for these had been met with in the hands of Portuguese half-castes, and the White men's Hottentots who were
regarded with contempt.

No! the root of the European's superiority lay in his possession of *ubu-kosi* – the quality and air of chieftainship – for which
only the Zulu language has a single word which fully defines
that otherwise indefinable aristocratic ascendancy which radiates
authority without any apparent effort. This *ubu-kosi* is instantly
and instinctively recognized by every Zulu among his own
people and the majority of Whites. Sigananda Cube of Rebellion
fame, who at the age of fourteen was at Bulawayo when the
Whites arrived, said of them: 'Their eyes have fire.' And whatever else Farewell and Fynn may otherwise have lacked, they
were resolute characters, and yet not unkindly, and their native
followers adored them. Nor did they and Lieutenant King, R.N.,
who arrived a year later, buy their way into the good graces of
Shaka, for they invariably received infinitely more than they gave
him in worldly goods, but in Shaka's mind made good this deficiency by imparting knowledge to him for which he had an
everlasting thirst. For Lieutenant King, who arrived a year later,
Shaka actually developed a great personal affection and sacrificed
many cattle to the spirits in the vain hope of staving off death
during his fatal illness.

Shaka gave the English a ceremonious farewell with a liberal
present of elephant tusks, milch cows, and slaughter oxen, 'In
order that "Joji" (King George) may not feel ashamed of me for
not taking care of his children whilst they are dwelling under my
shadow'. He assured them that they would be welcome at his
capital whenever they wished to call, individually or in parties.
That all homeless natives in Natal who sought asylum with them
would likewise enjoy his protection. He then instructed Chief
Mbikwane to escort them safely till they reached Port Natal
(Durban). As on their first journey, no military escort was
detailed to accompany the English – a tactful gesture to show

them that they were under no restrictions or surveillance, whatsoever.

When the English had left, Shaka called a meeting of his
whole council on whom he particularly impressed his wish that
every mark of respect and friendship should be shown to the
Whites. 'They have knowledge, and knowledge is strength, and
there is much we can learn from them.'

In spite of the attempt on his life Shaka took no steps to safeguard his person from a recurrence. He rigidly resisted all sug-
gestions to have a constant bodyguard posted around his hut at
night: neither his mother's tears, nor Pampata's, nor Mgobozi's
remonstrances, though they moved him deeply, could change
his mind.

But when Mgobozi risked his life by calling Shaka stupid and
thoughtless, concluding: 'Now kill me; for no one likes to hear
the truth,' then Shaka wept and said: 'If I killed you, Mgobozi,
I would be killing myself. If you tell me the truth, however unpleasant it may be, I mind it not, for well I know how your
loyal heart loves me. Wipe away your tears, my mother, as I now
do mine, and let us cheer our hearts with a pot of beer and a
friendly snuff of this latest tobacco. I will promise to have a few
guards around me on dark nights, but for the rest of the time
you must leave me to myself, for it irks me to be constantly
guarded like a sick child.'

Mdlaka and Nqoboka having arrived, the little gathering of
old friends recalled the earlier days of stress and strain, the only
comparative stranger present being Mbopa.

They discussed the White men and especially the military
problem posed by their firearms and horses in the event of war.
It was Shaka's opinion that these advantages could be overcome
by manoeuvring the White forces into broken country, forcing
them to dismount, and using the advantage of Zulu numbers
and, as Mgobozi added, Zulu courage. The King also worked out
a method of dealing with a defended *laager* of wagons by means
of fire. But he insisted that there should be no reason for war
between Whites and Blacks, and from the first he expressed his
intention of sending some of his young men, perhaps as many

as two regiments, to Britain, to learn the White man's arts. But when the question of possible intermarriages was raised, by Nandi, supported by Pampata, Shaka strongly supported Mgobozi's objections to anything of the sort. It would not do to allow good Zulu blood to be bastardized by a people not belonging to the Nguni race.

In this year of Shaka's first contact with Europeans an event occurred, at the Festival of the Little Umkosi, which greatly heightened Shaka's prestige, and therefore his power: he saved the sun from extinction.

The Zulu calendar was based on the flowering date of the *Umdubu* tree and was consequently self-rectifying, since if the year was forward the tree flowered early, if backward, then the flowering was late. As soon as the Pleiades (*Isi-Limela*, from *Lima*, to dig) appeared in the Zulu morning sky preparations for digging, or rather hoeing (and, by extension, nowadays, ploughing), were made. Early in July the Belt of Orion (*Impambana*, the Crossing) became visible, whereupon cultivation started. When the soil was ready for planting the people rested until heralds brought the news that the *Umdubu** trees in the Ngoye and Nkandla forests had flowered, which they do suddenly and in great beauty. Planting could then begin. Of course the elders of the tribes kept some account of time and season, but by July they were generally out in their reckoning, that is, they were said to be lost, and the *Umdubu* helped them to find themselves again, whence it was also known as *Mdukwa*.

In 1824 the flowering of the *Umdubu* was early and so, therefore, was the festival of Little Umkosi, or First Fruits, which was advanced to 20 December. On that day, one of rejoicing and feasting, Shaka had gone through the ceremony of squirting at the sun and also stabbing at it with the royal red-shafted spear as usual. The medicine for this purpose was always prepared by Shaka's war-doctor Mqalane, who also had the duty at this time of adding to the 'power' of the Zulus' sacred coil, the *inkata*, a ring made of woven grass and about one yard in diameter and of growing thickness, for the personal *inkata* of each chief was

* In the low veld it was the *Imhliziyo Nkulu*, meaning 'Great Heart'.

added to the national one. These rings were impregnated with all the war and strengthening medicines which were used in a chief's or king's lifetime, bits of his hair, nail-parings and sweat, together with such body matter as could be purloined from neighbouring chiefs. The net result was supposed to give the owner of the *inkata* all the power of the persons who were thus partly incorporated in it, as well as all the magic they ever possessed. The whole *inkata* was encased in a python skin. This Zulu national coil was finally a foot thick, and an outsize python's skin had to be specially stretched to encompass it. It was captured by the British after the Zulu power had been destroyed at the Battle of Ulundi in 1879, and was burnt to make sure that this power did not revive ! – logic to the modern Zulu !

There now occurred an event subsequently much used by writers of fiction.

At the height of the festivities Shaka and his entourage were watching the multitude. They were standing under the big, shady fig tree at the top end of the kraal, for it was a hot summer's day. Everybody looked happy, and sounds of singing floated everywhere. Even the birds in the tree added to the general gaiety with their lively twittering. Suddenly all bird-life seemed to cease. Shaka and Mqalane looked into the tree with a mystified air, and then the rest of the party, including Mdlaka and Mgobozi, did the same.

This silence and uneasiness of the birds was, as Shaka at once remarked, an *umhlolo*, an evil occurrence. Soon the people, too, were silent, for they saw that at the perimeter of the shade cast by the Court tree, the flecks of sunshine were taking grotesque and unreal shapes. And although there was not a cloud in the sky, it grew darker.

Then Shaka, followed by his party, strode out of the shade of the tree and glanced upwards.

'Wo!' he exclaimed with cupped hands to his mouth. 'Wo! umhlolo,' repeated all the others with hands to their mouths. All except Mqalane, who was silent.

Rapidly the sunlight faded as the disk of the moon covered more than half of the fiery orb and continued to invade the rest.

A heart-breaking wail arose from the multitude. 'The sun is being devoured; we are lost, for we shall be eaten too.'

'What is it, Mqalane?' Shaka said in a low aside. 'I have heard the old people say it has happened before, but I don't like it.'

As the eclipse advanced beyond three-quarters Shaka muttered to Mqalane: 'If it does not come back we are finished,' whereupon Mqalane at last replied: 'Have no fear. It will return. Chew this quickly, and then spit at the sun, commanding it to return. It is powerful medicine,' and he handed a black little ball to Shaka.

Mgobozi looked grave, but dauntless. '*Safa sapela*' (We are dead and finished.)

Seven-eighths of the sun was eclipsed. The light was weird and ghostly. The whole countryside began to look like an antechamber of Hades, and to the cowering, superstitious multitude it seemed like the approach of the nether world. They were numbed. This sudden transformation of a brilliant mid-summer's day of national feasting and rejoicing into an exact picture of what they imagined the underworld to be like paralysed them all. The cocks began to crow.

Then Mqalane's great voice boomed out: 'Have no fear, people of Zulu. Your mighty King is now going to spurt at the monster devouring the sun, and then he will stab it, and, mortally wounded, it will recede into its hole in the sky. Behold! all you people; he is doing it now, and soon the light will return.'

Shaka stood on the clay mound whence he made national announcements. The people gazed at him with fearful hope. His commanding figure seemed to be magnified to majestic proportions in that weird and unreal light. In his right hand he held the red-shafted spear, and in his left the Royal stick. Then he spurted at the sun. He commanded it to return. His spear lunged in the direction of the sun and he kept it pointing there as immobile as a statue. The vast concourse held its breath. The sun was nearly gone.

An incredulous gasp arose from the multitude. For when the sun was all but gone, it began to wax again. The black shadow of the moon was receding, and the sun's disk rapidly growing.

'It is true. It is true,' bellowed the multitude. 'The black monster is creeping back, and the sun is chasing it now. Our King has stabbed the beast and it is losing power.'

Like Joshua of old, Shaka continued to exploit the dramatic possibilities of the situation, and he continued in his statuesque posture; as the sun rapidly regained its ascendancy, tumultuous shouts arose from the populace. First with trembling hope as the sun reclaimed one-quarter of its own. Then with firm conviction as it recovered half. As three-quarters of it emerged, the tumult became deafening; and finally when the full sun shone forth again, there was one continuous roar of victory, which continued in triumphant waves of adulation for the all-powerful Warrior-King who had saved the nation.

At last Shaka held up his hand, commanding silence. Then bidding Mqalane to take his stand in front of, and a little below him, he bade him address the people.

'Children of Zulu,' began Mqalane. 'Behold your King! It was he, and he alone, who saved you and the nation today. Without him we would all have perished; but he slew the black monster which nearly succeeded in devouring our life-giving sun. Give thanks to him, and forget not to say it with cattle and comely damsels. For where would you all be, if it were not for him? Give thanks, I say.'

'*Bayete!*' they roared in joyful gratitude. '*Bayete!* King of kings, and devourer of all your enemies. Mighty Elephant who stamps but once!'

It is appropriate at this point to note that Shaka was far too wary to engage in the very uncertain business of rain-making, which all other chiefs, and kings, dabbled in. By custom he was required to do so, but he did not care to make himself look foolish, in case of failure. Mqalane, the war-doctor, would not touch the business either, but there were plenty of charlatans in the country who were prepared to risk the hazardous undertaking, for the rewards of success were great, even if the penalties of failure were drastic and certain.

Shaka argued that it was best to employ a rain-maker of little account, for if he failed, as any other rain-maker would, the populace would require a scapegoat, and little would be lost in sacrificing a man of no consequence.

The King's terms were perfectly clear and concise. 'Bring the rain and your reward is great. Fail, and the birds will have a meal.'

On one occasion when the rains had been tardy, the rainmakers were summoned before the King. After questioning them all in a grimly humorous way, one of them succeeded in securing the royal tender, as it were.

Shaka: 'How soon are we to get rain?'

Rain-Maker: 'My Father, I must procure some sea-water, and then an "*isiqalaba*" (Sugar Bush, Protea) branch from the Drakensberg. These mixed will pave the way.'

Shaka: 'In that way you will gain ten days, but you will need the time, for my old aunt Mkabayi's gouty big toe has not started to ache yet. It is always a sure sign of approaching rain, for even when I was a herd-boy we relied on that. You should go into business with her, and on the day she throws her stick at your head, you can proclaim to all the people that you are now ready to bring the rain.'

Rain-Maker: '*Hau! Baba*' (reproachfully).

Shaka: 'If somebody's toe does not ache, after ten days, presumably you will need a fish from the Pongola river, and the eyelashes of a hippopotamus from the Umzimvubu ("Home of the Hippos") river' – these rivers are 400 miles apart.

Rain-Maker: 'I was thinking of something very much nearer home, my Father – in this very river which flows past here.'

Shaka: 'What can it be?'

Rain-Maker: 'A white crocodile, my Father.'

Shaka: 'How so? There are hardly any ordinary crocodiles in this river, then where would an unheard-of white one come from?'

Rain-Maker: 'It would be hard to get, my Father – as hard as making rain in dry weather.'

Shaka: 'You are a bold rascal, but I like your answers. You give as good as you get, and that may save your neck. I will pass the word to you when Mkabayi starts to throw things.'

Rain-Maker: 'I thank you, my Father, for you are the greatest rain-maker in the country.'

But Shaka was not, of course, free from all the superstitions of his people and he had been much disturbed by the eclipse. That it was an omen, and an unpleasant one, he was convinced. He now awaited an interpretation from Mqalane.

Mqalane was wise in his generation, for he knew that he was dealing with the most precocious and unusual sample of his race. Not for nothing had he kept his position from the beginning of Shaka's reign as chief war-doctor and personal fortifier of this most exacting sovereign. Shaka, whilst publicly acknowledging the efficacies of the various prescribed charms and magical medicines, privately scoffed at Mqalane's efforts, and only encouraged them because he knew that their psychological effects were great on the army, which believed in them.

When Shaka therefore asked Mqalane what action should be taken following the eclipse, the war-doctor told him:

'It is not for me to say, but the old people held that when the sun died as it did today, it is an evil omen, and a warning not to embark on any major enterprise for a whole year.'

Shaka complained that this meant that the army, already idle and eating up the State cattle, could not be sent beyond the frontier. Mqalane replied, says the Chronicle, that the people must be taxed in cattle to support the army which should be strengthened, for trouble was brewing in the north where Sikunyana son of Zwide was active and resourceful.

And Mqalane advised the King: 'Let the enemy come into your fold and there destroy him.'

'You speak words of wisdom and truth, Mqalane, and I shall heed them. They walk side by side with those of Mdlaka and are near my own thoughts, which, however, sometimes get clouded at the sight of so many idle warriors. For the thing I created to make me great and powerful is now eating me up. I think we understand one another, and you may go now. I shall not forget what I owe you for today's work – when the cattle and the girls come in.'

'*Baba! Nkosi! Ndabezita!* Father – King – Illustrious Sir,' said the grateful Mqalane, taking his leave.

Throughout the year 1825 the Zulu army was not employed on

any large-scale operation but spent most of its time in the cantonments provided by the great military kraals. The absence of disease in the army was a remarkable fact, especially when compared with the heavy mortality in Napoleon's forces.*

It was only when the Zulu army later penetrated to the lowlands of the north, which were heavily infested with malaria, that they sustained devastating losses, and were also badly inflicted with dysentery. On their return to Zululand the survivors usually recovered rapidly. Partly, these ravages could also be accounted for by the inadequacy of food for months on end, during the two abortive expeditions to the north. In fact there were periods of absolute famine, which seriously undermined all resistance to disease. Shaka's last campaign into the healthy Cape Colony in 1828 was completely free of disease, although he had 20,000 men in the field.

Shaka ultimately had 1200 young women, his 'sisters', at Bulawayo, and his various military kraals: the people generally referred to them as the 'Great House'. Three miles from Bulawayo Shaka had his relaxation or pleasure kraal, which he aptly named 'Em-Tandeni' – the Place of Love – where he kept his specially chosen women.

It was here that Shaka's stormy petrel of love, Mbuzikazi Cele, reigned as self-appointed queen of the harem, but not of the kraal as a whole, which was ruled by a stern and apparently harsh Royal matron – a distant relative of Shaka's. It needed a firm hand to keep the Royal concubines in order, for with high living, a great deal of idleness, and the inexorable demands of nature, particularly of these very children of nature, they would take the most fantastic risks to 'get their man'.

The harem guards, known as Qwayi-Nyanga – moon-gazers – had their hands full. As the Zulus knew nothing about eunuchs, and in any case would have regarded human castration as a revolting abomination, Shaka hit on the next best idea. He chose

* Napoleon remarked that, as his monthly losses from disease often amounted to 20,000 men, there was no reason why he should not have a bloody battle every month.

as harem guards the most unprepossessing males in his realm. Even so, these Calibans found that it was not enough to guard the harem against the ingress of males from without, for the better they performed their duties, the graver the risk to their own persons from man-starved, idle women. These harem nymphs, in extreme cases, found their vision gradually clouded by passion, and one by one they began to discount the ugly characteristics of their guardians, and somewhat hopefully began to imagine that kindly nature must assuredly have given them some compensating point.

In selecting these ugliest specimens as guards, Shaka made a serious error of judgement, for they too suffered from pent-up passions, the simple reason being that they had no natural outlets, being more or less avoided by the free girls outside the harem. It was tantamount to supplying one party with food and no water and the other with water and no food. Inevitably it led to exchange! Moreover, some of the girls used it as a bribe in order to get to their real lovers. In this, and innumerable other ways, the nimble-witted concubines almost invariably outwitted the more ponderously thinking male guardians.

Whereas these harem women had deadly feuds against each other – usually on the score of jealousy – in one matter they stuck together absolutely, namely, the keeping of each other's guilty secrets. They all enjoyed quite a measure of freedom in the daytime as they went out to draw water and bathe, or collect firewood, besides attending to the daily calls of nature. But the areas they were allowed to visit were completely taboo to all males, on pain of summary death. It must be emphasized here, however, that the average normal Zulu girl was continent, and it was only when she became a harem (or seraglio) girl, deprived of all male company, that she ultimately rebelled when her years began to mount up to twenty-five and more. For Shaka could not possibly satisfy more than a dozen or so, let alone 1200.

The diarist Nathaniel Isaacs, who arrived at Port Natal when the brig *Mary* was grounded there on 1 October 1825, kept a record of his life in Zululand for six years. He was allowed to visit the harem but found the experience embarrassing. He confirms the Zulu chronicler as to the wild spirits of the harem girls.

'They gathered round me and began to examine me with no little scrutiny, without perceiving my diffidence or displeasure, and heedless of the King who, if he had seen them, would instantly have put them to death. They, however, on these occasions are pretty wary, and know when they can take such liberties with impunity.'

Shaka came and went several times on his periodical visits to *Em-Tandeni*. Then the utmost caution was observed by all those engaged in illicit affairs, whilst the King disported himself with the stars among his favourites, and particularly with Mbuzikazi Cele, who had the power of completely enthralling his senses. Mbuzikazi had discovered that she had a peculiar charm, and, like Cleopatra, she possessed the brains to develop it for holding Shaka, as the Egyptian Queen had done with Caesar and Mark Antony.

Nevertheless she only captured Shaka's senses, and Pampata remained the unquestioned Queen of his heart, of whom he never tired as he did of Mbuzikazi, after a hectic day or so. This permanent preference of Shaka for Pampata was the bane of Mbuzikazi's existence, for well she knew that she was only the mistress of his lust, and that when that was spent she meant little to him. Shaka enjoyed some of her sharp-tongued sallies, for she was a genius at non-repetitive invective, with which she lashed the other harem lilies to shreds. She was disliked and feared as much as Pampata was universally loved.

Mbuzikazi spared no women – not even Pampata in her high position as first favourite. Even Mbopa feared her, for she did not hesitate to tell any man what she thought of him. In one matter she was, however, extraordinarily noble, and that was in the way she protected the guilty secrets of her 'sisters', even though it might endanger her own life.

There is a story that Mbuzikazi, coming face to face with Pampata one day at Bulawayo, scornfully looked her up and down, and then in withering accents said: 'What the King sees in a smug-faced insipid old bitch like you surpasses my understanding. There is nothing in your ageing body which can in any way compare with mine. When it comes to talking you have not a single opinion of your own, but meekly echo everyone else's. Then in your sly way, with many little "buts", you slowly twist these opinions around, till people go in the opposite way they started from. You may think it clever, but I call it deceitful ... Why don't you answer, or are you a deaf mute, and an imbecile as well, judging by your idiotic grin?'

Pampata merely smiled in her gentle way, and shook her head. Had she wanted to, she could not have chosen a better way of raising the growing rage of Mbuzikazi. A knot of harem girls had gathered to watch this strange duel, for all knew that their favourite was using the only weapon – smiling silence – which could beat that cascade of acrimony. 'It makes me want to vomit every time I see your face,' continued Mbuzikazi. 'Your proper name should have been "Emetic", which, as you know, also means "fish". You are just as talkative and a great deal colder. So cold, in fact, that any man's manliness must be chilled to nothingness on contact with you.'

Still Pampata merely smiled and said nothing, whereupon Mbuzikazi tore her hair, and screaming with baffled fury, ran away shrieking unprintable imprecations at her calm rival.

It was after this that Shaka decided for the sake of peace to send Mbuzikazi to *Em-Tandeni*, where he knew she would soon arrogate to herself the premier position in the harem – and this she did!

CHAPTER 21

The English return

WITH Nathaniel Isaacs in the brig *Mary*, when she stranded on
1 October 1825, within the entrance to Port Natal (Durban), were
Lieutenant King, R.N., and a Scottish boy, John Ross. Most of the
cargo and all the medicines were lost.

The seamen, under the direction of their carpenter, Hutton,
immediately set about building another ship from the timbers
recovered from the wreck, supplemented by local wood obtained
from selected trees. The latter, however, had to be seasoned before
use. It took them nearly three years to complete a barque, which
they named *Chaka*. The delay was partly due to the excursions
the sailors made with Shaka's armies and hunting parties. In
the meantime they soon became ill, and they had no medicines.
The most accessible place from which these could be obtained was
the Portuguese Settlement at Delagoa Bay, and since there was
nobody else who could be spared, they decided to send John Ross
– a boy only fourteen years of age.

The distance from Durban to Delagoa Bay is 300 miles as the
crow flies, and at least 400 miles by the tortuous land-route which
Ross would have to follow. The whole journey would be through
country infested with wild animals, and beyond Zululand even
native paths would largely cease to exist; the boy would therefore
have to negotiate wild wooded country inhabited here and there
by scattered, hostile tribes, and bands of the fiercest marauders –
the heritage left behind by Soshangane, Zwangendaba and
Nxaba, on their destructive trails to the north.

Arriving at Shaka's capital on his march to Delagoa Bay, young
Ross called on the King, who received him kindly. Great was
Shaka's astonishment on hearing that this mere child contem-
plated so hazardous a journey, accompanied only by two native

300

servants, who even then had already acquired an abounding faith in the protective powers of a European, even though he was but a boy!

'*Mamo!*' exclaimed Shaka with surprise, '*Kodwa unesibindi*' 'My mother! but he has a liver!' (meaning courage) – 'Nevertheless what can courage alone do against the terrible hazards he has to face?' And filled with generous admiration Shaka provided Ross with an escort of two companies of soldiers and with ten pairs of elephant tusks to trade with the Portuguese. He sent ahead messages that Ross and his party were to be provided with food and slaughter oxen. Before they left, after the King had given careful instructions to the commanding officer as to the conduct of the expedition, he said to Ross: 'By what means would you have prevailed over the difficulties without my help?' To which Ross answered: 'My head, my heart and my gun.'

During two months Ross and his two companies met and overcame many dangers, from every kind of wild beast, and from hostile tribesmen beyond Shaka's borders who frequently attacked the expedition.

When in due course Ross presented himself to the astonished Portuguese at Delagoa Bay they could hardly believe their eyes. In fact they regarded him with suspicion, because, they said, no Christian would think of sending a boy of his age alone among a body of savage warriors on such a terrible journey. They thought at first that he was the spy and spearhead of one of Shaka's armies. But Ross and the Zulu leader convinced them of the peaceful nature of the mission, and they gave the boy all the medicines he needed as a free gift. They accepted Shaka's gift of two big elephant tusks, and traded in the others for beads. And so this stouthearted youngster accomplished his mission and on his return to Bulawayo gratefully reported his success to Shaka, to whom he gave all the credit.

'Not so, Child of the White man,' the King replied with dancing eyes. 'It was your bravery which warmed my heart, and caused me to give you a fitting shield and blade for your otherwise hopeless venture. How could I have let you go forth alone, knowing the dangers as I do? My heart would have bled, for though the death of many ordinary people affects me not, the death of one brave man does. And you are a man now, even though your body be that of a boy.'

After Ross had left, Shaka said to his entourage: 'If their children are like that what must their men be like! Small wonder that they brave the ocean waves, which fill even our bravest warriors with fear. True, we only fear that which we do not know, but these White people do not even fear that.'

There is nothing to commemorate the great deed of this brave Scots boy. The trail he blazed is now closely followed by the great north road from Durban via Swaziland to Delagoa Bay. Surely this highway could be aptly named after this heroic boy? Shaka rose nobly to the occasion and set an inspiring example to the fellow countrymen of John Ross. The Zulus salute John Ross as *I-Qawu* – The Hero.

At about the time of Ross's visit, and despite Shaka's good-natured dealings with the boy, the King was in a bad mood. He was worried about the great idle army, 30,000 men who were 'eating him up'; he glowered sourly at his councillors whenever he saw them, disgusted by the comfortable paunch which many of them were developing in the benign conditions of *Pax Zulu* – Shaka's Peace.

'Even I, myself,' he complained, 'am beginning to look like a woman just starting a pregnancy. As for the rest of you, excepting Mgobozi and Mdlaka, you are all eight months with child!'

The King decided on a forced route march through the whole realm. The council would be accompanied by slayers who would have orders to kill stragglers. Army exercises would follow.

Without delay Shaka arose and led the way, with his thunder-struck councillors and generals following in his wake. Mbopa had only time to issue the necessary instructions to the heralds who preceded the King, the slayers and the Fasimba regiment, which escorted the Court, and then followed after his Royal master, who was closely followed by Mgobozi. Mdlaka was ordered to stay behind to attend to all matters of State in the King's absence.

Thus, in single file, Shaka led the way at a steady loping march of nearly five miles an hour. The councillors each carried the customary stick without which no Zulu travels. Behind them came the two sinister army 'slayers of stragglers', each armed with a broad-bladed assegai and carrying a shield. The Fasimba regiment followed, and ahead of the King ran the Royal heralds and a detachment of guards.

Hour after hour Shaka kept up the devastating pace. He was sweating freely although it was late autumn, and streams poured from the fat councillors. That night there was a brilliant moon and the King continued the march relentlessly up to the cold Nkandla highlands. Silently, inexorably, the slayers followed. A short halt was called at midnight next to a stream, and everyone drank some water – but sparingly, as they knew what the consequences would otherwise be. Then they all sat down and ate a few mouthfuls of the iron ration of the army – kota. So far the councillors were all still present.

Then the gruelling march was resumed. Past the Nkandla forest and the Etaleni mountain, until Mount Hlazakazi, on the Buffalo river, came into view. At dawn Shaka called a halt. More than sixty miles had been covered. The roll-call revealed that only two councillors were missing, although the rest all looked exhausted, and even the King and Mgobozi showed signs of strain. Shaka looked at them all and remarked that they were harder than he had supposed, and had now all earned a long rest. Whereupon everyone lay down and slept, and the day was well advanced before the march was resumed.

For six days Shaka kept up the march, averaging some fifty miles a day. He inspected every military kraal on the way and, when he finally returned to Bulawayo, all the councillors and senior officers looked relatively slim, for 300 miles and more of forced marches, on a meagre diet, had worked wonders. No further casualties had occurred amongst them after the first night's march.

No sooner had Shaka returned to his capital than he summoned Mdlaka to take a strong division of some seven regiments, with which he was to proceed to Thaba Bosiu to the aid of Mshweshe (Moshesh), the king of the Ba-Sutu, who was hard pressed by Matiwane and his Ngwanes. Shaka also meant to show the Matabele that they must not encroach into that neighbourhood as it was now under his protection.

For Mshweshwe – wise statesman that he was – had foreseen that he would be crushed between Matiwane's Ngwanes and the other migrating hordes, not to mention Mzilikazi's Matabele, who had now also put in an appearance. He was struggling desperately to consolidate the many remnants of scattered Sutu tribes which had found a rallying point around his great stronghold, Ntaba Bosiu (Mountain of the Night).

Mshweshwe, in his extremity, had, therefore, appealed to Shaka for protection by suggesting that he should 'throw his blanket over him', that is, become his suzerain Lord. He had managed this adroitly by first sending Shaka extensive presents of ostrich feathers for his regiments. He sent these gifts over the almost impassable mountainous hinterland of Basutoland, over the 11,000-foot-high Drakensberg, through the Ndidimeni Pass, after Matiwane had been cleared from that neighbourhood by the Zulus in 1822.

Then Mshweshwe stopped the consignments and reported to Shaka that the stoppage was due to Matiwane and his ilk, and could only be resumed if the Zulu King afforded him protection. Hence Shaka's orders to Mdlaka to proceed to Ntaba Bosiu. As the crow flies this was over 400 miles from the Zulu capital, for even crows did not fly across a mountain range over 10,000 feet high. On foot the distance was 500 miles, via present-day van Reenen's Pass, Harrismith, Ficksburg and Ladybrand.

Mdlaka's army felt the bitter winter cold of the highlands after crossing the Drakensberg Mountains. They carried hide blankets and karosses, and were well provided with slaughter oxen. Dingane and Mhlangana – Shaka's half-brothers – accompanied this expedition. The King had opined that Dingane was getting too soft and fat and, much to the latter's disgust, had bundled him off with the expedition.

At Likhoele, not far from Ladybrand, Mdlaka came up with Matiwane and his Ngwanes, and again at Kolonyama, where he captured all the Ngwane cattle, which Matiwane had perforce to abandon in order to save his skin. The latter, however, only gained time, for the Zulus hung on to his heels till they chased him over the Orange river at Aliwal North. Then Mdlaka thought it was time to return, for he was now 600 miles from his base. On his way back he paid a friendly call on Mshweshwe at Ntaba Bosiu and assured him of Shaka's continued protection.

This show of strength by the Zulus did, indeed, safeguard Mshweshwe from all further serious attacks, and he was able to build up the Ba-Sutu (Basuto) nation without any further molestation of a serious nature from native tribes. He did come into collision with the Whites, later, but his shrewd diplomacy enabled him to steer successfully between Scylla and Charybdis, represented by Briton and Boer, and to this day his nation occupies Basutoland as a semi-independent State, in the form of a British Protectorate.

It is said that from this expedition Dingane and Mhlangana brought back the honourable scars of war, which would account for their brother's indulgence towards them, for the surest way to Shaka's heart was an act of bravery.

It was about this time that Shaka's grandmother, Mtaniya, died. She was the daughter of Manyelela of the Sibiya clan and supposed to be between 90 and 100 years of age. Shaka was deeply grieved, and the nation went into mourning for a month. About a score of people were executed for not showing sufficient sorrow, or for transgressing the rules against shaving and having their hair cut.

How great Shaka's affection was for his grandmother is related by Fynn. 'Shaka requested me to attend his grandmother, who was dangerously ill with dysentery and fever. I accordingly went to see her. As her age was about eighty, I saw no hope of recovery, and candidly told the King my fears. He requested me to put a white shirt on her. I did so. He then began to cry bitterly. Jacob, the interpreter, told me of Shaka's great affection for his grandmother. When she happened to visit him he frequently washed her eyes and ears, which were in a sad state because of her age; he also pared her nails and otherwise treated her as a father might his child. We could hardly believe that a man of an apparent unfeeling disposition could be possessed of such affection and consideration for others. Further observation, however, convinced us that this was indeed the case.'

When Lieutenant Farewell and H. F. Fynn called soon after his grandmother's death to offer their condolences, Shaka raised the question of the possibility of securing an elixir which would prolong life. His mother Nandi was then approaching the age of sixty; her hair was thinning and had turned grey, and he was perturbed lest advancing age snatch her away from him.

Fynn, who could now converse without the aid of an interpreter, told him that the Europeans had no elixir of life, but they did have a hair-restorer and dye which would turn her hair into its original youthful colour. As Fynn was not as yet very proficient in expressing himself in Zulu, Shaka may have misunderstood him, for he seized on this one point of restoring hair to its pristine youthfulness and exclaimed: 'It must indeed be the elixir of life! Procure for me, therefore, this hair-restorer, and if it works on the body as well as it does on the hair – for I would have it rubbed all over my mother – then you may name the price of your reward, and if it be half the cattle in Zululand and all the elephant tusks, they shall be yours.'

It has been suggested that Fynn had a base motive in keeping up the King's faith in this hair preparation, but it is possible that, having mentioned the hair-restorer, and Shaka having jumped to a wrong conclusion as to its possibilities, Fynn may have found himself in a cleft stick. For, in bluntly disillusioning the King, he may have raised a suspicion in his mind that Fynn did not wish him to become the possessor of this potent medicine. And to baulk Shaka was dangerous.

Be that as it may, Fynn and all his companions were thenceforth committed to do all in their power to secure a bottle of the hair-restorer, and Shaka basked in the hope of what it would mean to his mother, and to himself, too. It cannot be gainsaid that the prospects opened up by the 'elixir' were of immense benefit to the whole White settlement; for Shaka rendered them every assistance in his power, particularly to hasten the building of their new ship which should carry the order for the hair-restorer, failing any vessel calling in the meantime.

Nandi's kraal, Emkindini, was only three miles from Bulawayo, and two from Em-Tandeni, and Shaka frequently strolled over from one or the other to see his mother. With the prospects of the 'elixir' bubbling in his heart, Shaka could not restrain himself but immediately called on his mother, whom he greeted most joyfully.

'*Sakubona Mame*' ('Greetings, my mother!') he called out. 'I have great news for you. Hitherto, with all my power, I could not prevent the years from eating you up. But now the White men are going to procure for me a magic medicine which will make your grey hair black again and, where it is thin or falling out, it will grow again. That is certain. Then we will rub the rest of your body with the medicine, and of a surety it must act as beneficially there as it does on the head. In this way, then, you will become young and strong again and live with me far beyond the normal span, and I will use it, too, when the need arises.'

Nandi thanked her son but took the promise of longevity very coolly. And when Shaka asked what ailed her she again raised the matter of his marriage. Shaka defended his celibacy with the usual arguments and, when Nandi saw that she was still to be denied grandchildren, she wept. Shaka tried to console her but she became angry and, among other things, accused him of folly in trying to keep more than a thousand young and unsatisfied women in purdah. She ended her tirade with a deadly sneer:

'Sometimes,' she said meaningly, 'I wonder if there is not something in the jibes the herd-boys made at you concerning your sexual development. Perhaps you do lack potency.'

Shaka was stung to the quick, for it was still a sore point with him. For a moment or two his face became distorted with rage.

After a long pause, Shaka took his leave. 'Stay you well, my mother, and grieve not.'

'Go you well, my son,' returned Nandi and watched him stride away. And shortly hereafter, as if in reply to this taunt, Shaka's manhood was proved beyond a question: Mbuzikazi conceived. There was nothing strange about this, except that it had been so long delayed. From the very start she had been determined to have a child by Shaka, whilst he, with equal determination, had taken every precaution to avoid having one. Mbuzikazi had ultimately won; and when in the third month she failed 'to go to the river', both she and the Royal matron in charge of Em-Tandeni knew what to expect, and they both immediately made a secret report to Nandi.

The Queen-Mother was delighted, for she knew that this girl with the volcanic temperament, whatever her faults might be, was faithful to her son. The difficulty was to convince Shaka of this, for he had lately become very suspicious of his whole harem, and had declared that he would kill any of his women who became pregnant, as he refused to have any cuckoos brought into his hut. He maintained that he took such precautions that it was virtually impossible for any of his harem to become pregnant through him.

Whether this general statement applied to Mbuzikazi, too, Nandi was afraid to elicit, as Shaka had lately become too short-tempered on this subject. The girl maintained that his iron will had been overcome on several occasions, and Nandi believed her implicitly, and rightly, too.

In any case Nandi took no chances, as she was determined to become a grandmother. She therefore made all the necessary arrangements for spiriting the girl away, just before her condition became noticeable. Here she received fortuitous help, for Mbuzikazi was one of those women whose condition showed remarkably little, and even then only towards the end.

Soon after she became pregnant a marked change came over the temperament of the girl. She developed a purring gentleness which astonished everyone who knew her. This did not fall in with Nandi's plans, for she wanted Mbuzikazi to stage a jealousy scene with Shaka, and at the right moment Nandi would appear in the guise of protector, which would give her the excuse for taking the girl away to the old Emkindini kraal, which was far away and was presided over by Nomcoba, her only daughter and confidante.

Nandi was nonplussed, when kindly nature came to her assistance, without any planning at all: when Shaka was about to leave after one of his visits to Em-Tandeni, Mbuzikazi became so tearfully cloying, after experiencing the first quickening of her babe, that the King tired of her, and ordered her to take a lengthy holiday. This played into Nandi's hands.

In due course a boy was born, who, to Nandi's delight, bore a striking resemblance to Shaka as a baby. Mbuzikazi was only allowed to suckle the infant a few times, lest her breasts later betray her, and a wet nurse named Nomagwebu was duly installed. Nandi's greatest difficulty now was to tear herself away from the child, as she frequently had to do, to return to her own kraal. Between her, Mbuzikazi and Nomcoba, the baby did not lack for love and attention, and grew apace at the old Emkindini kraal.

When Shaka presently moved his Royal residence to Dukuza (present-day Stanger) more than half-way nearer to Port Natal than Bulawayo – in order to be nearer the White settlement – Nandi could not resist the temptation of bringing the child into her own kraal, the new Emkindini. There she could cherish it to her heart's content, although she was in a constant state of tension, as she was never quite certain when the King would call, in spite of the warning system she had devised. To all intents and purposes, however, the child belonged to Nomagwebu, even if it was a little strange that Nandi and Mbuzikazi should hover over him so much.

CHAPTER 22

Death of a warrior

ONE day, early in October 1826, Shaka was sitting among his headmen at Bulawayo. He was bemoaning the unhealthy condition into which, for lack of war-like exercise, the nation was degenerating, when a runner suddenly appeared, perspiring and breathless, and announced the stimulating tidings that Sikunyana, with the whole host of the resurrected northern confederation of the Ndwandwes, was approaching the frontier. He was bringing with him the women and the wealth of the confederation to retake possession of the Ndwandwe country which his late father, Zwide, had lost.

Shaka was delighted and immediately ordered a general mobilization, *uku-kulela ngoqo*, and summoned the great war-doctor, Mqalane, from the Mfule district to get ready for the sprinkling of the army – and also to receive the thanks of his King for having so accurately foretold the plans of Sikunyana, the heir of Zwide.

According to Fynn, Mqalane doctored more than 40,000 warriors, of whom 30,000 were active soldiers, and the rest reserves who had been permitted to marry. The effect of the doctoring was, of course, in Zulu eyes, instant and infallible; and on this occasion it was indeed so, for, even before the army had so much as moved from home, the enemy became so overcome with trepidation that he backed away for full two days' march. Strange to say, this interesting fact was first brought to Shaka's knowledge by a pretty augury, a shower of blossom petals – an augury, of course, which only Shaka could divine. Isaacs says that whilst he and his European companions were seated on the ground in front of Shaka's door, they ... 'observed a large quantity of small white flowers, blown from the shrubs in their vicinity, floating in the air, covering the whole space of the kraal and which were carried off by the first ripple of breeze that sprang up. The King asked us the cause of this, when, we being at a loss for a plausible reason, he observed, "that it was a sign the enemy had retreated from his position". While we were communicating with him, messengers arrived to announce the fact.

'Meanwhile, too, the "English musket corps" – consisting of the White settlers at Port Natal augmented by seamen – had been hastily summoned, with special instructions on no account to leave behind their magic tent – to say nothing of the blunder-busses, mostly out of repair and short of powder. "Hau!" Shaka declared, when he saw the tent erected, "if that does not paralyse them with terror, nothing will. An easy victory is obvious." Indeed, so convinced was he of the effectiveness of the tent, that he immediately dismissed the whole "musket corps" as relieved of further service. So back they tramped to Port Natal – all save Fynn, who marched off with Shaka to the great battle of Ndolol-wane.'

Shaka marched at the head of the main division, with Nzobo and Ndlela each commanding a wing; Mdlaka was in charge of the second and lesser division. Mgobozi was at Shaka's side. The division averaged about forty miles a day, and without complaint suffered the heat, thirst and dust in the lowlands, which alternated with the very chilly nights on the bare highlands of the present Vryheid district.

Several days of great hardship had thus to be endured before the Pongola river was reached and forded. This river was regarded as the northern border of Zululand proper. Then the Zulu host directed its course towards the En-Tombe river, and, within the sheltered nooks of a forest there, encamped in normal style behind comfortable wind-screens of leafy boughs (*ezi-honqeni*). In the vicinity stood the twin hills, Ndololwane and Ncaka; and high on the slopes of the former, just beneath its rocky summit, the Ndwandwe host stood assembled, warriors below, women and children above, cattle in between.

Early on the morrow Shaka and his staff stole from the forest (wherein his own forces lay concealed) and up the Ncaka hill to reconnoitre. He soon discovered that his spies had not exaggerated when reporting the enemy's might and magnitude as prodigious, demanding an equally prodigious offensive. Sikunyana had chosen a very strong position which could not be outflanked or turned. Of the 40,000 souls he had with him, according to Fynn, about one-half were warriors, as Sikunyana had only brought a portion of his women and children with him. Shaka had rather more than 20,000 warriors and Mdlaka the balance, which made up the Zulu total of 40,000 men. But Mdlaka was far away to the north-west executing his enveloping movement. The Zulus had, in addition, their *u-dibi*.

Returning in the afternoon from his reconnaissance, Shaka had his regiments assembled around him and harangued them with an inspiring address as to what he had seen and what he expected them to do. He asked for champions to cleave a way through the solid phalanx of the massed enemy ranks.

Mgobozi, who was conducting a tour of inspection, saw his chance of getting into the thick of the fighting and instantly he took it. Bryant says: 'Then rushed forth from the ranks the incomparable brave, Mgobozi, leaping fiercely as a madman around the arena, wildly brandishing his shield and with his spear dealing death to right and left on numberless invisible foes. All which wild mimicry is called in local parlance "*giya*". Having in imagination satisfactorily cleared the field, he stood, with outstretched legs, exhausted, and addressed the gathering: "Thus shall I go, spearing my way through the serried ranks of the foe, until I emerge in their rear or die – and so must we all do for our Father." '

Mgobozi had thus definitely committed himself, and Shaka had to support his act as a matter of honour. But Shaka was greatly worried for the safety of his old friend.

Other champions now emulated the example set by Mgobozi, and it was an understood matter that they would all have to honour their undertaking on the morrow and cleave a path through the enemy ranks. Their example would be an inspiration to all.

That evening Shaka, Mgobozi and Nqoboka, the Sokulu chief, sat alone at the small fire in the forest conversing. But Shaka was silent and moody, for he believed that Mgobozi would die on the morrow and there was nothing he could do to save his old friend. To this Mgobozi answered the king: 'My Father, we must all die sooner or later, and if my time has come nothing will hold it back. It is far, far, better to die with the joy of battle in the heart than to pine away with age, or like a sick ox in a kraal. I have lived by the spear and I shall die by it. That is a man's death. You would not deprive me of that, who are my friend as well as my father?'

'Nay, Mgobozi, but the parting would be heavy.'

Then Shaka sent for beer and, drinking only a little, he passed it on to Nqoboka, saying: 'We need but little. It is Mgobozi's night.'

'Nobela prophesied my end,' cheerfully chattered the irrepressible Mgobozi, 'and she knew a thing or two. In her last moments she realized that I could not stomach the impalement cruelties, and that I was for terminating everything quickly. For the first time I saw her eyes softening and she looked at me like a mother. Then she told me I had 'nothing to fear, and that when my end came I would be rich in honours and die the most glorious and enviable death ever known in Zululand. And, furthermore, she said the ancestral spirits of the House of Zulu would arrange a great reception for me – their adopted son – and see that I had a pleasant life in the Underworld.'

Then Mgobozi did an unusual thing, for when he had emptied another pot of beer he declined to have any more. 'It would not be seemly for my "boys" to see me "driving goats" on the eve of a battle. In any case I am full to my Adam's apple, thanks to the gracious bounty of my Father. Also I must not outstay my welcome, for I know my Father would be alone with his thoughts to arrange the order of our going tomorrow. I await his order to *valelisa* (to say goodbye).'

'*Hamba gahle, Mgobozi-ovela-entabeni.* (Go you well, Mgobozi-from-over-the-hill.) Go well, son of the Msane clan, who taught my regiments so well. You have been my dearest friend.'

'*Sala gahle, Baba* – (Stay you well, my Father) – and stay you well, too, Chief of the Sokulus,' and Mgobozi strode into the gloom of the night to his sleeping quarters. Shaka and Nqoboka watched him go in silence. There was nothing to say, for each knew the other's thoughts.

Of the great battle on the morrow, Njengabantu Ema-Bomvini, and Chief Sigananda Cube, who was present as Shaka's own *u-dibi*, say this:

When the first clash took place Mgobozi, with a number of ardent supporters, bored straight into the Ndwandwe ranks like a wedge, and so furious was their onslaught that they shore clean through all the numerous ranks of their foes, including the veteran regiments in the rear. Having thus cut their way right through, they found themselves confronted by an enormous rock, the size of a house, such as are frequently found below the crests of hills lined by precipices, from which they have broken away in ages past. As the Ndwandwe veterans turned on them, Mgobozi and his gallant band backed against the sheer wall formed by this rock. They barely had time for a breather before the Ndwandwes hurled themselves against the Zulus, and a fight of unprecedented ferocity ensued. The Ndwandwe veterans were furious, for they had recognized Mgobozi, and knew that he had killed most of their princes at the battle of Qokli.

Mgobozi was at his best now. He had already received a few flesh wounds, but these he hardly noticed. Cut off from the Zulu army and with his back literally to the wall, a savage, reasoning power asserted itself and took the place of mere blind blood-lust. Perhaps it was because he sensed that he was responsible for the lives of his 'boys' who had followed him that for once he acted as a real leader in a mêlée; for he formed his men in a compact semicircle against the rock face, and thus they met the impact of the Ndwandwes. The Zulus showed superb spear and footwork, for they were all champions, and Mgobozi grunted and growled his approbation. The first enemy wave broke against the fierce defence and receded. Mgobozi drew in his half-circle to close the gaps in the line. This lull coincided with the general lull on the main battle-front.

As soon as Mgobozi had partially recovered his breath he

314

bawled over the heads of the enemy to the main Zulu army, which was less than 100 yards away: 'We have got the bull by the testicles here. Do you now stab him in the chest!' Mgobozi's 'boys' in front recognized the voice of their beloved drill-instructor, and a howl of savage glee greeted this typical sally. It also ushered in the next general clash.

'*Si-gī-di,*' yelled the Zulus in front. '*Si-gī-di,*' echoed Mgobozi and his dauntless little company.

'*Ya-ntsini za-nja! nje-ya, nje-ya, nje-ya!*' yelled back the Ndwandwes, and the murderous battle was resumed.

'*Ngadla! Ngadla!* I have eaten! I have eaten!' The triumphant yells of warriors inflicting the death stab were now the only intelligible sounds which could be heard above the roar of the battle. Stamping feet, bumping and scraping shields, the thud of homing spears, and the answering death bellows of the victims, with all the tumult of some 40,000 desperately fighting warriors, made an indescribable din in that sea of waving, warring plumes.

Mgobozi's semicircle of heroes was shrinking ominously as his warriors fell on either side of him. They were exacting a terrible toll before they fell. Deadliest of all was Mgobozi, now bleeding in many places. Not a word did he utter now, for he needed all his breath. But his eyes shone when he looked at his men.

The second general pause set in, and, like the second clash, it lasted much longer than the first interval.

Mgobozi and his band had shrunk to half a dozen, and they were all bearing severe wounds. When he got back his breath he praised and thanked his comrades. 'What a fight!' he exclaimed hoarsely. 'This is what I always wished for.' Then, with a grin, he added: 'What about a pot of beer now? I could pour it down without a stop. It would be a fitting farewell, too, for in the next clash we will all eat earth. For us the sun will rise no more, but I for one do not regret it. I have lived by the spear, and today I die by the spear. That is how it should be. Look at the "mat" of corpses we have made for ourselves. It is a fit resting place for a king – and you are kings – all of you. Our enemies are men, too, and have fought well, but they no longer relish closing with us, even though we are but few now, and sorely stricken.'

There was a long pause. Mgobozi and his stricken remnant were leaning heavily on their shields, with their enemies a dozen yards away glaring at them with a mixture of hate and admiration. Then said Mashaya (the Striker), 'My Father, we all die gladly with you, for who would live when you are gone?'

'I thank you, Mashaya,' said Mgobozi. 'Your words put a stone into my stomach, for I liked not to drag you to certain death. And now, my children, let us say farewell, for the enemy is stirring and will soon be upon us. That will be our last fight. Let us call our final message to our brothers over there – a message of good cheer, for one more thrust will bring the Ndwandwe bull to his knees. Then let us give praise to our King. Thereafter, my children, I will say no more, for I feel the battle madness coming over me, and already the whole world looks red to me, like the blood dripping from my body. Now, all together!'

'*U-ZULU! U-Qobolwayo!* * *Bayete! Nkosi yama Kosi!*' (The Zulu! Their very essence! Hail, King of Kings! Thy will be done!)

'Our Mgobozi is still there,' yelled the Zulu army. '*Mayihlome!* To arms! and to his rescue.'

'*Si-gī-di*' roared Mgobozi and his handful of wounded lion-hearts, and the final clash was on.

Mgobozi went berserk. He was the personification of a battle-mad war-god. He vaulted at and among his enemies with such utterly reckless fury and death-dealing agility that they frequently scattered. Most of the Ndwandwes were dismayed. Then their champions engaged him in twos and threes, and, whilst he was so occupied, his companions were brought down, one after the other, until only Mashaya was left. Both he and Mgobozi were now grievously wounded but nëither recked his hurts. With their backs to the wall they still presented a deadly hazard to their enemies who stared at them with wonder. Then the Ndwandwes made a concerted rush, but once more they were scattered by the fury of the two warriors. Mashaya had, however, received mortal stabs through the lungs. As he panted for breath he looked mutely at Mgobozi with blood-streaming nostrils and

* Nearest pronunciation: '*Oo-Zoo-loo! Oo-ko-bol-why-yo!*' *Bayete* '*Buy-yeh-teh!*'

316

mouth. Without a word he sank slowly to the ground and was gone.

Mgobozi stood alone. His mouth was flecked with bloody foam. His madly staring eyes were red as blood: so he waited with heaving chest for the last rush. Already he could see the swaying tumult of the attacking Zulu army drawing near.

With a yell the Ndwandwes flung themselves at him, but the old lion met them like a pack of African wolves (wild dogs). Again and again he killed them right and left. Again and again he was pierced through and through, but for thirty seconds more he piled up the deadly score as his life-blood gushed from many gaping wounds. And so the indomitable warrior subsided amid a sea of his foes. Mgobozi was no more.

The triumph of the Ndwandwes was short-lived, for already vengeance was near. The Zulu army, fired by the deathless glory of Mgobozi's epic fight, was relentlessly stabbing its way through the dwindling Ndwandwe ranks. It was, therefore, not long after Mgobozi's death that the avengers came sweeping past in an irresistible wave which pushed the now retreating Ndwandwes farther up the hill to their doom.

When it was fighting, the Zulu army lost no time in looking for any of the fallen. Their Spartan code forbade that. So Mgobozi's body was passed in the rush after the Ndwandwes, who were now fleeing to, and through, their herds of cattle, and then on, and up the hill, where they made a last stand in front of their women and children. But it was of no avail. They were all massacred – men, women and children – except the few who managed to escape with their chief, Sikunyana, and hide in a near-by forest.

By the time the cattle had been rounded up and driven to water – always a task of first priority – the day was well advanced.*

When Shaka the King heard that Mgobozi was dead, he groaned aloud. 'Alas!' he said, 'Zwide's son I have conquered, indeed, but he has killed me in Mgobozi.' He went to look at his friend; his eyes were streaming, and for a long time he gazed in silence. Then he turned to Nqoboka and said abruptly: 'Let us go. My heart is

*For a European account of this battle see Bryant, *op. cit.*

bitter. Every Ndwandwe not yet dead shall pay for this.' And so they silently went down the hill, back to their forest camp.

The army mourned deeply. That night, in spite of great supplies of meat which usually cheered every warrior's heart, there was a silence around the innumerable camps fires in the forest. The celebration of a great victory, which had not been too costly in lives, should have been a joyful occasion, but it was not. Most of the conversations were in undertones, and almost exclusively concerned 'Our Mgobozi'.

Mgobozi's immense popularity may be summed up in one sentence. He typified the ideal of the Zulu warrior. Conservative, reluctant to learn 'new-fangled ideas' but, having learned them, like the use of the stabbing blade, obstinately clinging to them. Contemptuous of all strategy and tactics, except the encircling movement. A fixed idea that you must fight the enemy where you find him, irrespective of the strength of his position or numbers. A haughty scorn of sheltering behind any defences – even natural ones – let alone erecting any. Savage and bloodthirsty in battle. Slaying swiftly and surely, and without mercy, but never stooping to torture. No Zulu warrior would ever sully his name by using an impalement stick. The honour of any woman, friend or foe, was safe in the keeping of any Zulu warrior. Even in the flush of battle, as at Ndololwane, he would not dream of dishonouring any woman, though he would have no compunction in killing her according to instructions. Lastly, the Zulu warrior was imbued with an intense sense of loyalty, and unquestioning self-sacrifice to his chief and comrades, which, with the fanatical pride he took in his regiment, bred that *esprit de corps* which made him prefer annihilation to defeat.

All the qualities enumerated above were possessed by Mgobozi, but to such an outstanding degree that he became the guiding beacon of the whole army. The example which every newly enrolled recruit strove to emulate.

The Ndwandwes having been finally annihilated except for a sorry remnant which had escaped with their chief Sikunyana, Shaka's army had nothing further to do but return home. In doing so it skirted the Kumalo country and discovered that that will-o-the-wisp, Beje, had reappeared as arrogant as ever.

It will have been noticed how lenient Shaka was to Mzilikazi and his Kumalo clan. He had, in fact, a very soft spot for all the Kumalos, including the sub-clans under the chiefs, Beje and Mlotsha. All the Kumalos were real die-hards. As Shaka always had a weakness for the brave, this seems to be the most plausible explanation of his extraordinary leniency towards them all, which often amounted to a high degree of chivalry. When Beje and Mlotsha rebelled against Shaka he did not annihilate them, as he so easily could have done, but instead conducted openly ludicrous actions against them, suspending all his usual drastic measures. For instance, whenever the Kumalos repulsed the unaccountably weak forces Shaka sent against them, he took none of the customary action of weeding out cowards as scapegoats. In fact, he treated these repulses with high good humour, and refused to send any reinforcements.

With his huge, idle army on the way home it would have needed but a nod from Shaka to extinguish both Beje and Mlotsha, the other Kumalo chief. But, again, Shaka refused to use drastic measures against the favoured Kumalos and sent instead only one weak young regiment – the Ulu-Tuli (Dust Boys) – to put Beje in his place. Beje lured the inexperienced 'Dust Boys' into the recesses of his forest lair, and there administered such a dusting to them that they were forced to retreat and report failure.

Then something happened which gave Shaka a way out of his dilemma with honour vindicated on all sides. This happening was a gross transgression of the Zulu criminal code: Michael and John, a couple of lascivious Hottentots in Farewell's employ, had just then indulged in the rape of a young Zulu bride, a capital crime in Zulu society. So enraged thereat was Shaka, that he threatened there and then to kill every White man, Hottentot and Zulu girl within his reach. It was in reality mere stage rage, a hollow blind to placate the angry headmen round about. 'And yet,' he whispered to the Whites, 'something must be done to appease the chiefs, or they will say I am not fit to command; you must, therefore, go and fight Beje.' That something had to be done was equally manifest to the Whites; so, to appease the King, off went Isaacs, Cane, five seamen, and the offending Hottentots on the war-path.

The Belebele Division, 5000 strong, made up the Zulu contribution of this expedition. Arrived at Beje's stronghold – a mountain bordering on the Ngome forest, and not the gorge where the Um-Ota regiment fought – Isaacs and his contingent waited in vain for the Belebele Division to attack, or even show signs of activity.

So unusual was the whole conduct of the Zulus that it was clearly apparent that the commander of the division had received secret instructions to let the Whites fight it out alone with the Kumalos, and merely to afford them protection if they were too severely pressed by Beje's warriors. Shaka was evidently trying to see what effect the musketry of the Whites would have on the Kumalos.

Isaacs' party, numbering about one dozen muskets, for they included Jacob, the Swimmer – Shaka's interpreter – and some armed Natal natives, resolutely advanced on the Kumalos, of whom about fifty were visible among the great rocks near the summit of the hill. They fired an effective volley at them. Isaacs writes: 'The report of our muskets reverberated from the rocks, and struck terror into the enemy; they shouted and ran in all directions, and the Zoolas [Zulus] some considerable distance behind us, were observed all lying on the ground with their faces under, and their shields on their backs. This singular manoeuvre of the Zoolas had a terrible effect on the enemy, who on seeing the others [Zulus] fall at the report of the musketry, concluded they were all dead, and ran off to avoid coming into contact with us.'

The Kumalos were, however, die-hards, for, continues Isaacs: 'We had just finished loading, when we perceived a large body of them approaching us, in the height of rage, and menacing us with destruction; my party for a moment felt some doubt; on perceiving it I rushed forward and got on top of a rock; one of the enemy came out to meet me, and at a short distance threw his spear at me with astonishing force, which I evaded by stooping. I levelled at him and shot him dead. My party also fired, and wounded some others, when the whole ran off in great disorder and trepidation. We now felt some confidence, exulted in our success, and advanced along the side of rocks to dislodge some few who had halted with a design to oppose us again; they had got behind the bushes and large trees, and hurled stones at us with prodigious force, the women and children aiding them with extraordinary alacrity. I received a contusion on my shoulder from one of their missiles ... Advancing a little further we reached some huts, which we burnt, and killed their dogs ...'

After several days' desultory fighting in which Isaacs was wounded and many Kumalos shot, the Kumalos sued for peace as 'they did not understand this manner of fighting'. They consented to give up their cattle and to become tributary to Shaka.

'One of our seamen proposed', says Isaacs, 'that they should give ten young maidens by way of cementing their friendship by natural ties. To this they also assented with the same willingness as they gave up their cattle.'

So Beje was left once again in his Ngome forest, impoverished indeed – but only to a degree, for that wily old fox only handed in the worst half of his stock – but for the rest of Shaka's reign he remained unmolested, nor was he ever required to pocket his pride, by paying personal homage to the King.

When Shaka saw all the toothless old cows and goats Beje had parted with, he was not angry. He merely chuckled and said: 'Hau! Beje must have found a new grazing-ground for all his good stock. Perhaps it was in the tree tops, and you forgot to look there; this was a mistake, as you should know, for Beje and the Kumalos were not born yesterday.'

On seeing the five seamen with their ten prize Kumalo maidens Shaka exclaimed with delight: 'Mamo! these are discerning men. No toothless old cows for them. Did they shake them out of the trees? For of a truth I can say that never before have the Kumalos parted with a maiden without heavy payment of cattle.'

Mlotsha, head of the junior branch of the royal Kumalo house, had a stronghold on the Pondwane hill, a solitary and rugged mass in a wide plain.

From this inaccessible eyrie the Kumalo eagle ruled his clan, and extracted tribute from the neighbouring clans beyond. The cattle he collected as a leading rain-doctor provided a steady income, for during good rainy seasons he claimed a retainer, failing which he threatened to cut off supplies. Thus he instituted the quite novel concept that a rain-maker must be paid in times of plenty as well as in times of dearth; for, argued Mlotsha, if he had the power to make rain, in which all the people believed, then it was absurd to think that he could not also stop it. With which devastating logic the people agreed, and if they were tardy or forgetful in paying their water rates, the deeply grieved Mlotsha, with right on his side, sent a raiding party to distrain the necessary number of fat kine.

When Mlotsha felt bored he indulged in the highly dangerous game of twisting the Zulu Lion's tail. But as we have seen, the 'Lion' was very indulgent to all the Kumalos – Mzilikazi, Beje and Mlotsha – and allowed them the same liberties which a lioness allows her playful cubs, until one of them gives her an extra sharp nip. Then there would be a warning growl, and if that was not heeded, a little fur would fly to put the cub in its place.

Time and again Mlotsha had indulged in this tail-twisting, and as often overstepped the mark. Time and again he was chivalrously warned by the 'Lion' himself that his paw would sweep at him in the form of an expedition, which was invariably no stronger than Mlotsha's own forces. A number of single combats would then take place among the champions of both sides, and an occasional sharp skirmish if the Kumalos left their stronghold. In the meantime Mlotsha's cattle began to get thin without their usual grazing, and the Zulus were not getting fat either, even though they raided a Kumalo grain cache from time to time.

Now when the Zulu army returned from the battle of Ndolol-wane in October 1826, it had to pass not far from Mlotsha's fortress, and his latest delinquencies were remembered by the Zulus. Haplessly on that occasion he was taken unawares, without Shaka intending it. He bottled himself up indeed in time, along with his people, within the stronghold; but the stronghold was unprovisioned and the unhappy inmates soon discovered they had but

fled into a death-trap. Hunger was not long in forcing them out
again to surrender humbly to the inevitable. Shaka, however,
graciously received the Kumalo patriot back again into his family
and his favour.

Shaka did more than that. He spared Mlotsha's feelings as he
did Beje's by not requiring him to make personal obeisance to the
Zulu King. But he sent him this message: 'You are the greatest
rain-chief, and I am the greatest war-chief. Let each stick to his
own business and there will be no clash. As I have spared the
blood of your clan, maybe you will spare me a little of your
surplus rain – the next time your big toe aches.'

Hardly had Shaka and the army returned to Bulawayo from
the Ndololwane campaign when, in November 1826, he decided to
erect a new capital fifty miles south as the crow flies, and rather
more than half-way to the English settlement at Port Natal. This
was a genial gesture to the Whites, as it made it so much easier
for them to visit the King and eliminated the formidable hazard
which the broad and turbulent Tugela river presented during the
rainy season. At the same time it pleased Shaka, as it would enable
him to see more of the Europeans, whose conversations had become
a source of much pleasure to him.

The site of the new capital was some two miles north of the
Umvoti river and about the same distance from the sea, and
covered approximately the same area which is occupied by the
present town of Stanger. Shaka named his new kraal 'Dukuza',
derived from the Zulu word '*duka*', to get lost; this is said to have
been in allusion to its maze of huts in which newcomers lost their
way.

Thus Shaka moved his headquarters into Natal, which, from
the Umvoti river to the Tugela, he now began to colonize with
his own chosen settlers. The greater portion of the rest of Natal
served as Royal grazing-grounds in which uniformly coloured
herds had their apportioned districts. This colour scheme was an
excellent device for immediately spotting any beast which had
strayed from its own herd.

At the great annual national festival – the *Umkosi* or First Fruits ceremony of 1826 – all the nation assembled in full gala attire at the Royal kraal, at Bulawayo, for Dukuza had not yet been finished. The young and idle warriors plagued Shaka to lead them to war. And they chanted in his honour:

Wa qeda qeda izizwe (Thou hast finished off the tribes).
Uya kuhlasela-pi na (Where wilt thou wage war?).
He! uya kuhlasela-pi na (Yes! where wilt thou wage war?).
Wa-hlula amakosi (Thou hast conquered the Kings).
Uya kuhlasela-pi na (Where wilt thou wage war?).
Wa qeda qeda izizwe (Thou hast finished off the tribes).
Uya kuhlasela-pi na (Where wilt thou wage war?).
He! he! he! uya kuhlasela-pi na (Yes! yes! yes! where wilt thou wage war?).

But the chant exasperated the King. He had not finished off the tribes or conquered all the kings. What about Sobuza and his Swazis in the north and the Pedi-Sutus still farther on? Then there was Faku, the King of the Pondos in the south, but his territory bordered on King George's sphere of influence and that matter needed some tact and diplomacy before it could be handled.

So Shaka decided to send the army north to cool its ardour there, and off they went under Mdlaka, immediately the festivities were over. That is to say, all the younger regiments, for the Bele-bele veterans' division, as we have seen, was earmarked for the Beje campaign, accompanied by Isaacs and his party of musketeers.

The purpose of the expedition was not territorial conquest but one simply of pillage and to impress the northern tribes with the fact of Zulu supremacy, and to replenish the nation's beef supply. It was not a success: Sobuza and his Swazis took refuge in their mountain fortress from which it proved impossible to dislodge them. Farther north in the torrid and malarious bush-veld of the Oliphants river, the Ba-Pedi and Sutu country, the army was short of provisions and, encamped by the broad and turbulent river which they could not cross, subsisted on locusts and caterpillars and such 'small deer'. Then a third of the army went down with malaria and dysentery.

Mdlaka deemed it expedient to withdraw with his unaffected

warriors, westwards, up the Oliphants river to a higher altitude.
The *In-Dabankulu* regiment was hardest hit of all, with nearly all
its members *hors de combat*. With them Mdlaka left all the other
unfit and an appropriate guard of fit warriors, with a promise to
send them any spare cattle he could capture. It was all he could do
under the circumstances.

As Mdlaka forged westwards and upwards into the middle highlands the Zulu army was suddenly confronted by an appalling
apparition. A multitude of fearsome, yellow-skinned men, mounted on wild and prancing beasts – they were the Griquas, or bastard
descendants of Europeans and Hottentots, led by Barend Barends,
then hunting elephants in the neighbourhood – unexpectedly
charged down upon them amidst a terrifying flash and roar of
elephant-guns, the whole effect heightened by the billowing puffs
of black powder smoke.

The Zulus were completely taken by surprise but stood their
ground, for they knew what guns and horses were. They at first,
however, mistook the Griquas for Europeans. When the Zulus
charged forward the Griquas retired and reloaded, only to advance
again and fire. Mdlaka, remembering his talks with Shaka, then
withdrew his regiments into broken ground, where the Griquas
could not make much use of their horses, whereupon they broke
off the action. They then rode right out of the ken of the Zulus,
and Mdlaka was unable to gratify his wish to try out Shaka's
methods on them. These same Griquas – 1000 strong – were annihilated four years later by Mzilikazi and his Matabele.

When Mdlaka sent the promised cattle, with a relieving regiment, to the stricken *In-Dabankulu* regiment they found a sorry
state of affairs. For no sooner had Mdlaka left them than the
neighbouring Sutus grew suddenly bellicose and came out of their
rocky strongholds. They believed they could really tackle an army
of incapacitated Zulus with some prospect of success. And yet
they hesitated till the guards left by Mdlaka were also nearly all
stricken by illness. Then they swooped down upon the encampment of the *In-Dabankulu* regiment and executed tremendous
slaughter among them.

The survivors were helped along by the relieving regiment and tailed after Mdlaka's army, which was now homeward bound, but raiding to right and left of the direct route, which enabled the *In-Dabankulu* remnant finally to rejoin the main body.

Reaching Bulawayo (whither Shaka had meanwhile returned from Dukuza) on 18 March 1827, the expedition laid before Shaka the insignificant proceeds of a raid which had taken nearly three months.

Shaka was very annoyed at the meagre results, but much more so at the humiliating thought that mere despised Sutus should have nearly annihilated the *In-Dabankulu* in their own encampment. He could not imagine what the ravages of malaria and dysentery could do, as his army had hitherto been superbly healthy; he therefore heavily discounted all reports of incapacitation through disease, and preferred to believe that it was caused through hunger. This was the warriors' own fault, for if they were men they should by now have learnt how to live in a country which was well peopled by their enemies.

'How did the enemy live and remain robust?' Shaka asked the *In-Dabankulu* remnant before him. 'He must have had food, and it was your own incompetence and cowardice which shirked the task of dislodging the Pedi-Sutus from their rockeries, where you would have found all the food you needed. I am not speaking of the Swazis who are warriors, and who, perched on the top of inaccessible mountains, present an impossible task. But these Pedi-Sutus who live with rock-rabbits and their fleas are of no account as fighters, nor are their rockeries and the caves within them such formidable obstacles which cannot be overcome by determined men. At the most you had to face stone-throwing, which is child's play, and not to be compared with the deadly rock-rolling of the Swazis, down a long and steep declivity. It would be folly to attack the Swazis so placed. It was cowardice not to attack the Pedi-Sutus. Your cowardice brought on the hunger which weakened you, and then the Pedis and their rock-rabbits came out of their holes to look at you and were unafraid for they saw you were Zulus no more. Therefore they came forth boldly as rock-rabbits do when they see no man, and they attacked you there in the open and slew most of you, as if you were of no more account than a multitude of women. It makes my eyes sore with shame to look at you, the *In-Dabankulu* which clamoured loudest to go on the war-path. You were but a bladder full of wind and words, and now that these are gone, you have shrunk into the sorry spectacle I see before me – a proud regiment reduced to a company of sick-looking feathers with nothing to show for it.'

Shaka then turned to Mbopa, who was carrying the King's kaross of glossy leopard skins. 'Give me my kaross that I may hide my shamed head and eyes from this disgrace to the name of Zulu. Then take away this worthless remnant and have them stoned to death. For he who fears a spear, shall die by the spear, and he who fears stones shall die by them. Take them away.'

'*Bayete!*' saluted the doomed company and Shaka covered his head with the kaross. Without another word the condemned men walked with military precision to their appointed fate.

Mdlaka had done his best to intercede for his warriors, before the parade. He took whatever blame there might have been on himself, and told Shaka bluntly that he should kill the father of the erring household and not the innocent children who had but obeyed the paternal orders – that is, Mdlaka's orders. But it was all in vain. Shaka was in a bad mood, and apart from the *In-Dabankulu* regiment and the general failure of the expedition, he was greatly piqued that Barend Barends and his Griquas had made a clean getaway with the loss of but three men. Moreover, he was still very bitter at Mgobozi's death and the latter's restraining influence was no longer there. The friend of Shaka's early youth, Mbikwane, whom he had made into the chief, or king, of the Mtetwas, had also recently died. This was the same kindly man who had acted as first ambassador and guide to the Whites on their initial visit to Shaka. His moderating counsel was therefore also gone. Only Ngomane, now the Prime Minister, was left of the old friends of Mtetwa days, and Pampata. Nandi was away and too busy secretly cherishing her little grandson.

CHAPTER 23

The death of Nandi

ALTHOUGH Nandi had taken every precaution to hide the existence, or rather the identity, of the sturdy boy-child which Mbuzikazi had given birth to, her grand-maternal love for this replica of Shaka led her to one indiscretion after another. She loved the baby boy even more dearly than Mbuzikazi did herself. Never was Nandi so happy as when she was fondling him and calling him her little 'Bull-Calf' and other endearing names. She insisted on teaching him how to walk and talk and gave delighted squeaks if he belaboured her with the wooden porridge spoon he was wont to play with.

As Shaka was now principally at his new kraal Dukuza – fifty miles away – Nandi took ever greater liberties to enjoy the new happiness she found in her one and only Royal grandchild; for Nandi did not count the children of her younger son Ngwadi, whom she had had by a commoner, Gendeyana, after she left Senzangakona.

Thus it came about that whispers began to reach Shaka's ears and he decided to investigate in person, and whenever he did so, he invariably arrived most unexpectedly with practically no retinue at all, for it was nothing for Shaka to cover fifty miles or so in a night march. This ability alone distinguished him from the vast majority of native chiefs, let alone kings, who usually led a soft life and were overburdened with fat at an early age.

When Shaka therefore quietly strolled into Nandi's Emkindini kraal one early morning he was fifty miles nearer than where he was supposed to be. As he passed the opening of the reed fence screening the inner courtyard he beheld Nandi literally gambolling with the young 'Bull-Calf' in the early morning sunshine, with Mbuzikazi in close attendance.

'Greetings my mother.'

Nandi, though greatly startled at Shaka's sudden appearance, responded quietly, 'Greetings my child.'

'You appear to be very fond of the child. Pray tell me whose is it?'

'It is my grandchild,' Nandi declared with determination.

'What! Another one of Ngwadi's, for surely it could not be my sister Nomcoba's?'

'Nay, it is the grandchild I have always wanted, and had to wait so long to get it. It is yours and Mbuzikazi's.'

'Mamo!' said Shaka in affected surprise. 'You don't say so? How could that have come about?'

'That is best known to you and Mbuzikazi, and at least proves your virility, for this little Bull is the image of you, and just as fearless.'

'And what makes you think he is fearless, my mother?'

'You try and take that spoon away from him and see what you will get.'

Shaka approached and made as if to take away the spoon and saw it lifted defiantly against him, whilst a steady, hostile gaze was directed at him by the child.

'At least he has courage,' Shaka admitted with grudging admiration, 'but not long after he reaches the age of puberty he will challenge the older bull. I know not what to do with him, as Mbuzikazi is not of Royal blood, and in any case I will not acknowledge, and still less proclaim, an heir. Their best place is under the ground.'

'You would not kill this joy of my old age?' Nandi asked in great alarm, 'and yet permit the far greater danger represented by your brothers, Dingane and Mhlangana, and that evil, cringing hyaena Mbopa? Kill these three, but not this innocent child.'

'Nay, my mother, the child is safe. If only for the reason that he is a joy to you, and also because I kill not the brave. As for my brothers, how could I kill the children of my father?'

'You will not see your real danger,' Nandi said sadly and began to weep. 'I, for one, know that the real danger to this child will henceforth be your brothers and Mbopa, and I ask your permission

329

to send him far away, for much as I love him I would rather he were safe.'

Shaka then picked up his son and gazed at him long and earnestly, and turning him half around drew attention to the peculiar tuft of hair in the nape of his neck, which was identical with the one on his own. The child bore the scrutiny with a dignified silence pregnant with hostility. Then Shaka smiled and presently the bellicose look of his offspring also thawed into an answering smile, but not before Nandi had petted him and urged him to do so. Thereupon Shaka put him down, and after saying farewell to Nandi and Mbuzikazi he extended his hand to the 'Little Bull' and said '*Xaula*' (Shake hands).* The child complied in a friendly manner, whereupon Shaka bade him '*Sala gahle, Ndoda*' (Stay you well, Man). And Shaka left.

Soon thereafter Mbuzikazi and Shaka's son, with his wet-nurse Nomagwebu, accompanied by a suitable escort, left for Tembeland.

Perhaps the loss of her, grandson may have contributed to Nandi's sudden decline and death, which occurred not long thereafter.

The death of Nandi, which has generally, though falsely, been attributed to Shaka himself, took place in October 1827. At the time of her fatal illness Shaka was sixty miles away from Nandi's Emkindini kraal, hunting elephants with Henry Francis Fynn. One evening breathless messengers arrived to state that the greatest elephant of all, Nandi the Ndlovukazi,† lay critically ill.

In spite of the lateness of the hour Shaka immediately set out to bring what comfort he could to his stricken mother, and whatever medical aid Fynn could provide.

Over a continuous succession of great hills and deep valleys, in the darkness of the night, Shaka led one of the most gruelling marches on record. In silence he bore alone through thorn-bush country over rough and mostly pathless ground, for he cared not

* This custom was adopted by Shaka from the Europeans.
† 'The Female Elephant' – courtesy title conferred on Zulu Queens.

how arduous the short-cut might be so long as it reduced the distance to a minimum. Fynn was only able to keep up because he was mounted, and even then it was all he could do.

Just before noon the next day – 10 October 1827 – the great distance had been covered and Emkindini reached.

Nandi's hut was filled with mourning women and such clouds of smoke that Fynn had to bid them retire and ventilate the hut before he could breathe. Nandi was already in a coma and her grieving son could not communicate with her. Fynn says: 'Her complaint was dysentery; and I reported at once to Shaka that her case was hopeless and that I did not expect that she would live through the day.'

The regiments which had begun to assemble around the Queen's kraal were ordered to their barracks by Shaka; he himself sat in dejected silence with several of the elder chiefs around him. For two hours the King sat thus without a word escaping from his lips. Then the news he dreaded more than anything else was brought to him. Nandi was dead.

With unseeing eyes and uneven steps Shaka immediately sought the seclusion of his special hut. Thence an order was issued to the chiefs and headmen to don their war dresses. When Shaka reappeared after a time he was dressed in simple war kit and Ngomane, the Prime Minister, thereupon publicly announced that the 'mother of the nation' was no more. Upon hearing this everyone present instantly tore from their persons every ornament.

Shaka now appeared before the hut in which the body of Nandi lay. In a semicircle behind him stood his principal chiefs, also dressed in their war attire.

'For about twenty minutes,' says Fynn, 'he stood in a silent, mournful attitude, with his head bowed upon his shield, on which I saw large tears fall, occasionally wiping them away with his right hand. He presented the appearance of a brave warrior in extreme distress, sufficient to extort pity and commiseration from the hardest of hearts. After two or three deep sighs, his feelings becoming ungovernable, he broke out into frantic yells, which fearfully contrasted with the silence that had hitherto prevailed. The signal was enough. The chiefs and people to the number of about

15,000, commenced the most dismal and horrid lamentations ...

'The people from neighbouring kraals, male and female, came pouring in, each body as they came in sight, at a distance of half a mile, joining to swell the terrible cry. Through the whole night it continued, none daring to rest or refresh themselves with water; while at short intervals, fresh bursts were heard as more distant regiments approached. The morning dawned without any relaxation; and before noon the number had increased to about 60,000. The cries now became indescribably horrid. Hundreds were lying faint from excessive fatigue and want of nourishment; while the carcasses of forty oxen lay in a heap, which had been slaughtered as an offering to the guardian spirits of the tribe.

'At noon the whole force formed a circle, with Shaka in the centre, and sang a war-song, which afforded them some relaxation during its continuance. At the close of it, Shaka ordered several men to be executed on the spot; and the cries became, if possible, more violent than ever. No further orders were needed; but as if bent on convincing their chief of their extreme grief, the multitude commenced a general massacre. Many of them received the blow of death while inflicting it on others, each taking the opportunity of revenging his injuries real or imaginary. Those who could no more force tears from their eyes – those who were found near the river panting for water – were beaten to death by others who were mad with excitement.

'Towards afternoon I calculated that not fewer than 7000 people had fallen in this frightful indiscriminate massacre. The adjacent stream, to which many had fled exhausted to wet their parched tongues, became impassable from the number of corpses which lay on each side of it; while the kraal in which the scene took place was flowing with blood.'

According to Chief Sigananda Cube, Shaka was so overwhelmed with sorrow that he lost control of himself and the situation, and surrounded as he was by a crowd of sycophants he had no idea of the extent of the destruction which was going on during that tragic afternoon, but as soon as he began to grasp what was really happening he put a stop to the massacre. Fynn corroborates this. The time was about sunset. The wailing, however, continued till mid-morning on the following day, when the multitude was invited to eat.

Later in the day Nandi's remains were placed in a grave which had been dug near the spot* where she had died. It was an orthodox chief's grave about nine feet deep with one side hollowed out to make an artificial cave. In this, the body, sitting upright in the orthodox contracted posture, was deposited. This posture is ensured by binding the body before *rigor mortis* sets in.

Fynn was not allowed to witness the burial, for this would have entailed remaining in the vicinity of the grave for a year. His report that two girls were buried alive with Nandi's body is probably incorrect; more probably, as Bryant says,† the victims were first broken and killed in the manner described in an earlier chapter.

Some 12,000 warriors were present at the burial and were formed into a special division to guard the grave for a year. Fifteen thousand head of cattle were set apart for their use, as well as providing a fitting sacrifice to the ancestral spirits of Nandi. All the cattle owners in the country contributed to this as well as the King himself.

Subsequent to the burial, says Fynn, Ngomane, the Prime Minister, rose and addressed the multitude. 'As the great Female Elephant with the small breasts – the ever-ruling spirit of Vegetation – had died, and as it was probable that the heavens and the earth would unite in bewailing her death, the sacrifice should be a great one: no cultivation should be allowed during the following year; no milk should be used, but as drawn from the cow it should be all poured upon the earth; and all women who should be found with child (thereafter) during the year should, with their husbands, be put to death.'

As Nandi died on 10 October and all crops had been planted by early September the non-cultivation ordinance could only affect the weeding from 12 October onwards. This in itself was serious

---

*A decayed Um-Lahlankosi tree – chief's burial tree (*Zyzyphus mucronata*) – marks the grave. Vide Bryant, *Olden Times in Zululand and Natal*, p. 610.

†Op. cit.

enough, in spite of the fact that the crops by then had had an average start of from six weeks to two months. The loss of the milk was a real hardship. The taboo on sexual intercourse could be overcome by married couples provided there were no evident consequences.

Shaka developed a brooding and bitter spirit. On the one hand he was constantly 'pinching himself' – Zulu expression for 'self-reproach' – for not getting betimes the 'elixir of life' for which he also blamed the Whites, who should have seen to it that vessels called more frequently, or hastened the building of the brig from the timbers of the wrecked *Mary.*

'I have conquered the world but lost my mother,' was his poignant cry. 'Bitter aloes fill my mouth and all taste has gone out of my life.'

Anyone who had not shown the deepest manifestations of mourning became repugnant to him. Anyone except those strange Europeans who had different ways. He therefore ordered companies of warriors to scour the country and to kill all those who had manifestly not mourned, or else sent a 'wreath', as it were, in the form of sacrificial cattle for Nandi's grave. Fynn blames the chiefs for these further killings.

So deep and sustained became Shaka's melancholia that he seemed to have lost all interest in governing the country. Many self-seekers were quick to take advantage of this; for they merely had to suggest that so-and-so had shown no sympathy, and unless it happened to be someone who had shared the early years of trial, or some person of acknowledged courage, Shaka would point his finger, or nod his head, which became tantamount to a sentence of death to the unfortunate one thus indicated.

Shaka sought no solace in beer, but felt greatly drawn towards Pampata, who alone appeared to be able to prevent his brooding madness from flaring into that of an uncontrollable homicidal maniac. Some time previous to this she had been made 'Colonel' of the new, strongest and finest Maidens' regiment which was called U-Ngisimane (the Englishman) in honour of Shaka's new friends, and the King's affection for her was greater than ever. Ngomane and Mdlaka also used all their great moderating influence in restraining Shaka, but in their absence it was as dangerous to be in the King's presence as to be near a hungry man-eating lion.

Amongst other idiosyncrasies Shaka now developed the unheard of habit of taking his meals whilst lying flat on his stomach. His chiefs and courtiers had to do likewise, and anyone who coughed or sneezed whilst the King was eating would be 'indicated' for instant death by that fatal nod of the Royal head, 'for the eating "Lion" must not be disturbed'.

One day it was reported to Shaka by self-seekers that the small Mfekane clan had shown little sympathy for the King's great bereavement, and Shaka gave the order for their annihilation. Ngomane then drew his attention to a little incident when Shaka was but one of Dingiswayo's ordinary warriors. This was when a girl of the Mfekane clan at Chief Mzingeli's kraal, insisted on Shaka sitting on a mat instead of the bare ground in a hut, and had fed him when he was hungry. Shaka instantly countermanded the order against the Mfekane clan and commanded that their traducers should be killed instead.

Shaka at this time complained much about his dreams, in which his long-deceased foster-father, Mbiya, appeared to him. Mbiya was usually crying and telling Shaka that notwithstanding the killings which had taken place there were sorcerers in the country who had brought about the death of his mother through witchcraft. These sorcerers were women whom Mbiya named, or at least indicated.

Half a dozen luckless women were soon afterwards brought before Shaka and he denounced them as being instrumental in causing Nandi's death, for how otherwise could she have died, when, but shortly before, he had left her hale and hearty? In a fearful rage he ordered that their hands be tied behind their backs and that thatching grass should be tied thickly around their bodies. Then he commanded the slayers to set the grass alight and drive the women upwind. And so the unfortunate human torches ran screaming about in their agony until they collapsed. When the grass was consumed by the fire the slayers crushed the victims' skulls.

After three months (some say two) of intensive mourning over Nandi's death, the country was in a parlous state. The fields were overgrown with weeds and one of the staple diets, namely milk, was no longer on the food list as it had to be poured on the ground immediately after milking.

Now the more courageous and intelligent of Shaka's people began to grow rebellious: the Zulus were disciplined but they were never servile. One Gala of the Biyela clan determined to end the tyranny. Cudgel in hand he went to Bulawayo and halting at the private enclosure of the royal kraal, he shouted to the King within:

'Hau! O King, you have destroyed your country. What will you reign over? Will you create a new race? Shall all die because your mother died? Senzangakona died too; but there was not done what you do. And your grandfather, Jama, died; yet these things were not done. You have destroyed the country. Your country will be inhabited by other kings; for your people will perish of famine. The fields are no longer weeded, the cows no longer milked. They will be milked by those kings who will cultivate the soil; for your people no longer eat, no longer bear, and the cattle are no longer milked. As for me, O King, I say you are dead yourself through this mother of yours. Stuff a stone into your stomach (brace yourself up, be not downhearted). This is not the first time anyone has died in Zululand.'*

Then Shaka roused himself and summoned all the Councillors and rebuked them.

'Of what use are you? Did you ever tell me to stuff a stone in my stomach?'

To Gala he gave fat cattle, acknowledging that the man had advised him well, and he gave permission for Gala and all his ward to assume the head-ring.

This assumption of the head-ring meant release from the active army, and the right to marry, and was usually only granted to a commander and his regiment for specially distinguishing themselves.

Thus the ice of Shaka's distemper broken, a rapid thaw set in

*Bryant, *op. cit.*

336

and the oppressive food restrictions were removed, automatically opening the sluice-gates to a whole flood of thankofferings, streaming in droves into Shaka's Treasury from every quarter of his land.

But still Shaka mourned the death of his mother and still was he troubled with dreams of his foster-father Mbiya, who this time warned the King that the girls of his harem were playing him false. To his council he said: 'What shall I do with these wicked debauchees?'

'Kill them,' was the answer.

By a stratagem of absence the King and his guards surrounded the harem kraals by surprise and no less than eighty-five warriors were taken, with the girls of their choice. Some of the men were beaten to death with sticks; others, with the girls, were strangled. And in this massacre Shaka was supported by the people, for it was according to the law that adulterers should die.

But another killing must have aroused more horror than approval. Some of the junior *u-dibi* attached to the court had developed the habit of peeping into the King's hut while he fondled his girls. They were warned that this conduct merited death, but ignored the warning and grew bolder. Shaka ordered them to be caught, but as the guilty boys always scampered away and mingled with their friends before the guards could catch them, it was impossible to arrest them. This was reported to the King.

'Then kill them all,' Shaka said, 'every one, for then I shall have peace and their death will be an example to others in the land.'

The boys were clubbed to death.

One of Shaka's harem women had given birth to a child. The pregnancy and birth had been concealed from him until the child was some six months old. Concealment being no longer possible the woman and her child were brought before Shaka.

'So this is supposed to be my child?' said the King, addressing the mother.

'Yes, O King,' was the faint and trembling response.

'Will you tell me when I slept with you to make this possible?' Shaka asked in a very low voice.

337

'A long time ago,' was the almost inaudible reply.

'Can you remember some details? For instance, which other women were present in the hut with us?'

There was no response.

'You know very well that all that happened between us was a little love-play which quite precludes the possibility of any pregnancy. Have you any reply to that?'

The woman gazed silently at her feet.

'Many of my women go whoring about with my guards and warriors. Some of the less clever ones become pregnant, and then try to plant someone else's child on me.* That is what you have done. Can you deny it?'

The unhappy woman said nothing.

'Speak!' Shaka roared at her, but she remained a frozen mute.

Thereupon, in an ungovernable rage, Shaka seized the little child by the heels, and swinging it on high crushed its head by bringing it down violently against the floor.

The horrified mother looked on in mute anguish and at a sign from the King a slayer crushed her skull with a club.

A man condemned to death for failing to observe the mourning regulations was asked by Shaka: 'As you are about to die what nice thing do you leave behind on earth?'

'Great Elephant,' he replied with seasonable tact, 'I leave my King. And I leave as well my little child just beginning to smile and my calf beginning to frolic.' Hearing which, the heart of Shaka was touched and he ordered the man's release.

Shaka spent very many hours in seclusion with Pampata after his mother's death. In her quiet way she rebuked his every excess of killing. Not so much in words, as by her silent attitude and many tears.

'You at least, Pampata, genuinely mourn the "going down" of my mother,' Shaka remarked on one occasion.

*Fynn in *The Diary*, p. 300, records that Shaka only begat one child. This was Mbuzikazi Cele's son who was sent to Tembeland as recorded in a previous chapter.

'I mourn because I know she is unhappy on account of all these cruel killings, which must fill her with horror.'

'You speak true, but I was ill, for the pain in my heart was only exceeded by the pain in my head, which felt full of boring brain maggots.'

'You are ill no more, and yet you kill a man because he does not stoop sufficiently, or crawl to you on his belly like a whipped dog. There was a time when the whole nation loved you, but now you only inspire terror.'

'Terror is the only thing they understand, and you can only rule the Zulus by killing them. Who are the Zulus? They are parts of two hundred or more unruly clans which I had to break up and reshape, and only the fear of death will hold them together. The time will come when they will be as one nation, and the clans will only be remembered as their *izibongo* (surnames). In the meantime my very name must inspire them with terror.'

'You will need a constant bodyguard around you, for people will suffer so much and no more.'

'I need no bodyguard at all, for even the bravest men who approach me get weak at the knees and their hearts turn to water, whilst their heads become giddy and incapable of thinking as the sweat of fear paralyses them. They know no other will except that of their King, who is something above, and below, this earth.'

Pampata sighed, and remarked: 'What would our good father Mbiya say to all this, when, as you know, he warned you that too much power was worse than the excessive use of the hemp-horn. What is worse, you now make it appear that it is Mbiya who urges you to kill, when he speaks to you in your dreams, when you know very well that he is crying all the time. For thus he appears to me nearly every night.'

'There is a reason for everything that I do. When I look up and see the vultures circling and say that the birds of the King are hungry, it gives me an opportunity of "smelling out" those whom I consider to be a danger to the nation, and at the same time providing a drastic example to the others.'

'Mbiya told you to beware of the time when you were the

only great bull left in the kraal, and drunk with power, you started to kill your harmless oxen and cows and even calves. Even the White men, who are your great friends, have heavy hearts, and it sickens them to see what they see every day. You say they are greater than we are, then why do you not listen to what their hearts say to you without words?'

Yet still Shaka mourned, and while he mourned the sufferings of his people were not to end. A final and grotesque instance of his melancholy temper must be given, for it throws light upon the singularity of his nature; and if it offends against taste, we shall hope to be forgiven in the name of truth. The Fasimba and other regiments were paraded stark naked, and with them Pampata's Ngisimane regiment, three thousand of the youngest and comeliest women in the kingdom, not in the nude, of course – that would have been out of the question – but wearing their scantiest string aprons four inches long. It should be recalled that during six months all sexual intercourse had been a capital crime, even the customary *uku-hlobonga*.

'My children!' said Shaka, addressing the parade. 'I have called you together in order that I may feast my eyes on the true sorrow in your hearts for my sad bereavement. Whoever feels this sorrow will have no thought of love when the maidens present their charms, as they will presently do. They will only be filled with sorrow and not with voluptuous thoughts. There may be those who are callous and regardless of my sorrow and their thoughts will betray them by an unseemly rise of their passions which will be immediately evident to us all. Such men are of no use to me and will go to the birds.'

Then Shaka addressed the maidens and exhorted them to do all in their power to awaken the hidden passions of the disloyal ones in order that their lack of piety and loyalty might be revealed to all. They were to advance slowly in high-stepping lines, till they came very near, then recede and advance again. They were to sing and clap their hands. Then turning once more to the guards regiment he bade them remain stationary but to clap their hands in unison with the maidens. Thereupon Shaka, in regimental uniform, took up a position facing the Fasimba, with half a dozen slayers armed with massive clubs behind him.

The consternation of the regiments on receiving the order to parade in the nude, and the events thereafter, are best related by Jabula Ema-Bomvini, one of the senior Fasimba guards :

'My father, when we got the order to parade without even wearing our *um-ncedo* (prepuce-cover) our hearts were heavy, for we knew not what was in the mind of the Great Elephant. Many strange things were happening since the death of Nandi, but this was the strangest of all. We slept with very bad dreams that night.

'When we learnt the truth next morning on the parade ground our forebodings increased ; for, my Father will understand, we had been through a woman-famine for many moons, and when a man has been starved for over-long it is but natural that he should get excited at the sudden sight of much food – especially when it is surpassing good.

'As we saw the maidens advance we tried to look sad, but those beautiful, undulating forms fired our blood with the madness of desire which will not be subdued by the exercise of the will. As they came nearer, stepping as high as they could, we all felt that we were birds' food already, and that the Great One had only made one mistake by not providing enough slayers.

'Our commander had to turn round and face us from time to time to see that we carried out our duty, as commanders have to do on parade. Then, my Father, we observed that he was as guilty as all the rest of us, for even he could not hide what was going on in his mind, for like us he had not the wherewithal to hide it with.

'The platoon immediately in front of the Great Elephant went to the birds to the last man, but even that did not seem to dampen our manhood. How much our manhood was rebellious, my Father will gather from the dying of this platoon, for even when the slayers seized the warriors their strength was as evident as that of a cow-starved bull. The Great One roared with rage when he saw that not even the descending clubs could quell the ardour of the guilty ones till they actually struck their heads. "Look at them !" the Nameless One bellowed. "They have no respect for my

341

poor mother or my grieving heart. Their words of sorrow were but lying froth to cover up their low and disloyal thoughts. Behold! their *imi-shiza* (thick fighting-sticks: a Zulu euphemism). Instead of pointing sorrowfully downwards they brazenly stare upwards into my face. Ho! slayers, massacre the disgusting brutes." '

'Not for nothing did our Fasimba regiment bear the nickname 'The Maidens' Delight' (*Umtando* * *we Ntombi*), and although we felt sad to see the warriors die we were proud of them. Yes, my Father, they died like men and for all time confirmed the regimental nickname.

'Fortunately for us the Terrible One could not be everywhere at once, and for the time being we were safe. Our wits were dull and would not counsel us, and we were all as good as dead when our guilt stood forth everywhere, as the maidens came up close to us. It was then that their nimble wits came to our aid, for they hissed to us *"shayani amasende"*. (Which delicately expressed meant "Hit yourselves where we cannot hit ourselves".) And we did; but even now, my Father, the memory of it is so painful that I like not to think of it, although it saved us from becoming birds' food on that day.

'As the maidens receded the Great One strode down our line inspecting us closely. But the manhood of every one of us looked as dejected as our faces and not a single man could he find, from the commander downwards, who showed any evidence of guilt, thus proving that none of us had any lowly thoughts unworthy of the memory of his mother.

'The Terrible One seemed pleased, but as yet he was not satisfied till once more the "Ngisimane" maidens had approached us, and there he kept them, exhorting them to tantalize us to the utmost of their ability. Today, my Father, although I am grown old, the memory of those sights stirs me, and I feel that I am not as old as I might think. But on that day I had to suppress the groans of self-inflicted pain, and I was no more interested than an ox is in a

* The 'A' sound in this word was sometimes changed to an 'O' thus giving it an obscene twist, at least to European ears, but to the natural Zulu it represented a logical synonym. '*Umtando*' means love or delight. '*Umtondo*' means penis.

cow. From a regiment of bulls we had all been temporarily transformed into a regiment of oxen. Still it is better to be a live ox
than a dead bull, particularly if the disability is but temporary.

'At last the Great Elephant was satisfied. Indeed he was so
pleased with our victory that he ordered the whole regiment to
don a single red loury feather, which, as my Father knows, is the
insignia of honour and victory which is accorded to but few
regiments. Thus, then, my Father, our outstanding virility for the
first time brought our regiment to the verge of defeat and shame,
and yet when we had ceased to be men we were awarded the
honours of victory. Nevertheless, for a victorious regiment we
looked singularly crestfallen and woebegone as we painfully
marched off the parade ground to seek the comfort of our barracks,
where we were glad to stay for a day or two till the pain had
subsided.

'What more is there to say, my Father, except that the regiments
behind us profited by our experience, and with their need being less
urgent than ours they were able to subdue themselves with lesser
harshness than we had to apply to ourselves. They were fortunate
too, inasmuch that they lost no warriors as birds' food.'

CHAPTER 24

Embassy to King George IV

As Shaka was about to dispatch an embassy to King George he took some preliminary steps which he considered necessary for so important a venture. It had been decided at a formal meeting of the Zulu King-in-Council with his chiefs and White friends that the embassy should travel under the aegis of Lieutenant King, R.N.

Shaka therefore decided to give Lieutenant King an official status in his realm by appointing him to the command of the crack regiment *Gibabanye* then stationed just south of the Umvoti river, near Dukuza, the capital. Fynn says it was the *Dukuza* regiment but this mistake arose from the fact that a Zulu regiment was sometimes referred to by the name of the military kraal where it was stationed. There was, in fact, no *Dukuza* regiment.

Lieutenant King was issued with the full ceremonial dress of a commander of a guards regiment, for such the *Gibabanye* was. Whether he ever wore it is not recorded, but if he did, he would have presented an imposing appearance with a plume of white ostrich and blue crane feathers, mounted on a fur busby, whose base was encircled by a band of leopard skin, from which hung lappets of leopard skin down the cheeks and the back of the neck. Over the shoulders an ornate cape of many dark fur tails, with the chest covered by similar tails, but white in colour. A kilt of loose tails hanging to just above the knees with more fur tails around the calves. And finally he would have carried a white shield and a stabbing assegai. If the reader will compare this description with the painting by Angas of three Zulu warriors as they were dressed in King Mpande's reign he will get a clearer conception of the artistic achievements of the Zulu army.

King Shaka wanted his 'brother', King George IV, to know how the Zulus dressed, and a few other things about them. He therefore selected six of his choicest and most virginal 'harem lilies', which the blushing Lieutenant was to present to the head of the House of Hanover in their all but nude glory.

As Shaka's only knowledge of European architecture was limited to the crude and inartistic adobe edifices of the White settlers, he decided to supply Lieutenant King with six expert Zulu hut-builders who would show *Um-Joji* how to build a really neat-looking hut, which though small compared with his big buildings would not be as ugly.

The main business of the embassy was to secure the 'elixir of life' in the form of the hair-restoring oil and dye, and to propose an offensive and defensive alliance between Shaka and King George. In this connection Shaka said it would be well for *Um-Joji* to get his military chiefs to study the Zulu methods of warfare. For, argued Shaka, 'If it always rains in your country of what use are your flintlock muskets, which are useless on a rainy day here as I have seen?' If the English Army were then equipped with spears and shields they could choose a rainy day for attacking their enemies with these good weapons which did not depend on the weather. The enemies' bayonets would be no match against English shields, which would turn them aside, and then the enemy would be exposed to the stabbing assegai and easily slain.

Shaka then averred that on a wet day, which rendered muskets useless, he would take on any European army of equal numbers to his own and issue victorious from such a contest. Cannon intrigued him, but he maintained that they must retard the speed of any army, and thus frustrate the acme of good generalship, namely, a war of rapid movement. This led him to advise *Um-Joji* to do away with boots and reserve his hides for shields. 'Look at you White people here; when you first arrived most of you had boots and walked so badly that we felt sorry for you. Now, barefooted, you have vastly improved, and one day you may be able to march nearly as well as the Zulus.'

To defray the cost of the embassy Shaka gave Lieutenant King eighty-six elephant tusks, and one or two large ones which, he said, were to be his mouth (Zulu, meaning introduction) to King George.

Shaka expressed a hope that *Um-Joji* would take the Zulu embassy under his 'armpits and shadow' as he (Shaka) had done to the English in Zululand. It may here be remarked that Shaka was ever generous in his attitude to the Whites, for when an increasing number of Zulu delinquents deserted from Shaka to the English settlement at Port Natal the chiefs made many vehement protests to him, with requests to demand their extradition. His invariable reply was: 'No matter. They have gone to my friends and not to my enemies. Leave them alone.' In this connection Fynn later also mentioned Shaka's 'noble spirit'.

Through adroit diplomacy Lieutenant King somehow managed to avoid the embarrassing responsibilities of becoming the chaperon of the six almost nude harem beauties, and of the half a dozen hut-builders.

The brig *Mary*, it will be remembered, was wrecked just within Port Natal on 1 October 1825, with Lieutenant J. S. King, Nathaniel Isaacs and others on board. After nearly three years' hard work Hatton, the carpenter, had reconstructed a new schooner from the salvaged timbers of the wrecked vessel. 'The schooner was christened the *Chaka* (Shaka) and on 10 March 1828, the little craft glided smoothly down the slip-way to the placid bosom of the lagoon; and on 30 April amidst the lamentations and tears of their faithful servants left behind, sailed over the bar of the harbour with Farewell and his lady, Isaacs and King on board bound for the Cape.'

There was also on board Shaka's embassy to King George IV. The personnel of the embassy consisted of Sotobe (of the Gazu Sibiyas and accompanied by two wives), Mbozamboza (of the Ema-Ngwaneni), Pikwane son of Bizwayo, Shaka's trusty body servant, and Jacob the Swimmer, Shaka's interpreter.

On 4 May 1828, after five days at sea, the *Chaka* dropped anchor at Algoa Bay (Port Elizabeth) and at once bumped into soulless officialdom. The authorities frowned on the *Chaka* as coming from a foreign port and being unregistered. The vessel was consequently confiscated and allowed to rot.

The embassy which was destined to go to Cape Town to interview the Governor was detained at Port Elizabeth, with instructions from the Governor that the Zulus were to be entertained at the Government's expense, which was largely done with grog. The deeper they drank the lower their spirits sank, till at length they grew so 'exceedingly impatient and became so alarmed, that they made several attempts to run off, and find their way to their country by land' – a contingency which, had it happened, would have jeopardized very seriously the safety of their European guardians when returning to Natal.

For nearly three months the Zulu embassy was kept cooling its heels when at last the officer commanding his Britannic Majesty's troops at Port Elizabeth was commissioned to interrogate the Zulus. This was Major Cloete, resplendent in scarlet uniform and gold lace. He subjected the embassy to an interminable barrage of questions, which they answered with all the dignity of their race.

Lieutenant King was absent at the earlier interview. Isaacs, who was there, records the following questions and answers.

Question by Major Cloete: 'Can Shaka write, or make any characters whereby to show his authority?'

Answered by Sotobe. 'No. He cannot write or make characters.'

'How is Sotobe to be known as a chief? And how is he distinguished as such?'

'By the bunch of red feathers; and there is no one allowed to wear them but the King, and two or three of his principal chiefs.'

'Did you come by your own free will and consent?'

'We were sent by our King to show his friendly disposition towards the Governor and the White people; also to ask for medicines and so on.'

'What authority have you from your King to show that you are sent by him?'

'We have nothing. We were sent with Lieutenant King.'

'Have you no sign, or token, or feather, or tiger's tail, or tooth, to show you were sent by Shaka?'

'We generally send cattle, but as the vessel could not take them, Shaka has sent an ivory tusk.'

'Will Sotobe go to Cape Town with me?'

'No; we have been here so long, that we are quite tired, and we wish to go back to our King.'

'What was your motive for coming here, if you did not intend to see the Governor?'

'We have heard that our King is near the Colony, and we want to return, as we understand that the Governor will protect the neighbouring tribes, and our King was not aware of it before our leaving Natal. We also hear that Lieutenant King is going to meet Shaka, and we cannot leave him, and we know no other person. We look upon him as our father and protector. Unbosom Boser (Mbozamboza) ought to have returned long ago, and then I could have gone to see the Governor, as my King wished me to do.'

'Provided Unbosom Boser returns from hence will Sotobe go and see the Governor?'

'As Lieutenant King is absent, we cannot say anything about it; we will not leave him, as he is sent with us, and he is one of our mission.'

And the futile questioning continued for hours; at a subsequent interview the same interminable cross-examination continued. Lieutenant King was present during the latter half. This is Isaacs' summing-up of the treatment of the embassy:

'It was in this manner that the chiefs were subjected to annoyance, and by an insignificant display of paltry authority and petty power, which commanded no respect, but rather excited feelings of no ordinary indignation. A species of perplexing interrogation that might have been resorted to by an Old Bailey pleader, but little becoming the dignity of a British Officer deputed by the Governor of a high British dependency. What could have called for such an attempt to confound two or three unlettered people on an especial mission from their King ... I know not, nor can I divine, but I have no hesitation in declaring unequivocally, that it redounded but little to the credit of the Officer who was the Governor's organ.'

To the unspeakable relief, as well as surprise, of the whole party, on 2 August (1828) H.M.S. *Helicon* sailed into the Bay for the purpose of returning the Zulu Ambassadors to Natal. These latter refused to board the vessel unless accompanied by their protector, Lieutenant King, who consented to their request. The vessel sailed away amidst great rejoicings, bearing to Shaka a present from the Cape Government and reaching Port Natal on 17 August. Though the Zulu mission had proved abortive, it was at least enabled to carry home the weighty intelligence that any irruption into Native Territories adjoining the Kaffrarian frontier would be repelled by British Arms.

Almost immediately after dispatching his embassy Shaka felt the time was ripe to start the Pondoland campaign, which he had long had in mind. The preliminary steps had been taken a month before his mother's death when Shaka had dispatched his spies to reconnoitre the country. These spies were the remnants of Ngoza's Tembus who had found refuge in Zululand. They knew Pondoland well.

Shaka reasoned that with his ambassadors within the British domain he had good advocates at court in case he should have any friction with the British border-guards 100 miles beyond the southern border of Pondoland. In any case he would warily probe how far in his direction the British sphere of influence extended. It was a delicate position which needed tact.

This campaign, although originally planned as a purely military expedition, would now also serve as the *i-hlambo* or mourning hunt for his mother's death, which like all such ceremonies necessitated the warriors washing their spears in blood. This would be a very great washing of spears, as befitted the outstanding status of the late Nandi. The Tembu spies and scouts led the army, not by the regular route along the coast, but by the path they knew farther inland.

Ogle with his and Fynn's Hottentots and Natives, formed a special company of musketeers which was attached to the army.

Fynn had established a kraal on the Umzimkulu river and here Shaka formed his headquarters. Fynn says: 'I went to meet him. I found him about forty miles from my place; he was resting there for the night, having left the whole of his forces about five miles in the rear. We went forward the next morning and, in the afternoon, arrived at one of my kraals, where I had about 100 muids of Indian corn. On his asking, therefore, I gave him the whole of it for the use of his army.

'On the following day we arrived at my residence (at the Umzimkulu river). Knowing it to be the custom for me as host to present the King with a bullock, I produced my herd and requested him to make himself welcome to as many as he thought fit. He selected seventeen and thereupon made my place his headquarters.

'By this time I had acquired a thorough knowledge of the Zulu language, manners and customs, hence was able to spend my time pleasantly with Shaka; he always demanded my attendance during his leisure moments. All this, moreover, gave me an opportunity of minutely ascertaining the basis on which he acted.'

Fynn's kraal was the farthest point south Shaka personally ever went. Here, with Fynn, he stayed for the remainder of the campaign directing the two divisions into which he divided the army. The first was commanded by his generalissimo Mdlaka, who was to operate along the coast and tackle Faku, the King of the Pondo; the other, commanded by Manyundela, son of Mabuya, had to deal with the Tembus and Natal refugees more inland. The company of musketeers was likewise duly apportioned, the one section under Ogle accompanying Mdlaka; the other Manyundela.

Shaka was kept busy attending to the reports or dispatches which he received several times daily through runners from his two generals heading south, and issuing instructions to them according to these reports. There was a similar direct liaison between the generals themselves. At Fynn's kraal Shaka kept a relatively small strategic reserve. Couriers from the capital also engaged some of Shaka's time with affairs of State remitted to him by the Prime Minister, Ngomane, his boyhood patron, whom he regarded with great affection for the favours then shown to him.

When Shaka was not thus engaged with State affairs he turned his interest on Fynn, who was then teaching some of the King's harem maids how to make pancakes from crushed green maize mixed with fat, and how to fry a beef steak in the English manner. Shaka was so pleased with the results that he sent a courier to Port

Natal to obtain a frying-pan for himself, similar to the one used by Fynn, whom he encouraged to demonstrate all his culinary arts.

Fynn proved to be an excellent host and the Zulu Dictator greatly enjoyed the novelty of eating at a table, seated on a chair, with the food served on enamel plates and dishes instead of the Zulu wooden ones. When Fynn tried to introduce forks Shaka waved them away with 'A fork is a dangerous and useless implement. Dangerous because it could cause bodily harm to the user, and useless because in an emergency it could not be used as a stabbing weapon. Now a spoon such as the Zulus use is a useful article, especially for eating soft foods.'

Fynn's 'place' was his home, and an 'Englishman's home is his castle'. Shaka, with two regiments in close attendance, and a great army not far away, had such complete power over the lives of all that he literally merely had to wink an eye, or half crook a finger, or give the slightest nod with his head, and anyone's life was terminated. Yet Fynn had made it perfectly and forcibly clear to the 'Great One' that he objected to any executions being carried out in 'his place'. And Shaka conceded the point, saying that it would indeed be unseemly to have blood spilt in his host's home or its immediate surroundings, and the King therefore gave strict instructions that all people condemned by him whilst staying with Fynn had to be taken some distance before they were executed. Shaka believed in etiquette as much as he did in dictatorship!

Meanwhile, Fynn was acting as Shaka's adviser:

'Owing to the knowledge I had of Faku, the King of the Pondos, Shaka asked me one morning if I thought, were he to withdraw his army, Faku would consent to becoming his tributary. I replied in the affirmative and recommended, as an inducement, the return of the girls who had been captured and sent to him by the army, and refraining from destroying more corn. To this he assented. He accordingly sent messengers to Faku with proposals for peace, at the same time returning the females as proof of his *bona fides*; he, moreover, directed his army to withdraw and to stop destroying the corn. Several chiefs of petty tribes in Faku's neighbourhood, with messengers from Faku, returned with the army to thank him for his liberality in thus sparing their lives. They were rewarded with presents of cattle selected from those that had been taken from them.'

News of the Zulu advance towards the south had been received by the British, and an account, grossly exaggerated, of their depredations in Kaffraria. It may have been this which caused Major Cloete's curious behaviour to the Zulu embassy. Although alarmed, the British were slow to act, and it took General Bourke, Commanding Officer at Grahamstown, so long to muster his forces that he arrived in the field a month after the Zulu raid was over. Meanwhile, during May, June and July, the Zulus were killing and plundering their way southward, while the Pondos fled out of their path, with their cattle, into the jungles and forests where the enemy could not find them. After crossing the Umzimvubu and Umtata rivers, into the territory of the Bomvana who also took refuge in the bush, the army was out of Faku's country. The Pondos emerged from hiding. The Zulus turned and struck, seized Faku's capital, and captured a treasure of 30,000 head of cattle.

Major Dundas, Civil Commissioner of Albany and Somerset, arrived in Pondoland a month later, with about forty British and Dutch young men, making a reconnaissance in force for General Bourke. While questioning the ruined and prostrate Faku, Dundas received intelligence that the Zulus were operating among the Tembus, on the Umtata river. But the invaders turned out to be Matiwane and his migrating Ngwanes, down from Basutoland. Dundas, either ignorant of or indifferent to their identity, attacked and scattered the migrants, and returned to his H.Q. to report.

At the Cape frontier he met Colonel Somerset at the head of a thousand mounted Colonists and eighteen thousand Xoza and Tembu warriors. Somerset, with apparently little idea of what he was about, advanced, attacked the unfortunate Matiwane and his Ngwanes, and wiped them out.

Meanwhile, the Whites had never come near the Zulus and Shaka was, on Fynn's advice, ordering his generals to avoid battle if they did so. Mdlaka's division, with the 30,000 Pondo cattle and other spoils, was back with the King at Umzimkulu, feasting and receiving the rewards of their success.

In the meantime the upper army, under Manyundela, had operated in the cold highlands of the Ingeli mountains and forest, and the Mount Ayliff and Mount Frere districts, where it had some sharp fights with the Zelemu-Wushes and the Bacas generally, but as they were largely impoverished the gains in cattle were small.

In one of the sharp brushes with the enemy in a wild defile, the commanding general Manyundela was cut off and killed, as were also the warriors forming his bodyguard. When Manyundela's division rejoined the main army at Fynn's kraal on the Umzimkulu they found their comrades making merry in a great feast of meat. As soon as Manyundela's death was reported to Shaka he flew into a rage and accused the army of cowardice, for allowing its general to be killed. He was very fond of Manyundela and nothing would appease him until a large number of warriors had been condemned for cowardice and these luckless ones had been executed. Thus the merriment of the warriors was changed into sadness and gloom.

After another day's subdued feasting the call was given to break camp and march back home. 'On our crossing the Umzimkulu', writes Fynn, 'where the tide was high, many little boys would have been carried down with the stream. Shaka, foreseeing this, plunged into the river, with only his head-dress on, and remained one and a half hours in the water, giving the boys to the care of the men, who otherwise would have left them to their fate, and collecting the calves, which were nearly drowned, ordered fires to be made to assist their recovery.

'In the evening he slept in the kraal where I had given him the corn. Here he put to death one of his "sisters" (harem girls) for having taken a pinch of snuff out of his snuff-box. Such opposed kinds of conduct in one person appeared to me to be strange, but I afterwards became convinced that both the contradictory dispositions, delicate feeling and extreme brutality, were intimately blended in him.

'As soon as we came in sight of Dukuza, the new capital, we rested near a drove of cattle. He called the boys employed in herding them and asked them if they sucked the cows that had small calves. They denied having done that, upon which he directed them to take the usual oath (that is, to swear by Shaka). This they refused to do, knowing they were guilty. He then told them to go to the army about a mile distant, and say he had ordered them to be put to death. They did what he told them and were instantly killed.'

Fynn did not see the boys die but Zulu tradition says that when they brought the order for their own execution to the grim old commander of the Belebele veteran regiment his eyes streamed as he said, 'Ni *ngama qawu*' ('You are heroes – and as men and heroes you shall die by the spear, and not by the felon's club'). Thereupon the boys stood proudly in a line, automatically ranged according to their ages, and the eight-year-olds were as steadfast as their seniors when the line of death advanced on them in the form of silent and sorrowful warriors who had been deputed to kill them. 'They died like men.'

Fynn censured Shaka for this and other barbarously harsh punishments. To this Shaka replied that an order was an order and the whole nation knew what to expect for disregarding his wish or command. Laws and commands were promulgated with the object that they should be obeyed, and any slackening of this rule would soon lead to licentiousness, and then to chaos. 'It is merely a question of establishing guilt, no matter how trivial the offence may seem. The punishment is death. If I should put you in my place for the space of a moon, Zululand would fall to pieces; for with your stupid White man's reasoning you would first condone the little offences, which, like the little rents in your shirt – a fabric of your people – if unattended to, soon become big holes, and then tear into the shreds I see hanging around you. Therefore learn from your shirt if you would govern a nation – especially an unruly and warlike one like the Zulus. Truly, Mbuyazi (Fynn's Zulu name), when I look at you and your shirt I want to laugh, for already you look like a '*Sakabula*' (male widow-bird with long tail feathers) which has only just managed to escape from the rending claws of the hawk. Why? Because you overlooked the first harmless-looking rents. When you put on your next good shirt attend to it, and until you have learnt to do that, do not try to teach me how to rule the Zulus; for your ideas on that subject are as foolish as a man who urinates against the wind' (lacking in common sense).

Shaka was so feverishly active himself that he became more and more intolerant of an idle army. Already at the Umzimkulu he had discussed the problem with the Army Council, and without waiting for any opinions to be expressed, decided that without even one day for breathing-time at home, his army should from the extreme south proceed to the extreme north round about Delagoa Bay where Soshangane had established himself as a potentate with rapidly growing power. So complete was Shaka's ascendancy now that none in the council – not even Mdlaka – dared to gainsay his wishes. When the army, therefore, arrived at the Umgeni river and camped where the two golf courses now are he promulgated the '*ukase*' – 'off with you, all and straightway, to the land of Soshangane'.

Shaka was without a doubt the most popular and respected King and national hero of the Zulus – up to the death of his mother. But a revulsion had occurred since Nandi's death and the ugly consequences of the King's melancholy.

As is not unusual in such cases, active revolt began in the Court circle. Mkabayi and M-Mama, Shaka's aunts, the former an iron-willed intriguing virago, with a poisonous tongue, whispered rebellion to the King's brothers, Mhlangana and Dingane. 'How long shall the Zulus suffer? The country cries out to you! Hasten, or you will be the next victims!' And she made of Shaka's chamberlain, the wily Mbopa, an even more willing instrument. For the King had alienated nearly all his friends, and everyone feared him.

Mkabayi also inflamed the friends of Nandi by insiduously propagating the false rumour that she had not died of illness but that Shaka had murdered her. (This story, incidentally, was later taken up by the Colony of Native refugees at Port Natal, who enthusiastically added the crime of matricide to the list of abominations they saddled on Shaka. Such, then, is the origin of the calumny which was later spread by popular fiction writers and others.)

The expedition to the north, by an army tired out in the Pondo campaign, was the last straw. And the King, left among the women at home, turned his malice against them. In his insatiable quest of those who had killed his mother by sorcery he had discovered that certain women were the owners of domestic cats which had been brought into the country via Delagoa Bay. These women were, therefore, sinister witches, and he had them killed by the score till he had ultimately accounted for about 300. These killings provided special fuel to the smouldering hate in Mkabayi's heart.

But the act which finally drove the King's brothers to revolt was an order from Shaka, received when the army had reached Sitayi's kraal at Kwa-Ceza, that the *u-dibi* were to be sent home to be formed into a new regiment, The Bees, and that henceforth all warriors, officers as well as men, were to carry their own baggage. Sitayi was the father of Mbopa. At his kraal Dingane and Mhlangana discussed their plan. Announcing that they were unwell, they returned to Dukuza accompanied by Nkunzi-Yezindlovu of Mbopa's clan, but leaving their half-brother, Mpande, unaware of the plot, behind with the army.

On approaching Dukuza their courage, however, failed them, for they remembered the terrible majesty of their half-brother. They, therefore, each repaired to his respective kraal in the vicinity of Dukuza and sent messages to Shaka that they were ill. Shaka used some forcible language about the softness of his brothers and let it rest there, to the intense relief of Dingane and Mhlangana. Mkabayi, however, kept up a relentless pressure on them, especially as the killings of cat owners, or those suspected of owning them, continued. Meanwhile Mdlaka, outgeneralled by Soshangane and with a starving army, was making his way home by the coastal route.

CHAPTER 25

Death at Dukuza

SHAKA was forty-one years of age, but already his sun was setting, although he knew it not. For hours at a time the Zulu emperor would sit dreaming and brooding in lonely grandeur at Dukuza, on a great rock overlooking his capital, with but a single attendant within hailing distance. The mental miasma which had settled on him since the death of his mother was clearing away as time began to cure the all but mortal blow he had suffered. But it was clearing only slowly as far as his misanthropy, and its resulting savagery, were concerned. In all other directions his thoughts were clear as crystal, notably his ambitious plans for the Zulu nation.

As Bryant says of him,* Shaka was not a 'normal' Zulu. If he had used force to make a great nation, had created an invincible and uniquely disciplined army as his instrument, he well knew that this was not enough. He was for ever dissatisfied with his own results; he sought, by questioning the White men on every possible occasion, a way to raise the standard of his people, and their own indifference to his plans for them distressed and angered him.

It would be instructive to consider Shaka and his people in the light of Dr Arnold Toynbee's theory of 'Challenge and response'. We know, today, that the African people are as well endowed with minds as ourselves. That none of them had ever cast off the enormously ancient tribal way to make a higher civilization may be due to the fact that the challenge of their environment was inadequate. But contact with the outposts of Western Civilization might have constituted that challenge. It is impossible not to see, in Dingiswayo, with his association with a White man of

*Op. cit.

education and character, the initiator of a great change among Africans; and in Shaka a man destined to realize that change. But, as Toynbee has suggested, if a people remain unmoved by an urge to progress because the challenge of their environment and contacts with the rest of the world is inadequate, they may, equally, fail because the challenge when it comes, is more than they can respond to successfully. Even had Shaka lived to be seventy and carried out his plan of sending his younger regiments to England, to learn Western techniques, the rising Nguni people would have been overwhelmed by the radiant energy of Western Civilization.

Says Bryant:

Strange, but true, this Shaka was as sublime a moral teacher as martial genius. Submission to authority, obedience to the law, respect for superiors, order and self-restraint, fearlessness and self-sacrifice, constant work and civic duty – in a word all the noblest disciplines of life were the very foundation-stones upon which he built his nation. So rigorously enforced was the lifelong practice of all these excellencies, that he left them all a spontaneous habit, a second nature amongst his people.

In assessing the actions of Shaka we must never overlook the fact that he lived in a social organization reflecting a stage in human development infinitely older than archaic Greece – say, at least 1000 years B.C. Zulu architecture had, for instance, not risen above huts made of a lattice-work of laths covered with thatch. Building with stone or green brick was still entirely foreign to them. A wheel or any kind of conveyance was quite unknown to them. On water they had not advanced beyond a bundle of dry reeds on which a person would lie half submerged and propel himself with his hands and feet as in swimming. How unsophisticated they were will be gathered from the fact that when they were first presented with a mirror by the Europeans they viewed it with alarm as an uncanny charm, and after a while made passes behind it to catch, as they thought, the person whom they saw.

Shaka, no doubt, was cruel at times: what great soldier is

not? Titus, most 'humane' of Roman emperors, crucified 1000 Jews a day at the siege of Jerusalem – *pour encourager les autres!* Shaka burnt sixteen women alive. Crassus, after defeating Spartacus, crucified 6000 of the revolted slaves. When Tilly sacked Magdeburg in 1631, the women of the town were raped. Shaka's troops would have been put to death for this crime. Before judging the Zulus, we must recall the behaviour of all the belligerents in the last war.

Of Shaka's native intelligence we may judge from the brief accounts of his conversations with White men. The King greatly enjoyed his talks with Isaacs, whom he incessantly plied with questions in his thirst for knowledge. He was particularly keen to know the nature of the stars and the universe generally. He flatly refused to believe that the stars were suns, bigger than the earth and moving freely in fixed orbits.

'Has anybody ever been there and measured them?' The answer being in the negative Shaka abruptly told Isaacs not to stuff him with children's fairy tales. Shaka suggested that the stars must be stuck into a vast blue canopy of rock which revolved around the earth. Alternatively, that the canopy was composed of a dense cloud of blue smoke resulting from all the fires on earth.

During Fynn's first visit to Shaka, when the latter was still suffering from the stab wound which was inflicted on him by the would-be assassin, a European carpenter in the employ of Lieutenant Farewell arrived at the Royal residence. 'He had been sent', writes Fynn, 'to build for Shaka a house like those used by Europeans.' He brought with him a saw, a hammer, a gimlet, and an adze, also some nails. Shaka wished to know the uses of these things, except the hammer, for he knew that a tool of that description was used by Zulu blacksmiths. After the uses of the gimlet and nails had been explained, he sent for a piece of the hardest wood grown in his country, namely, a species of ironwood. He desired that the gimlet should be tried on that. It snapped at once. Then he said the nails must be used without the gimlet. These, on being hammered, bent into all kinds of shapes. Much pleased with his own cunning, he declined to have the house built, directing the carpenter to build them in England where the wood was softer than the iron, and not attempt to build in Zululand where English iron was softer than his wood. After this, he frequently talked of sending six of his men to build a house for King George in the Zulu style, for, though assured that King George's houses were much larger than his, he would not be convinced that they were as neatly constructed.

On another occasion, Lieutenant King tried to explain that the earth was a sphere. Shaka was prepared to accept that it was half a sphere, or a dish, for how, otherwise, would the waters of the ocean remain on it.

When Lieutenant King tried to tell him that the earth revolved from west to east, Shaka immediately asked him to demonstrate it with a pumpkin on which he placed some grains of corn to represent people. 'Now turn it and see what will happen,' and the upshot was that the Lieutenant looked rather foolish and Shaka laughed heartily.

The representative of the Royal Navy, however, refused to accept defeat, and pointed out to Shaka that a ship sailing due east from a promontory like Cape Town would eventually return from the west. Shaka asked him whether it was possible to sail in that direction without striking other land masses. Lieutenant King averred that an allowance had to be made for that by altering course to north and south.

Shaka pondered for a time then exclaimed: 'In other words, you go to the right and to the left to avoid the obstacles as we do on the land to by-pass hills, clusters of dense bush and rocky masses?'

'That is quite correct,' answered the delighted Lieutenant as he felt that his arguments were striking root.

'You are the "pathfinding headman" (navigator) of your ship with which you would, or could, leave one of King Joji's ships' kraals (ports) in an easterly direction and return to it after many moons from the west?'

'Yebo, Baba.'

'When you and your seamen left your hunting camp the other night, without Zulu guides, to get to Bulawayo, you

started off in an easterly direction, and at dawn you arrived back
in your own camp from the west. How did that happen?'

Lieutenant King looked sheepish and admitted they had got
lost and wandered in a complete circle.

'*Utshilo!*' (You have said it) exclaimed Shaka triumphantly.
'That is the sort of flat circle you make with your ships, for in
trying to avoid the land masses you lose your direction as you
did in your night march, when perforce you had to get around
the obstacles in your path.

'That disposes of the nonsense that you sail around the dish
or open pumpkin from top to bottom instead of the flat circle
on its surface. Truly, M'Kingi (Lieutenant King's Zulu name),
if I did not know you better I would think you had "*ama-bungezi*"
(big maggots found in sheep's brains) in your head. I must offer
Zulu guides to "Joji" for they at least would never lose their
direction as they know how to gauge it through the prevailing
winds.'

When Isaacs explained to Shaka 'that the religion of our
nation taught us to believe in a Supreme Being, a First Cause,
named God, who had'created all things, Shaka paid marked
attention yet evinced no conception of any idea of religion.'
... According to Bryant this 'marked attention' was really
surprise at the striking resemblance between this White man's
'Supreme Being' and his own U-*Kulu-kulwane* (Great-Great Little
One). 'Certainly he possessed a hazy acquaintance with *Kulu-
kulwane*; for he was his own Great-Great-Ancestor (and, incidentally, the proud possessor of two fruitful wives). He it was who
"made" the first man, and then for man the world. Where
Kulukulwane himself came from no Zulu ever asked; any more
than we, whence God? In him they had arrived at the "Beginning o fthings" and at the end of their range of thought. Having
made man and set the world a-rolling, *Kulu Kulwane* graciously
retired and was never heard of more – save on that one
momentous occasion when he sent along a salamander (*in-tulo*)
to order man to die, then a chameleon (*u-nwabu*) to tell him
not to; but the latter – slow motion personified – dilly-dallied
on the way and the former got there first, and man accordingly

died – died, indeed, but not before having left behind another to carry on the procreative function and to venerate himself in turn as a minor *Kulukulwane.*

'Shaka, too, knew his ancestral Kulukulwanes right enough, great and small; and if he feared no living man, he entertained a holy and wholesome dread of them. Though no longer in the flesh, he knew they were living still, for he often saw them in his dreams, received their counsel and suffered their rebuke. Of all of them, he most revered Mbiya, who was really no ancestor at all but his adopted "father" who had cared for him, a little exile, during his childhood and youth in Mtetwaland.'

Shaka was anxiously and impatiently awaiting the return of his ambassadors. His Pondoland campaign had enlarged his knowledge of geography, and he had discovered that the British sphere of influence was closer than he had supposed. The disadvantages of this were offset by the advantage that there was no real obstacle to establishing friendly contacts overland. For a long time he had been toying with the idea of sending one or more of his youngest regiments overseas, to be taught such arts and crafts, besides reading and writing, as were known by the subjects of King George. The scarcity of ships, however, ruled this out. Now he had discovered that King George had quite a sizeable outpost within reach by the overland route. This completely altered matters. If the embassy returned with a favourable report he could forthwith take steps to send two regiments to the Cape on foot. One of them should be composed of the youngsters whom he was now forming into the *Izi-Nyosi* regiment for this very purpose. Once these regiments had been taught they could return – possibly with a nucleus of White teachers – and in their turn teach the rest of the Zulu nation. Thus they would acquire the knowledge which made the Whites so powerful.

In the meantime Shaka developed his cult that he needed no bodyguard and that his terrible presence alone was sufficient to keep away all persons with evil intent. Indeed, he carried this idea so far that even the fledglings of the new regiment were ordered to have their barracks several miles away from Dukuza.

On 17 August 1828, the returning Zulu embassy, accompanied by King, Farewell and Isaacs landed at Port Natal. Lieutenant King, however, was a sick man, suffering from a dangerous disease of the liver which finally killed him on 7 September. Shaka had been greatly distressed at his friend's illness, causing two bulls to be sacrificed for his recovery. Shaka was very anxious for the embassy to complete the journey to Dukuza, for he believed that they brought with them the 'Elixir of Life'.

Owing to King's illness, his friends opened the heavy case of presents from 'King George' (The Cape Government) to Shaka, in order to facilitate their transport. They found the only gift of value to be a piece of scarlet broadcloth, together with some sheets of copper, some medicines, knives and other worthless geegaws. To these Lieutenant King had added a handsome looking-glass, beads and other trifles.

'Sotobe's first endeavour was to assuage his Sovereign's raving wrath by piling on the flattery. While this hymn of praise was being sung, the presents were being spread out at Shaka's feet. He affected not to see them and demanded, "Where is the big case sent by the Governor?" True, but unsatisfactory, explanations having been given, "You see," he roared, indicating Sotobe and company, "these rascals have not attended to my interests; they have been deceiving me. It is all that fellow Fynn's fault, for putting Lieutenant King up to opening my chest; he is like a monkey, he wants to peep into everything." '

Shaka decided to send a more reliable ambassador and he chose John Cane, whom he sent away accompanied by Mbozamboza and Nomandlambi. Subsequently, however, they were recalled and Isaacs was chosen in their place. Meanwhile Shaka was perfectly well aware of the quality of his presents. He regarded them, says Bryant, as contemptible rubbish. In the course of looking through them for the Elixir, he was accompanied by Isaacs who recorded that when the King found it was not there, 'Shaka was grievously disappointed. Heaving a subdued and bitter sigh he lay down on his mat – and went to sleep.'

On 7 September 1828, Shaka deemed that the 'Year' of mourning for his mother had been fulfilled, and the time had come to 'bring her spirit home' (*uku-buyisa*) and for the Court and country to go out of mourning. Accordingly, he went through the process of purification from the 'darkness' (Zulu – *um-nyama*) which since Nandi's death had overshadowed him. 'Every cattle-owner had brought calves for this purpose, each of which was ripped open on its right side, the owner taking out the gall of the living animal, which was then left to die in its agonies and not allowed to be eaten.' For Shaka thought it fitting that a last great lament should be raised by the animals themselves. Reserve regiments had been specially mobilized for the occasion and 'each regiment in succession then presented itself before Shaka; and as it passed in a circle around him, each individual, holding the gall-bladder in his hand, sprinkled the gall over him.'

Prior to this ceremony Fynn had feared that Shaka might require more human sacrifices for terminating the mourning; he had, therefore, approached the King and told him he had a request to make, in a matter which weighed heavily upon him.

'What troubles you so sorely, Mbuyazi?' Shaka inquired, adding : 'If I can help you I will do so.'

'I fear that more people will be butchered,' Fynn replied.

'If that is all,' Shaka said with a smile, 'have no more fears for I promise you that no one will be killed.' And Shaka kept his promise, records Fynn.

Long-pent-up spirits now found vent in lusty jollification. A riotous dance, accompanied by joyful song, was revelled in; 'several droves of oxen were slaughtered; and Shaka was finally washed with certain decoctions prepared by the native doctors'. Subsequently 'the King went with the greater part of his people to a distant forest to perform the national ceremony of discarding their mourning dress ... They then proceeded to the river to perform the customary ablutions. Mourning, after this, was permitted to cease throughout his dominions.'

Then the Prime Minister, Ngomane, delivered the Court's farewell address. 'The nation,' he said, 'had now lamented for a year the death of her who had become a spirit and would continue to watch over Shaka's welfare. But there were nations of men inhabiting distant countries who, because they had not yet been conquered, supposed that they never would be. This was plain from the fact that they had not come forward to lament the death of the Great Mother of Earth and Corn. And, as tears could not be forced from these distant nations, war should be made against them, and the cattle taken should be the tears shed on her grave.'

The reserve regiments were thereupon demobilized and sent to their respective homes, in order that Shaka could continue his life of 'splendid isolation' from all warriors and guards, which he said were only needed by the timid and the weak, or the ordinary.

Thus, in Olympian loneliness, the sands of Shaka's life began to run out. He had accomplished the seemingly impossible in the twelve years since he had succeeded to the petty Zulu chieftaincy and the tiny principality, from the heart of which he could walk to any of its borders within an hour. His sway then extended over a paltry 100 square miles, but now it covered 200,000, whilst the fragments broken off from his empire were rapidly expanding till they would ultimately extend far over another million square miles. From a rabble of 500 men he had increased his army to 50,000 warriors whose discipline exceeded that of the Roman legions at their best. The very name of Shaka made every tribe tremble from the Great Kei river in the Cape to the Zambezi, and from the Indian Ocean to the farthest confines of Bechuanaland.

Sitting on his rock at Dukuza like an eagle in its eyrie, Shaka surveyed the hinterland, with just a glimpse of the sea on his left. He would colonize the empty land of Natal with Swazis from the north, and Swaziland with Xozas, Tembus and Bacas from the south – all Zulu-speaking people these, or at least dialects which were closely akin. The next dozen years would be devoted to this work of colonization and consolidation, and, above all, his subjects should all go to school and learn the White man's knowledge. In a dozen years he would fight and conquer ignorance with the same zeal as he had shown in building up the Zulu nation thus far. Then, indeed, he thought, they could measure themselves with the greatest nations on earth. By that time, too, he should be in possession of the 'elixir' which should extend his life beyond the normal span, thus giving him ample time to carry out all his ambitions. On one other thing he was firmly resolved and that was never to incur the enmity of the British but, on the contrary, to weave the strongest bonds between the two nations, for he argued that if they fought one another they would both get hurt to the abiding disadvantage of each.

Such were the fragments of Shaka's dreams which he threw to Mbopa and Pampata during this period of meditation.

All this time Dingane and Mhlangana were given no peace by Mkabayi, who, with all the venom at her command, ceased not to urge them to pluck up courage and kill their half-brother. Time and again these two went to Dukuza with the intention of acting, but every time they saw the athletic Colossus with those penetrating eyes their blood turned to water and their courage froze. '*Uya sabeka!*' ('He is terrible!') they whispered, and they slunk homewards again. Unguarded, alone and unarmed, Shaka was still more than a match for them, although they had shortened assegais concealed beneath their karosses.

Again and again Pampata remonstrated with Shaka for dispensing with all his guards. Ngomane, the Prime Minister, ably supported her. 'It is madness to invite your enemies to kill you by exposing yourself as you do.'

'Who are my enemies?' Shaka inquired.

'Who knows?' Pampata countered. 'It may be anyone who bears you a grudge, or some ambitious person who would like to take your place; or someone who fears you may kill you some day.'

Shaka laughed. 'My brothers have no ambition. Dingane is a milksop who cannot think beyond women, and Mhlangana is too much of an honest warrior to harbour any designs against me. Moreover, I have treated them well, so why should they turn against me? In any case they are both afraid of me.'

'And Mbopa?'

'He is too frightened to do anything. But why should he want to harm me when I have done so much for him?'

'Your two brothers and Mbopa may be egged on by someone else. Somebody who may be telling them that they will be killed next. And nobody is so desperate as a frightened man.'

'Who could egg them on?'

'Mkabayi has hatred in her heart.'

'She is a venomous old toad, but all her sting is in her tongue, and apart from that she has a white heart. Look how she flayed poor Mgobozi with her tongue, but on the day of the great "smelling out", when she thought he was doomed, the motherly tears ran down her face.'

'But she hates you all the same; on account of all the killings since the death of "our mother", when the "darkness" came over you.'

'The "darkness" has left me now, as you also know, Pampata.'

'True; but a fire once started will not go out as long as there is any fuel. And fear is a very inflammable fuel.'

'How do you know these things, Pampata? I mean about Mkabayi?'

'There are some things we women can hear with our hearts, without the necessity of words.'

'Well, what do you expect me to do?'

'Kill Mkabayi and Mbopa, and banish Dingane and Mhlangana.'

'What! Kill my father's sister and my bodyservant! Never yet have I laid hands on any of my relatives, or my close servants.'

Mhlangana, Dingane, Mbopa! They were overmuch together lately and Shaka began to think. But still he could see no wrong in his brothers. On the night of 21 September 1828, he had hideous dreams. He dreamed that he was a dead man, and that Mbopa was serving another King! On waking he confided the awful vision to his tattling harem girl of the night, and she, within an hour, confided it to Mbopa. The tocsin had sounded. Mbopa sharpened his weapons.

Shaka was getting distinctly suspicious now, but as yet he would take no steps. He could not get it into his head that his brothers and Mbopa could possibly turn against him.

That afternoon an ex-captain of the guard was brought before him, charged with a crime which merited death according to the Zulu code. The ex-captain, who only had one arm, was found guilty and Shaka condemned him to death, but asked him if he had anything to say before the sentence was carried out.

'Nothing, Great Elephant, except to praise my King for allowing me the honour to lose this arm in his service, and the boon of seeing my child before I die.'

'Where is your child?' demanded Shaka.

'But a spear's throw away.'

'Then fetch it and kill it in front of me, before you are led away.'

'*Bayete!*' saluted the ex-captain and went to fetch his child, to carry out the order.

As the grief-stricken father led the child into the Royal presence, Shaka's eyes streamed with tears. 'Nay, man, I was but testing you. You gave your arm for me and that washes away your crime. Your loyalty shall be rewarded with three cows. Go in peace.'

Dark thunderclouds gathered in the late afternoon, presaging the first heavy electric storm of the season, and a yellowish-green light suffused everything while crimson clouds glowed in the west.

It was towards sundown on this day, 22* September 1828, that some *Izi-Yendane* (Natal men) arrived from Pondoland and vicinity, whither they had been dispatched to procure crane feathers and monkey, genet and other skins for the Royal wardrobe.

Shaka led the way from the Dukuza kraal to the small kraal, called *Kwa-Nyakamubi*, near by, where he sat to watch his cattle being driven in from the veld and to hear the report of his men from Pondoland.

Dingane and Mhlangana arrived to 'pay their respects' to the King. They were now ready to act but were disconcerted to find

* Isaacs gives this date. Fynn says it was the 24th. Isaacs is more reliable as he quotes from his diary, whereas Fynn wrote from memory many years later after his own diary had been lost. A. T. Bryant accepts Isaacs' date.

Shaka not alone, as they had expected, but surrounded by men. They withdrew to consult with Mbopa, who advised them to take up their position behind a certain reed fence, their weapons hidden beneath their cloaks. The chamberlain, with wealth and power within sight, showed more resolution than the assassins. He went off to prepare the way for his associates. Shaka was upbraiding the messengers for their delay and Mbopa seized this opportunity:

'Mbopa burst upon the assembly, bearing an ugly *in-gcula* assegai in the one hand, a heavy stick in the other. With feigned concern for his royal master's comfort, he rushed menacingly at the messengers and belaboured them with his cudgel, shouting, "How dare they pester Majesty with their lying tales !"

'The messengers took to their heels immediately. The aged attendants rose to remonstrate with the over-zealous servant. Shaka held his mouth, dumbfounded – then, in that instant, uttered a piercing cry! His two aged attendants disappeared into space! Mhlangana had, at the psychological moment, rushed forward from behind, planted his assegai, as he thought, deep into the King's left side, but, owing to the cloak, only through his arm. Dingane seconded with another thrust; when Shaka, sharply rising and turning, was amazed to find himself face to face with the murderous glare of his brothers.

'It is you, children of my father, who are killing me,' Shaka addressed them as he towered over them. The awful majesty of their brother made them quail and shrink back. Was he human to survive two such lethal stabs? 'What have I done, Dingane?' Shaka continued more in sorrow than in anger. 'What have I done, Mhlangana, that you should kill me thus? You think you will rule this country, but already I see the "swallows"* coming. You will not rule it when I am dead. The White people have already arrived.'† Blood trickled from Shaka's mouth, and he let the cloak slip from his shoulders. Then he turned his back on his brothers, and with Royal dignity strode towards the kraal-

*The allusion being to the Whites who built adobe houses with mud like the swallows.

† R. R. R. Dhlomo, *Shaka* (Zulu language).

gate. Mbopa intercepted him and stabbed him in the back, whereupon Shaka turned once more and exclaimed:

'*Hau! Nawe Mbopa ka Sitayi, usungi-bulala*' – ('*Hau!* You, too,
Mbopa, son of Sitayi, you too, are killing me.') Blood now spurted
from Shaka's mouth. 'I ... I ...' but the tide of life was exhausted
and, like a felled tree, he slowly toppled over backwards and
crashed rigidly to the ground, thus even in his death striking awe
into the three assassins, for who had ever before seen a man
die like that?

For a long time the assassins stood hand to mouth in deathly
silence, gazing on the great corpse lying on its back, which even
in death retained a halo of majesty. Not until the widely staring
eyes began to glaze did they feel sure that he was really dead.
Then they quietly faded away – the Royal brothers to their
kraals, some three or four miles away, and Mbopa to hunt down
and kill the only two witnesses – the aged attendants. Thereafter he spread the rumour that the messengers who had brought
the feathers and the skins had carried out the awful deed.

Thereupon the whole population of the Dukuza capital took
to the forests with the wail, '*Ku dilike intaba. Inkosi ye lizwe
ishonile.*' ('The mountain has collapsed. The lord of the world
is dead.') They feared that the heavens would fall in, and that
every imaginable catastrophe would follow.

Even Mbopa quitted the capital for the night and sought refuge
at Dingane's kraal. The eerie loneliness of those 2000 empty
huts, emphasized by the horrid howling and cackling of hyaenas,
broke his already over-strained nerves.

One, and only one, living person stayed on in that utterly
deserted capital – Pampata. When the dread news reached her
with the rest of the populace, darkness was already gathering.
She could get no information from anybody, for nobody seemed
to know anything, and everyone was in a panic and with only
one idea: to get away from Dukuza. As she began to search for
Shaka's body a stab of lightning tore the skies, and a crashing
reverberation immediately shook the earth.

Only Pampata was not dismayed and, as the lightning gathered violence, flash after flash vividly lit up her surroundings and the thunder crashed with tremendous detonations. As yet the rain had not come, which accounted for the brilliance of the lightning, always at its worst in a dry storm.

As Pampata approached the little *Nyakamubi* kraal, an almost blinding flash illuminated the scene – and there, a few yards away, she saw the body of the King.

With a sob she threw herself beside the beloved figure and, as her fingers began to caress his face, she could not, and would not, believe that her lover – the Titan of her world – was dead. Presently the lightning lit up his face, and she beheld his glazed eyes, and as the inescapable truth was forced upon her, she uttered a piercing cry of anguish. For a long time she remained in a petrified trance.

At last the rain came in torrents. This seemed to loosen the flood of her own tears, which hitherto had refused to flow. And so the tribute of her heart mingled with that of the skies, and washed away the unsightly stains from the blood-flecked mouth and gory body.

Presently the storm ceased. Then the hyaenas came, for their instinct quickly told them that the whole town was deserted. Their keen noses soon led them to the corpse; they were no respecters of rank or royalty after death; though after this night the legend arose that they will not touch a dead chief. For Pampata guarded the body of her King throughout that dreadful night.

The cowardly hyaenas would not approach nearer than a dozen yards, for they fear the living as much as they disregard the dead or dying, or those who are otherwise incapacitated, or maybe only asleep. Robbed of their prey, they formed a circle around Pampata and set up a hideous howling, like cackling, demented laughter. Time and time again Pampata drove them away, which she did with one of the poles picked up from the near-by gate. The mere fact that she carried this ponderous pole kept them at a respectful distance. Then she would return to kneel beside her King, forsaken by all but herself.

At last the dawn came, and with it the hyaenas slunk away to their forest hide-outs, but they left behind a wide and regular circle of their footprints, which did not fail to strike awe into the hearts of all beholders later on that day. Her own footprints Pampata obliterated and, after a last, lingering farewell, she took refuge in the nearest hut.

At first it was her intention to kill herself on the body of her love, but then, she argued, she could not be sure that he would be properly buried. Then again she knew that his wish would be for her to act in at least two other directions; namely, to warn Ngomane, the Prime Minister, who was away at his Nonoti kraal; and Ngwadi (Shaka's dearly loved half-brother, through Nandi and the commoner, Gendeyana), who lived as a semi-independent prince, with his own private army, in the original principality which Shaka had inherited. Her intuition told her that the assassins would assuredly try to destroy Ngomane and Ngwadi next, and she felt certain that the foul deed had been carried out by Dingane, Mhlangana and Mbopa. It therefore behoved her to use her wits until she had warned her friends, and then, and only then, would she be free to destroy herself.

The morning had not advanced far before Dingane, Mhlangana, and Mbopa arrived with some members of the Nyakamubi kraal, which latter was in effect a sub-division of the Dukuza capital. They all came to see how much, if anything, of the corpse the hyaenas had left, and were thunderstruck to see that the body was still intact, although a kraalful of hyaenas had circled all around it.

There were too few men available to dig the customary grave such as was needed for a chief. But there were many empty grain-storage pits within the Nyakamubi kraal. Mhlangana was for pitching the body unceremoniously into one of them, but Dingane demurred, saying that it savoured of sacrilege to do such a thing to the child of their father. A black ox was accordingly slaughtered, and the body of Shaka was wrapped in its skin and bound with *umtwazi* cords. As *rigor mortis* had already set in, the body could not be bound in the usual recumbent posture, which is done as soon as a Zulu dies.

Shaka's body was therefore put into the pit in a standing position, and all the Royal clothes, food vessels and weapons were deposited around him. The pit was then closed with its stone lid, a heap of stones raised over the grave, and the whole covered with thorn bushes. The flesh of the slaughtered ox was put into an adjoining pit, and this was also sealed, in order to serve his spirit as a dining-room. All the surrounding pits were thereafter carefully closed up, lest Shaka's spirit might thereby find a channel of escape, and return to take revenge.

As soon as Pampata had made sure that Shaka had been decently buried she hastened northwards, carrying with her Shaka's little toy spear with the red wood handle, carefully concealed; firstly she made for Ngomane's kraal ten miles away on the Nonoti river, where she told the Prime Minister what had happened; for, although news travels with remarkable rapidity among Africans, the death of Shaka was considered such an overwhelming event that 'it was a matter which is not spoken of', and in any case all those in the know were either in hiding, or, having linked their fortunes with those of the assassins, they maintained a conspiracy of silence.

Normally, when a chief or king dies, it is given out that he is 'indisposed' or 'not seeing anyone', and this myth is kept up till the successor has firmly established himself. Pampata was therefore the first to break the news to Ngomane, who was completely shattered by it; for from the very first day he had seen the then seventeen-year-old herd-boy, he had taken a liking to Shaka, who, in return for this early affectionate patronage, had heaped every reward within his power on the kindly man who was now growing old.

Ngomane considered that all was lost, and he and his family took to the bush country; but not before giving Pampata a youth to accompany her on her further mission to Shaka's half-brother Ngwadi, for it was against custom for a woman to travel alone for any considerable distance. Arriving on the banks of the Tugela river, they were amazed and perplexed to find that it was in flood, thus early in the season, for they did not know that exceptionally heavy rains had fallen in the Drakensberg catchment area. For days they were held up whilst anxiety gnawed at Pampata's heart, for she guessed that Mbopa would waste no time in organizing a strong force to annihilate Ngwadi and all his kraal.

And so it proved to be. For Mbopa, as major-domo of the capital, had made himself the chief executive during the inter-regnum, until Mdlaka's army should return, with all the nobles accompanying it, and proclaim the new king. Mbopa at once realized that he could do nothing without an adequate force. He could not mobilize the reserve regiments, for they would not recognize his authority. He accordingly swept together the several hundred *Izi-Yendane* (mop-headers or Natal Natives) serving as menials or cattle-guards in the numerous Royal cattle-kraals scattered about Natal and incorporated them into a single regiment, the *U-Hlomendlini* (The Home Guards).

Squads of the new soldiery were at once dispatched to round up and bring north all the Royal cattle scattered about the southern parts of Natal as far as the Umzimkulu river, lest the Pondos, Bacas, and other southern tribes, upon hearing the report of Shaka's death, be tempted to indulge in raids on their own stolen property. For Shaka alone and alive was the equivalent of a great army.

With the rest of the Home Guards and the *Izinyosi* regiment of newly enrolled lads, Mbopa formed an effective striking force. The latter were now told that they were the avengers for the 'Great Elephant's' assassination, which had been planned by an evil relative in the north. Placing himself at the head of this force, Mbopa now hurried northwards to eliminate Ngwadi.

Pampata and her youthful companion had just managed to cross the subsiding Tugela river when, in the distance, they saw the glint of numerous spears behind them. Pampata's worst fears were realized, and on the wings of anxiety she and the youth flew onwards.

Mbopa knew that Ngwadi had a well-disciplined little army, which, even numerically, was superior to his own. This little army had been exempted from the general mobilization for the

Soshangane campaign, and was therefore in garrison at home, but in a state of semi-mobilization. Mbopa consequently had to move warily, and reach his objective before Ngwadi's army could be mustered.

Pampata had a start of about ten miles, but Ngwadi's kraal was over 100 miles away. She had no illusions about the marching power of Zulu warriors, but woman though she was, she was determined to out-distance them. All that day she kept up a steady jog-trot, pausing only to drink a very little water at some of the streams she had to cross. To the astonished inquiries of passers-by at the unusual spectacle of a running woman, she called out that she was hastening to the side of her dying mother.

And so Pampata and the youth went on the whole night long, frequently taking the wrong path and compelled to make detours to get into the right direction again. When daylight came the two utterly exhausted runners looked more like fugitives than anything else and presently they were stopped by a party of dignified elderly 'ring-heads'. Pampata now played her trump card. She produced the little toy spear which everyone knew belonged to the 'Great Elephant'. This instantly cleared her path, on this and subsequent occasions. Each time she adjured the beholders, on pain of death, to mention to no one what they had seen.

As they wearily climbed the Melmoth heights they saw again, far behind them, and beyond the Umhlatuzi river, that tell-tale glint of assegais. But now they had appreciably lengthened the distance between themselves and Mbopa's slayers. Only her will-power kept Pampata going now, for she was in a grievous state. All her toes were battered, and her feet were swollen. She was afraid to stop and rest, for she felt she would not be able to get up again. The youth was also just about finished, although his feet were in better trim, and he kept on eating a handful of the army 'iron' rations, *kota*, and insisted that Pampata also eat a mouthful or two.

When they arrived at the Melmoth plateau they ran into a dense mist, and wearily limping, Pampata almost gave up hope, for frequently they lost their bearings altogether, and had to retrace their footsteps. At last the youth gave in. Human nature could endure no more, for he lacked the almost supernatural will-power of Pampata.

Arrived in the lowlands, she got below the canopy of mist, and although the night was dark, she was again able to pick her way, and so at a late hour she stumbled, rather than walked, into Ngwadi's kraal, to the amazement of the warrior who guarded the gate. She was immediately taken to Ngwadi's hut, who had to be awakened, and who was no less astonished at the piteous sight he saw. He knew at once that something dreadful had happened, for Pampata was unable to speak for a while. Then she told him the dread news. Ngwadi could hardly grasp it at first. The great half-brother whom he deified, had seemed immortal to him. He immediately called the whole kraal to arms, and mustered about fifty spears. Then he dispatched runners to the other kraals and military units, to mobilize his whole little army. By this time it was cock-crow.

Meanwhile Pampata was being revived with beer and milk, and soothing applications of medicinal herbs to her battered feet, and Ngwadi's veterans took up battle stations, besides posting pickets outside the kraal.

Just before dawn the pickets came in and whispered, 'They are here. They are surrounding the kraal now.'

In the first light of dawn the defenders saw Mbopa's 'Home Guards' stealthily creeping towards the outer stockade of the kraal from all sides, with several massed platoons making for the kraal gate, where Ngwadi stood with a chosen bodyguard. Silently, like cats, they clambered up the stockade, and just as they thought that the surprise was complete they were confronted by jabbing spears, which caught them mostly under their chins. At the same time the fight was on at the gate and Ngwadi gave the old national war-cry 'Si-gī-di' ('One thousand', which was one of Shaka's praise names) and his personal war-cry 'Um-joji'.* These cries were now taken up by all the defenders. who gave the two or three hundred 'Home Guards' such a hot

* By George! – curious evidence of Ngwadi's feeling for the British.

and unexpected reception, that they reeled back, and away from the furiously defended stockade.

Urged by Mbopa they attacked twice more, only to be hurled back with bloody losses. Mbopa now called off the Home Guard and sent orders to the youthful Bees regiment to muster for the attack. When Ngwadi saw this overwhelming force move up, he withdrew into the inner cattle-kraal with all his womenfolk and children, Pampata in their midst. This shortened his line of defence very considerably, and he gazed anxiously over hill and dale for his expected reinforcements, but as yet there was no sign of them.

Mbopa first infuriated the unsophisticated Bees by giving them a harangue, and accusing Ngwadi as the instigator of his half-brother's death.

With a fierce cry of vengeance they swarmed over the outer stockade, which was now undefended, and rushed at the inner kraal. A murderous fight ensued, and soon Ngwadi was defending his last line of resistance, the calf enclosure within the cattle-kraal, where all his dependants were now gathered.

For a space there was a lull, and Mbopa looked at Ngwadi from behind the safety of the main cattle-kraal. 'It is you who will be hyaena's meat soon now – you and your whole kraal,' he said with an evil grin.

'*Mbopa ka Sitayi*,' Pampata said with the dignity of a queen, 'You laugh today, but Dingane will soon laugh at you, when he sees the vultures eating your worthless carcass. Remember Nobela's prophecy.' And Mbopa heard and was never quite happy again, for he lived in fear until in due course he was brutally killed by order of Dingane.

There was a sudden shout by the attackers. They had seen several bodies of warriors approaching in the distance. They were Ngwadi's reinforcements.

'At them,' yelled Mbopa. 'Finish them, before help comes, and capture Pampata alive.'

A furious clash now began; but with his reduced numbers pitted against a whole regiment, Ngwadi had no hope: Ngwadi alone killed eight of the attackers, and all his men fought with magnificent valour, but it was of no avail. As Ngwadi fell at last Pampata knew her time had come, and taking the little toy spear she placed the point between two ribs opposite her heart; then she gave a vigorous push and with a cry collapsed dead, just before the massacre of the women and children took place.

Some say that her last cry was *U-Shaka!*

MAPS

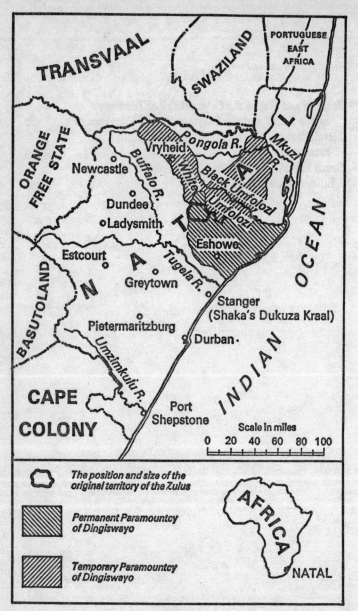

TRANSVAAL

SWAZILAND

PORTUGUESE
EAST
AFRICA

ORANGE
FREE STATE

Newcastle

Vryheid

Pongola R.

Mkuzi
R.

Buffalo R.

White Umfolozi

Black Umfolozi

Dundee

Umfolozi-

Ladysmith

Eshowe

BASUTOLAND

Estcourt

N A T A L

Tugela R.

Greytown

Stanger
(Shaka's Dukuza Kraal)

Pietermaritzburg

Umzimkulu R.

Durban

CAPE
COLONY

INDIAN OCEAN

Port
Shepstone

Scale in miles

0   20   40   60   80   100

The position and size of the
original territory of the Zulus

Permanent Paramountcy
of Dingiswayo

Temporary Paramountcy
of Dingiswayo

AFRICA

NATAL

380

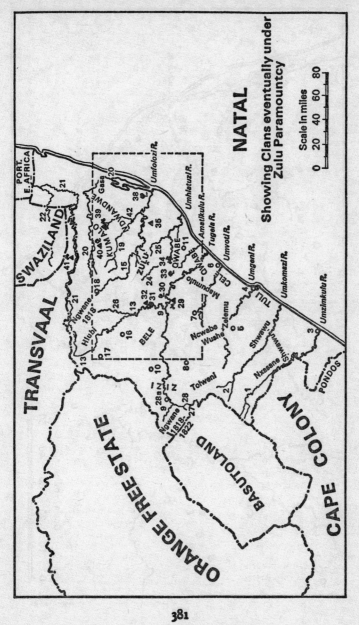

NATAL

Showing Clans eventually under
Zulu Paramountcy

Scale in miles

0 20 40 60 80

TRANSVAAL

SWAZILAND

PORT.
E. AFRICA

ORANGE FREE STATE

BASUTOLAND

CAPE COLONY

PONDOS

Umfolozi R.

Umhletuzi R.

Amatikulu R.

Tugela R.

Umvoti R.

Umgeni R.

Umkomezi R.

Umzimkulu R.

Ngwene
1818

Hlubi

BELE

Ngwene
1818-
1822

Mapumulo

Ncwabe
Wushe

Zelemu

Shwawu

Shwawu

Nxasane

Tolweni

Gasa

KUMALO

NDWANDWE

ZULU

QWABE

QWABE

CELE

TULU

Tchweni

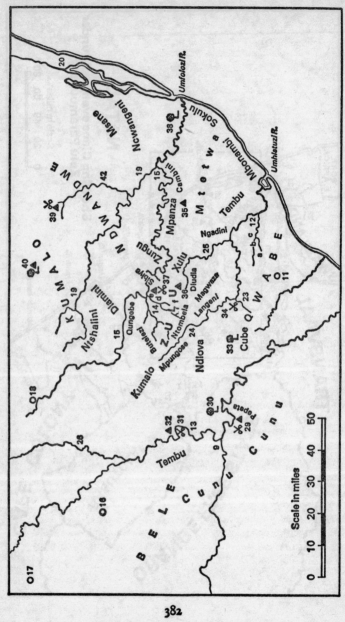

Scale in miles

0 10 20 30 40 50

KEY TO MAPS OPPOSITE AND ON PAGE 381

1. Umzimkulu, *River*
2. Umkomazi, *River*
3. Port Shepstone, *Town*
4. Durban, *Town*
5. Pietermaritzburg, *Town*
6. Stanger, *Town* (Shaka's Dukuza *Kraal*)
7. Greytown, *Town*
8. Estcourt, *Town*
9. Tugela, *River*
10. Ladysmith, *Town*
11. Eshowe, *Town*
12. Umhlatuzana, *River*
    - (a) Em-Tandeni, *Kraal*
    - (b) Nandi's *Kraal*
    - (c) Bulawayo (No. 2), *Kraal*
13. Buffalo, *River*
14. Umkumbane, *River*
    - (d) Esi-Klebeni, *Kraal*
    - (e) Belebele, *Kraal*
    - (f) Bulawayo (No. 1), *Kraal*
15. White Umfolozi, *River*
16. Dundee, *Town*
17. Newcastle, *Town*
18. Vryheid, *Town*
19. Black Umfolozi, *River*
20. Umkuze, *River*
21. Pongola, *River*
22. Ngwavuma, *River*
23. Mvuzane, *River*
24. Umhlatuzi, *River*
25. Mfule, *River*
26. Blood, *River*
27. Lambonja, *River*
28. Ndidimeni, *River*
    - (a) Bergville, *Town*
29. O-Pisweni, *Mountain* and *Battle*
30. Qudeni, *Mountain* and *Forest*
31. Tembu, *Battle* (Shaka's first and only reverse)
32. Hlazakazi, *Mountain*
33. Nkandla, *Forest*
34. Umhlatuze, *Battle*
35. Tzangonyana, *Mountain*
    - (a) Dingiswayo's O-Yengweni *Kraal*
36. Tonjaneni, *Heights*
37. Qokli, *Hill* and *Battle*
38. Duku-duku, *Forest*
39. Nongoma, *Heights* and Zwide's *Kraal*
40. Ngome, *Mountain* and *Forest*
41. Ndololwane, *Mountain* and *Battle*
42. Um-Mona, *River* and *Battle* (which extended to No. 39)

383

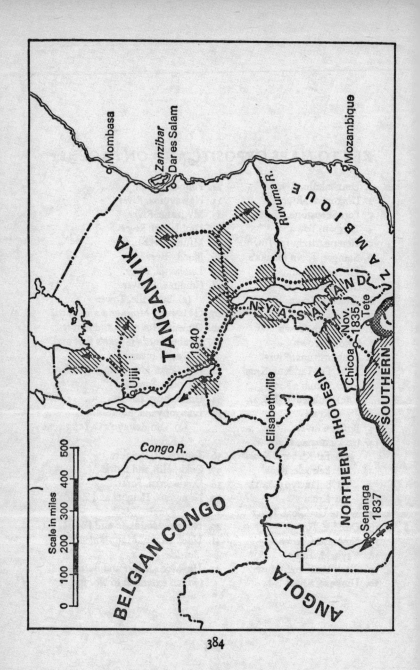

Mombasa

Zanzibar
Dar es Salam

Mozambique

TANGANYIKA

Ruvuma R.

ZAMBIQUE

N · Y · A · S · A · L · A · N · D

Nov.
1835

Tete

Chicoa

840

Ujiji

SOUTHERN

Elisabethville

NORTHERN RHODESIA

Congo R.

Scale in miles

500
400
300
200
100
0

BELGIAN CONGO

Senanga
1837

ANGOLA

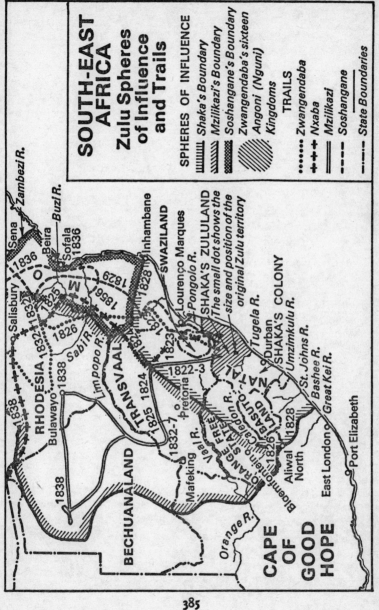

SOUTH-EAST AFRICA

Zulu Spheres of Influence and Trails

SPHERES OF INFLUENCE

Shaka's Boundary
Mzilikazi's Boundary
Soshangane's Boundary
Zwangendaba's sixteen
Angoni (Nguni)
Kingdoms

TRAILS

Zwangendaba
Nxaba
Mzilikazi
Soshangane
State Boundaries

Zambezi R.
Sena
Beira
Buzi R.
Sofala 1836
1836
Inhambane
SWAZILAND
Lourenço Marques
Pongolo R.
SHAKA'S ZULULAND
The small dot shows the size and position of the original Zulu territory
Salisbury 1832–1832
1825
1856
1829
1828
1826
1838
Sabi R.
RHODESIA
Bulawayo
Limpopo R.
TRANSVAAL
1825 1824
1832-7
Pretoria
1822-3
Tugela R.
Durban
SHAKA'S COLONY
Umzimkulu R.
St. Johns R.
Bashee R.
Great Kei R.
NATAL
BECHUANALAND
1838
Mafeking
Vaal R.
ORANGE FREE STATE
Bloemfontein
Caledon R.
BASUTOLAND
1826
1828
Aliwal North
East London
Port Elizabeth
Orange R.
CAPE OF GOOD HOPE

385

APPENDIX

(a) SANDALS

FROM time immemorial until Shaka abolished them, the Zulus wore sandals made of cowhide. The Zulu name was *izi-xatuba* (singular: *isi xatuba*). This was established by Bishop Colenso, who published the first Zulu dictionary in 1860.

Finding the Zulus barefooted, the Europeans came to think that they had always been so. The missionaries, finding that the Zulus had no name for boots or shoes, coined the word *izi-xatulo*, which was obviously derived from *izi-xatuba*. In order further to differentiate the coined word they changed the initial x into c, to make *izi-catulo*, the current word for boots or shoes. The more modern Zulu–language lexicographers have lost Bishop Colenso's *izi-xatuba* and have tried to replace it in some cases with the coined monstrosity, *ama-slipusi*, from the English *slipper*.

Russel, in *Russel's Natal* (p. 134), notes: 'Sandals, worn before Chaka's [*sic*] time, were by him forbidden as they impeded the movements of his warriors.' Dr E. J. Krige (*The Social System of the Zulus*, p. 263) says: 'No sandals were worn because Shaka did away with them, believing that his soldiers would act more promptly without footwear.' Her authority is Delegorgue's *Voyage dans l'Afrique Australe*. Delegorgue was a recognized authority who was in the country with the Voortrekkers when Dingane still ruled. Dr Krige also mentions as an authority Mayr, *The Zulu Kaffirs of Natal* (Anthropos, vol. ii). In a list of early clothes Dr Krige mentions *isi-Qathuba* – sandal of hide worn with three straps. She thus uses the 'Q' click instead of the 'X' click. I have used Bishop Colenso's spelling in the first Zulu dictionary ever published.

In *Libertas*, Sept. 1947, vol. 7, no. 9, p. 40, Hermia Oliver has

an article, entitled 'Zululand's Lost Fashions', in which she says:
'Further to harden his fighting men Shaka abolished the sandals
that were formerly worn.' (*Libertas*, now defunct, was a monthly
magazine specializing in historical sketches.)

How Dr Bryant ever made the mistake he did on this subject
has always puzzled me. True, he dealt with this matter only
casually.

(b) ZULU OATHS

Dadewetu! literally 'our sister', but meaning 'my' sister. The
implication of this oath was, 'may I be found sleeping with my
sister if I do not speak the truth'. This would be one of the most
heinous social offences in the Zulu code. *Dadewetu!* was
also frequently used profanely as an expression of surprise.

Until Shaka rose to power the strongest affirmative oaths a
Zulu could use were to swear by the bones of his father, or just
simply 'by my father'. In Shaka's reign the most binding oath
was in his name. Women, however, never used this oath but
only swore by their father-in-law.

Shaka frequently swore by his dour maiden aunt Mkabayi,
but almost invariably as an expression of anger.

To this day Zulus affirm in Shaka's name, or in that of his
nephew King Cetewayo, who, next to Shaka, is regarded as the
greatest Zulu king. A few will swear by Mpande, but none by
Dingane.

(c) HERBALISTS, MEDICINES AND
WITCH-DOCTORS, OR DIVINERS

Every class of Zulu doctor is referred to as an *i-nyanga*, which
merely means a specialist, and may be given to any person qualified in some specific occupation or trade requiring skill. *I-nyanga*
is therefore analogous to our degree of doctor and is prefixed
to the specific calling of the person referred to. Thus the Zulus

had doctors of healing, divining, rain-making, war (*Inyanga yoku songa*), etc.

The healing doctors generally specialized in some particular ailment but were also herbalists generally. They did not do any divining but their patients were frequently sent to them by diviners. These healers supplied common sense, purgatives, emetics, enemas, poultices; performed simple operations such as the removal of piles; alleviated hydrocele, and applied the 'heroic' method in treating indolently healing wounds, etc.

They had some good remedies, but unfortunately they frequently mixed these with some rubbish to disguise the effective ingredient and thus caused more harm than good.

Their tape-worm specific (*inkoma-nkoma* or male fern) was very effective.

Poultices or aqueous solutions made from the *umtuma* fruit (*Solanum incanum*) were amazingly effective in removing external benign tumours.

An epithelioma on the back of a racehorse, and certified as such by a pathologist, was permanently cured by the application of solanum poultices. A mule with a certified carcinoma on the hock was successfully treated by an injection of the aqueous solution into the surrounding healthy tissue. A horse with half a dozen melanoma was likewise successfully treated. The two former cases were handled by a qualified veterinary surgeon, and the last by an M.D. Both were aged and died soon afterwards, but their equine patients flourished for many years, with never a sign of relapse. A scientific investigation of the merits of this widely distributed plant appears to be called for. It is definitely selective in its action.

For the sake of intending investigators the following detailed analysis is given of the aqueous solution which was used in the injections detailed above:

The solution or extract contained 1.5 (one point five per cent) of solids composed of:

Protein	0·21 per cent
Tannins	0·87 „
Sugars	0·11 „
Oil	0·01 „
Acid (as tartaric)	0·03 „
Undetermined (gums, etc.)	0·27 „
Alkaloids	slight trace

With the proteins and tannins removed the residual solanum extract was just as effective. The active principle could not be pin-pointed closer for lack of facilities.

The divining doctors, witch-doctors or witch-finders constituted a specialized profession of their own, divided into several classes.

The ordinary diviner, whose lowest fees were the equivalent of one fowl, was as much in demand as the modern tea-cup reader. Any trivial worry was brought to him for elucidation and he seldom 'threw the bones', which were reserved for more important occasions, with a correspondingly higher fee, namely a goat. His client always had to be accompanied by one or more friends or relatives.

Chanting his questions, the diviner would require his audience to reply to every one of them, *siya vuma* – we agree. The emphasis or lack of emphasis would then guide him to give his answer or divination, which was always clothed in self-evident ambiguity like the Oracle of Delphi.

The high-class diviner who had established a reputation charged accordingly, and was therefore only consulted in the more serious cases. He had to be given a *vula-mlomo* (literally, mouth-opener) goat before he would even deign to speak. Thereafter he would demand a goat to appease the spirits, and incidentally his own stomach, and another one for considering the case. Much of this considering consisted in assessing the fee, in which he would be guided by his almost census-like knowledge of the cattle owned by his clients.

Having named his fee, the diviner was proverbially tardy till it arrived, for he believed in payment before delivery. Moreover, this had the sound advantage that it enabled him to make secret inquiries into the case before him. If the client arrived with the payment on the hoof he could still gain time on the pretext of collecting the necessary medicines first, or consulting the spirits.

When all was ready the diviner would throw the indicating bones, or sticks, which each had a different name and significance. This procedure was not unlike the method of telling fortunes by cards. During the throwing of the bones, the audience was usually also subjected to the chanting questions which had to be answered by the invariable 'we agree'.

Every illness, death, misfortune or untoward event was ascribed to witchcraft, and the person who was supposed to be responsible for this was indicated. This was always done ambiguously, except at a proper 'smelling out', when the victim was openly denounced by striking him with the gnu or wildebeest tail. Some misfortunes, however, came from those ancestral spirits who had been angered.

Another and rarer type of diviner, or witch-doctor, was the *um-lozi* or whistling diviner. This type is a ventriloquist, and usually only divines in a hut filled with acrid smoke. Different 'spirit' voices will come from the roof and sides of the hut and from the very ground itself. The client and his friends are terrified by these supernatural manifestations, especially when the 'spirits' proceed to drop the medicines they have prescribed from the roof. The highlights are reached when freshly killed poisonous snakes, scorpions, etc., drop at the feet of the client. Sometimes the latter is given a body-shattering emetic and his eyes are half-blinded with acrid smoke which is held to his eyes with a bowl. After retching and vomiting desperately the client is shown what he is supposed to have brought up in the way of expelled witchcraft, for instance, a bloated puff adder three feet long and three inches thick. His gratitude knows no bounds and he is too shaken to even attempt to reason how such a monstrous thing could have passed his throat. To his way of thinking all things are possible to the beneficent witch-doctor, just as every evil can be perpetrated by witches and wizards, or sorcerers.

The rain-doctor belongs to a specific class, and the profession is generally hereditary.

Although all the witch-doctors or diviners have been referred to in the masculine gender the profession is open to both sexes and usually there was one female diviner for every two male ones. With this one exception, that all war-doctors were males only.

(d) OFFERINGS TO THE ANCESTRAL SPIRITS

These were frequently made either as thanks for a spell of prosperity and good luck, or in times of anxiety, loss and sorrow. The head of the kraal, as officiator, would call on all the ancestral spirits as far back as they were remembered, and as a precautionary measure all those whom he may have inadvertently forgotten. When misfortunes were attributed to an ancestral spirit named by the diviner, the officiator at the sacrifice would reprimand him, and ask him sorrowfully but outrightly why he, who had been so good and great in his lifetime, now made them all wonder at his underhand methods. A guarded hint would then be made that if the spirit continued to visit them with death there would soon be no worshippers left.

Special parts of the animal killed were placed in the *umsamo* or back portion of the 'great hut' of the kraal. This meat was reserved for the sole enjoyment of the ancestors, and needless to say the kraal-head would see to it that it never went bad through lack of attention by the 'spirits'. All the rest of the meat was divided up amongst the inmates of the kraal according to their status – special parts of the animal being reserved to the head of the kraal, the men, women, boys and girls. The Zulus were too practical to make wasteful burnt offerings, except only in the case of the residue of the black bull killed for war medicine.

Appendix

(e) THE MONTHLY EXAMINATION OF MAIDENS

Immediately after her 'moon' every unmarried maiden was subjected to a very careful pudendal examination by her mother, or the next nearest elderly relative, to make sure that her virginity remained intact. This was particularly necessary to ensure the strict observance of the rules laid down for the 'customary', or semi-external, intercourse described in the text.

The Guild 'Queen' and Actions against Slander

All the girls of the same age-group, and the same district, who went through the ceremonial rites of puberty in the same year, formed a guild who chose a 'Queen'. As a unit they now jealously guarded their own and each other's honour, which would not countenance any deflowering. If one of them were slandered the 'Queen' immediately took action. The slandered girl would be examined by her and a committee of maidens, and having established that her virginity was intact, the whole guild armed with sticks would proceed to the slanderer's kraal – almost invariably a boastful man; arrived there the 'Queen' would demand that the senior wives of the kraal should examine the girl and declare their finding publicly.

The matrons having done so and found the girl to be a virgin indeed, the irate maidens would proceed to the slanderer's hut and smash everything inside it. And woe betide any slanderer who had not got away betimes. He would be lucky to escape with his life.

Thereupon the 'Queen' would proceed to the cattle-kraal with her following and there she would select the fattest ox which would be driven to the slandered maiden's kraal. No one would even attempt to interfere with them as they were acting according to the law of the land.

The captured ox would be ceremoniously slaughtered and all the relatives of the maidens of the guild would partake of the meat, but not a single member of the guild itself. They were content that the honour of the girl, and therefore of the guild, had been vindicated.

Had the girl indeed been deflowered the whole guild would have turned against her and treated her with contempt ever afterwards.

(f) THE 'HLONIPA' CUSTOM

This custom is almost wholly confined to women. The word *hlonipa* means modesty, or 'to avoid out of respect', from using the ordinary names of certain near relatives-in-law, or to refer to an object by its usual name if it coincides with, or bears a close resemblance to such person's name, or the name of a living or deceased chief.

Thus if the husband's name is 'Tree' she must use some other arboreal name, or invent one. When a woman passes the child-bearing age the custom ceases, as she is then regarded as a man.

Both sexes and all ages must observe the *hlonipa* custom in the case of the chief of the clan. Thus when a chief 'Tshani' (Grass) ruled over the Ngwane clan, the whole tribe ceased to use that word for grass, and substituted the coined word '*ince*', which is still in use although Tshani died about 1793.

(g) 'LOBOLA' – OR PAYMENT FOR A BRIDE

Correctly speaking, it is not a payment at all. It is also incorrect to call it a dowry. Actually it is an irrevocable guarantee given by the intending bridegroom to his prospective father-in-law that he will take every care of his daughter when she becomes his wife, and also the resulting children. For, if he should ill-treat or neglect her, she has the right to return to her father, who is then able to provide for her and such children she may have borne. This would tend to bring the man into a reasonable frame of mind again, and usually a reconciliation takes place. It is extremely rare for a married woman to return to the protection of her father, for a mere threat to do so, if she has just cause, is sufficient to pull up a badly behaving husband.

394

On the other hand a wife will always take care not to antagonize her husband by bad behaviour; for this might mean that her father would have to take her back, and return at least a proportion of the cattle which had been given to him – depending on the number of children she had borne.

If a wife is barren, or should die before producing any children, her father has to provide her husband with another wife, without receiving any more *lobola* cattle.

The amount of *lobola* varied from three to five cattle in Shaka's days, to ten head nowadays, for a commoner's daughter. Headmen received many more for their daughters, and a chief could fix on any figure he chose.

It appears to be the rule that the more expensive *lobola* is, the more durable and satisfactory are the resulting ties. For a Zulu will always choose his bride very carefully as he has to work hard for many years to acquire the necessary cattle. As one proceeds farther north the *lobola* drops in value, until in Nyasaland a bride may be acquired for a goat. With the lessening *lobola* the value of a woman drops accordingly, with a corresponding lowering of the self-respect of the bride and the marital state.

(h) TREATMENT OF WOUNDS RECEIVED FROM THE SEPTIC CLAWS OF A LEOPARD

The *Inyanga yokwe lapa* or healing doctor immediately applied the following treatment. The wounds were thoroughly syringed with an antiseptic made of thoroughly boiled *Datura stramonium* leaves and nitrate of ammonium which was obtained by scraping the dried-out deposits of rock rabbits' (coney) urine which forms in white layers on the special rocks which are daily urinated on by members of a rock rabbit colony. As the doctors had no syringes they first took a mouthful of the fluid and after keeping it in the mouth they would spit it out. This was done three times with an invocation of the spirits. This, although they knew it not, obviously helped to sterilize their mouths before they filled them with the medical doses, and pressure-squirted the fluid through a reed tube into the patient's wounds. This they did with meticulous care. Thereafter the boiled stramonium leaves were packed into the larger gashes, and finally every wound was bound with a thick package of the leaves, which then came into operation with their phenomenal drawing powers and ability to form moulds. This treatment was continued daily till the doctor was satisfied that all danger was past.

A European acquaintance of the author, a Mr Sweetenham, was successfully treated by this method about 1910 in the wilds of the Sebungwe district of S. Rhodesia. Mr Sweetenham, a young giant, was pounced upon by a lightly wounded leopard which he ultimately succeeded in strangling and breaking its ribs with his knee. He suffered unbelievable lacerations from the claws of the leopard and for two months lost all count of time whilst the native doctor fought for his life. Nevertheless he completely recovered.

(i) LIST OF SHAKA'S REGIMENTS – MALE AND FEMALE. DECORATIONS FOR MERIT

When Shaka took over the Zulu chieftaincy in 1816 he inherited some 300 able-bodied men who were loosely formed into several so-called regiments – besides 200 youths not yet enrolled.

The eldest men, ranging from thirty to forty years, were known as the Ama-Wombe (Single Clash) and numbered about 100 men. Shaka retained the name and steadily increased their numbers until they became one of the strongest regiments, numerically and in prestige. They were the 'Old Guard' which was almost invariably held in reserve until the crisis of the battle was at hand. They were stationed at the Belebele (Everlasting Worry) military kraal. As other regiments were brigaded with them the whole brigade was known as the Belebele, and this was continued when the brigade became a division.

Regiments usually forming the Belebele Brigade or Division

Name of Regiments	When formed	Warriors born (about)
Ama-Wombe (Single Clash)	1816	1775–85
U-Kangela (Look-out)	1816	1785–90
Izin-Tenjana (ezakala O-Ngoye) (The Plovers who called out at Ngoye)	1818–19	1795–8
U-Nomdayana	1820	1800
Ama-Pela (The Cockroaches—adopted from Zwide)	1821	1801
Ama-Kwenkwe Izi-Kwembu Izi-Zimazane	1822–6	1802–6

The Izim-Pohlo (Bachelors') or Isi-Klebe Division

Name of Regiments	When formed	Warriors born (about)
Jubingqwanga (Shorn Head-rings)	1816	1785–90
U-Dlambedlu (Wild Men)	1816	1790–5
Um-Gumanqa (Heavy influx due to collapse Isi-Pezi of Mtetwas and Qwabes. U-Mbonambi These 4 Regts. sometimes U-Nteke formed a subdivision	1818–19	1797–8
U-Gibabanye or Kipabanye (The Expellers) U-Fojisa Im-Folozi In-Dabankulu (The Great Affair)	1820–5	1800–5

The 'Fasimba' (The Haze) regiment, or 'Shaka's Own', and the second 'Izi-cwe' (The Bushmen) regiment, or 'Ngomane's Own', formed the 'Young Guard', and were seldom, if ever, brigaded with the above divisions. They were both formed from the youngest men in 1816, the Izi-cwe coming over *en masse* with Ngomane on the dissolution of Dingiswayo's Mtetwa kingdom. As special Royal Guards they always received most favoured treatment.

There were three other unattached regiments, namely the 'U-Dlangezwa', 'Um-Ota' and 'Ulu-Tuli', all formed about 1923–4. The two latter were specially employed against Beje, the Kumalo Robin Hood.

Finally Shaka formed the 'Izi-Nyosi' (The Bees) from the senior *u-dibi* boys he withdrew from the Soshangane campaign in 1828.

What other regiments Shaka had is no longer ascertainable now. Other regiments are frequently mentioned, but are in fact only the names of the military kraals they occupied, and not regimental names at all. This has frequently led to an erroneous multiplication of the regiments themselves.

Maidens' Regiments

Name of Regiments	When formed	Maidens born (about)
Um-Vutwamini (Ripen-at-Noon, the name of a luscious wild fruit)	1817	1796
In-Tlabati (Sand)	1818	1797
Im-Babazane (Self-admirers)	1819	1799
Ulu-Siba (The Feather)	1823	1802
U-Ngisimane (The Englishman)	1827	1806

Decorations for Merit

When a Zulu warrior had slain an adversary in battle he was entitled to wear for each enemy slain a small piece of wood suspended by a string from his neck. It was about two inches long, half an inch wide, and a quarter of an inch thick. It was made from the *um-nyezane*, or indigenous willow tree, and the necklace itself was so named.

Prior to putting on this necklace the warrior wore a sprig of wild-asparagus (*I-Pinga-ntlola*), one sprig for each victim.

Although Shaka would at first allow nobody but himself to wear the brilliant scarlet feathers of the red loury (of which he wore 12 bunches), he presently allowed his most important chiefs to wear one bunch, and warriors who had distinguished themselves, one feather each. The crack regiment of Royal Guards – the Fasimba – as a whole, were allowed to wear this one feather per warrior.

The head-ring, or *isi-coco*, was probably the most universal and most coveted distinction of all, as it meant permission to marry. It was sometimes granted to a regiment as a whole for meritorious service.

(j) NGUNI (ZULU) LOVE-PLAY

The average Nguni benedict had several wives. The higher his social status the more wives he possessed. Perhaps it would be more correct to say that the more wives he had the higher his social status was. Usually his wealth and wives increased in the reverse ratio to his potency. An unsatisfied wife meant trouble.

The natural common sense of the Ngunis here came to the aid of the much married man. He profited from his sound knowledge of female physiology and called to his aid a delicate and highly developed technique of love-play. His infallible guide was that anything which was pleasing to his partner, and natural to average womanly desires, was right. The greatest satisfaction to a Nguni man was to impart sexual satisfaction to his partner. Therein lay his success in keeping happy a plurality of wives.

If, then, a husband had more wives than he could normally cope with, he would withhold or reserve his own orgasms by means of controlled intercourse, and yet with the auxiliary aids of love-play ensure that all his wives invariably had a satisfactory orgasm themselves. His prestige as a man demanded this. By these methods Ngunis, especially chiefs, were able to partner satisfactorily an astounding number of women, quite apart from the pregnancies they provided them with at determined intervals of three or four years. Shaka, of course, eschewed these. For a very potent and virile man, with a harem of 1200, he established something like a record in self-control, for he only caused one authenticated pregnancy. But then he largely relied on the *uku-hlobonga* type of intercourse described in the text. Nevertheless, he too gloried more in the satisfaction he was able to give rather than in that which he received.

Nguni women, too, believed in hearty cooperation with their spouses and never allowed the cult of Venus to degenerate into an act of dignified acquiescence.

BIBLIOGRAPHY AND SOURCES

As was explained in the Introduction to this work, a principal, and perhaps the principal, source of material was the Zulu oral tradition conveyed to the author through the mouths of Njengabantu Ema-Bomvini, Chief Sigananda Cube and other Zulu 'chroniclers', including notably Nqakamatshe Ntombela, Msuzeli Qwabe, Mtambokag-wayi Gcumisa and Chief Ncwadi Ngwane. The tactical and strategical details of the principal battle descriptions were supplied by the author's father, Captain C. L. A. Ritter. And the author has already put on record his indebtedness to Miss Killie Campbell, for access to her unrivalled collection of unpublished material.

The literary sources for any history or biography concerning South Africa are not extensive, but what there are are very good. In the following list three books have been of such very great help that they call for special mention.

First is Dr A. T. Bryant's *Olden Times in Zululand and Natal*. It is a thousand pities that this great book, the work of many years, by a man of outstanding talent and integrity, is not more widely read. It is very much to be hoped that in the future it will be more widely read: for it is and must remain *the* source book for historians of Natal and Zululand, and the author has written *Shaka Zulu* within the framework of Dr Bryant's history and consulted it extensively for almost every chapter ... so extensively that it was impossible to refer to every instance by an acknowledgment.

The Diary of Henry Francis Fynn has been invaluable because Fynn was constantly and frequently in Shaka's company, and it is a rule that no document has so much value to the historian as a contemporary one.

An author wishing to reconstruct the social life of a Zulu kraal in Shaka's time, or any other time, could not hope to do so without the aid of Dr E. J. Krige's *The Social System of the Zulus*. Where he has quoted from that admirable book the author has acknowledged the fact, but the scientific confirmation it has provided for his own observation of the Zulus has also been invaluable.

BOOKS CONSULTED

Olden Times in Zululand and Natal. Dr A. T. Bryant.

Bird's Annals of Natal.

The Diary of Henry Francis Fynn.

Russel's Natal History.

Moodie's British South Africa.

The Social System of the Zulus. Dr E. J. Krige.

Voyage dans l'Afrique Australe. Delegorgue.

Agricultural Ceremonies in Natal and Zululand. (Bantu Studies, vol. III.)

Long, Long Ago. R. C. Samuelson.

Wild Sports in Southern Africa. W. C. Harris.

Visit to Moselekatze 1844. Rev. R. Moffat.

'U-Hlanga Kulu. J. Stuart.

Travels and Adventures in Eastern Africa. Nathaniel Isaacs.

Cradle Days of Natal. Graham Mackeurtan.

Shaka. R. R. R. Dhlomo.

INDEX

Mdlaka, *continued*
324–6, 327; and King of
Pondos, 350
Mfusi, 248
Mgobozi, 48, 49, 50, 51; offered
post of C.-in-C. by Shaka, 83;
given permission to marry,
95–7; wedding of, 98–102; and
witch-finders, 113–15; and
battle of Qokli hill, 147–8,
150, 158–60, 163–5, 168, 200,
214, 216; and buffaloes, 230–31;
at Shaka's smelling-out parade,
262, 264, 265, 266–7; popularity
of, 267, 289, 291–2, 318; and
battle of Ndololwane, 311,
312–17; death of, 317
Mhlangana, 268
Mhlope, 275
Mkabayi, and revolt in Shaka's
court, 355–6
Mkabi, 217
Mlandela, becomes Mtetwa
chief, 167
Mlotsha, 321–3
M-Mama, and revolt in Shaka's
court, 355
Mpangazita, 124–5, 126
Mpepa, 159
Mqalane, 171, 290, 291–2, 293, 295
Mshika, 241, 243
Mshweshwe, aided by Mdlaka,
303–4; builds up Basuto
nation, 305
Msimbiti, Jacob, 276–7;
appointed Royal interpreter,
277; and attempt on Shaka's
life, 282, 320; and embassy
to George IV, 346
Mtaniya, 305
Mtetwa Chief, *see* Jobe

Mtetwa expedition, 51
Mudli, trial of, 76–9
Mvuzane river, 195, 198
Mzilikazi, 134, 167–8, 169, 186,
187, 200; given command of
two regiments by Shaka,
246–8; given plume of white
ostrich feathers, 248; and
Kumalos, 249–52; builds last
capital, 252; annihilates
Griquas, 325

Nameless One, 42–4
Nandi, and Senzangakona,
26; gives birth to Shaka, 26;
and Pampata, 52–3, 56, 66,
166; and Butelezi women, 92;
acts as 'mother' of
Mgobozi, 99; hears of victory
at Qokli hill, 166; and
Umkosi festival, 177; and
building of Emkindini, 216;
welcomes Shaka to Bulawayo,
234; and mother's death,
306; and grandson, 309, 327,
328–30; illness of, 330; death
of, 330, 331
Ncubeni, 168
Ndabazimbi, 257, 260
Ndlela, 138, 159, 198, 238, 311
Ndlovukazi, 178
Ndololwane, battle of, 311–17
Ndwandwes, 58; and battle of
Qokli hill, 145–66; second war,
182–201; and battle of
Ndololwane, 311–17;
annihilated by Zulu army,
317–18
Ngomane, 52, 68, 73–4, 133, 148,
163; becomes Zulu prime
minister, 167, 327; announces

FOR THE BEST IN PAPERBACKS, LOOK FOR THE

In every corner of the world, on every subject under the sun, Penguin represents quality and variety – the very best in publishing today.

For complete information about books available from Penguin – including Puffins, Penguin Classics and Arkana – and how to order them, write to us at the appropriate address below. Please note that for copyright reasons the selection of books varies from country to country.

In the United Kingdom: Please write to *Dept E.P., Penguin Books Ltd, Harmondsworth, Middlesex, UB7 0DA.*

If you have any difficulty in obtaining a title, please send your order with the correct money, plus ten per cent for postage and packaging, to *PO Box No 11, West Drayton, Middlesex*

In the United States: Please write to *Dept BA, Penguin, 299 Murray Hill Parkway, East Rutherford, New Jersey 07073*

In Canada: Please write to *Penguin Books Canada Ltd, 2801 John Street, Markham, Ontario L3R 1B4*

In Australia: Please write to the *Marketing Department, Penguin Books Australia Ltd, P.O. Box 257, Ringwood, Victoria 3134*

In New Zealand: Please write to the *Marketing Department, Penguin Books (NZ) Ltd, Private Bag, Takapuna, Auckland 9*

In India: Please write to *Penguin Overseas Ltd, 706 Eros Apartments, 56 Nehru Place, New Delhi, 110019*

In the Netherlands: Please write to *Penguin Books Netherlands B.V., Postbus 195, NL–1380AD Weesp*

In West Germany: Please write to *Penguin Books Ltd, Friedrichstrasse 10–12, D–6000 Frankfurt/Main 1*

In Spain: Please write to *Longman Penguin España, Calle San Nicolas 15, E–28013 Madrid*

In Italy: Please write to *Penguin Italia s.r.l., Via Como 4, I-20096 Pioltello (Milano)*

In France: Please write to *Penguin Books Ltd, 39 Rue de Montmorency, F-75003 Paris*

In Japan: Please write to *Longman Penguin Japan Co Ltd, Yamaguchi Building, 2–12–9 Kanda Jimbocho, Chiyoda-Ku, Tokyo 101*

FOR THE BEST IN PAPERBACKS, LOOK FOR THE

BIOGRAPHY AND AUTOBIOGRAPHY IN PENGUIN

Just for William   Nicholas Woolley and Sue Clayton

Originating as a film for the award-winning BBC2 documentary series *Forty Minutes*, *Just for William* is the story of William Clayton, diagnosed with leukaemia at the age of nine – and the story of a family who refused to give up hope in the battle against one of the deadliest diseases of all.

The Secret Lives of Trebitsch Lincoln   Bernard Wasserstein

Trebitsch Lincoln was Member of Parliament, international spy, right-wing revolutionary, Buddhist monk – and this century's most extra-ordinary conman. 'An utterly improbable story ... a biographical scoop' – *Guardian*

Tolstoy   A. N. Wilson

'One of the best biographies of our century' – Leon Edel. 'All his skills as a writer, his fire as a critic, his insight as a novelist and his experience of life have come together in this subject' – Peter Levi in the *Independent*

Fox on the Run   Graeme Fowler

The intimate diary of a dramatic eighteen months, in which Fowler became the first Englishman to score a double century in India – before being cast down by injury and forced to come to terms with loss of form. 'One of the finest cricket books this year' – *Yorkshire Post*. Winner of the first Observer/Running Late Sports Book Award.

Backcloth   Dirk Bogarde

The final volume of Dirk Bogarde's autobiography is not about his acting years but about Dirk Bogarde the man and the people and events that have shaped his life and character. All are remembered with affection, nostalgia and characteristic perception and eloquence.

Jackdaw Cake   Norman Lewis

From Carmarthen to Cuba, from Enfield to Algeria, Norman Lewis brilliantly recounts his transformation from stammering schoolboy to the man Auberon Waugh called 'the greatest travel writer alive, if not the greatest since Marco Polo'.

FOR THE BEST IN PAPERBACKS, LOOK FOR THE

Higher Than Hope Fatima Meer

The authorized biography of Nelson Mandela – imprisoned for twenty-seven years, released on 11 February 1990.

'A chronicle of persecution and exceptional courage, not simply of the Mandelas but of their friends and political colleagues' – *Sunday Telegraph*

Nelson Mandela Mary Benson

From his childhood in the royal family of the Thembu people to his membership and eventual leadership of the African National Congress, Mary Benson's biography illuminates the life, work and ideas of the man whose release is seen as the essential first step towards averting catastrophe in his tragic land.

also published:

Part of My Soul Winnie Mandela

Winnie Mandela has been described as 'the mother of the black people of South Africa ... the incarnation of the black spirit'.

In this collection of conversations, supplemented by letters, speeches and historical notes, she narrates the remarkable story of her life and political development. Courageous and humorous, it is a story as inspiring as that of her husband Nelson Mandela.

A Far Cry Mary Benson

'One of those rare autobiographies which can tell a moving personal story and illuminate a public and political drama. It recounts the South African battles against apartheid with a new freshness and intimacy, and it throws a bright sidelight on familiar figures who have been portrayed only from the front' – *Observer*